PUBLIC FUNDING OF RELIGIONS IN EUROPE

Public funding of religions is an important subject of debate today in Europe. Within eighteen well-documented chapters, gathering different national points of view with timely historical insights, this book represents a major contribution to this key question, so complex to solve. It is a high-level reflection led by the best specialists.

Vincente Fortier, National Center for Scientific Research (CNRS),
Strasbourg University, France

In contemporary Europe, direct and indirect financial aid to religious organizations represents a key testing ground for relations between religion and the State. This scholarly volume is ample testimony not only to the importance of the topic in our critical understanding of these relations but also of the value which the State places on religious activities as they contribute to social vitality. This impressive collection of studies offers profound insights on the issues, principles and challenges faced in this field of law and religion.

Norman Doe, Cardiff University, UK

From historical compensations and privileges to the status of not for profit organizations, this essential publication shows that public funding of religions in European legal systems is a clear expression of the evolution from institutionalized systems of church–state relationships to systems based on the fundamental rights of individuals.

Miguel Rodríguez Blanco, University of Alcalá, Spain

The views expressed during the execution of the RELIGARE project, in whatever form and or by whatever medium, are the sole responsibility of the authors. The European Union is not liable for any use that may be made of the information contained therein.

Cultural Diversity and Law in Association with RELIGARE

Series Editor: Prakash Shah, Queen Mary, University of London, UK

RELIGARE was a project on Religious Diversity and Secular Models in Europe funded by the European Commission under the Seventh Framework Programme. The project brought together an interdisciplinary team of high profile researchers and 13 academic institutions to collaborate on examining how existing policy and practice is suited to the demands of religious diversity within Europe and what legal models could be recommended to accommodate such diversity in future. More details on the project can be seen at its website: http://www.religareproject. eu/. Cultural Diversity and Law in Association with RELIGARE provided an outlet for the results of specific research undertaken within the RELIGARE project.

Other titles in this series:

Belief, Law and Politics
What Future for a Secular Europe?
Edited by Marie-Claire Foblets, Katayoun Alidadi,
Jørgen S. Nielsen and Zeynep Yanasmayan

Family, Religion and Law
Cultural Encounters in Europe
Edited by Prakash Shah with Marie-Claire Foblets
and Mathias Rohe

The Burqa Affair Across Europe
Between Public and Private Space
Edited by Alessandro Ferrari and Sabrina Pastorelli

Religion in Public Spaces
A European Perspective
Edited by Silvio Ferrari and Sabrina Pastorelli

A Test of Faith?
Religious Diversity and Accommodation in the European Workplace
Edited by Katayoun Alidadi, Marie-Claire Foblets and
Jogchum Vrielink

Public Funding of Religions in Europe

Edited by

FRANCIS MESSNER
University of Strasbourg, France

ASHGATE

Published by
Ashgate Publishing Limited
Wey Court East
Union Road
Farnham
Surrey, GU9 7PT
England

Ashgate Publishing Company
110 Cherry Street
Suite 3-1
Burlington, VT 05401-3818
USA

www.ashgate.com

British Library Cataloguing in Publication Data
A catalogue record for this book is available from the British Library

The Library of Congress has cataloged the printed edition as follows:
Public funding of religions in Europe / edited by Francis Messner.
    p. cm. – (Cultural diversity and law in association with RELIGARE)
  Includes bibliographical references and index.
  ISBN 978-1-4724-2891-2 (hardback) – ISBN 978-1-4724-2892-9 (ebook) –
ISBN 978-1-4724-2893-6 (epub) 1. Corporations, Religious – Finance – Law and legislation – Europe. 2. Church finance – Europe. 3. Ecclesiastical law – Europe.
I. Messner, Francis, 1947– editor.
  KJC5527.P83 2014
  254'.8094–dc23

                                                                              2014023420

ISBN 9781472428912 (hbk)
ISBN 9781472428929 (ebk – PDF)
ISBN 9781472428936 (ebk – ePUB)

Printed in the United Kingdom by Henry Ling Limited, at the Dorset Press, Dorchester, DT1 1HD

Contents

List of Figure and Tables

Figure

Tables

List of Contributors

Louis-Léon Christians is Professor and Head of the 'Chair for Law and Religion' at the Catholic University of Leuven and, since 2008, President of the interdisciplinary master in Religious Studies. He is also a visiting Professor at the Catholic Institute of Paris, and the University of Paris XI, and an expert for the Council of Europe on religious affairs and for the Fundamental Rights Platform (FRA-EU). His research interests, publications, and teaching cover the fields of Religious Freedom, Churches and States Relationships in Europe and International Law, Comparative Religious Laws and Canon Law.

Lisbet Christoffersen is Professor of Law, Religion and Society at the Department of Society and Globalisation, Roskilde University and part-time Professor of Law and Religion with Ecclesiastical law, Faculty of Theology, University of Copenhagen. She was leader of the NordForsk-funded Nordic Network on Law, Religion and Ethics 2003–2008 and in the same period research coordinator of the University of Copenhagen research initiative 'Religion in the 21st Century'. She was a member of the RELIGARE-project. She has published widely (books, book chapters and journal articles) in Danish and English on law and religion. In 2013, she was appointed a member of the committee entrusted by the Danish government with the task of analysing possible changes in the legal and economic structure of the Danish *folkekirke* and its relations to the State.

Zana Çitak is Vice-Chair of the Department of International Relations at Middle East Technical University. She works on issues in secularism, religion, nationalism, and politics. Her current research examines Islam in Europe from a comparative perspective.

Frank Cranmer is a Director of Central Lobby Consultants, Secretary of the Churches' Legislation Advisory Service and a Fellow of St Chad's College, Durham. He specializes in legislation as it affects the Churches, charity law, and religion and human rights. Previously Clerk of Bills at the House of Commons, he is an Honorary Research Fellow at the Centre for Law and Religion at Cardiff Law School. He has been a member of the editorial committees of the *Ecclesiastical Law Journal* since 2002 and of *Law and Justice* since 2006.

Françoise Curtit is research assistant in the research centre DRES – *Droits et religions* (CNRS/University of Strasbourg) in charge of law and religion projects: research dissemination, database management and monitoring of publications.

Her research interests focus on religion and sources of law, religious issues and European Union Law.

Raphaël Draï was Professor of Political Sciences at the Faculty of Law and Economic Sciences of the University of Nancy in 1977, Dean of the Faculty of Law and Political Sciences of the University of Amiens in 1990 and Professor of Political Sciences at the University of Aix-Marseille III in 1998. He is also Professor at the Political Studies Institute of Aix-en-Provence and Professor at the *Institute* for *Jewish Studies* and *Culture* of Aix-Marseille. He is a member of the World Religion Watch and he specializes in Hebraic Law. He is committed to inter-religious dialogue and gives lectures at the *Interuniversity Institute* for *Jewish Studies* and *Culture.*

Aykan Erdemir is Assistant Professor in the Department of Sociology of Middle East Technical University (METU) where he teaches courses on social and political anthropology, and the anthropology of Europe and the Middle East. He is also Deputy Dean of the Graduate School of Social Sciences and Director of the German-Turkish Masters Program in Social Sciences, a dual-diploma program of Humboldt-Universität and METU. His research covers faith-based collective action of Turkish and European Alevi communities, work and remittance strategies of Turkish immigrants in Europe, and competitive sharing and museumification of religious sites.

Anne Fornerod is researcher at the CNRS-University of Strasbourg centre of research, DRES. She took her PhD in public law at the University of Paris XI (2006). Her works address several issues in Law and Religion: principle of *laïcité*, State support for religions, chaplaincies, cemeteries, religious heritage and ECHR freedom of religion. She edited a book on chaplaincies in 2012 and published one book and several papers on cultural and religious heritage. She was a member of the RELIGARE-project.

Franck Frégosi took his PhD in Political Sciences, and is Research Director at CNRS, UMR DRES, University of Strasbourg, and Director of the Master Religion and Society, (*Institut d'études politiques d'Aix en Provence*, University of Aix-Marseille). His fields of research are Islam and secularism, public regulation of Islam in France and in Europe, and Islam and Politics in France.

Niels Kærgård is Professor at the Department of Food and Resource Economics, University of Copenhagen. His field of interest is agricultural politics, economic politics, econometrics, economic history and history of economic theory and welfare state research.

Francis Messner is Emeritus Director of Research at CNRS (University of Strasbourg/DRES-CNRS). He is involved in the Editorial Board of several reviews of law and sociology of religion. He was a member of the *commission for legal consideration of the relations between religions* and *public authorities,* appointed by the Minister of Interior in 2005. In addition to numerous publications on law and religion, he co-edited the *Traité de droit français des religions* (2003 and 2013). He was a member of the RELIGARE-project and as such managed the research group working on State support for religions.

Vincenzo Pacillo is Associate Professor at the Law Faculty of Modena and Reggio, where he teaches Canon Law. He is a member of the executive committee of the Institute of Canon Law and Comparative Law of Religion (DiReCom) at the Theological Faculty of Lugano.

Pierre-Henri Prélot is Professor of Public Law at the University of Cergy-Pontoise, where he teaches, among others, Constitutional Law and Human Rights. He was a member of the commission for legal consideration of the relations between religions and public authorities, appointed by the Minister of Interior in 2005. In addition to numerous publications on law and religion, he edited a handbook of Law of Human Rights (2010) and co-edited the *Traité de droit français des religions* (2003 and 2013).

Tuğba Tanyeri-Erdemir is the Director of the Science and Technology Museum, lecturer at the Graduate Program of Architectural History and a member of the Executive Board of the Centre for Society and Science at Middle East Technical University (Turkey). She has directed comparative projects on competitive sharing of religious sites and regulation and management of religious sites. She has extensive experience in dissemination and communication of scientific issues to the public.

Rik Torfs is Rector of the University of Leuven and Professor of Law and Canon Law at the Universities of Leuven and Stellenbosch. He was Dean of the Faculty of Canon Law (1994–2003, 2004 to date), president (2003) and member of the executive committee (1993–2003) of the European Consortium for Church and State Research. He is a member of the board of the International Academy for Freedom of Religion and Belief (Washington) and a member of the academic advisory board of the International Center for Law and Religious Studies (Brigham Young University Provo).

Jeanne-Marie Tuffery-Andrieu is Professor of Law at the University of Strasbourg. Her research interests cover the fields of History of Labor Law and History of Canon Law. She is responsible for the team of Labor Law of the UMR DRES and Deputy Director of the Doctoral School of Law (PhD) of the University of Strasbourg.

Patrick Valdrini was Dean of the Faculty of Canon Law of the Catholic University of Paris (1984–1992); Rector of the Catholic University of Paris (1992–2004); Director of the L'année canonique review (1985–2008); Chairman of the FUCE (European Federation of Catholic Universities) (2004–2006). Nowadays he is Professor of Canon Law at the Pontifical Lateran University and at the University Federico II of Naples. He is also Chairman of the Consociatio Internationalis Studio Juris Canonici Promovendo and Consultant to the Pontifical Council for the Laity. Since 2010, he has been Vice-Rector of the Pontifical Lateran University.

Paul van Sasse van Ysselt is Coordinating Legal Advisor, Constitutional Affairs Ministry of the Interior of the Netherlands.

Jean Volff is a French judge, *Honorary Advocate General at the Court of Cassation, and a* former Public Prosecutor of the Court of Appeal of Toulouse. He has been active in three fields: his career as a Public Prosecutor, his engagement as a reserve officer and several responsibilities in the service of the Protestant Churches. He has published widely, writing books about Law, Local History and Protestantism.

Heinrich de Wall is Professor of Ecclesiastical Law, Constitutional and Administrative Law at the University of Erlangen-Nürnberg and Director of the Hans-Liermann-Institut für Kirchenrecht. His fields of interest are in State/Church law, the law of the German Protestant churches, history of church law, German constitutional law and political thought in early modern Germany.

Stéphanie Wattier is a PhD candidate at the Catholic University of Leuven and an FNRS candidate. She was Research Assistant on the RELIGARE-project and Research Assistant in Teaching in Constitutional Law. She is a member of the Religions Law Chair at the Catholic University of Leuven and of the Research Center for State and Constitution at the Catholic University of Leuven.

Jean-Marie Woehrling studied at Strasbourg and Paris before starting the *Ecole Nationale d'Administration.* From 1975 to 1998 he was judge at the Administrative Court of Strasbourg, where he was successively commissioned as Advisor-rapporteur, Government commissioner, Vice-chairman and then Chairman. From 1998 to 2012 he held the position of General Secretary of the Central Commission for the Navigation of the Rhine, an international organization responsible for river transport. He was also Professor of Public Law at the University of Strasbourg, Fribourg en Brisgau, Spire and at the Euroinstitut in Kehl. He has worked on various research groups associated with the CNRS. Since 1999 he has been Chairman for *Alsace-Moselle Local Law Institute* and director of the collection 'Alsace Moselle', *Jurisclasseur* (Editions LexisNexis). With Francis Messner and Pierre Henri Prélot, he co-edited the book *Traité du droit français des religions.*

Introduction[1]

Francis Messner

This collective work on public or parapublic funding for religious denominations and philosophical groupings in Europe is the fruit of three international scientific meetings which were held in Strasbourg in 2010, in Copenhagen in 2011 and again in Strasbourg in 2012. They give an account of historical developments with regard to methods of funding, current laws and emerging practices and, lastly, the stances adopted by religious authorities on financial support from the State and local authorities, within the framework of the RELIGARE project funded by the European Commission.

Researchers affiliated with this working group set themselves the objective of reflecting on the legitimacy of public support for religious and philosophical groupings in a profoundly secularized society, while striving to contribute to the construction of a theoretical model compatible with transparency, the principle of state neutrality, with fundamental rights and, more precisely, a guarantee of freedom of religion and respect for the principles of equality and non-discrimination.

State funding of religious denominations developed gradually in Europe from the sixteenth century on, as a compensation mechanism following the secularization of Church property by public authorities. It was almost non-existent before that period; on the contrary, national Churches often replenished the State coffers, just like the procedure of voluntary donation in France under the *Ancien Régime*. It was finally called into question in some States at the beginning of the twentieth century, at the same time as policies to separate politics from religion were being implemented. Church officials being paid salaries by the State was considered contrary to the principle of separation and was associated with the public admission that religions could be 'bought'. Currently, methods of funding religious denominations are again being evaluated and reconsidered in the light of a newly emerging religious landscape that, paradoxically, is tending towards shrinking funding for religious denominations, while enlarging a perimeter traditionally reserved for national, majority religions.

This process of enlargement/shrinking is not homogeneous, varying greatly according to the States in question and being linked to the implementation of principles of non-discrimination and neutrality, but also to recent sociological developments. The end of salaries for ministers of worship was thus counterbalanced

---

1   The editor of this book would like to thank Ms. Laure Pubert and Lucie Veyretout warmly for their thorough corrections and review.

in the Netherlands in the 1980s by payment of a grant, while in France it came about in 1905 with the progressive loss of State support for ministers of religion. Funding in the latter case was entrusted to members of the religious communities concerned. This shrinking is also noticeable in the possibility given to taxpayers in some States to contribute a small part of their income tax to a religious denomination of their choice or else to the State which then allocates it to social and charitable causes. The shrinking then becomes symbolic, in that Churches and religions tend to resemble privileged NGOs as regards economic support.

Moreover, funding for religions is quantitatively in sharp decline for two reasons: the first is due to secularization and relative indifference, sometimes even animosity, towards 'recognized' religions. The example of Germany is significant in this respect. The number of people formally withdrawing from the two major Christian Churches incorporated under public law is having an impact on the collection of Church Tax by tax authorities. Moreover, the financial and economic crisis will probably have longer-term repercussions that are currently difficult to measure. The choices made by public authorities in terms of budgetary restrictions do not stop at the temple doors and they will affect the funding of religions in Europe and, as a consequence, impact how they function: ending tax niches, decreasing the number of ministers of worship paid for by the State (modelled on planned reductions in public officials), reassigning redundant buildings of worship.

In parallel, new convictional groups, both denominational and non-denominational, are growing in strength and giving rise to new public policies in terms of financial support for faiths. Non-denominational groups play a noticeable social role in this trend in States which have conferred upon them a status and funding similar to that accorded to religious denominations. They allow for the part of the population detached from religious institutions to be cared for and receive spiritual support, particularly during major life events (birth, marriage, death). Lastly, newly established religions and, more specifically, Islam are not always treated on an equal footing with 'recognized religions', which poses a problem in terms of integrating these populations into society.

This publication is divided into two parts. The first is devoted to presenting systems of funding for religious denominations and non-denominational organizations in Belgium, the Netherlands, Denmark, Germany, Italy, Turkey, France and the United Kingdom, in the light of European human rights law and European Union law. France's unique position – product of a turbulent history between the Catholic Church and the Republic and its upholding of regional statutes for faiths – deserves fuller explanation than is the case for other States. Contributions dealing with the theory of funding for religions and its place in economic theories will conclude this first part. The second part examines the doctrine of Catholic, Protestant, Jewish and Muslim faiths with respect to public authority funding for their personnel and activities.

Chapter 1

State Support for Religions: European Regulation

Françoise Curtit and Anne Fornerod

The issue of public funding for religions in Europe deals mainly with the various mechanisms put in place by domestic legal systems. However, in addition to financial relationships between the State and religions, we should take into account the European level as a regulatory framework. European Union policy, as well as European Court of Human Rights case law, could indeed affect state support for religions. The first section of this chapter will examine European Union tax policy on funding religious organizations, while the second section will analyse the case law of the European Court of Human Rights in this field.

European Union Tax Policy and Financial Relationships between States and Religions

Religious issues do not fall within European Union competence and in this respect Member State sovereignty continues to prevail.[1] In various areas, European Union law nevertheless provides exemptions from rules of general applicability to preserve the existing domestic provisions relating to the organizational autonomy of religious communities and to their role in society (for example, processing of sensitive data, labour law for organizations with an ethos based on religion or belief, ritual slaughter and so on). In these cases, religion is clearly distinguishable from economic activities and requires protection against market forces or economic regulation. On the other hand, if religious organizations are to be considered as serving economic purposes, they are subject to the same rules and principles as any other entities, particularly as regards public funding and state aid.

In this context, European Union regulation of Member States' tax policies could affect state support for religions, and we intend to show how European Union tax rules and the powers of investigation of the European Commission could interfere in, and even influence, financial relationships between States and religions.

---

1   See Article 17 § 1 of the Treaty on the Functioning of the European Union [30.03.2010] *OJ* C 83: 'The Union respects and does not prejudice the status under national law of churches and religious associations or communities in the Member States'.

The European Union's Role in Tax Coordination

Tax policy itself falls mainly within the competence of Member States, which may provide support for religions, in particular by granting them specific tax reliefs. However, the European Union plays a subsidiary role of tax coordination (and harmonization for value added tax) to maintain the fairness and balance of Member States' tax systems. In fact, the European Commission checks that national tax systems are compatible not only with each other, but also with the aims of the treaties, by ensuring that taxation (or non-taxation) does not create an obstacle to the free movement of goods and the free supply of services within the internal market. European Union law contains very few legal provisions relating to tax measures for religious activities and institutions.

Firstly, one could mention Article 103 of Regulation 1186/2009,[2] which provides that documentation for religious events (leaflets, books, magazines etc.) shall be free of import duties – which clearly has a very minor impact on funding for religions.

Secondly, and more relevant to our subject, the Value Added Tax (VAT) Directive 2006/112[3] obliges a Member State to tax supplies of goods and services as long as no specific exemption is provided. Public interest exemptions are strictly listed under Articles 132 and 133, relating in particular to welfare, social, medical or educational activities undertaken by bodies governed by public law and by non-profit organizations. VAT has to be harmonized at European Union level in order to ensure that goods and services can move freely and without hindrance between Member States, and exemptions constitute exceptions which must be strictly interpreted.[4] The impact of this directive and the 'Europeanization' of tax policy will be discussed further below.

European Union Investigative Power and Infringement Procedures: Recent Cases

The European Union single market is the cornerstone of European integration. As guardian of the treaties, the European Commission ensures that competition is not distorted and promotes the free movement of people, goods, services and capital. The Commission could, for example, control if state aid or taxation/non-taxation of activities are anti-competitive. To this end, the Commission has investigative powers, wielded at its own initiative or in response to a government request or an individual complainant. If the Commission detects a failure to comply with European Union law, it may initiate an infringement procedure (Article 258 of

---

2   Council Regulation (EC) 1186/2009 of 16 November 2009 setting up a Community system of reliefs from customs duty [10.12.2009] *OJ* L324, p. 23.

3   Council Directive 2006/112/EC of 28 November 2006 on the common system of value added tax [11.12.2006] *OJ* L347, p. 1.

4   See case *Temco Europe* [2004] ECR I–0000, C–284/03, pt 17.

the Treaty on the Functioning of the European Union) comprising several stages. At the beginning, the Commission sends the Member State concerned a letter of formal notice inviting it to submit its observations within two months and most differences of opinion are settled during this first stage. Otherwise, the Commission may issue a reasoned opinion, allowing the Member State an additional two-month period within which to comply. At the end, if the Member State fails to conform to European Union law, the Commission can refer the case to the Court of Justice of the European Union. Up to now, no case law has been brought before the Court relating to domestic tax systems as applied to churches and religious organizations. The Commission has recently opened a handful of investigations and proceedings in this area, involving Spain, Italy and, more recently, Denmark. Here, we will present the most significant of these.

VAT exemption in favour of the Catholic Church in Spain
The European Commission decided in December 2005 to issue a formal request to Spain to amend value added tax treatment of supplies of goods made to the Catholic Church (for example, Episcopal Conference, dioceses, parishes and other territorial constituencies, orders and religious congregations). Spain maintains that the Agreement between the Spanish State and the Holy See on Economic Affairs of 3 January 1979,[5] Article 4 1. B), obliges it to exempt from VAT certain supplies of goods (imports and acquisitions of movables and immovables) to the Catholic Church.[6] Such an exemption is not authorized under the European Union VAT system (according to the VAT Directive), even if the State makes a positive adjustment to the revenue. The Commission pointed out that the second paragraph of Article 307 of the European Community Treaty[7] obliges Spain – to the extent that the agreement is not compatible with the European Community Treaty – to 'take all appropriate steps to eliminate the incompatibilities established. This would even, following the case law of the European Court of Justice, include denunciation of the Agreement'.[8]

---

5   Instrumento de ratificación del Acuerdo entre el Estado español y la Santa Sede sobre asuntos económicos, firmado en la Ciudad del Vaticano el 3 de enero de 1979 [15.12.1979] *BOE* 300, p. 28782.

6   Press release IP/05/1620 of 16 December 2005, 'VAT – Commission asks Spain to amend treatment of supplies of goods made to the Catholic Church'.

7   Now, Article 351 TFEU: 'The rights and obligations arising from agreements concluded before 1 January 1958 or, for acceding States, before the date of their accession, between one or more Member States on the one hand, and one or more third countries on the other, shall not be affected by the provisions of the Treaties. To the extent that such agreements are not compatible with the Treaties, the Member State or States concerned shall take all appropriate steps to eliminate the incompatibilities established. Member States shall, where necessary, assist each other to this end and shall, where appropriate, adopt a common attitude.'

8   Press release IP/05/1620.

The Spanish Episcopal Conference and the Spanish government started negotiations and finally reached an agreement on funding the Church: from 1 January 2007, VAT exemptions were no longer to apply to the operations of the Catholic Church (except as provided by European Union tax law). The Commission had made it clear that this does not prevent Spain from paying financial compensation to the Catholic Church in return for VAT that the Church has to pay to the Spanish tax authorities.[9] In this regard, the Spanish Government chose to revise the state's tax allocation to the Catholic Church from 0.52 per cent to 0.70 per cent of the entire income tax revenue received from private individuals.[10]

ICIO exemption in favour of the Catholic Church in Spain
In 2007, a second investigation was initiated against Spain to review the Catholic Church's exemption from the 'Tax on construction, installation and repairs' (*Impuesto sobre construcciones, instalaciones y obras*, ICIO),[11] a municipal tax on building works requiring permits. This exemption was granted by a ministerial order of 5 June 2001,[12] a legal provision also pursuant to Article 4 1. B) of the Agreement of 3 January 1979 between the Spanish State and the Holy See.

This exemption also applied where constructions, installations or repairs were related to activities having nothing to do with worship, sometimes of a purely commercial nature. Here, the Church could be in competition with economic entities (e.g. companies), which had to pay tax and enjoyed no exemption. As the status of the supplier determines whether the activity is taxable or non-taxable, it may create distortions of competition. The Commission considered that this exemption was therefore a form of state aid,[13] incompatible with the common market since it distorts or falsifies competition, favouring bodies of the Catholic Church and being prejudicial to other Spanish or European businesses carrying out buildings or repairs for similar purposes.[14]

---

9   Press release IP/05/1620.
10 Ley 42/2006, de 28 de diciembre, de Presupuestos Generales del Estado para el año 2007. Disposición adicional decimoctava. Revisión del sistema de asignación tributaria a la Iglesia Católica [29.12.2006] *BOE* 311.
11 See Parliamentary questions: E–2578/06 of 12 June 2006 [30.12.2006] *OJ* C329; E–0829/07 of 20 February 2007 [5.12.2007] *OJ* C293; E–0774/08 of 18 February 2008 [13.11.2008] *OJ* C291.
12 Orden de 5 de junio de 2001 por la que se aclara la inclusión del Impuesto sobre Construcciones, Instalaciones y Obras en la letra B) del apartado 1 del artículo IV del Acuerdo entre el Estado Español y la Santa Sede sobre asuntos económicos, de 3 de enero de 1979 [16.06.2001] *BOE* 144, p. 21427.
13 Article 107 § 1 TFUE: '1. Save as otherwise provided in the Treaties, any aid granted by a Member State or through State resources in any form whatsoever which distorts or threatens to distort competition by favouring certain undertakings or the production of certain goods shall, in so far as it affects trade between Member States, be incompatible with the internal market'.
14 Parliamentary question E–2578/06 of 12 June 2006 [30.12.2006] *OJ* C329.

In 2009, the Spanish Government amended the legislation to eliminate any incompatibility between this tax exemption and European Union state aid rules.[15] The Spanish proposal consisted in limiting the scope of the ICIO exemption to real estate which is clearly used for religious purposes and is thus unrelated to an economic activity. For this reason, the European Commission considered that the Spanish proposal has satisfied its request, since it only covers buildings whose use is outside the scope of rules on state aid.[16]

Both cases in Spain have thereby been closed, as have other more recent cases in Italy. Acting upon complaints in relation to undertakings received from 2006, the European Commission sent several requests for information to the Italian authorities and in 2010 finally opened formal investigation proceedings related to two types of tax exemption.

Tax exemption from the municipal tax on real estate in Italy[17]

The first procedure relates to a municipal tax (*Imposta comunale sugli immobili*, ICI) exemption, which is granted on real estate used by non-commercial entities which exclusively fulfil specific purposes: activities such as social assistance, welfare, health, and religious and worship activities.[18] An entity can enjoy this exemption only if its commercial activities are non-prevalent: if they are neither marginal, nor directly related to the activity of worship, it will not benefit from the exemption. A circular from the Finance Ministry dated 26 January 2009[19] states that ecclesiastical organizations legally recognized according to the Lateran Treaty or agreements between the Italian State and other denominations are included among private, non-commercial entities.

The Commission considers that this tax exemption could constitute illegal state aid and therefore distort competition, because it constitutes an advantage for these organizations in comparison with commercial entities which provide the same activity. For instance, health-care or accommodation services provided by ecclesiastic institutions are in competition with similar services

---

15 Orden EHA/2814/2009, de 15 de octubre, por la que se modifica la Orden de 5 de junio de 2001, por la que se aclara la inclusión del Impuesto sobre Construcciones, Instalaciones y Obras en la letra B) del apartado 1 del artículo IV del Acuerdo entre el Estado Español y la Santa Sede sobre asuntos económicos, de 3 de enero de 1979 [21.10.2009] *BOE* 254, p. 88046.

16 Parliamentary questions P–1628/2009 of 15 April 2009 [13.07.2010] *OJ* C189.

17 State aid C 26/10 (ex NN 43/10) – Scheme concerning the municipal real estate tax exemption granted to real estate used by non-commercial entities for specific purposes. Invitation to submit comments pursuant to Article 108 § 2 of the Treaty on the Functioning of the European Union (text with EEA relevance) (2010/C 348/11), [21.12.2010] *OJ* C348, p. 17.

18 Decreto legislativo n. 504, 30 dicembre 1992, Article 7 § 1 i), [30.12.1992], *G.U.* 305, suppl. ord.

19 Circolare 26 gennaio 2009, n. 2, del Ministero delle Finanze, Imposta comunale sugli immobili (ICI), Article 7, comma 1, lettera i), del D. Lgs. 30 dicembre 1992, n. 504.

offered by economic operators.[20] Furthermore, the Commission considers that non-commercial entities may perform, in certain cases, economic activities and '[a]t this stage of the procedure, [it] also considers that the criteria used by the *Circolare* in order to exclude the *commercial nature* (under Italian law) of the activities listed in Article 7 i) cannot exclude the *economic nature* (under European competition law) of these activities'.[21]

In early 2012, the ICI was replaced by the IMU (*Imposta municipale unitaria*), and the Monti government drafted an amendment[22] which provides that, in cases of mixed commercial and non-profit use of the same building, the exemption will be strictly limited to the fraction of the property in which non-commercial activities take place. A declaration mechanism is also planned so as to identify the proportional relationship between commercial and non-commercial activities performed within the same building.

The European Commission has therefore closed its investigation, considering that, under these limitations, the IMU is in line with European Union state aid rules.[23]

Italian Unified Law on Income Tax: ecclesiastic institutions can never lose their non-commercial status[24]
As part of the same procedure, the Commission also investigated Article 149 4) of the Italian Unified Law on Income Tax (*Testo unico delle imposte sui redditi*, TUIR)[25] which provides favourable tax treatment for ecclesiastic institutions and amateur sports clubs. This law lays down the tax advantages applicable to non-commercial entities and identifies the conditions that can lead to the loss of the 'non-commercial status' of an entity. The provision of Article 149 4) appeared to exclude the application of the rules concerning the loss of 'non-commercial status' for ecclesiastic institutions with a civil status, even if they carry out commercial activities. 'As regards Article 149 4) TUIR, at this stage the Commission considers that the provision constitutes *prima facie* a selective measure, since the possibility to maintain the non-commercial status even when they would otherwise no longer

---

20   State aid C 26/10, pt 54.

21   State aid C 26/10, pt 38 [emphasis added].

22   Decreto-legge 24 gennaio 2012, n. 1, coordinato con la legge di conversione 24 marzo 2012, n. 27, Disposizioni urgenti per la concorrenza, lo sviluppo delle infrastrutture e la competitivita, Article 91–bis, [24.3.2012] *G.U.* 71, suppl. ord. 53.

23   Press release IP/12/1412 of 19 December 2012, 'State aid : Commission finds Italian ICI real estate tax exemptions for non-commercial entities incompatible and clears amended exemptions under new IMU law'.

24   Press release IP10/1319 of 12 October 2010, 'State aid: Commission opens probe into preferential real estate tax regime for non commercial entities in Italy'.

25   Decreto del Presidente della Repubblica, 22 dicembre 1986, n. 917 – Approvazione del Testo unico delle imposte sui redditi [31.12.1986] *G.U.* 302, (Article 149 was introduced in 1998).

be considered as non-commercial entities is granted only to ecclesiastic institutions and to amateur sport clubs'.[26]

But here again, the European Commission has closed its investigation. It had finally revealed 'that the controls carried out by the competent authorities include these entities and that there is no system of "perpetual non-commercial status"'.[27]

VAT exemption for charitable and non-profit making associations' supplies in Denmark

Finally, mention should be made of a last, pending case related to Denmark. Danish authorities exempt from VAT all activities carried out by charities or other non-profit associations (including religious organizations) in connection with the running of their businesses, as well as goods supplied by second-hand shops. In 2008, the European Commission sent a formal notice to Denmark[28] and stated that such a general exemption goes beyond what is allowed under Article 132 of the VAT Directive, which contains a detailed, restrictive description of the activities that can be exempted, as well as certain conditions related to the exemption. In 2010, the procedure continues as a reasoned opinion and the Commission has formally requested Denmark to change the law regarding the application of these exemptions. It is a recent, ongoing investigation and further information should be forthcoming.

Towards a New Funding Model in the Member States?

We will try to draw some conclusions from these few infringement cases, in order to assess factors involved in the emerging patterns of state support for religions.

Does the European Union interfere in the financial relationships between States and religions?

The European Union acts strictly within the limits of its competences conferred by the treaties (single market, competition, state aid and so on) and does not want to deal more precisely with state funding of religious institutions.[29] Its intervention on the matter mainly involves checking the implementation of European Union tax law within domestic legislation. Moreover, without needing to refer to the Court of Justice, at least for religion-related cases, the Commission succeeded in

---

26   State aid C 26/10, pt 56.

27   Press release IP/12/1412.

28   Press release IP/10/90 of 28 January 2010, 'VAT – Commission pursues infringement proceedings against Denmark regarding VAT exemptions'.

29   On the privileged situation of the Catholic Church relating to tax exemption in Spain, the Commission responded: 'the Commission would point out that, as Community law stands at present, the financing of religious institutions falls entirely within the sphere of competence of the Member States': Parliamentary question P–3773/2002 of 24 January 2003 [10.07.2003] *OJ* C161E, p. 142.

amending Spanish and Italian tax law, and perhaps soon Danish law. Therefore, we can say that the European Union does interfere in financial relationships between States and religions, at least as regards tax policy, which represents only one part of public support that they receive.

A 'banalization' of religious organizations?
We can identify two different tax policy approaches among the partners involved. On the one hand, Member States could apply differentiated treatment between religious and non-religious *organizations* (Catholic Church in Spain, ecclesiastic institutions in Italy) or between commercial and non-commercial *status* (non-commercial entities in Italy, non-profit associations in Denmark).

On the other hand, European Union authorities focus their approach on the *activities*,[30] regardless of the type of organization that carries them out. The justification for the exemption here lies in the nature of the tasks, and the status of the supplier cannot determine in itself whether the activity is taxable or not. In this regard, the European Union distinguishes more specifically between the *economic* nature and the *commercial* nature of activities[31] and considers that non-commercial entities – and among them religious organizations – may perform economic activities in various areas (health-care, housing, education etc.). They are therefore in competition with other operators offering the same services and fall within the scope of state aid rules. Under this broad interpretation and according to the case law provided by the European Court of Justice, 'any activity consisting in offering goods and services on a given market' is an economic activity.[32]

The European Union plays its role of tax coordination and harmonization in accordance with the primacy given to single market and competition rules. In this context, the same law applies to all legal entities (profit-making companies, non-profit organizations etc.): religious organizations are economic players like any others. As providers of social services, but also as institutions *per se*, religions are losing their specificities, at least regarding taxation: if the Catholic Church is subject to special rules pursuant to an international agreement (Concordat), this agreement has to be amended (see *supra*). In this matter, as in other areas (employment status of ministers of religion, denominational schools etc.), the prevailing market logic is progressively leading to a 'banalization' of religious organizations.

The European Union's aim is not to standardize national systems of financing and taxation, but European Union law creates a legal framework, an economic context to which Member States have to adapt their domestic legislation. In this light, in December 2010 the European Commission issued a Green Paper on VAT,[33]

---

30 See Article 132 of the VAT Directive 2006/112: '*Member States shall exempt the following transactions*' [emphasis added].

31 See *supra*, concerning the ICI tax in Italy.

32 *Ambulanz Glöckner* [2001] ECR I–8089, –475/99, pt 19.

33 *Green Paper on the future of VAT. Towards a simpler, more robust and efficient VAT system* COM (2010) 695 final.

proposing a comprehensive reform of the VAT system, because the existence of numerous options and derogations for Member States under European Union VAT law was leading to divergent rules across the European Union and may be an obstacle to the better functioning of the single market. There is a need to review these exemptions, and to 'reform the VAT rules in a "single market-friendly way"'.[34] After a consultation phase, the Commission's decision on such harmonization could be a new step towards fiscal integration into the European Union – and the disappearance of disparities within Member States.

'Coping mechanisms'

In this European legal context, various tax exceptions for operations of a purely religious nature remain possible in Member States, but only if they can strictly be considered as activities of social utility or public benefit which cannot distort competition.

However, this binding framework does not prevent any Member State from adapting its own legislation, for instance by implementing a tax refund mechanism (e.g. returning VAT to religious organizations or charities). Various VAT compensation systems are currently in operation in Member States (Austria, Denmark, Finland, France, Netherlands, Portugal, Sweden and UK) for certain public bodies or non-profit organizations.[35] As regards religious organizations, Portugal, for example, has chosen to operate a VAT refund mechanism, funded by the State, compensating various entities, including the Catholic Church. In 1991, the European Commission started an infringement procedure against Portugal related to VAT exemption for the delivery of objects of worship and for construction, maintenance and repairs to buildings belonging to the Catholic Church, intended exclusively for worship.[36] The Commission recognized that these were not 'economic activities', but it was nevertheless a breach of the VAT Directive. The Portuguese Government then solved this problem by passing a law stating that the Catholic Church would receive in return, every year, a subsidy equivalent to the amount of VAT paid. In the United Kingdom, the Listed Places of Worship Grant Scheme provides grants towards the VAT incurred in making repairs and carrying out necessary alterations to listed buildings mainly used for public worship. Places of worship 'listed' by Government as architecturally important benefit from the refund of the difference between five per cent and the actual amount spent on VAT on eligible repairs and maintenance.[37]

---

34 *Green Paper on the future of VAT*, p. 5.

35 Copenhagen Economics, *VAT in the public sector and exemptions in the public interest: final report for Taxud*, Taxud/2009/de/316. 1 March 2011 <http://ec.europa.eu/ taxation_customs/resources/documents/common/publications/studies/vat_public_sector. pdf> accessed 4 February 2013.

36 Decreto lei 20/90 de 13 de Janeiro [13.01.1990] *D.R.* 1 serie 11, p. 199.

37 See on this issue Franck Cranmer, *Paying the piper? Public Funding and Supervision of Religion in a Secular Society (United Kingdom)*, Chapter 10, this volume.

Several reports[38] suggest extending the VAT refund scheme throughout the European Union, especially for charities. This recommendation could be extended to the activities of religious organizations and perhaps for other categories of taxes, as far as it does not lead to competition distortion.

'Coping mechanisms' can thus be implemented in the Member States to ensure compliance between national practices and European Union law. This superposition of technical rules and complex mechanisms could nevertheless be an additional obstacle to an even greater transparency required in the financial relationships between States and religions. In this respect, European Union law and domestic legislation have to provide clear and reliable tax rules and selection criteria.

A market-oriented approach for emerging practices in State funding for religions
Public funding for religions is under pressure on all sides and, in a context of secularization of societies, growing pluralism and economic crisis, it may give rise to contestation within the States: 'privileges' are no longer applicable to religions, nor *among* religions. In Italy for instance, in summer 2011, a growing number of people were criticizing tax breaks given to the Catholic Church, using various methods, including an Internet campaign. Protesters were asking for numerous exemptions given to the Church to be reviewed and proposed the abolition of the *otto per mille* (part of the annual income tax revenue, paid to an organized religion or to a social assistance project run by the Italian State, mainly benefiting the Catholic Church). Supporters said that the tax breaks were justified, because the Catholic Church plays an important role in social welfare, but the debate is far from over.[39] In Greece, public controversy emerged in September 2011, as the Orthodox Church appeared to be largely exempt from a new property tax implemented to achieve Greece's austerity targets.[40] Here again, people are asking for religious organizations to be viewed as one among many economic players in a market society.

State funding for religions goes far beyond tax policy issues, and many other direct and indirect funding mechanisms are involved in Member States. Nevertheless, a market-oriented approach could also be applied in this larger context and on a national level, as an explanatory framework for legal adjustments, but also for emerging practices and ongoing discussions on the 'good standards' of state support for religions.

---

38   ISOBRO, *Denmark – VAT Compensation Scheme for Charities* 2006, 28 February 2007, <http://www.ictr.i.e./files/Danish%20Vat%20Compensation%20Scheme%20Summa ry%20-%20Feb%202007.pdf> accessed 4 February 2013.

39   Margherita Nasi, 'Italie: les privilèges fiscaux de l'Église en question' (2011) *Libération*, 30 August. And see Facebook *Vaticano pagaci tu la manovra finanziaria* and *Ma quali privilegi e ICI? La Chiesa le tasse le paga!*

40   Alain Salles, 'Orthodox Church appears to be exempt from austerity measures' (2011) *Guardian Weekly*, 4 October 2011.

Tax Policy and Financial Relationships between States and Religions before the European Court of Human Rights

Addressing the issue of state support for religions in the light of the European Convention of Human Rights raises at the outset one obvious question: does this matter fall within the scope of the Convention? No doubt the European Court is competent to rule on applications pertaining to freedom of religion, guaranteed by Article 9 § 1. Moreover, and despite the margin of appreciation often granted to Member States to regulate religious matters within national borders,[41] the Strasbourg Court no longer hesitates to take a stand against the national system of relationships between States and denominational groups and to align them with the requirements of the European Convention of Human Rights.[42]

In addition, state support takes on several forms, such as the use of tax instruments or direct or indirect funding through subsidies. An in-depth analysis shows that the main – and even the sole – aspect dealt with by the Court is the tax legislation of the various domestic systems of state support for religions. As the European Court of Human Rights itself points out in its case law, the power of taxation in general is expressly recognized by the Convention and is ascribed to the State by Article 1 of Protocol No. 1,[43] concerning the protection of property.[44] The relevant provisions lie in section 2 of this article, allowing States to 'secure the payment of taxes'.

The European Court has a long tradition of dealing with tax issues related to religions: decisions have been regularly issued since the 1980s and they will require some elucidation in the context of the sample under study here. This sample comprises only sixteen cases, including four judgments and in the main, decisions on admissibility. It should be noted that an overwhelming majority of applications have been declared inadmissible. The only three cases that confirmed a violation of the Convention[45] are rather disappointing in that the religious tax

---

41   Raffaella Nigro, 'The margin of appreciation doctrine and the case-law of the European Court of human rights on the Islamic veil' (2010) *Human Rights Review* 531.

42   See for example, *Sviato-Mykhaïlivska Parafiya v Ukraine*, no. 77703/01 (ECHR, 14 June 2007), § 114 and § 121, and *Lang v Autriche*, no. 28648/03 (ECHR, 19 March 2009), § 24–5.

43   Precisely, this provides that: 'Every natural or legal person is entitled to the peaceful enjoyment of his possessions. No-one shall be deprived of his possessions except in the public interest and subject to the conditions provided for by law and by the general principles of international law. The preceding provisions shall not, however, in any way impair the right of a State to enforce such laws as it deems necessary to control the use of property in accordance with the general interest or to secure the payment of taxes or other contributions or penalties'.

44   *C. v the United Kingdom*, no. 10358/83 (EComHR, 15 December 1983); *Alujer Fernandez and Caballero Garcia v Spain*, no. 53072/99 (ECtHR, 14 June 2001).

45   *Darby v Sweden*, No. 11581/85 (ECHR, 23 October 1990); *Jehovah's Witnesses v France*, no. 8916/05 (ECHR, 30 June 2011). In the *Darby* case, the Court concludes

systems in question are either only a secondary consideration or are very much linked to national legislation. This limited number of cases could be an illustration of the specificity of case law related to taxation based on Article 1 of Protocol No. 1. Indeed, most of the applications highlight the procedural aspects of national taxation processes, leaving limited space for Article 1 of Protocol No. 1 taken in conjunction with other substantive rights – opposed to procedural ones – of the Convention.[46]

Concerning specifically the combining of provisions related to religious issues – mainly Article 9 – and Article 1 of Protocol No. 1, no real leading case can be found which would provide a framework for case law in this field. Nevertheless, what emerges from this small number of cases is the Court's amazingly steadfast position, and its guidelines are worth examining. It seems that unshakeable protection is granted to State sovereignty in taxation and, furthermore, that the financial dimension of the system of Church–State relationships benefits from an important stability.

Tax System and Religious Freedom before the European Court: the Reduced Protection of Freedom of Religion

The tax system applicable to religious groups seems to offer nearly absolute power for state authorities to decide on how they should be taxed. In comparison, freedom of religion, negative or positive, seems to benefit from very limited protection and does so in several respects and under varying circumstances.

The impression of reduced protection of freedom of religion firstly results from the Court very exceptionally accepting to consider taxation itself as interference in religious freedom, while freely admitting that taxation amounts to interference in Article 1 of Protocol No. 1. Indeed, the Court seems much more cautious when religious taxation is at stake or when the applicants claim that taxation has an impact on their religious freedom. The impression prevails that taxation and the free exercise of freedom of religion are two separate processes, largely disconnected. This starts with the fact that tax cannot be characterized as a 'manifestation of

---

that there was a violation of Article 14 combined with Article 1 Protocol 1, but without carrying out a real examination of the claim under Article 9. In addition, the violation relies on a lack of legitimate aim pursued by the Swedish legislation, the scope of which is very limited. In the same vein, the recent *Association of Jehovah's Witnesses* case led to a decision confirming a violation of Article 9, but only because of the gifts received by the association being taxed under a law that was too imprecise. In the *Wasmuth v Germany* case no. 12884/03 (ECHR 17 February 2011), it is without doubt the difficulties surrounding negative freedom of religion raised by the application which eventually justified an examination of the merits.

46　See Vincent Berger, 'La jurisprudence de la Cour européenne des droits de l'homme et le droit fiscal' (2010) 24 *Droit Fiscal* 367; Ali Riza Çoban, *Protection of property rights within the European Convention on Human Rights* (Ashgate 2004) 218.

one's religion'[47] and that 'the obligation to pay taxes is a general one which has no specific conscientious implications in itself'.[48] As a consequence, already in 1983 in the *C. v United Kingdom* case, the Commission and then regularly the Court have stated that 'Article 9 does not confer on the applicant the right to refuse, on the basis of his convictions to abide by [tax] legislation'.[49] Moreover, as considered in the *Iglesia Bautista 'El Salvador' and José Aquilino Ortega Moratilla v Spain* case,[50] 'the right to freedom of religion by no means implies that churches or their adherents must be granted a different tax status from that of other taxpayers'. In addition, case law related to '*prima facie* neutral legislation' applies here, as is proven in the decision *Skugar and others v Russia.*[51] The applicants complained that they had been assigned taxpayer numbers which were incompatible with their religious beliefs.[52] The Court very clearly answered that 'general legislation which applies on a neutral basis without any link whatsoever with an applicant's personal beliefs cannot in principle be regarded as an interference with his or her rights under Article 9 of the Convention'.

The sole possible evolution in case law linking taxation and freedom of religion could arise from situations in which taxation leads to material consequences in that it deprives the applicants of the concrete conditions of worship. As mentioned before, in the *Iglesia Bautista 'El Salvador' and José Aquilino Ortega Moratilla v Spain* case,[53] the applicants argued that levying property tax infringes their freedom of religion set forth in Article 9. The Commission holds however that it 'fails to see how a right to exemption of places of worship from all forms of taxation can be derived from Article 9 of the Convention. It considers that the right to freedom of religion by no means implies that churches or their adherents must be granted a different tax status from that of other taxpayers'.

It should be noticed that, in this case, the application was declared inadmissible by a majority only, suggesting that some disagreement had occurred among the judges about the eventual decision. Since the Court does not provide dissenting opinions at the admissibility stage, it is difficult to know the underlying reasoning.

---

47   *Bruno v Sweden*, no. 32196/96 (ECtHR, 28 August 2001).

48   *Iglesia Bautista 'El Salvador' and José Aquilino Ortega Moratilla v Spain*, no. 17522/90 (ECHR, 11 January 1992).

49   *C. v the United Kingdom*, no. 10358/83 (EComHR, 15 December 1983); *Hubaux v Belgium*, no. 11088/84 (EComHR, 9 May 1988).

50   *Iglesia Bautista 'El Salvador' and José Aquilino Ortega Moratilla v Spain*. The applicants argued that levying property tax infringes their freedom of religion set forth in Article 9. The commission holds however that it 'fails to see how a right to exemption of places of worship from all forms of taxation can be derived from Article 9 of the Convention'.

51   *Skugar and others v Russia*, no. 40010/04 (ECtHR, 3 December 2009). See also *Vergos v Greece*, no. 65501/01 (ECHR, 24 September 2004), § 40.

52   In the case at hand, the number in question contained the figure '6' three times and therefore corresponded to the image of the beast in Saint John's apocalypse.

53   *Iglesia Bautista 'El Salvador' and José Aquilino Ortega Moratilla v Spain.*

In the 1992 case, the complaint was three-fold and, since both of the applicants' arguments may be considered to be well-established case law, one could suggest that the disagreement within the Commission could be explained by the alleged unequal treatment of the Catholic Church, which would infringe Article 14 in conjunction with Article 9. The intransigence of the Court gave way only recently in the 2011 *Jehovah's Witnesses v France* case, which throws new light on the 1992 Spanish case. Indeed, although the eventual solution did not deal with this point, it seems that for the first time the Court recognized in unambiguous terms that 'the taxation imposed on the applicant had threatened, if not severely hindered, the internal organization and its functioning, given that, in particular, places of worship were targeted' (§ 53).[54]

In addition, one observes an unequal balance between freedom of religion and religious organizations' taxation rights. Although the Court commonly holds that no-one should be constrained to be involved in religious activities against their will, it remains shy when it comes to questioning the tax system.

The case *Bruno v Sweden*[55] could have us think and believe in the prospect of protection of the freedom of religion through Article 9 § 1 in taxation litigation. Indeed, in its reasoning, the Court includes the duty to pay church tax within the constraints of being involved in religious activities against one's will. However, the Court combines this statement with the nuance that it is 'in certain circumstances' a condition that was not met in this case. The applicant claimed that 'the levying of church tax on him, who is not a member of the Church of Sweden, violated his freedom of religion as protected by Article 9 of the Convention'. His complaint was more precisely directed at the administration of burials, which the Church of Sweden is entrusted with. It should be specified that the sums levied by the Church of Sweden – at the time of application – were partly justified by the carrying out of certain tasks in the common interest, by the Church instead of public authorities. Non-members of the Church might be partially exempted from this tax. In addition, in this case, the reference to the *Darby v Sweden* is only half convincing in that, although the Court concluded here that there was a violation of Article 14 taken together with Article 1 of Protocol No. 1, it drew this conclusion irrespective of the religious background of the case. The impugned discrimination came from the illegitimate aim of the distinction between residents and non-residents in Sweden, and not from the distinction between members and non-members of the Church of Sweden. The applicant worked in Sweden, but lived in Finland.

The protection of freedom of religion rests at first sight on the principle according to which 'a Church tax regime is not incompatible with the individual's freedom of religion so long as he or she is free to leave the Church in question'.[56] Nevertheless, the formalities of departure depend on the conditions fixed by the

---

54   *Jehovah's Witnesses v France*, no. 8916/05 (ECHR, 30 June 2011).

55   *Bruno v Sweden*, no. 32196/96 (ECtHR, 28 August 2001).

56   Julian Rivers, *The Law of organized Religions: between Establishment and Secularism* (OUP 2010) 61.

State. But this position is an old one, as the Commission already held in 1984 that 'a requirement to pay a tax for belonging to a specific Church is not an interference with the exercise of freedom of religion where the law allows individuals to leave the Church'.[57] It shows that from the moment a case deals with the heart of religious freedom, the Court could modify its position. The case *Sukyo Mahikari v France* also dealt with the taxation of manual gifts, but, unlike the *Jehovah's Witnesses v France* case, the basis of taxation did not prevent the association from practising worship by depriving it of its places of worship.[58]

Negative freedom of religion is equally dealt with by the Court within this tax litigation context. In general, negative freedom of religion has a double meaning: it consists in the right to confess no religion or in the right not to be compelled to disclose one's religious beliefs. It appears that, connected to the taxation issue, the applicants complained that they had been led to reveal their religious beliefs while filling in their tax return.

In the *Spampinato v Italy* case, the applicant had decided to grant the State the eight thousandths of the amount due for income tax. Before the European Court of Human Rights, he complained under Articles 9 and 14 of the Convention that he had been obliged to reveal his religious convictions while drawing up his tax return. The Court rejected the argument, saying that the choice of assignment of income tax would not necessarily involve revealing one's belonging to a religious denomination. Indeed, the Court observes that, pursuant to Article 47 § 3 of Act No. 222 of 1985 – pertaining to the 0.8 per cent system – taxpayers can express their choice as to the assignment of sums thus perceived. In the *Wasmuth v Germany* case,[59] the tax return was at issue against the backdrop of the German tax system. For some years, the applicant's wage tax cards had included a section 'Church Tax deducted', which was left blank, thereby informing his employer that he did not have to deduct any Church Tax for Mr Wasmuth. He unsuccessfully asked the local authorities to provide him with a wage tax card disclosing no information related to his religious belonging. He lodged an appeal with various German courts arguing that this refusal amounted to a breach of his right not to disclose his religious opinions. The European Court concluded that there had not been a violation of Article 9 – notably for two reasons. As to whether the interference had been proportionate to the legitimate aim of ensuring the right of churches and religious societies to levy religious tax, the European Court followed the German jurisdiction in thinking that the reference to the applicant's religious or philosophical beliefs on the wage tax card had limited influence. Indeed, it only indicated to the fiscal authorities that he did not belong to one of the six churches of religious communities that can levy tax. In addition, the tax card is

---

57 *E. v Austria*, no. 9781/82 (EComHR, 14 May 1984); see also *Gottesmann v Switzerland*, no. 10616/83 (EComHR, 4 December 1984).

58 *Sukyo Mahikari v France*, no. 41729/09 (ECHR, 8 January 2013).

59 *Wasmuth v Germany*, no. 12884/03 (ECHR, 17 February 2011).

not publicly used and has no utility outside the relationship between employee and fiscal authorities.

All this contributes to ensuring stability for the state support issue within the premises of systems of Church–State relationships.

Impregnable Tax Sovereignty?

The main statement likely to sum up the European Court's position here is that freedom of religion has limited impact on tax legislation enforcement, be it general and neutral legislation or religion-oriented tax legislation on the one hand, or positive or negative freedom of religion on the other hand. Indeed, the Strasbourg Court case law seemingly reflects the principle according to which 'tax sovereignty is a fundamental part of national sovereignty'.[60] Before the European Court of Human Rights, this results in a wide margin of appreciation generally granted to Member States in deciding upon tax matters and the limited room granted to the principle of discrimination.

A wide margin of appreciation, the pillar of tax sovereignty
In general, and like other European Union institutions, the Strasbourg Court is very cautious about evolving within the context of Church–State relationships.[61] Although freedom of religion undeniably benefits from protection through the enforcement of the European Convention by the Court, Member States nevertheless have an important margin of appreciation justified by the specificity of their relationships with churches and religious groups.

A historical inheritance, these relationships reflect a part of the deep identity of the States and lead to the subsidiarity of European systems. This is all the more visible when it comes to the tax system applicable to religious groups. The unchanged position of the European Court is summarized in the decision *José Alujer Fernandez and Rosa Caballero Garcia v Espagne*:[62] 'such a margin of appreciation is all the more warranted in that there is no common European standard governing the financing of churches or religions, such questions being closely related to the history and traditions of each country'. The Court has us understand that it does not intend to intrude into this exclusive domain of the States. Among several examples, the dissenting opinion of judges Berro-Lefèvre and Kalaydjieva following the case *Wasmuth v Germany* should be considered here. Their criticism focuses on the analysis of negative freedom of religion

---

60   Ben Terra et al. *European Tax Law* (Kluwer Law International 2005) 3.

61   In the relevant law section, it refers to Article 17 § 1 of the Treaty on the Functioning of the European Union, which provides that: 'the Union respects and does not prejudice the status under national law of churches and associations or communities in the Member States'.

62   *Alujer Fernández and Caballero Garcia v Espagne*, no. 53072/99 (EComHR, 14 June 2001); see also *Spampinato v Italy*, no. 23123/04 (ECtHR, 29 March 2007).

adopted by the Court and they go to the trouble of expressing their adhesion to 'the financing of churches as existing in Germany' and their 'possibility to levy the Church Tax' that 'it is out of their purpose to question'.

It seems that the freedom granted to the States when it comes to taxation questions is added to the traditional margin of appreciation usually left to the domestic authorities in religious matters. In the *Spampinato* case, the Court openly justifies the eventual solution by referring to its overall case law on state economical and tax policies.[63]

Such rooting in history is especially tangible when the Court is led to go into the details of Church–State relationship systems. In several countries, historically dominant churches are in charge of social tasks pertaining to the general interest or public good. In this regard, litigation brought before the Strasbourg judges shows how the borders between the civil or religious nature of these tasks prove difficult to establish. The tasks thus carried out directly or indirectly benefit all citizens, regardless of their religious beliefs. In the *Bruno v Sweden* case, 'the Court agrees with the Government that the administration of burials, the care and maintenance of Church property and buildings of historic value and the care of old population records can reasonably be considered as tasks of a non-religious nature which are performed in the interest of society as a whole. It must be left to the State to decide who should be entrusted with the responsibility of carrying out these tasks and how they should be financed'.[64] In the same vein, the *Iglesia Bautista 'El Salvador' and José Aquilino Ortega Moratilla v Spain* case justifies the differential treatment between the Catholic Church and other denominations on the grounds that the Catholic Church is entrusted with specific missions like the maintenance of cultural heritage, in the knowledge that 'the Catholic Church has undertaken to place its historical, artistic and documentary heritage at the service of the Spanish people'.

This case law allows a great stability of the domestic tax system. But the diversity of the status granted to religious denominations in various national Church–State relationship systems in Europe logically leads us to consider the discrimination argument, which very often forms the basis of applicants' claims before the Court.

Impregnable case law? Power of taxation v discrimination
The question arises whether this case law could remain apart from the now well-established trend impacting all the European Union Member States, which consists in questioning the current systems of state support for religious groups and activities in the light of the requirements of equality of treatment and the related

---

63   *Gasus Dosier – und Fördertechnik GmbH v Netherlands*, no. 306–B, series A, p. 49 (ECHR, 23 February 1995), § 60; *National & Provincial Building Society, Leeds Permanent Building Society and Yorkshire Building Society v United Kingdom*, coll. 1997–VII (ECHR of 23 October 1997), § 80–82.
64   *Bruno v Sweden*, no. 32196/96 (ECtHR, 28 August 2001).

principle of non-discrimination. Indeed, the contemporary religious landscape is characterized by neutrality and pluralism, leading States to the dilemma of funding no, or all, denominations to avoid discrimination on religious grounds. Will the principle of non-discrimination challenge the Strasbourg Court's position on these premises? Or will the Court maintain the disconnection between its case law on discrimination between religious denominations and its position regarding tax applied to individuals and denominational groups?

In general, the position of the Court on the principle of non-discrimination rests on Article 14 and consists in considering that 'this provision does not prohibit all differences in treatment in the exercise of the rights and freedoms recognized, equality of treatment being violated only where the difference in treatment has no objective and reasonable justification' (a reference to ECHR, Belgian linguistic judgment of 9 February 1967). Hence, on the one hand, as noted above, the Court is much more attentive to the discrimination issue when it applies to religious denominations prevented from benefiting from the advantages normally granted to already established religious groups or from acceding to the same legal status as exists for them.[65] On the other hand, very little room, if any, is given to the discrimination parameter in the case law under study here. Indeed, one observes that very regularly not only is Article 9 invoked but also Article 14, related to discrimination, taken together with Article 1 of Protocol No. 1. The Strasbourg Court regularly, if not systematically, opposes the very important margin of appreciation allotted to the Member States in this respect. Its position is clearly expressed in the *Alujer Fernandez v Spain* case: 'Regard being had to the margin of appreciation left to Contracting States … particularly as regards building the fragile relations that exist between the State and religions, it cannot be considered as amounting to discriminatory interference with the applicants' right to freedom of religion'. However, as noted above, within the sample under study here, three cases conclude that there was a violation of the Convention: *Darby v Sweden* (1990), *Jehovah's Witnesses v France* (2011) and *Association Culturelle du Temple Pyramide v France* (31 January 2013). In the *Darby* case, the Court precisely concludes that there was a violation of Article 14 combined with Article 1 Protocol No. 1, but without carrying out a real examination of the claim under Article 9. In addition, the violation relies on a lack of legitimate aim pursued by the Swedish legislation, the scope of which is very limited. Moreover, it should be noted that, in the *Jehovah's Witnesses v France* case, the claim relating to discrimination had been overturned at the admissibility stage. Lastly, the range of French cases of January 2013 does not allow comparison, since the discrimination issue was not dealt with.[66]

---

65   See cases *Lang v Austria*, No. 28648/03 (ECHR, 12 March 2009), *Gütl v Austria*, No. 49686/99 (ECHR, 12 March 2009) and *Löffelman v Austria*, No. 42967/98 (ECHR, 12 March 2009).

66   Besides the case of *Association Culturelle du Temple Pyramide v France*, the Court delivered judgments on two other cases on a similar issue and with identical solutions; case

The case *Jehovas Zeugen in Österreich v Austria*[67] could announce a less clement position adopted by the Court towards the Member States, as it paves the way to a link between non-discrimination requirements and tax law. The applicant was granted the status of religious society under the Religious Communities Act in May 2009. It claimed that before this date, as a mere religious community, it had been subject to laws concerning employees and tax from which it would have been exempt, had it been a recognized religious society and treated accordingly. In particular, it could have been exempt from inheritance and gift tax for a donation made to it in 1999. On this point, it invoked Article 14 and Article 1 of Protocol No. 1. The Court deemed that there had been a violation of these provisions. The reason very likely lies in the fact that 'the Government has not given any reason justifying the difference in treatment regarding the liability to inheritance and gift tax between the applicant community and religious communities recognized as religious societies and merely indicated that inheritance and gift tax had ceased to be collected after 31 July 2008' (§ 47). Hence, the Court could only apply the reasoning according to which a difference in treatment between two religious groups cannot only depend on 'whether or not the applicant community was a recognized religious society' (§ 35–7 and 47–9).

The question remains open about how these cases are likely to determine the orientation the Court has adopted so far. Should the Court follow this pathway, the consequences for States could be serious.

List of References

Berger V, 'La jurisprudence de la Cour européenne des droits de l'homme et le droit fiscal' (2010) 24 *Droit Fiscal* 367

Copenhagen Economics, *VAT in the Public Sector and Exemptions in the Public Interest: Final Report for Taxud*, March 1 2011 <http://ec.europa.eu/taxation_customs/resources/documents/common/publications/studies/vat_public_sector.pdf> accessed 4 February 2013

Cranmer F, *Paying the Piper? Public Funding and Supervision of Religion in a Secular Society (United Kingdom)* Chapter 10, this volume

ISOBRO, *Denmark – VAT Compensation Scheme for Charities* 2006, 28 February 2007, see summary at <http://www.ictr.i.e./files/Danish Vat Compensation Scheme Summary – Feb 2007.pdf> accessed 4 February 2013

Nasi M, 'Italie: les privilèges fiscaux de l'Église en question' (2011) *Libération*, 30 August

---

Association des Chevaliers du Lotus d'or v France, No. 50615/07 (ECHR, 31 January 2013), case Église Évangélique Missionnaire and Salaûn v France, No. 25502/07 (ECHR, 31 January 2013).

67 *Jehovas Zeugen in Österreich v Austria*, No. 27540/05 (ECHR, 25 September 2012).

Nigro R, 'The Margin of Appreciation Doctrine and the Case-law of the European Court of Human Rights on the Islamic Veil' (2010) 11, 4 *Human Rights Review* 531–64

Rivers J, *The Law of Organized Religions: Between Establishment and Secularism* (OUP 2010)

Riza Çoban A, *Protection of Property Rights within the European Convention on Human Rights* (Ashgate 2004)

Salles A, 'Orthodox Church Appears to be Exempt from Austerity Measures' (2011) *Guardian Weekly*, 4 October

Terra B. et al., *European Tax Law* (Kluwer Law International 2005)

Chapter 2

Public Funding of Religious Organizations in the Netherlands

Paul van Sasse van Ysselt

Introduction

Public funding of religious organizations is one of the issues surrounding the relationship between religion and the State that is much debated in many European countries.[1] This is also true for the Netherlands, where other issues involving this relationship are also the subject of debate and research, such as expressions inspired by religion, religious symbols in the public domain or in schools, and religious rites such as ritual slaughtering. These topics have many legal questions in common and share a relevant common constitutional and historical background. This would theoretically justify general research into the different issues combined.[2] However, for practical reasons, *inter alia*, this chapter will limit itself to dealing only with the first topic: public support for religious organizations in the Netherlands.

Focusing on the situation in the Netherlands, it seems worthwhile taking note of some key statistics and developments in the country on the topic in order to have a better understanding of the Dutch context and the challenges to which the Netherlands are exposed. This will be dealt with in the second part of this chapter. In the third part, the constitutional context will be treated in short, as well as its history and general meaning nowadays. The following part will address the current situation of different issues related to public support of religious organizations. Next, some sociological/political challenges will be mentioned, as well as some good practice. The last part will deal with the question of how it is possible to change the current situation, if need be, and whether, in the process, state support would be a legitimate aim.

---

1 The concept of 'religious organizations' is not particularly satisfactory, but there are also drawbacks attached to the possible alternatives. See, for some deliberations on this point, Julian Rivers, *Law of the Organised Religions. Between Establishment and Secularism* (OUP 2010), Preface.

2 For an excellent general overview, see Sophie C Van Bijsterveld, 'Religion and the Secular State' in W C Durham et al. (eds), *Religion and the Secular State: Interim National Reports* (The International Center for Law and Religion Studies, Brigham Young University 2010) 523–48.

The Netherlands: Facts and Figures

The Netherlands is part of the Kingdom of the Netherlands, which was modified on 10 October 2010. As a consequence, the Kingdom now includes four countries – the Netherlands, Aruba, Curaçao and St. Maarten. The three islands – Bonaire, St. Eustatius and Saba – formerly part of the Netherlands Antilles in the Caribbean, together with Curaçao and St. Maarten, have become special municipalities and therefore part of the country of the Netherlands under an amendment to the Charter for the Kingdom.[3] The Netherlands have 16.7 million inhabitants.

A uniform and well-defined notion of church membership does not, however, exist. Each church has its own criteria for membership and these may differ widely from one church to another. Figures on religious affiliation, as presented in statistical surveys, tend to be quite approximate, because there is no census in the Netherlands. A fairly recent statistical survey has shown that 58 per cent of the population over 18 regards itself as having a religious affiliation: 29 per cent of them Catholic, 19 per cent larger Protestant denominations, since 2004 united under the Protestant Church in the Netherlands, 5 per cent Islamic and 6 per cent affiliated with another religion or belief.[4]

Besides these figures, some key developments in societal and political life in the Netherlands deserve to be mentioned here. First of all, religion seems to have returned to the public arena as a result of the strongly perceived presence of Islam and political issues such as integration, pluralism and social cohesion. Furthermore, over the last two decades, the secularization thesis has experienced the most sustained challenge in its long history, and Western and therefore Dutch society has not been left untouched by this phenomenon. Secularization has been challenged and instead, the transformation of religion seems better to reflect changes in the role of religion in the public domain nowadays.[5] Churchgoing is in decline, especially in the Netherlands and more especially among Catholics and Muslims, but religion and belief have not disappeared and are unlikely to do so.[6] Besides, the traditional social welfare state is in a process of transformation. The so-called pillarization

----

3   This change raised one particular legal issue related to the topic discussed here, which will be developed in Section 4.

4   Centraal Bureau voor de Statistiek, *Religie aan het begin van de 21e eeuw* (Centraal Bureau voor de Statistiek 2009) 7–14. See for a slightly different overview, for example, Ton Bernts et al., 'A religious Atlas of the Netherlands' in Wetenschappelijke Raad voor het Regeringsbeleid, *Geloven in het publieke domein. Verkenningen van een dubbele transformatie* (2006) [Scientific Council for Governmental Policy, *The role of religion in the public domain*. Explorations of a double transformation] 90–91. <www.wrr.nl>

5   Scientific Council for Governmental Policy (2006). See also, among others, Charles Taylor, *A Secular Age* (Belknap/Harvard University Press 2007).

6   Centraal Bureau voor de Statistiek (2009) 13–25; Philip Jenkins, *God's Continent* (OUP 2009). See for an 'update' of the secularization thesis, among others, Pippa Norris et al., *Sacred and Secular. Religion and Politics Worldwide* (CUP 2004).

of Dutch society is a further feature that should be mentioned.[7] Traditionally, churches or church-affiliated organizations in the Netherlands have been active in the social and cultural domains (for example, schooling, youth activities, health care institutions, social support and mass media). With the expansion of the State into these domains from the nineteenth century – and particularly in the twentieth century – the State has accommodated these initiatives.[8] This has resulted in a system of state facilities in these domains, namely religiously neutral entities and confessional facilities. Quality requirements and the funding system are usually the same for these religious and non-religious facilities.

Another characteristic of Dutch society is the organization of political activities along confessional lines. The Christian Democratic Party (CDA: result of the fusion of the former Roman Catholic Party and two reformed parties) and its predecessors have been part of government coalitions ever since the establishment of the modern party system, apart from during two periods of government in the 1980s. Besides the Christian Democratic Party, two other Christian parties are represented in both Houses of Parliament (the Christian Union and the State Reformed Party). A variety of political parties and opinions exists in parliament as a result of Dutch electoral laws which are based on the model of proportional representation and a low electoral threshold. For this reason, there is always a need to build coalitions between the larger parties. A fairly new party, the Party for Freedom (PVV), has a strong anti-Islamic profile. At national level, it is currently represented in the directly elected House of Representatives with 24 of the 150 seats and so it is ranked third among the 10 parties represented. In the indirectly elected Senate, the party occupies 10 of the 75 seats, as such ranked fourth of twelve. The current government, formed by the People's Party for Freedom and Democracy (VVD: Conservatives and Liberals) and the Christian Democratic Party is a so-called 'minority cabinet', which benefits from the tolerant support of the PVV as an opposition party.

The Constitutional and Legal Context

When analysing the Dutch situation on public support for religious organizations, three main constitutional concepts or rights are relevant. These are the principle of

---

7 See, among others, Arend Lijphardt, *The Politics of Accommodation. Pluralism and Democracy in the Netherlands* (University of California Press 1968); James C Kennedy, *Dutch and their Gods. Secularisation and transformation of religion in the Netherlands since 1950* (Uitgeverij Verloren 2005); Hans Knippenberg, 'The Changing Relationship Between State and Church/Religion in the Netherlands' 67 *GeoJournal* 4, 317–30; see for a critical view on this basic approach, Peter Van Dam, *Staat van verzuiling. Over een Nederlandse mythe* [State of pillarization. On a Dutch myth] (Wereldbibliotheek 2011).

8 For example, Annemarie Houkes, *Christelijke vaderlanders. Godsdienst, burgerschap en de Nederlandse natie (1850–1900)* [Christian patriots. Religion, citizenship and the Dutch nation (1850–1900)] (Wereldbibliotheek 2009).

separation of Church and State, neutrality of the State with regard to religion and belief, and freedom of religion and belief. The latter is explicitly guaranteed in the Constitution (Article 6),[9] while the principle of neutrality can be found in Article 6 in conjunction with Article 1,[10] which guarantees equal treatment on the basis of religion and belief. Separation of Church and State is not explicitly mentioned in the Constitution or in any other legislation. It is an unwritten principle of the law and is implicitly embodied in a combination of constitutional guarantees, notably those of Articles 6 and 1. In conjunction with these two articles, Article 23 of the Constitution should also be mentioned; it guarantees freedom of education and establishes the dual system of education with public (State) schools and private (usually denominational) schools, which are funded on an equal footing with State schools. Apart from that, a preamble with an '*invocation dei*' does not exist, unlike in constitutions in some other countries. A State commission set up to review the Dutch Constitution has advised the government not to revise this aspect of the Constitution.[11]

The formulation of the aforementioned constitutional provisions dates from the general constitutional revision of 1983. This Constitution abolished the former chapter VI 'On Religion', which had originated in 1814 and was amended in 1815, 1848, 1917 and 1972. One of the most relevant changes of the 1983 Constitution with respect to the issue relevant here was the fact that 'churches' were no longer mentioned. In addition, belief was introduced as being equally protected as religion. As the fundamental rights in the Constitution protect individuals and organizations (as far as applicable), churches as organizations enjoy religious freedom and are treated equally. While a *specific* 'law on churches' or 'law on religion' does not exist any more, religion is taken into account by the law, for example, certain forms of conscientious objection, law relating to burial, ritual slaughter, processions and church bell ringing, education, mass media and chaplaincy services. A specific law on the financial relationship between Church and State no longer exists.

Historical Explanation

The constitutional provisions and principles and (other) legislation reflect the process of the so-called 'disentangling' [*ontvlechting*] of Church and State in

---

9   Article 6 of the Constitution: '1. Everyone shall have the right to profess freely his religion or belief, either individually or in community with others, without prejudice to his responsibility under the law. 2. Rules concerning the exercise of this right other than in buildings and enclosed places may be laid down by Act of Parliament for the protection of health, in the interest of traffic and to combat or prevent disorders'.

10   Article 1 of the Constitution: 'All persons in the Netherlands shall be treated equally in equal circumstances. Discrimination on the grounds of religion, belief, political opinion, race or sex or on any other grounds whatsoever shall not be permitted'.

11   Staatscommissie Grondwet (2010) *Rapport staatscommissie Grondwet* [Report, State Commission on the review of the Dutch Constitution].

the Netherlands.[12] The principle of separation of Church and State originated in the Batavian Revolution of 1795. In 1796, the constitutional body of the Batavian Republic decreed the separation of Church and State and full freedom of religion for all. This put an end to the privileged status enjoyed by the Dutch Reformed Church since the Union of Utrecht (1579) – when freedom of religion was also first recognized[13] – and government interference in religious matters also declined. This disentangling of Church and State was continued via the Batavian Constitution and later constitutions and legislation with their ups and downs.

In 1798, the separation of Church and State was formalized in the Constitution of the Batavian Republic. Article 20 stipulated that 'no civil advantages or disadvantages are attached to the confession of any religious doctrine'. The Constitution also declared that churches were responsible for supporting themselves, and that no-one was permitted to appear in public 'in a religious order's dress or with the symbol of a religious community'. In addition, the State's right to nominate or appoint a minister when a vacancy arose (right of collation) was abolished. This strict separation between Church and State was primarily due to French influence in the Netherlands in 1798. In 1808, a regulation by decree concerning state financial support for churches was implemented nevertheless. Napoleon Bonaparte declared, however, that: 'everyone ... has equal claim to the same encouragement, to the same assistance. I sense and acknowledge that the Constitution, my feelings and my principles bind me to permit the same privileges and benefits to all clergymen and all members of every faith or community, without distinction'.[14]

After the period of French rule had ended in 1813, the separation of Church and State was abandoned again. The Constitution of the Kingdom of the Netherlands enacted in 1814 once again provided the State with complete latitude with regard to religion. Article 139 enabled the State 'without prejudice to the right and obligation of the Sovereign Ruler, to supervise all religious convictions, if deemed to be of benefit to the interests of the State'. This Constitution also benefited the Dutch Reformed Church again. Although it was decreed that all existing religions would receive equal protection and that everyone would have the same right to public functions, it was explicitly stipulated that the sovereign ruler had to belong

---

12   See for a more elaborated historical overview in English, Constantijn AJM Kormann et al., *Dutch Constitutional Law* (Kluwer 2000). Focussed on the current issue for the period 1813–1855, E Bos, *Soevereiniteit en religie. Godsdienstvrijheid onder de eerste oranjevorsten* (Verloren 2009) 512–21; from a more liberal perspective: Fleur de Beaufort et al. (eds), *Separation of Church and State in Europe with views on Sweden, Norway, the Netherlands, Belgium, France, Spain, Italy, Slovenia and Greece* (European Liberal Forum 2008).

13   Article 13 stipulated that each province possessed legislative power over religious matters, 'provided that every private person shall remain free in religion and that no-one may be persecuted or investigated because of religion'.

14   Sophie C Van Bijsterveld, *De verhouding tussen kerk en staat in het licht van de grondrechten* (Tjeenk Willink 1988) 33.

to the Protestant Christian Reformed Church. Moreover, this church also received State funding. The right of collation was therefore restored as well. After all, payments meant that influence could be exerted.

The Reformed Church's privileged position had officially ended when Catholic Belgium became part of the Kingdom of the Netherlands in 1815. The constitutional provision on financial ties between the Church and State remained. Article 194 stipulated that 'salaries, pensions and other income, of whatever nature, currently received by various denominations or their exponents, will continue to be guaranteed to the same religious persuasions. Exponents who to this date do not receive a salary or a sufficient amount from the State's coffers may be given a salary or the existing salary may be augmented'. Additionally, religious communities other than those of the Reformed Church became entitled to state funding.

In 1848, an extensive constitutional revision was endorsed, but the chapter on religion did not undergo any fundamental changes. The separation of Church and State was confirmed. Religious denominations were given a greater degree of control over their own organization. A new article stipulated that 'Government intervention is required neither in correspondence with leaders of various religious denominations, nor, except for responsibilities in accordance with the law, during the proclamation of ecclesiastical orders'. The freedom of church organizations was confirmed in the Law on Religious Denominations of 1853,[15] rescinding the 'Loi relative à l'organisation des Cultes du 18 Germinal, An X (1802)'.[16] Furthermore, the right of collation was rescinded by means of an Act of 1861, just as the ministries of worship were in 1870 and the State's influence on the content of the education programme for clergymen was in 1876. In 1983, the financial separation of Church and State was ensured by a law that put an end to traditional government obligations with regard to salaries, pensions and suchlike for church ministers (see Section 4). In 1988, the Law on Religious Denominations of 1853 ended with the entering into force of the Law on Public Manifestations.

---

15   At the time of its enactment, the Law did not have a broader significance than appeasing tensions between Protestants and Catholics which had surfaced after the restoration of the Roman Catholic hierarchy in the Netherlands in 1853. It only dealt with a few elements of the vast array of church and state issues. Its main importance at the time was the unequivocal acknowledgement of Church autonomy. At present, this principle is expressed in the Civil Code in the provision dealing with the Church as a legal person (Article 2:20).

16   In this law, the Concordat between the French government and the Pope was laid down. The Law restricted the freedom of the Roman Catholic Church and arranged the organization of the Protestant, the Reformed and the Lutheran Churches. The Law entered into force on 15 May 1810 for the southern provinces and on 29 October for the rest of Holland.

Meaning and Interpretation Nowadays

The principle of the separation of Church and State is used in many debates to justify or reject governmental or (other) institutional policies, laws or practices. This does not always seem very fruitful. On the contrary, it seems reasonable to recognize that the principle seems to be overestimated in the Netherlands nowadays.[17] One could argue that the meaning of the principle of the separation of Church and State in today's society is essentially still an institutional one, namely that State and Churches and other spiritual organizations function as independent bodies. For the spiritual organizations, this means, among other things, that they choose their officials independently and that they (and their members separately or jointly) can freely determine or confess their faith or beliefs. They determine their spiritual and institutional order according to their own views. The State respects this independence. It may not bring any pressure to bear on the administrative organization.

The State must refrain from any interference in the confession of faith or beliefs, without prejudice to its authority and obligation to act against those who violate the law. Spiritual organizations must be treated equally by the State. The government may not, therefore, side with a particular religious or ideological belief. It is, in the words of the European Court of Human Rights, a 'neutral organizer'. On the other hand, the independence of the State *vis-à-vis* these organizations is expressed in the fact that the organizations and their officers do not as such have any public law powers.[18] As long as the government does not act in a discriminatory way, the principle of separation of Church and State does not prevent the government from concerning itself, under certain circumstances, with religious matters or from referring to religious sources or allowing itself to be inspired by these.[19]

It would be clearer, however, not to include all the topics addressing the relationship between State and religion within the principle of separation of Church and State, but rather within the constitutional notion of neutrality. In the current

---

17   Sophie C Van Bijsterveld, 'Scheiding van kerk en staat: een klassieke norm in een moderne tijd' [Separation of Church and State: a classic norm in modern times], in Wetenschappelijke Raad voor het Regeringsbeleid (ed.) *Geloven in het publieke Domein – Verkenningen van een dubbele transformatie* (Amsterdam University Press 2006) 227–60.

18   The policy paper on fundamental rights in a pluralistic society, *Parliamentary Documents II*, 29614, no. 2; Ministerie van Bannlandse Zaken, *Overheid, godsdienst en levensovertuiging:* indrapport van de Commissie van advies inzake de criteria voor steunverlening aan kerkgenootschappen en andere genootschappen op. geestelijke grondslag (ingesteld bij ministerieel besluit van 17 februari 1986, Stcrt. 1986, nr. 51) [Final Report *Government, religion and belief* Commission for advice on the criteria for the provision of support to church organizations and other spiritual organizations], (Ministerie van Bannlandse Zaken 1988).

19   International standards, such as those of the European Convention for the protection of Human Rights and Fundamental Freedoms, offer scope for this. They presuppose the existence of national structures in respect of religion and law and proceed on the recognition that there is a wide variety of relationships between Church and State.

debate, three modes of neutrality may be distinguished: exclusive, inclusive and compensational neutrality.[20] While the first form of neutrality implies excluding religious manifestations from the public domain, the second form includes them in order to be 'neutral'. The compensational form of neutrality implies the possibility of positive action and intends to allow certain religious organizations, practices etc. to be accommodated, in order to let them function or enjoy rights on the same, equal footing as others. This active involvement by the government has, in addition, to be distinguished from involvement that is sometimes necessary to create opportunities and facilities through which freedom of religion can actually be experienced or professed as a result of (positive) human rights obligations. Such obligations (of care) in respect of facilitating the manifestation of a religion – such as offering spiritual care, a prayer area and a special diet – arise especially where there are special legal relationships of dependency between State and individuals, as in the case of prisoners.

Traditionally, the Dutch concept of neutrality is an inclusive one. The funding of general social activities of religious and ideological organizations in the areas of education, social work, aid and suchlike is accepted, as is indirect support in the form of general granting of subsidies for monuments, including church buildings.[21] This inclusive form of neutrality applied nowadays is highly debated, however. A good example of this is Amsterdam's Burgomaster, Van der Laan, who rejected the concept of compensational neutrality, adhered to – along with inclusive neutrality – by his predecessor, Cohen, member of the same political party in 2007, while public demands for a more exclusive neutrality have become more obvious.

Financial Relationship between Church and State

In the Netherlands, there is no generalized state funding of churches or other religious buildings and religious (inspired) activities as such. This is the result of the system of Church and State relations that has developed over recent centuries, as described above and which will be elaborated hereafter. However, there are different ways in which funding of religious (inspired) activities takes place. The following analysis provides an overview of key topics involving state support in some way, whether direct or indirect. The topics focused upon, elaborated to a greater or lesser extent, are: church buildings, clerical offices, chaplaincy or spiritual care services (army, detainees, healthcare institutes), education, social activities, mass media, tax services and political parties. Although the focus is primarily on State funding, the final sub-paragraph will partly address the public, 'financial' value of parishes and communities.

---

20   Wibren Van den Burg, *Het ideaal van de neutrale staat. Inclusieve, exclusieve en compenserende visies op. godsdienst en cultuur* (Boom 2009).

21   See for example the Report on government, religion and beliefs (1988), and the government paper approving this: *Parliamentary Documents II* 1989/90, 20 868, 2, 3.

Churches (Buildings)

In the Netherlands 8,323 church buildings (churches, church buildings, synagogues, temples, mosques) exist with a religious function.[22] As a general rule, church buildings are funded by the churches or believers themselves. However, State funding occurs in different, more or less direct, ways.

Firstly, many church buildings, notably Christian church buildings, are designated 'ancient monuments', like other monuments that also form part of the country's cultural heritage. For such buildings, possibilities for using public funds for conservation and restoration exist under the *Besluit rijkssubsidiëring instandhouding monumenten* [Resolution on State Subsidies for the Preservation of Ancient Monuments].[23] In the Netherlands, there are 3,676 church buildings which have the status of ancient state monument,[24] about 2,600 of which are churches.[25] About 1,750 of these belong to municipalities and parishes, 850 to other entities (for example, religious organizations, private persons or companies). The costs of conservation and restoration of the 1,750 churches with 'monument status' are met by the government up to a maximum of 65 per cent in order to accomplish a six-year conservation plan,[26] with a maximum of €700,000 per application.[27]

Subsidies for the period 2012–2017
In 2011, the Public Service for Cultural Heritage granted subsidies of €58 million for the conservation and restoration of about 500 ancient monuments. The allowance was based on 477 requests; 1,700 requests had to be refused, because the budget was insufficient. €31 million of the allowed subsidies were reserved for the conservation of 230 church buildings. Requests in 2011 concern plans for conservation/restoration during the period 2012–2017.

---

22 Nicolaas Nelissen, *Strategisch Plan voor het Religieus Erfgoed* [Strategic Plan for Religious Heritage] (Uitgeverij Berne-Heeswijk 2008).
23 Besluit van 27 september 2010, *Stb.* 2010, 708 (entered into force 1 January 2011).
24 Nelissen (n 22).
25 Public Service for Cultural Heritage. Other church buildings are, for example, parsonages, presbyteries, chapels, monasteries and cloisters, but also church buildings which no longer have any religious functions, but fulfil instead the function of homes, cultural centres or libraries.
26 Article 15, section 1, subsection b), Besluit rijkssubsidiëring instandhouding monumenten [Resolution on state subsidies for the preservation of ancient monuments], *Stb.* 2010, 708.
27 Article 4, section 1, subsection b), Regeling rijkssubsidiëring instandhouding monumenten 2011 [Ministerial regulation on state subsidies for the preservation of ancient monuments], *Stcrt.* 2010, no. 15658, 7 oktober 2010. Article 4, section 1, subsection d), of this regulation provides the possibility of a higher amount up to a maximum of €1 million, in the case of special projects which cost more than €700,000.

Although the State allocates considerable funds in this way to churches, as it does for monuments,[28] subsidies will always be in great demand, as is recognized in the explanatory memorandum of the 2011 Resolution on State Subsidies for the Preservation of Ancient Monuments.[29] So, the funds are not available for everyone and only cover part of the costs. For this reason, and as a result of the ongoing decline of churchgoing and the resulting lack of finances as well, it is becoming increasingly difficult for churches to find the financial resources for the upkeep and restoration of their buildings, whether monuments or not.[30] This seems particularly the case for migrant religious organizations that have no historical roots and infrastructure in the Netherlands, although their churchgoing tends to be on the increase, rather than on the decline. Nevertheless, it is expected that even 25–30 per cent of Catholic and Protestant Churches will have to be closed and therefore lose at least their religious function during the next decade.[31]

Three other arrangements for state funding do not alter the fact that the situation is worsening. Some specific and indirect arrangements in the fiscal sphere – the purpose of which was to prevent the creation of undue burdens on the owners of church buildings – will be dealt with further below. Another arrangement, which is sometimes available, is foreign funding. This could be welcomed and motivated by charity; funding by foreign (mission) organizations and especially by States, could also bring with it risks of unsuitable influence – but for different reasons, such as safety and integration.[32] At the same time, as a consequence of the separation of Church and State, it is undesirable for the State to intervene in this area when no law has been violated. Instead, the Dutch government has developed, *inter alia*, a set of helpful guidelines for municipalities and organizations in recognizing and dealing with possible façade politics.[33] Finally, one cannot exclude religious buildings which are not ancient monuments being subsidized (locally) for their construction, conservation or restoration. This approach to their funding seems, however, to be rather controversial.[34]

In the past, temporary arrangements existed to support church communities in the establishment of new church buildings. This was the case, for instance,

---

28   *Parliamentary Documents II* 2008/09, 31 700 VIII, 212 (policy letter of 9 July 2009).

29   Resolution on State subsidies for the preservation of ancient monuments, *Stb.* 2010, 708, p. 18.

30   Nelissen (n 22), 130–31.

31   <http://www.kerknieuws.nl/nieuws.asp?oId=20566> accessed 19 May 2011; <http://www.trouw.nl/tr/nl/5091/Religie/article/detail/2883824/2011/09/02/Kwart-kerken-gaat-binnen-tien-jaar-dicht.dhtml> accessed 2 November 2011.

32   Different publications on the influence of ultra-orthodox Salafism by the Saudi government and Saudi Islamic organizations as part of the General Intelligence Service (AIVD), e.g. AIVD, *Radical Dawa in change. The rise of Islamic neo radicalism in the Netherlands* (The Hague 2007).

33   *Parliamentary Documents II* 2008/09, 29754, 145.

34   *Parliamentary Documents II* 2008/09, 29754, 145, 1.

where churches were demolished as a result of war or flooding, where land was reclaimed from inland waterways and where new villages and cities were erected.[35] A law on church building was enacted in 1962.[36] Once it expired in 1975, 770 churches were set up at a cost of 112 million guilders (€50 million).[37] Afterwards, a temporary ministerial regulation on subsidies was accepted on two more occasions that provided financial assistance to places of worship for religious minorities in particular, but these have now expired.[38] The House of Representatives did pass a motion several times during the same period, indicating that such subsidies contravened the separation of Church and State.[39] Today, there are about 475 mosques in the Netherlands.[40]

Clerical Offices

Clerical offices are not funded by the State. For a long period, this was otherwise, as described in the section above. The establishment of the Van Walsum State Commission in 1946 marked the first serious step towards a review of constitutional payment obligations.[41] This commission released its report in 1967; it considered religion to be of such value that government financial support was justified as a rule and proposed an annual donation of 50 million guilders (then about €24 million). The government, however, wanted a complete separation and ignored the recommendation in 1969. The Verdam Commission was established to advise on a regulation addressing a one-off surrender of payment obligations concerning salaries and pensions of church ministers.[42] Such a regulation was included in the

35   See respectively: Oorlogschaderegeling kerkelijke gebouwen (*Stcrt.* 1949, no. 92), Wet op. de Watersnoodschade (Stb. 1953, no. 92) and the Regeling financiering kerkenbouw in de IJsselmeerpolders (1962–1984).

36   Wet van 29 november 1962, *Stb.* 1962, 538 (Premie Kerkenbouw [Church Construction Premium Act]).

37   Final Report *Government, Religion and Belief* (1988) 28–33.

38   Global ministerial subsidy regulation governing (Islamic) places of worship 1976–1981 (31 mosques); Temporary ministerial subsidy regulation governing (Islamic) places of worship 1981–1984 (69 mosques).

39   *Parliamentary Documents II* 1983/84, 16102, 5 (motie-Krajenbrink); *Parliamentary Documents II*, 1984/85, 16102, 99 (motie-Wiebenga/Dales); *Parliamentary Documents II* 1985/86, 16635, 11 (motie-Wiebenga/Dales).

40   See Institute for Multicultural Affairs, *The Position of Muslims in the Netherlands. Facts and figures* (FORUM 2010) 35, <http://www.forum.nl/Portals/Res/res-pdf/Moslims-in-Nederland-2010.pdf> accessed 15 August 2014.

41   The payment obligation was originally compensation for the 'nationalization' of spiritual and ecclesiastical funds from which clergymen's salaries were paid during the period of the Republic.

42   These financial obligations originated as compensation for the annexation of Church goods and property during the eighteenth century. The compensation arrangements had been incorporated into the Constitution of 1814.

partial constitutional revision of 1972 in an additional article of the Constitution, and the former article stipulating payment obligations disappeared. In 1983, government and churches, united in the Inter-Church Contact in Government Affairs (CIO), concluded an agreement that was ratified that same year by a law terminating the financial relationship between the Church and State.[43] The government committed itself to a one-off surrender payment of 250 million guilders (then about €120 million).

Transition period for Bonaire as part of the Netherlands
Since 10 October 2010, the Caribbean island of Bonaire – formerly known as the Netherlands Antilles – has become part of the country known as the Netherlands. As a consequence, churches on Bonaire are (financially) disconnected from the government. Therefore, appointment of new clerical officers paid for by the government will no longer take place. At the same time, the legal position of clerical offices on Bonaire will be respected, until the moment of termination of the employment.[1] Should a new appointment still be pending at the moment of the transition, an exception to the aforementioned might be made under the Law of 1997 on the other subsidies of the Ministry of the Interior and Kingdom Relations.[2]

---

[1]   Second Chamber of Parliament, 2010–2011, appendix, no. 2508. The issue here dealt with Bonaire, but the same would be the case for the islands of St. Eustatius and Saba.
[2]   Whether the former Netherlands Antilles fulfilled their obligations in general before 10 October 2010 or not, will be the subject for a commission on the liquidation of an estate.

Chaplaincy/Spiritual Care Services

Chaplaincy services are provided for in public institutions such as the armed forces or penitentiary institutions. These services are funded by the State. The justification for them is individuals' freedom of religion. For instance, individuals in the armed forces or in penitentiary institutions live under extraordinary circumstances which mean that they cannot take part in ordinary religious life. Since the State bears some responsibility for people living in these circumstances, it has a positive obligation to provide for their religious needs. Chaplains are appointed by the Ministers of Defence and Justice respectively. Religious denominations involved put forward the chaplain to be nominated (whether Christian, Jewish or other). The Protestant Churches cooperate for this purpose. Of course, numbers must be such that the employment of a chaplain of a certain denomination makes sense. Where this is not the case (certainly in the beginning for the Islamic faith), the practice of contracting chaplaincy services developed.

---

43   Act of 7 December 1983 on the termination of the financial relationship between Church and State [Wet tot beeindiging van de financiele verhouding tussen Kerk en Staat].

Each penitentiary is obliged to have sufficient spiritual care, linked as much as possible to the religion or beliefs of its detainees.[44] The budget for chaplaincy services in penitentiaries is based upon the total number of detainees. In addition to this, a norm is applied of one spiritual caretaker for every 90 detainees. Application of this norm in combination with the outcome of an opinion poll held in 2008–2010 resulted in the need for 43 full-time units for Islamic spiritual care. This means an increase in the number of imams (approaching 21 per cent) and less humanist care (12.3 per cent).[45]

As hospitals and other so-called *zorginstellingen* (care institutions like nursing homes and homes for the elderly) are organized, run and funded in a different way to prisons and the armed forces, the organization of the chaplaincy service is slightly different. Hospital boards employ chaplains or involve them on a contractual basis. They are funded through general hospital funds. An act of Parliament guarantees the availability of such spiritual care as part of the overall care that the institution provides.[46] About 800 of the 1,000 spiritual caretakers in care institutions are members of the Trade Association of Spiritual Caretakers in Care Institutions (VGVZ), an association with the aim of advancing spiritual care in care institutions, active in six professional fields (hospitals, nursing homes, psychiatry, youth care, persons with mental disabilities and rehabilitation) and in six sectors as well: Catholic, Protestant, Humanist, Jewish, Islamic and Hindu. Each sector and professional field has a supervising body: the sector/professional field council. The General Board is composed of representatives from the sectors and professional fields.[47]

Education

The Dutch education system distinguishes public (State) and private education. Under Article 23, Section 7 of the Constitution, both forms are funded on an equal footing. This means that denominational schools are fully funded by public funds if they fulfil certain financial conditions and educational standards: a State–religion relationship viewed as a mode of 'inclusive neutrality'. As a consequence, these (publicly funded) denominational schools are, in principle, allowed, for example, to deny admission to prospective pupils on denominational grounds and to not allow pupils of other denominations – when admitted – to abstain on religious

---

44 Articles 41 and 44, section 3, Prisons Act [Penitentiaire Beginselenwet]. See also: Recommendation R(87)3 of the Committee of Ministers of the Council of Europe regarding prison rules (rules 46 and 47) (www.coe.int), *Parliamentary Documents II* 1989/90, 20868, 2, 4–5; European prison rules; Malcolm D Evans, *Religious Liberty and International Law in Europe* (CUP 1997) 216.

45 Second Chamber of Parliament, 2010–2011, appendix, no. 1666.

46 Article 3 of the Act on the Quality of Care Institutions [*Kwaliteitswet Zorginstellingen*].

47 See, among others, <www.vgvz.nl> accessed 15 August 2014.

grounds from, for example, gymnastics. Furthermore, parents are not entitled to withhold their pupils from religious education in such a school. Furthermore, the school may require staff to be loyal with regard to its denominational views. The extent to which it may do so depends, as is the case in exercising other rights or requirements it has, on the exact case. There are a fair number of decisions made by the Commission on Equal Treatment relating to these issues, which receive fairly significant attention in the media, society and politics/parliament. Recently, the Amsterdam Court overruled a decision by the Equal Treatment Commission and allowed a Catholic secondary school to forbid a pupil from wearing a headscarf so that it could maintain its (Catholic) identity.[48]

Undoubtedly, denominational schools are characterized, *inter alia*, by their attention to religious education. Public schools do, however, also offer religious (GVO) or humanist (HVO) education. In 2007, religious/humanist education (G/HVO) was offered in 56 per cent of public schools and in 30 per cent of public schools such education was desirable, although it was not offered.[49] The right to religious education in public schools has existed since 1857, enshrined in Articles 50 and 51 of the Law on Primary Education. According to the present law, public schools have to pay attention to religious, philosophical and social values existing in Dutch society and to acknowledge the meaning of the variety of these values (among others, Article 46 of the Law on Primary Education). Of course, public schools do not promote a specific conviction, while religious schools do, under Articles 50 and 51 of the Law on Primary Education. Public schools are not responsible for the content of religious education and only organize the facilities; lessons are aimed at pupils who participate on a voluntary basis, mostly for one hour a week. In general, the teachers in these lessons are employees of churches, mosques or other religious/philosophical organizations. In the past, Parliament made several requests to the Government to subsidize the G/HVO and establish an adequate (national) organizational structure. As a consequence, the Welfare Centre G/HVO (*Dienstencentrum G/HVO*) was established in 2009, which is governed by five organizations cooperating together. Since that time, religious and/or humanist education (G/HVO) in public schools has been subsidized by the government. In 2010–11, €10 million were spent on these lessons, attended by 70,000 pupils in 1,400 of the 2,600 public schools (53 per cent).[50] A total of 95 per cent of the budget was used to pay personnel costs, as well as any extra training. The remaining 5 per cent of the budget is reserved for the Welfare Centre G/HVO (*Dienstencentrum G/HVO*) and to meet the costs of the different employers who are responsible for

---

48   Amsterdam Court, 6 September 2011, LJN: BR6764.

49   This appears from an investigation under the authority of the Ministry of Education, Culture and Sciences (2007), see reference made at <http://www.gvoenhvo.nl/organisatie. html> accessed 15 August 2014.

50   Protestant lessons 45 per cent, Humanist 45 per cent, Roman Catholic five per cent, Islamic five per cent and Hindu lessons one per cent; see also the website: <http:// www.gvoenhvo.nl/organisatie/enkele-kerncijfers.html> accessed 15 August 2014.

the execution and content of the G/HVO programme.[51] The Education Council argued that government funding of the G/HVO did not contravene the Constitution and, specifically, the principle of separation of Church and State.[52]

The training of religious leaders and spiritual caretakers is no longer a specific government task, as has been described above. Nevertheless, general financial state support for the education programmes of some denominations is still granted. This has been the case recently under the '*Wet op. het hoger onderwijs en wetenschappen*' [Law on Higher Education and Sciences], amended by the '*Wet versterking besturing*' [Law strengthening steering].[53] One result of this, is that the special legal status of different denominations – regarding their right to state funding for their training programme for religious leaders – has been abolished. The possibility of obtaining funds has become more difficult.[54]

In recent years, however, one specific issue in this area came to the fore. It concerns support for so-called moderate Islam by providing (financial) support for the training of imams or similar educational programmes. In 2005, as a result of motions by the Parliament asking for 'home-grown' imams,[55] the government funded a four-year Bachelor's programme entitled, 'Imam/Islamic servant of spiritual care' offered by the Amsterdam-based Inholland College. That same year, the government granted Amsterdam's VU–University a Master's programme in 'Islamic Spiritual Care' and the Bachelor's programme 'Islamic Theology' and Leiden University could offer the Bachelor's and Master's programme in 'Islamic Theology'.[56] Although the State does not focus specifically on moderate religious organizations, the reason behind this effort seems to be to progress towards a liberal Islam delivered by imams and Islamic spiritual care courses in the Netherlands, in order to speed up the integration of Islamic minorities. The government is not involved, however, with the content of the education programme, bearing in mind the separation of Church and State. Since 2005/06, education programmes have received one-off subsidies for the period to 2010/11, in addition to the regular funds provided by the Ministry of Education.

---

51   Second Chamber of Parliament, 2010–2011, appendix, no. 2176.

52   Education Council, 'Dienstverband, godsdienst en openbare school' [Employment, religion and public school], 31 maart 2006.

53   Wet van 4 februari 2010, *Stb.* 2010, 119.

54   *Parliamentary Documents II* 2009/10, 31821, no. 80.

55   *Parliamentary Documents II* 2003/04, 29 200 VI, no. 155 (motion-Sterk); *Parliamentary Documents II* 2004/05, 29854, no. 10 (motion-Bos).

56   These subsidies concern the so-called 'development subsidies' offered by the Ministries of Education, Culture and Sciences (OCW) and the former Ministry of Justice: €1.5 million for the VU–University Amsterdam (for the period 2005–2011); €2.35 million for Leiden University (period 2006–2011) and €1.2 million for INHOLLAND (period 2007–2010). See: *Parliamentary Documents II* 2008/09, 31700 XVII, no. 6.

Social Activities/Accommodation

Church-affiliated organizations have long been active in the fields of education and health, as well as in other fields of social life, such as care for the elderly and activities for young people. Since the end of the nineteenth century, but particularly with the development of the social welfare state ever since the 1960s, the State has started to organize, provide and accommodate more activities in these areas as well.[57] Thus, a system of parallel activities has developed: those offered on a private, often denominational basis, and those offered by public authorities on a neutral, non-religious basis. This continues to the present day. The growth of regulation and financial intervention of the State in these domains has also extended to private providers. As a result, these activities are usually regulated by the same body of law and share the same funding system. The denominational background and inspiration of the activities provided on a confessional basis is respected in law.

In general, no special arrangements exist between governments/municipalities and organizations. Subsidies are granted within the framework of regulations governing regular subsidies for activities, whether carried out by organizations which are founded on religion or beliefs or not. Nevertheless, different approaches and visions relating to subsidies do exist, especially at a local level. The local context – the denominations which are present, the historical traditions, size of the municipality, the nature of any social problems – seems to play a role in this, as well as the difficulty in practice of making the difference between public policies and religious ones.[58] This has been demonstrated in some municipalities where religious denominations are funded for their activities in general, but this amount is based on their member numbers (€1 per member). Other cases concern activities by, for example, the organizations 'Youth for Christ' (youth care), *De Hoop* (care and treatment of drug addicts), *Scharlaken Koord* (care for prostitutes) and *Leger des Heils* (health care).

---

57 Houkes (n 8); Van Dam (n 7).

58 See for example, Maarten Davelaar, Eliane Smits van Waesberghe (eds), *Tussen principes en pragmatisme. Een onderzoek onder Nederlandse gemeenten naar de subsidiëring van levensbeschouwelijke organisaties* [Between principles and pragmatism. Research among municipalities on subsidizing organizations on a religious or philosophical basis] (FORUM 2010) 95.

Youth for Christ: religious or public policy goal?
In 2009, the organization 'Youth for Christ' won the tender for a contract to provide care for young people in the De Baarsjes district of Amsterdam. Both the local area and Youth for Christ were criticized vehemently, because an organization with the mission of 'bringing young people into contact with Jesus Christ' would not be able to take care of young people in a 'neutral' way. In addition, people feared that young people of a different religious background might be excluded by the organization or there was the risk that young people in De Baarsjes – a district with many young people of Islamic background – would give up. Furthermore, there were concerns about personnel management: 'Youth for Christ' wanted, just as for its other activities, only to recruit Christian personnel to care for young people. As a result of its critics, new negotiations started and led to an agreement that non-Christian personnel would be recruited as well via a separate corporation (*stichting*) and a website would be launched.

Afterwards, a comparable issue arose, when the West district decided not to extend a contract with 'Youth for Christ' for providing youth projects in the district of The Mall Westerwijk,[1] after having taken advice from the Equal Treatment Commission in the municipality of Amsterdam on the issue of which recruitment and selection requirements an organization based on religion or belief is allowed to impose within the framework of the Equal Treatment Act.[2]

---

[1] Second Chamber of Parliament, 2009–2010, appendix, no. 3036.
[2] Advice on the stipulation of conditions at recruitment and selection policies of organizations performing tasks for municipalities, CGB–advice 2010–1, January 2010.

The funding of activities organized or provided by religious organizations has gained greater attention over the last five years, especially at a local level. Local questions on the allocation of subsidies for such activities have also attracted the attention of the national Parliament. In order to pass a parliamentary motion, the government joined with the Association of Dutch Municipalities to develop a guide for municipalities on how to deal with concrete issues of the relationship between religion and State and, in particular, on the possibilities of granting subsidies to organizations with a religious or philosophical basis.[59] Also, other organizations have contributed in this regard with research, interviews, conferences and publications.[60]

One of the main guidelines is that public authorities may not exclude organizations solely on the grounds of their denominational background[61] and may (thus) not discriminate between organizations. Municipalities are allowed to enter into financial arrangements, as long as the aims of the voluntary/non-profit organizations with a denominational focus coincide with public policy goals;

---

59 Joyce Overdijk-Francis et al., *Tweeluik religie en publiek domein* – Handvatten voor gemeenten [Diptych Religion and Public domain] (VNG en Ministerie van Binnenlandse Zaken en Koninkrijksrelaties 2009).

60 See for example Davelaar and van Waesberghe (n 60); Marcel Maussen, *Ruimte voor islam? Stedelijk beleid, voorzieningen, organisaties* (Het Spinhuis 2006).

61 ARRS [Council of State] 18 December 1986, AB 1987, 260.

religious education in itself is not interpreted as such.[62] These guidelines are used by municipalities and reference has been made to them in parliamentary questions and answers. For example, questions were raised and answered about the General Regulation on Subsidies (*Algemene Subsidieverordening*) by the Municipality of Rhenen, which stipulated that 'activities which are political and/or religious/ philosophical in nature, resulting from political and/or religious/philosophical motives or having as an aim education or dissemination in this area, cannot receive subsidies'.[63]

Media

Churches, as well as organizations founded on a religious or philosophical basis, have participated in broadcasting ever since the development of the broadcasting system. This was reflected in legislation up until the current Mass Media Act 2008, although various changes have taken place.[64] In general, broadcasting time is allocated in the first instance to broadcasting associations, which must represent a particular societal, cultural, religious or spiritual tendency to meet the corresponding programming needs; broadcasts are also allocated, however, to individual organizations, such as political parties, educational organizations and churches. In order to retain spiritual multiformity in society and to promote the representation of different denominations within the public domain, the government funds – via the Broadcasting Commission (*Commissariaat voor de Media*) – small, spiritual channels, the so-called '2.42 broadcasting organizations', referring to the relevant section of the Mass Media Act 2008. Currently, there are Protestant, Catholic, Evangelical, socialist, liberal and 'neutral' broadcasting organizations (IKON, RKK, ZVK, Humanist and Buddhist, Jewish and Hindu channels).

Under the Mass Media Act 2008, denominations or organizations founded on a religious or philosophical basis have to be allocated airtime by the Broadcasting Commission for a period of five years. In the recent past, Islamic and Hindu organizations succeeded in obtaining broadcasting time, in addition to Christian and Humanist organizations, which have enjoyed a longer tradition in this regard. Recently, Muslims have not received airtime due to organizational problems. It seems that this will be impossible for new broadcasting corporations in the future, so that Muslims will be permanently excluded – although they are, apart from Catholics and churches united in IKON, the third largest denomination or movement in the Netherlands.

---

62   ARRS [Council of State] 19 December 1996, AB 1997, 414.

63   Second Chamber of Parliament, 2009–2010, appendix, no. 1033.

64   Johan Wolswinkel et al. (eds), 'Velen zijn geroepen, maar weinigen uitverkoren. Zendtijd onder kerken en geestelijke genootschappen in de Mediawet 2008' (2009) 9 *Mediaforum* 310–23.

One of the government's main reform and cost-saving measures is a wide-ranging review of the national channel (*publieke omroep*);[65] €127.3 million have to be saved in 2015, of which €13 million concern small, spiritual channels, which will have their budgets cut in half.[66] This is intended to favour the broadcasting companies. One of the arguments in favour of this is the government's opinion that the '2.42 channels' have to 'restrict themselves henceforth to specifically spiritual tasks; the more general programming could be supplied perfectly well by the broadcasting companies'.[67] One could seriously doubt whether – and if so, to what extent – this approach is still in conformity with the principle of separation of Church and State, because here the government is deciding what belongs to the core and what does not, while indicators seem even not to be available.[68]

Tax Services

An indirect way of funding religious denominations is for them to enjoy certain tax benefits, especially under (a) their formal status as Institutes for General Benefit (*ANBI; Algemeen Nut Beogende Instelling*) and (b) of the fiscal exemption of churches from property tax (*kerkenvrijstelling in de Onroerend Zaak Belasting, OZB*). These facilities are not exclusively available for the religious sector, but are available for all sorts of charitable organizations/purposes.

An ANBI has to fulfil two categories of conditions, concerning: (a) the object and factual activities of the institutions and (b) regulations on the organization and financial accounting within the ANBI. The second condition of the first category has been highlighted since 1 January 2010; at least 90 per cent of the factual activities of an ANBI must now contribute to the General Benefit.[69] The first and second categories of conditions are linked via 10 (sub-) conditions which have to be fulfilled in order to obtain ANBI status.[70] Since 1 January 2008, it is up to the tax inspector to decide in a binding ordinance whether an institute fulfils the

---

65   For example, based on research done in 2010, see: *Parliamentary Documents II* 2009/10, 31804, 83 (Report 'Partners in levensbeschouwing' as Annex).

66   *Parliamentary Documents II* 2010/11, 32827, 1, 11.

67   *Parliamentary Documents II* 2010/11, 32827, 1, 15.

68   WibrenVan den Burg, 'Afrekenen met de linkse kerk' [Put behind the left church] (2011) *Nederlands Juristenblad* 26 August, 1473.

69   Article 6.33, section 1, subsection b) Act on Income Tax (*Stb.* 2009, 564) and *Parliamentary Documents II* 2009/09, 31930, 3, 17.

70   See eight conditions mentioned in Articles 41a, and 41b, Regulation (*Uitvoeringregeling*) Income Tax 2001, *Stcrt.* 2000, 250, amended 1 February 2007, *Scrt.* 2007, 28; an additional condition in Article 6.33, section 4, Act on Income Tax (Wet van 17 December 2009, Stb. 2009, 564), and one in Regulation (Besluit) of 6 April 2010, *Stcrt.* 2010, 5278, no. 4.

conditions for ANBI status to be granted.[71] As a result, a register of institutions has been created for those considered to have ANBI status.

One could seriously doubt whether these criteria and procedures do still respect the separation of Church and State and freedom of religion, which is distinct from this; the (ex-ante) influence of the Tax Department on the internal structure and policies of denominations is rather severe,[72] which is quite different from (ex-post) judgements which sometimes indicate a rather severe review of the notion of General Benefit too.[73] Of course, one is not obliged to obtain ANBI status, one could argue. This does not seem very realistic, however, because of the far reaching financial consequences of such a status, which seems to be the more the case when bearing in mind the worsening financial situation of denominations mentioned above, as well as some statistics on donations by groups and individuals to churches, which are tax-deductible thanks to a special tax ruling. Thus, ANBI status seems to encourage private financial donations to churches (and, more generally, to religious causes). The Netherlands donates 0.8 per cent (€4.7 billion) of its Gross Domestic Product (GDP of €572 billion in 2009), while 19 per cent of this (€891 million) – the highest amount – was donated to religion, despite falling from one billion in 2007.[74]

Although tensions seem to arise with the separation of Church and State, these tensions might be diminished by procedural arrangements agreed upon on 30 November 2007 in a covenant between the 25 (in 2011: 30) denominations represented in the CIO (*Interkerkelijk Contact in Overheidszaken;* Inter-Church Contact in Governmental Affairs) and the Tax Department concerning the application of the ANBI regulation.[75] The flip side of the coin seems, however, to be possible unequal treatment between religious denominations which are members of the CIO and those who are not. In this regard, serious evaluation is rather difficult, because the conditions for membership of the CIO are not very clear. What is clear, however, is that only (some) Christian and Jewish denominations are members of the CIO. One can have doubts about the presence of an objective justification in order to legitimate possible discrimination.

Finally, and in short, exemptions or reduced tariffs for churches are also available under the *Successiewet* [Inheritance Tax Act] and laws on property tax.

---

71   As a result of case law, especially that concerning the Scientology Church of Amsterdam, Supreme Court, 7 November 2003, LJN:AN7741. The Tax Department responsible for this is the Tax Office Oost Brabant. See: article 13a Uitvoeringsregeling Belastingdinest 2003.

72   Teunis Van Kooten, 'Kerk en fiscus: de zilveren koorde te nauw aangehaald?' in Broeksteeg, Hansko et al. (eds), *Overheid, recht en religie* [Government, law and religion] (Kluwer 2011).

73   Richard Steenvoorde, 'In het algemeen belang?' [For the General benefit?] (2011) 2 *Tijdschrift voor Religie, Recht en Beleid* 1, 30–42.

74   Theo NM Schuyt et al. (eds), *Giving in the Netherlands: Donations, Bequests, Sponsorships and Volunteering* (Reed Business 2011).

75   <www.cioweb.nl> accessed 15 August 2014.

Church buildings, for example, are exempted from property tax under a local government law, provided the building is used for religious worship for at least 70 per cent of the time. The legal base for this tax is Article 132, Section 6 of the Constitution and Article 219 of the Municipality Act.

Public (Financial) Value of Parishes and Communities

The topics mentioned above are approached from a perspective that mainly emphasizes how religious organizations benefit from state aid. The rationale behind this funding, as described above, is scarcely made explicit and is not translated in financial terms. This has, however, been undertaken in some recent research studies, the findings of which will now be summarized.[76]

Research has been undertaken into the financial value of funding to 1,375 Catholic parishes and 2,270 communities of the Protestant Church in the Netherlands. Their members represent about 90 per cent of all Christians in the Netherlands. The financial value is linked to a social and cultural domain. In the first domain, four types of social activities practised by community parishes have been distinguished: (a) pastoral care and support from the diocese; (b) juvenile and youth work; (c) social cohesion activities and recreation; and (d) education and courses. In total, these activities reach 1.4 million people, half of them with the first activity. All activities combined require the efforts of 165,000 volunteers, whose reward would be on average about €33 an hour. Their financial value therefore amounts to €325 million. As to the second category – cultural activities, such as festivals, concerts or pilgrimages – these reach 1.7 million people each year. About 30,000 volunteers make these activities possible. Their efforts represent a value of €45 million. Furthermore, parishes and communities contribute to the conservation and restoration of church buildings as ancient monuments for €30 million a year. Taken together, both activities represent a value of €400 million a year.

Research has also been conducted into the social return of mosques. About 475 mosques are present in the Netherlands and they save the rest of Dutch society €150 million a year in their role as contributors and taxpayers.[77] Research into the social return of migrant churches, which play a very central role in the (daily) life of many migrants, indicates that the efforts of migrant churches in The Hague represent a financial value of €17.5 million a year.[78] These churches help,

76   Ton Bernts et al., *Kaski Report no. 594 – De kerk telt. De maatschappelijke waarde en parochies en gemeenten* [The Church matters. The social value of parishes and communities] (*Giving in the Netherlands: Donations, Bequests, Sponsorships and Volunteering* (Kaski 2010).

77   Jaap Van der Sar et al., *Maatschappelijk rendement van moskeeën* [Social return of mosques], (Ministerie van Binnenlandse Zaken en Koninkrijksrelaties 2008); <http://www.stichtingoikos.nl/?nid=48010> accessed 15 August 2014.

78   Jaap Van der Sar et al., *Gratis en waardevol: rol, positie en maatschappelijk rendement van migrantenkerken in Den Haag* [Free and Valuable. Role, position and social

inter alia, with the organization of language courses and support people when contacting official bodies.

Sociological and/or Political Challenges

Since the 1960s, some central developments have characterized the Netherlands and had their impact on the country of today. These could be summarized as: (a) individualization as a result of, for example, increased welfare, social and geographical mobility and social security; (b) different methods of secularization; and (c) changes to (the organization of) politics and the (social) welfare state. An important notion related to these developments is the transformation of so-called big or 'heavy' communities into smaller communities, whose transformation might be a better indication of the different changes in society and politics and their relation to religion rather than the notion of depillarization.[79] The latter notion suggests a transformation of Dutch society that was more radical and internationally more distinctive than seems to be the case.

Although society has been individualized and has become more 'fluid', as Zygmund Baumann elaborates in his standard work on this issue,[80] people are not detached from communities. Religion plays another, but still obvious role (again) in public debate and in the public domain. Although religion has become something that one 'just opts for', as Charles Taylor points out,[81] it has not gone away. This does not mean, however, that religion is becoming more accepted in this domain, quite the contrary: there seems to be a tendency to limit the role of religion in the public sphere. Besides, politics has transformed into a search for identity and contact with its unknown citizens, which has partly resulted in more technocratic (1980s) and, since 2001, more populist styles and programmes. Even the existence of freedom of religion and belief among other freedoms has been questioned in the Netherlands by some politicians and legal scientists. In a post-modern, fluid and networked society, the role of religion is no longer evident. Therefore, arrangements between governmental and religious organizations are not that evident either and request permanent legitimacy.

This request for legitimacy cannot be fulfilled or answered by the constitutional framework (alone), which must therefore not be overestimated, although this must be explained again and again. But, on the positive side, one is looking for people's real needs for services, activities, social cohesion, security and so on, and the possibility of organizations based on religion or belief contributing to this. Such organizations have a long tradition and expertise in this regard and

---

return of migrant churches in The Hague], (Digicopy 2006).

   79   Van Dam (n 7).

   80   Zygmunt Bauman, *Liquid Life* (Polity Press 2005); Zygmunt Bauman, *The Individualised Society* (Blackwell Press 2001).

   81   Taylor (n 5).

represent both a social and a financial capital, as described above. Besides the possible contribution of organizations based on religion or belief to society and the reasoning behind funding them, other sub-items and challenges to public funding have been described in this chapter, such as increasing numbers of church closures (both monumental and non-monumental buildings), possible risks from foreign financing and the changed needs for chaplaincy services in penitentiary institutions as a result of the changing population and migration. One political challenge will be maintaining tolerance and keeping up the ideal and guarantee of living peacefully in one society with different religions, believers and non-believers and religious orthodoxy.

Good Practice

This chapter deals with different subtopics of the general theme. At the general and more abstract level, one could identify some good practices involving ways of managing or dealing with debates and emotions in society around this theme. When debate in society heats up and the existing relations between rights and institutions are questioned, it is seems helpful when the government releases a *policy letter*, like that on fundamental rights in a pluralistic society; a two-day debate was held in Parliament and two international conferences were organized in cooperation with the Council of Europe,[82] which resulted, *inter alia*, in a Political Declaration by the Committee of Ministers of the Council of Europe.[83]

Another policy letter on the separation of Church and State and fundamental rights was released in the autumn of 2011 after a public hearing in Parliament on the same issue involving 13 experts. Among these experts were professors in constitutional law, human rights and legal philosophy, a rabbi, a chief of the chaplaincy services and others. They mainly drew attention to the positive aspects of religion for society and urged dialogue on difficult questions instead of resorting too hastily to the courts. Both the policy letter and the public hearing served as input for parliamentarians ahead of a political debate with the cabinet along the same theme.

A second good practice seems to have been the release of *guidelines* by the Ministry of the Interior in cooperation with the Association of Dutch Municipalities (VNG) on how to deal with concrete issues of the relationship between religion

---

82 See Constitutional Affairs and Legislation Department (ed.), *Report of the International Conference on Fundamental Rights in a Pluralistic Society* (Ministry of the Interior and Kingdom Relations 2004); Directorate General of Human Rights and Legal Affairs – Council of Europe, *Human rights in culturally diverse societies. Challenges and perspectives*, Conference proceedings, The Hague, 12–13 November 2008 (Council of Europe 2009).

83 CM (2005)56 final 13 May 2005, *Declaration of the Committee of Ministers on human rights and the rule of law in the Information Society.*

and State, especially on possibilities for subsidizing organizations founded on a religious or philosophical basis.[84] Also, other organizations have contributed in this regard with fruitful research, interviews and publications.[85] Furthermore, guidelines were released for municipalities and organizations for recognizing and dealing with possible façade politics in the context of foreign funding.[86]

The establishment in 2008 of the foundation for the Year of the Religious Heritage and its strategic 2008 Plan for Religious Heritage, in which it made several recommendations, could be regarded as further good practice, in this case for bringing to the State's attention the artistic significance of church buildings and the financial and funding aspects of it. With respect to chaplaincy services in prisons and other institutions, it seems worthwhile having opinion polls on a regular basis in order to identify which denominations should be represented in the services, in order to permit the most effective and legitimate allocation of budgets.

Conclusion

This chapter has illustrated some of the main issues affecting the public funding of organizations based on religion or belief in the Netherlands. These topics include the funding of church buildings, clerical offices, chaplaincy or spiritual care services, education, social activities, mass media, tax services and political parties. They show that a relationship between national and/or local government and religious organizations does still exist. In order to interpret this relationship, the topics and examples were illustrated against the backdrop of the constitutional framework. Then, it became clear that there is a continuum of this relationship throughout Dutch (constitutional) history. Although such a relationship has existed for a long time, the motives for this have differed from time to time, and especially from the motives existing pre-1850, when the principle of separation of Church and State was confirmed with the constitutional revision of 1848 and further developed.

The separation of Church and State has been further elaborated in our present time. The concept is nevertheless the subject of rather heated debate in Dutch society. However, in many cases, it is linked to many different topics which relate to the role of religion in the public domain, rather than the separation of Church and State in a stricter sense, which is more an institutional concept. In this regard, the principle seems to be overestimated. When we look to the role of religion in the public domain, we realize that an equally intensive debate is taking place, as a result of different developments mentioned previously in this chapter. This debate gives rise to a trend of limiting the role of religion in the public sphere and away

---

84   Overdijk-Francis et al. (n 63).
85   See, for example, Davelaar and van Waesberghe (eds) (n 60).
86   *Parliamentary Documents II* 2008/09, 29754, no. 145.

from pluralist accommodation towards monist secularism.[87] Institutions and laws respecting religion and beliefs do still rather solidly exist, however.

A rather less controversial domain where government and religious organizations still encounter one another is that of general benefit. In this context, it is worthwhile realizing the public (financial) value of parishes and communities, as has been illustrated above. Public funding to religious organizations is accepted and legitimate as long as it serves the general benefit. Of course, the general benefit is no neutral concept in itself, as has been shown by, for example, the issue of tax arrangements or funding youth care, but it seems nevertheless to give more guidance to – and be accepted by – both government and religious organizations. An important condition for the legitimacy of funding in this regard is the applicability of the obligation not to discriminate between different organizations.

On the other hand, fundamental rights sometimes even oblige the State or government to fund or otherwise enable religious practices and thereby religious organizations. Against this background, a key challenge is to keep trying not to intervene in the content of religion or beliefs (mass media, tax), while funding organizations based on that religion or belief and to organize a political and public climate where tolerance and respect for both religious minorities and religious orthodoxy on the one hand and non-believers on the other is achieved. This seems necessarily to be a non-stop process in any democracy. It is especially the case in a time of financial crisis when States are in a phase of cost-cutting measures. Good practice could be helpful for both governments and religious organizations in this regard.

List of References

AIVD, *Radical Dawa in Change. The Rise of Islamic Neo Radicalism in the Netherlands* (The Hague 2007)

Bauman Z, *The Individualised Society* (Blackwell Press 2001)
—— *Liquid Life* (Polity Press 2005)

Bernts T et al., *Kaski Report no. 594 – De kerk telt. De maatschappelijke waarde en parochies en gemeenten* (Kaski 2010)
—— 'A Religious Atlas of the Netherlands' in Wetenschappelijke Raad voor het Regeringsbeleid, *Geloven in het publieke domein. Verkenningen van een dubbele transformative* (2006)

Bos E, *Soevereiniteit en religie. Godsdienstvrijheid onder de eerste oranjevorsten* (Verloren 2009)

---

87 Ben P Vermeulen, 'On Freedom, Equality and Citizenship. Changing Fundamentals of Dutch Minority Policy and Law (immigration, integration, education and religion)' in Marie-Claire Foblets et al. (eds), *The Response of State Law to the Expression of Cultural Diversity* (Bruylant/Yvon Blais 2010) 45–143 (para.12–13).

Centraal Bureau voor de Statistiek (CBS), *Religie aan het begin van de 21e eeuw* (Centraal Bureau voor de Statistiek 2009)

Constitutional Affairs and Legislation Department (ed.), *Report of the International Conference on Fundamental Rights in a Pluralistic Society* (Ministry of the Interior and Kingdom Relations 2004)

Davelaar M and van Waesberghe ES (eds), *Tussen principes en pragmatisme. Een onderzoek onder Nederlandse gemeenten naar de subsidiëring van levensbeschouwelijke organisaties* (FORUM 2010)

De Beaufort F et al. (eds), *Separation of Church and State in Europe with views on Sweden, Norway, the Netherlands, Belgium, France, Spain, Italy, Slovenia and Greece* (European Liberal Forum 2008)

Directorate General of Human Rights and Legal Affairs – Council of Europe, *Human Rights in Culturally Diverse Societies. Challenges and Perspectives*, Conference proceedings, The Hague, 12–13 November 2008 (Council of Europe 2009)

Education Council, *Dienstverband, godsdienst en openbare school*, 31 maart (2006)

Evans MD, *Religious Liberty and International Law in Europe* (CUP 1997)

Houkes A, *Christelijke vaderlanders. Godsdienst, burgerschap en de Nederlandse natie (1850–1900)* (Wereldbibliotheek 2009)

Institute for Multicultural Affairs, *The position of Muslims in the Netherlands. Facts and figures* (FORUM 2010)

Jenkins P, *God's Continent* (OUP 2009)

Kennedy JC, *Dutch and their Gods. Secularisation and Transformation of Religion in the Netherlands since 1950* (Uitgeverij Verloren 2005)

Knippenberg H, 'The Changing Relationship Between State and Church/Religion in the Netherlands' 67 *GeoJournal* 4

Kormann CAJM et al., *Dutch Constitutional Law* (Kluwer 2000)

Lijphardt A, *The Politics of Accommodation. Pluralism and Democracy in the Netherlands* (University of California Press 1968)

Maussen M, *Ruimte voor islam? Stedelijk beleid, voorzieningen, organisaties* (Het Spinhuis 2006). Ministerie van Bannlandse Zaken, *Overheid, godsdienst en levensovertuiging:* indrapport van de Commissie van advies inzake de criteria voor steunverlening aan kerkgenootschappen en andere genootschappen op. geestelijke grondslag (ingesteld bij ministerieel besluit van 17 februari 1986, Stcrt. 1986, nr. 51), (Ministerie van Bannlandse Zaken 1988)

Nelissen N, *Strategisch Plan voor het Religieus Erfgoed* (Uitgeverij Berne-Heeswijk 2008)

Norris P et al., *Sacred and Secular. Religion and Politics Worldwide* (CUP 2004)

Overdijk-Francis J et al., *Tweeluik religie en publiek domein* – Handvatten voor gemeenten (VNG en Ministerie van Binnenlandse Zaken en Koninkrijksrelaties 2009)

Parliamentary Documents II 1983/84, 16102, no. 5 (motie-Krajenbrink)

Parliamentary Documents II 1984/85, 16102, no. 99 (motie-Wiebenga/Dales)

Parliamentary Documents II 1985/86, 16635, no. 11 (motie-Wiebenga/Dales)

Parliamentary Documents II 1989/90, 20868, no. 2
Parliamentary Documents II 2003/04, 29200 VI, no. 155 (motion-Sterk)
Parliamentary Documents II 2004/05, 29854, no. 10 (motion-Bos)
Parliamentary Documents II 2008/09, 29754, no. 145
Parliamentary Documents II 2008/09, 31700 VIII, no. 212 (policy letter of 9 July 2009)
Parliamentary Documents II 2008/09, 31700 XVII, no. 6
Parliamentary Documents II 2009/10, 31804, no. 83 (Report 'Partners in levensbeschouwing' as Annex)
Parliamentary Documents II 2009/10, 31821, no. 80
Parliamentary Documents II 2010/11, 32827, no. 1
Parliamentary Documents II, 29614, no. 2
Rivers J, *Law of the Organised Religions. Between Establishment and Secularism* (OUP 2010) Preface.
Schuyt TNM et al. (eds), *Giving in the Netherlands: Donations, Bequests, Sponsorships and Volunteering* (Reed Business 2011)
Staatscommissie Grondwet, *Rapport staatscommissie Grondwet* (2010)
Steenvoorde R, 'In het algemeen belang?' (2011) 2 *Tijdschrift voor Religie, Recht en Beleid* 1, 30–42
Taylor C, *A Secular Age* (Belknap/Harvard University Press 2007)
Van Bijsterveld SC, *De verhouding tussen kerk en staat in het licht van de grondrechten* (Tjeenk Willink 1988)
—— 'Scheiding van kerk en staat: een klassieke norm in een moderne tijd' in Wetenschappelijke Raad voor het Regeringsbeleid (ed.) *Geloven in het publieke Domein – Verkenningen van een dubbele transformatie* (Amsterdam University Press 2006)
—— 'Religion and the Secular State' in WC Durham et al. (eds), *Religion and the Secular State: Interim National Reports* (The International Center for Law and Religion Studies, Brigham Young University 2010)
Van Dam P, *Staat van verzuiling. Over een Nederlandse mythe* (Wereldbibliotheek 2011)
Van den Burg W, *Het ideaal van de neutrale staat. Inclusieve, exclusieve en compenserende visies op. godsdienst en cultuur* (Boom 2009)
—— 'Afrekenen met de linkse kerk' (2011) *Nederlands Juristenblad* 26 August, 1473
Van der Sar, J et al., *Gratis en waardevol: rol, positie en maatschappelijk rendement van migrantenkerken in Den Haag* (Digicopy 2006)
—— *Maatschappelijk rendement van moskeeën* (Ministerie van Binnenlandse Zaken en Koninkrijksrelaties 2008)
Van Kooten T, 'Kerk en fiscus: de zilveren koorde te nauw aangehaald?' in H Broeksteeg et al. (eds), *Overheid, recht en religie* (Kluwer 2011)
Vermeulen BP, 'On Freedom, Equality and Citizenship. Changing Fundamentals of Dutch Minority Policy and Law (immigration, integration, education

and religion)' in MC Foblets et al. (eds), *The Response of State Law to the Expression of Cultural Diversity* (Bruylant/Yvon Blais 2010)

Wolswinkel J et al., 'Velen zijn geroepen, maar weinigen uitverkoren. Zendtijd onder kerken en geestelijke genootschappen in de Mediawet 2008' (2009) 9 *Mediaforum*

Chapter 3

Funding of Religious and Non-confessional Organizations: the Case of Belgium

Louis-Léon Christians and Stéphanie Wattier

Introduction

State funding of religions has been part of the Belgian constitutional system since its beginning in 1830. It has never been questioned since, as it is considered the heart of the Belgian principle of State neutrality. Started in the nineteenth century for the diverse religious denominations historically located on the territory (Catholic, Anglican, Jewish, Protestant), the funding scheme was expanded in the twentieth century to Islam (1974–2005), to Orthodoxy (1985) and finally to non-confessional philosophical groups (1993–2002), who were before 1981 the most active minority opposed to State funding of religions. While State support has continuously been reaffirmed, after the Second World War, however, new controversies arose focusing on the 'opacity' of allocation methods, the historical inertia of administrative criteria used for distributing funds and, finally (perhaps mainly), the Catholic Church's disproportionate share of State funding. There is no doubt that the Belgian administrative and legal structure – based on a stability-oriented policy – is unable to provide adjustments as promptly as required by the secularization of the Belgian Catholic population, coupled with the diversification of minority religions. Despite a large consensus in favour of these findings, huge controversies remain about the best way to improve the flexibility and the fairness of the system, without endangering the specificity of Belgian active pluralism.

Sociological Approach

Since the Second World War, the secularization process in Belgian society has been progressively increasing. Catholic religious practice has been gradually declining and religious indifference growing rapidly (Table 3.1). Nevertheless, sociological data is complex: when parents have to choose between religious or non-confessional courses for their children at school, they continue to predominantly choose the Catholic ones, with only one exception in favour of Islamic courses in Brussels (Table 3.2). Between 1964 and 1984, Islamic immigration was encouraged. In 2012, from a global population of 11 million inhabitants, more than 450,000 are Muslim, mainly based in central Brussels and other main Belgian

Table 3.1   Catholic religious practices in Belgium (compared to the global population, 1980–2006)

%	Wallonia				Flanders				Brussels				Kingdom				
	1980	1990	1995	2006	1980	1990	1995	2006	1980	1990	1995	2006	1967	1980	1990	1995	2006
Baptisms	82.3	74.2	70.6	54	89.0	83.1	79.1	67.8	44.9	36.9	29.7	17.1	93.6	82.4	75.0	70.9	58
Marriages	73.4	58.1	55.1	28.6	81.5	64.5	54.5	29.7	44.7	28.1	26.3	25	86.1	75.7	59.1	52.0	28
Funerals	78.2	76.8	75.1	50	90.7	88.8	86.0	70	64.2	60.4	51.7	29.8	84.3	83.0	81.6	78.6	63
Attendance	21.5	14.6	11.2	6.8	32.2	21.3	15.2	14.4	12.0	8.8	7.6	6.2		26.7	17.9	13.1	7

Source: La Libre Belgique, 30 June 1997 and 9 July 2008, survey by the Catholic University Leuven and the Bishops' Conference.

Table 3.2   Choice of religious/non-confessional courses at school (2010–2011)

%	Catholicism	Islam	Protestantism	Orthodoxy	Judaism	Non-confessional ethics
Wallonia	71.8	4.7	1.1	0.1	0.04	22.2
French-speaking Brussels	55.2	23.7	2.2	1.1	0.8	17.1
Flanders	82.6	4.1	0.5	0.1	0.3	11.6
Flemish-speaking Brussels	62.5	25.8	1.7	0.5	0.04	8.8

Source: Caroline Sagesser (2012), 'Les cours de religion et de morale dans l'enseignement obligatoire' (2012) 2140–41 *Courrier du CRISP.*

cities. The relative importance of atheism or secularity is very controversial, because of the ambiguity of the individual meaning of 'religious indifference' in different surveys. The Humanist movement has a relatively low membership (1 per cent–13 per cent), but claims to represent all the indifferent people. Judaism, Protestantism, Orthodoxy, Buddhism and Hinduism are also active minorities in Belgium, but represent a very small part of the population.

Historical Approach

Looking back in history is certainly one of the best ways to understand the present legal system of Church funding. When choices were being made by the Belgian First Parliament (*le Congrès National*) in 1830 during the adoption of the Constitution, Belgian society was predominantly Catholic, although a very active, liberal, political minority was also significant.

The political compromise in favour of a regime of mutual independence between the Church and the Belgian State is important to our understanding of the funding mechanisms pertaining to religious and non-confessional organizations.

Influences of Previous Regimes (before Independence)

First of all, Belgium was dominated by the Austrian Netherlands (until 1795) and was regulated by innumerable customs. There were two funding systems *vis-à-vis* recognized religions: (1) using income from property distributed to religious institutions over the course of history and (2) collecting tithes.[1] At that time, the ambition of the Habsburgs was to transform 'the Church of the Austrians into a nationalized "Belgium Church" with the loosest possible ties to Rome'.[2]

After being annexed by the French Republic in 1795, Belgium became subject to French legislation. In 1797, presbyteries and churches were put under sequestration. Then, they were reopened thanks to Napoleon's *coup d'état*.

In 1801, Napoleon signed a convention – called 'Concordat' – with the Holy See.[3] This Concordat is considered as one of the historical bases for the funding of recognized religions in Belgium, because it ended the conflict between State and Church that was born during the French Revolution and because the aim of the Concordat would be transposed into the Belgian Constitution.[4] Indeed,

1   Jean-Pierre Delville, 'Le financement des cultes en Belgique: approche historique' in Jean-François Husson (ed.), *Le financement des cultes et de la laïcité: comparaisons internationales et perspectives* (Editions namuroises 2005) 79–80.

2   Hervé Hasquin, 'Is Belgium a *laïque* State?' in Fleur de Beaufort et al. (eds), *Separation of Church and State in Europe* (European Liberal Forum 2008) 92.

3   Delville (n 1) 80–81.

4   Francis Delpérée, 'Les aspects constitutionnels, budgétaires et fiscaux du financement des cultes' (2001) 61, 4 *Les Annales de Droit de Louvain* 447.

the French Revolution having suppressed most Church revenues – such as the dime – and confiscated its lands and properties, the Concordat was also compensating this in a way, by providing financial support paid for by local authorities (municipalities and departments) for church councils (or *fabriques d'églises*), cathedrals and seminaries, whenever their income was insufficient to maintain buildings and organize the [religion].[5]

In 1808, there was much tension surrounding religion. In fact, opposition to the regime was strong and 'revived by the Imperial Catechism and the virtual deification of the Emperor; the "war" between Napoleon and the Pope from 1808 onwards precipitated the rupture, especially with an increasing number of bishops and priests who were being arrested'.[6] Therefore, the fall of the imperial regime was interpreted as deliverance.

In 1815, the United Kingdom of the Low Countries (today, the Netherlands and Belgium) was founded and 'the Church entertained hopes of winning back its former freedom and even of regaining the right to collect tithes: there was no better way to escape financial dependency on the Government'.[7] Those hopes did not last for long: they vanished in 1817 when the autocratic sovereign, King William I, decided to create special training for priests. Then, in 1825, the King 'closed a string of episcopal seminaries and established a state-controlled philosophical college intended to cast all future priests from the same mould'.[8]

In 1827, King William I signed a convention with the Church. This Concordat contained the same principles as that of 1801.[9]

After the Belgian Revolution (1830), the State became independent. Globally, Belgian independence was the result of a coalition of Liberals and Catholics.[10] When writing the Constitution, its Belgian authors were faced with two different tendencies: on the one hand, the Liberals wanted the principle of separation between State and Church to be adopted; on the other hand, Catholics wanted a specific dependence between state sphere and religious sphere.[11] They were politically obliged to build an original compromise into the Constitution. Finally, there would be some continuity between the old Netherlands and the new independent

---

5   Jean-François Husson, 'New policies with old instruments? Financing religious and philosophical communities in Belgium' in M Moravcikova et al. (eds), *Financing of Churches and Religious Societies in the 21st Century* (Bratislava: Institute for Church–State Relations 2010) 148–9.

6   Hasquin (n 2) 92.

7   Hasquin (n 2) 92.

8   Hasquin (n 2) 92.

9   Stéphanie Wattier, 'Le financement des cultes au XXIe siècle: faut-il réviser l'article 181 de la Constitution?' (2011) *Revue Belge de Droit Constitutionnel* 28.

10   Aloïs Victor Jacques Marie Simon, 'Le Saint-Siège et l'Union Catholico-Libérale (1828–1846)' (1962) 34 *Bulletin de l'Institut Historique Belge de Rome* 595–615.

11   Emile Huyttens, *Discussions du Congrès national de Belgique*, tome 1 (Bruxelles: Société typographique belge 1834) 525.

Belgian State. For that reason, Article 117 of the Belgian Constitution of 1831 (now Article 181) mandated – and still mandates – the State to fund ministers of recognized religions. This article specifies that 'the salaries and pensions of ministers of religion are paid for by the State; the amounts required are charged annually to the budget'.

But it would be wrong just to conclude that Belgium simply re-assumed its previous obligations towards religious organizations during the French and Dutch regimes. These existing obligations were linked with a new liberal approach to Church autonomy in its own sphere. They were no longer justified through formal concordats.[12] Independent Belgium has never signed a Concordat with the Holy See. In fact, a 'Concordat regime' would have meant reciprocal rights and obligations between State and Church. As mentioned above, it is only the principle of funding of recognized religions that was transposed into the new Belgian Constitution in 1831. In short, the funding of the salaries of ministers of recognized religions was maintained, but linked to a new formal ban on political control over religious issues.

A Regime of Mutual Independence

Adopted on 7 February 1831, the Belgian Constitution did not explicitly refer to *laïcité* of the State, or to a *séparation* between State and Church.[13] Three articles of the new Constitution were – and are – important as far as freedom of religion and Church autonomy are concerned.

Article 19 of the Constitution[14] guarantees freedom of religion; Article 20[15] specifies that 'no one can be obliged to contribute in any way whatsoever to the acts and ceremonies of a religion or to observe its days of rest'; Article 21 § 1[16] stipulates that 'the State does not have the right to intervene either in the appointment or in the installation of ministers of any religion whatsoever or to forbid these ministers from corresponding with their superiors, from publishing the acts of these superiors, but, in this latter case, normal responsibilities as regards the press and publishing apply'.

Those three articles have never been modified since 1831 – except for the new numbering of the Constitution that took place in 1994.

As far as the funding of recognized religions is concerned, Article 181[17] of the Constitution mandates the State to fund their ministers. Concretely, this article

---

12 Henri Wagnon, 'Le concordat de 1801–1827 et la Belgique indépendante' in *L'Eglise et l'Etat à l'époque contemporaine – Mélanges dédiés à la mémoire de Mgr Aloïs Simon* (Facultés universitaires Saint-Louis 1975) 547–63.

13 Hasquin (n 2) 93.

14 Article 14 of the Constitution of 1831 (since 1994, Article 19).

15 Article 15 of the Constitution of 1831 (since 1994, Article 20).

16 Article 16 § 1 of the Constitution of 1831 (since 1994, Article 21).

17 Article 117 of the Constitution of 1831 (since 1994, Article 181).

specifies that 'the salaries and pensions of ministers of religion are paid for by the State; the amounts required are charged annually to the budget'. Article 181 has only been modified once, in 1993, in order to extend the funding obligation for the benefit of non-confessional organizations (like the Humanist movement).

Fundamentally, the combination of Articles 21 § 1 and 181 of the Constitution is considered as the main rationale that justifies the assertion that Belgium represents a *regime of mutual independence or active neutrality* between Church and State. As such, it is a combination of State funding and Church autonomy. It has been clear since 1831 that control of public order and the enforcement of criminal law may and must be imposed by the State on all religions, but precisely without formalizing more intrusive lowering of autonomy for *funded* religions.

In 1859, Jules Bara, a famous Belgian legal scholar, Senator and Minister of Justice, explained that the salaries granted to ministers of religions

> are an exception with no influence on the constitutional system. No special power of control resulted from this public funding. The State's power and rights remain independent from these salaries, and the equality of religions affirmed by our Basic Law would break down if greater powers were exercised over ministers. Salaries do not justify any special obligations nor privileges for the clergy *vis-à-vis* the State.[18]

For Rik Torfs,[19] Articles 19, 20, 21 and 181 of the Constitution 'governing Church–State relations are an early example of the Belgian political tradition of consensus. Though bright, young, liberal and sometimes anticlerical politicians wanted to propagate modern freedoms, they also wanted to retain absolute governmental supervision of the Church. Catholic politicians and the Belgian Church, however, were unwilling to allow their voices go unheard'. Torfs concludes that 'the final constitutional articles have produced an equilibrium which, although not perfect, has remained unchallenged'.[20]

---

18   Hasquin (n 2) 96.

19   Rik Torfs, 'Church and State in France, Belgium, and the Netherlands: Unexpected Similarities and Hidden Differences' (1996) *Brigham Young University Law Review* 956.

20   On the other hand, some very narrow public limitations of Church autonomy have been allowed by the National Congress and enacted by the Constitution: Article 21 § 2 stipulates that 'a civil wedding should always precede the blessing of the marriage, apart from the exceptions to be established by the law, if needed' (without distinction as to whether the religion is funded or not by the State). This shows the incorrectness of any idea of radical separation. In 1831, the argument used to sustain this principle was fear of family disorder. In fact, in support of the precedence of civil marriage, 'several speakers have referred to abuse reported to have been suffered by women and children between October 1814 and January 1817, a period during which Napoleon's legislation had been held in abeyance'. Hasquin (n 2) 94–5.

Justifications for the Funding of (Recognized) Religions

From the beginning, in 1830, justification for the State's financial support has been a mix of (mainly Catholic) history and new liberal trends, both united in common opposition to the intrusive policies used by previous regimes.

Defenders of the Catholic religion considered that payments made to (Catholic) ministers were *compensation* 'for the nationalization of Church assets that had occurred under the French regime and the effects of which had lasted throughout the Dutch regime between 1815 and 1830'.[21]

Liberals finally reached a compromise with Catholics to guarantee a *status quo* via the Constitution, i.e. the State's obligation to fund ministers of religion. In other words, the funding of Catholic ministers in Belgium is founded on 'reparation for the despoilment of Church assets for the benefit of the Nation which occurred at the end of the eighteenth century'.[22] Nowadays, this argument is still used by Catholic authorities to justify their salaries.

The first draft of the Belgian Constitution narrowed this support to '*already funded religions*' or to '*Christian churches*',[23] but, at the request of Jewish communities, it was finally agreed to include Jewish rabbis in the State support regime. The phrasing of the Constitution changed in consequence into a new, broader formula referring to 'ministers of *all* religions' ('*ministres de tous les cultes*'). This phrasing was however criticized as a formula that went too far and was finally replaced by the words 'ministers of religions' ('*ministres des cultes*'), designed to allow the legislator some choice.

The rationale for this expansion was to respect the new constitutional trends of freedom and liberalism towards religions,[24] but also to free the State from the systematic obligation to fund any new religions. Very early on, constitutional literature proposed a new criterion: the concept of 'reasonable' ('*sérieuses*') religions.[25] As far as non-Christian religions were concerned, allocated salaries were – and still are – progressively founded on the principle of *social utility* within society. This more recent criterion has been criticized by some Catholic scholars,[26]

---

21 ibid.

22 ibid.

23 Isidore Van Overloop, *Exposé des motifs de la Constitution belge* (H. Goemaere 1864), tome 4, 106.

24 Huyttens (n 11), tome 2, 280. See also Van Overloop (n 23) 222: 'Quant aux cultes et aux communions dissidentes, c'est une conséquence de la liberté accordée aux opinions religieuses, c'est à ce seul titre que l'Etat peut leur devoir un traitement: la justice exige qu'il soit alloué à ces communions les sommes nécessaires aux frais de leur culte; passé cela, nous ne leur devons rien' (Baron de Sécus).

25 For example, Philippe Vandevivere, 'Du culte et du clergé sous l'empire de la constitution belge' (1851) *Belgique judiciaire*, tome 9, 1265.

26 For an early use of the criteria of 'social utility': *cf.* Joseph Daris, *La liberté de la religion catholique et le projet de loi sur le temporel des cultes* (H. Dessain 1865), *spec.* p. 26 ('Ce sera donc à la législature à apprécier si le nouveau culte qui sollicite la

but finally accepted in the main and applied to the funding of Catholic ministers. As Vincent De Coorebyter explained, 'the social value given to ministers of religion is above all, not their acts of charity (which are primarily a matter of congregations and associations), but their contribution to maintaining public order, a critical issue in the aftermath of a revolution'.[27] During the twentieth century, ministers of religions were progressively considered as providing not only a form of social control, but also a true social solidarity and moral support throughout life (birth, marriage, death...). In this regard, guaranteeing an adequate social status to ministers was also important: 'These salaries must also correspond to the needs of life and the necessities inherent to the social position of ministers of religion'.[28]

It is worth noting that, since the beginning, the concept of 'recognized religion' was used by scholars, in keeping with the vocabulary of the French regime, but was formally ignored by the Belgian Constitution until 1988. As already mentioned, the system was intended to be formally open to all religions. However, according to Article 117 (now 181), a law is necessary to determine the budget each year. Consequently, the legislator might decide each year which denominations are to be funded. No general legislation has ever been enacted to define criteria or general rules on 'recognition'. Extending State funding to new denominations remains a 'sovereign' and unilateral decision of the Belgian Federal Parliament, confirming the result of previous governmental negotiations with denominational representatives. What is usually called 'legal recognition' involves simply *introducing the new denomination's name* onto the existing list of denomination names, within the phrasing of different particular acts and laws (namely, laws on salaries, budget, administration, religious broadcasting, religious education in public schools, chaplaincies, and so on).

Since 1974, some Members of Parliament have questioned the Minister of Justice about the Government's recognition policy. The regularly reiterated answer given by the Minister mentions five criteria: (1) having a relatively large number of followers (several tens of thousands); (2) being structured in such way that there is a representative body that can represent the religion in question in its relations with civil authorities; (3) having been established in the country for a fairly long period; (4) having a social interest for people; (5) not having any

---

personification civile, le mérite réellement par son utilité sociale'). This criterion was, however, controversial: see Anonymous, *Mémorial belge des conseils de fabriques, du contentieux des cultes, des bureaux de bienfaisance, des hospices et de l'administration en général* (Verhoven–Debeur 1860) 4, 247: 'L'Etat n'est-il pas constitutionnellement incompétent pour connaître de la vérité ou de la fausseté d'un culte et par conséquent de son utilité sociale?' For a contemporary reference to this criterion, see, for example, written parliamentary question no. 219 of 25 October 1996 by Alain Destexhe to the Minister of Justice, Sénat sess. ord. 1996–7, *Q.R.* 1–34, p. 1708.

27   Vincent De Coorebyter, 'Retour sur la naissance d'un système paradoxal', in Jean-François Husson (ed.), *Le financement des cultes et de la laïcité: comparaisons internationales et perspectives* (Editions namuroises 2005) 91.

28   Hasquin (n 2) 95.

activity that is contrary to public order.[29] It is important to underline that 'the basis for such recognition is not religious content – such a basis would directly violate religious freedom – but a religion's social value as a service to the population'.[30] Ministers have never provided further explanation. Up to now, these criteria have remained a mere administrative custom. In 2004, the Minister of Justice launched a new dialogue with religious leaders and proposed to enforce these criteria with a specific law. More recently, the proposal formally to enforce these criteria (by a general administrative decree) was also supported by two Expert Committees appointed by the Minister (2006 and 2011). Both of these committees confirmed the importance of a 'social utility' test as the central justification of a State support policy.

From Formal Federal Recognition to Local and Regional Implementation of Objective Funding

To obtain this specific funding, it is not sufficient to become a 'recognized' denomination. The Belgian funding system has never been a global subsidy system. Recognized religions do not obtain a global amount of public money, nor any privilege to become discretionary administrators of any funds. The administration retains complete control over the payment of salaries and other specific financial aid.

The federal recognition of a religious denomination only enables subsequent local application in diverse fields (worship, education, chaplaincies etc.) via several administrative levels (federal, regional and local) and specific additional conditions.

Since 2001, the local objectivity of the funding, linked to the numbers of recognized local communities, ceased to be federal and became a matter of regional legal competence. This very important reform resulted in the establishment of four different regional systems for the recognition of local communities in Wallonia, the German-speaking region, Flanders and Brussels-Capital. The results were so complex that, in 2004 and 2008, the four regions and the federal Government signed a special 'cooperation agreement' in order to coordinate the concrete cross-influences of all these competencies and norms.

Each of these norms defines concrete objects and timely intervention, which are not interchangeable at the discretion of religious authorities. For example, each priest or religious minister involved in a recognized local community receives his or her individual salary directly from the State, and not through a global fund managed by religious authorities.

The Belgian system of sub-recognition may be compared to a kind of 'Russian doll' system. Each sub-recognition may be understood as a test of local objectivity and proportionality. For example, in order for a priest to obtain a public salary,

---

29   [20.02.2004], *Q.R.* 51/20, 2843.
30   Torfs (n 19) 957.

it is required that, after recognition of his global denomination, his specific local community is also (sub)recognized by regional authorities through specific regional conditions and, finally, that his name is put forward by religious authorities and not refused for public order reasons by the Government.

This 'Russian doll' system has transformed the 'social interest' test from a socio-political appreciation to a concrete, quantitative and local test.[31] For example, the number of priests paid by the State depends on the number of religious territorial units, which have to reach a certain demographic level to be recognized and provided with a corresponding number of salaried offices for the religious ministers to be appointed in each unit (for example, a parish). The actual justification of the global level of funding is nothing more than the addition of all this local data. Due to its grass-roots approach, the system seems transparent enough to compare the level of public funding for each religious denomination and to test their proportionality.

Although this system was quite objective in a stable society, such as in nineteenth-century Belgium, some problems occurred with the growing sociological complexity of Belgian society during the twentieth century. The political stability of this very segmented system was high. This was convenient for the objectivity of a non-evolving society and also for the autonomy of well-established religions (whose local communities had long been recognized). But for new insiders, this system was seen as too slow and unresponsive. Moreover, since 2001, recognition of each new local community is subject to an additional stage of negotiation between federal and regional governments and this is precisely of special concern for new Muslim communities.

Another problem was due to an outdated legal difference between the demographic evaluation of Catholic communities (based on the number of *inhabitants*) and that of minority communities (based on the number of *believers*). Such a legal system facilitated (too) high a stability and even inertia in respect of Catholic funding. This inertia was further reinforced by the lack of periodical review of demographic evolution within already recognized local communities. Only competent religious authorities can submit an application to end the recognition of an old and depopulated parish.

It is worth noting that, instead of reforming the system (as undertaken by the Flemish Parliament),[32] the Federal Parliament chose in 2002 to extend the Catholic 'privilege' to the Humanist movement (recognized since 1993): instead

---

31   See Louis-Léon Christians, 'Le financement des cultes en droit belge: bilan et perspectives' (2006) *Quaderni di diritto e politica ecclesiastica* 83–107.

32   Flemish Decree of 20 September 2005 (concerning religious communities in Flanders): Catholic communities too are now evaluated in Flanders according to their member numbers. Moreover, this Decree also provides for new requirements relating to the 'social utility' test: it requires that the local community itself has to describe (in the application for recognition) its own understanding of its social utility. This Decree also requires that, inter alia, the local community use the Flemish language and declare its

of requiring a precise number of 'Humanist members' in order to determine the number of Humanist counsellors to be paid by the State, the new law simply has no other criteria than a number of administrative districts, that is to say, indirectly a number of unqualified *inhabitants*.[33] The potential bias of the Belgian system is due to its inability to evolve and to take into account variations in member numbers (i.e. fewer Catholics) in each local community. In fact, for a long while, this bias did not impede objective evaluation of decreasing Catholic dynamism in Belgium, because of an alternative system of evaluation: the decreasing number of Catholic vocations to priesthood and, consequently, the decreasing number of Catholic priests to be paid for by the State. This parallel between the decreasing dynamism of members of Catholicism and the decreasing dynamism of vocations to priesthood was nevertheless upset in the mid-1990s. In 1996, Catholic bishops successfully negotiated with the Belgian Government that lay pastoral actors obtain a salary from the State. Even if the Socialist Party contested the possibility for non-priests to be appointed as Catholic ministers by the Church and paid for by the State, a specific law finally allowed this new practice in 2008, for a limited, fixed number (360) of lay ministers. Another decision by (French-speaking) Catholic bishops also aggravated the same problem: a growing number of *foreign priests*, mainly from the Congo and Poland, had been appointed to fill vacant positions (to be paid for by the State) and this artificially counterbalanced the reduction in local priests.

Both of these developments completely upset the sociological soundness of the system. It resulted in an *increasing* number of new 'lay' ministers and foreign priests, breaking the parallel between declining local Catholic practice and decreasing numbers of Catholics, which had until then been linked to the decreasing number of *Belgian priests* paid for by the State.

New controversies arose in Belgium precisely at that time, but it is worth noting that criticisms did not address the *principle* of State support, but were only intended to improve the *fairness* and proportionality of the system. One of the main reasons of such limited criticism may be explained by a historical coincidence: the State recognized, supported and included since 1981, 1993 and most recently 2002 the main opponent to State support – the Humanist movement. It is clear that, ever since this recognition of the Humanist movement, debates have only focused on *distributive* issues.

These criticisms have become almost unanimous. They cover not only the differences between Humanism and religions but also between the religions themselves. Professor (and Liberal Minister) Hervé Hasquin perfectly summarized these kinds of criticisms limited to technical aspects: 'While the basic clergy

---

'commitment to exclude anyone who would call upon to violate the Constitution or the European Convention on Human Rights'.

33   There are no such difficulties in the funding system for teachers of religion in public (state) schools, because teacher numbers are determined in proportion to the numbers of pupils choosing each denomination's class.

(priests and vicars, auxiliary pastors, Orthodox archpriests, officiating Jewish ministers, Islamic imams) receive the same salaries, there are, on the other hand, significant disparities among the high clergy, with considerable advantage being given to Catholicism'.[34]

Recognized Denominations

Six religious and two non-confessional denominations have been recognized and funded by the State.

Recognized Religious Denominations

Catholicism and Protestantism have been recognized ever since the independence of Belgium (Laws of 18 Germinal Year X and 18 April 1802). Judaism was organized according to three Decrees of 17 March 1806. Then, three other religions were recognized: Anglicanism (by royal Decrees of 18 and 24 April 1835), Islam (Law of 19 July 1947) and Orthodoxy (Law of 17 April 1985).[35]

Non-Confessional Recognized Denominations

In 1993, a second paragraph was added to Article 181 § 1 of the Constitution. This new paragraph mandates the Belgian State also to fund non-confessional organizations. The adoption of this paragraph was the result of a political evolution that had begun in 1980.

Article 181 of the Constitution had been open for revision in 1978, 1981 and 1987 without being effectively revised.[36] Then, a new proposition was introduced on the basis of Resolution 36/15 of the United Nations General Assembly of 28 October 1981 on the elimination of all forms of intolerance and discrimination based on religion or conviction.[37] This proposal showed the importance of pluralism in Belgium and the necessity to fund non-confessional organizations. After being discussed for years in Parliament, new Article 181 § 2 of the Constitution was adopted with quasi-unanimity in 1993.

Soon after this vote, the Lay Central Council asked to be recognized as a non-confessional organization. This recognition took place in the Law of 21 June 2002.

Recently, the Belgian Buddhist Union has asked to be recognized on the basis of Article 181 § 2 of the Constitution. The legislator has not yet accepted or

---

34   Hasquin (n 2) 98.

35   ibid 97.

36   Caroline Sägesser et al., 'La reconnaissance et le financement de la laïcité organisée' (2002) *Courrier hebdomadaire du CRISP* 1756, 26.

37   ibid 26.

refused this demand, but has formulated some preparatory measures to structure this non-confessional organization.[38]

The Extent of Belgian State Support

Of all the different kinds of support, only a few are guaranteed at constitutional level. The Constitution narrows its guarantee to the funding of *salaries and pensions* of ministers of religion and non-confessional philosophies (Article 181); another constitutional provision (Article 24) guarantees the salaries of teachers of religious instruction provided by recognized denominations in public (State) and subsidized schools, but these expenses are usually not included in the debate about State funding of religions.

Other funding is provided by the federal legislature and regional (since 2001) or local authorities, without being required to do so by any constitutional obligations: housing for ministers, church councils (*fabriques d'églises*) in charge of local communities, maintenance of religious buildings are all supported by municipalities and provinces under four regional legal jurisdictions (Wallonia, Flanders, Brussels, German-speaking communities). Other public support is provided on a linguistic basis (French-speaking, Flanders, German-speaking): religious and Humanist radio and TV broadcasts, religious and Humanist education in public schools etc.

Finally, we can also mention that Belgian Law incorporates a specific tax regime for religious buildings.

Salaries

In Belgium, 'salaries are directly paid by the Ministry of Justice' and are paid to local ministers of religion and Humanist delegates working for local communities, but also to some staff who may include lay administrative staff (except for Anglicans)'.[39]

However, some differences exist between ministers of religion and Humanist delegates. As Belgian economist and expert Jean-François Husson explains, '[f]or instance, salaries for Humanist delegates are higher than those of ministers. Unlike the latter, they have also regular, planned salary increases during their career'.[40]

Such increases are logical: Humanist delegates are subject to employment contracts, which is not the case for ministers of religion, who cannot be considered as employees of either Church or State.[41]

---

38 Loi du 24 juillet 2008 portant des dispositions diverses [07.08.2008] *M.B.*, 41186.

39 Husson (n 5) 150.

40 ibid.

41 Patrick De Pooter, *De rechtspositie van de erkende erediensten en levensbeschouwingen in Staat en maatschappij* (Larcier 2003) 316–18.

Furthermore, most ministers of religion 'have housing provided by local authorities and Catholic ministers can add an extra 50 per cent to their salary, if they are assigned to more than one parish'.[42]

Finally, Humanists argue that their delegates necessarily hold a university degree, i.e. higher than spiritual training.

In 2008, Humanist delegates' salaries cost the Belgian State €11 million and ministers of religions €90.7 million (including €81.2 for Catholic ministers, as in 1996).[43] Spread across the entire Belgian population, the cost is about €10 per capita.

Pensions

Pensions for ministers of religion and Humanist delegates are paid by the Pensions Administration.

Pensions cost the federal State approximately €35.5 million each year.[44] This amount mainly goes to the Catholic Church, 'as other groups are either smaller and draw a limited number of pensions (Protestants, Anglicans, Jews) or are more recently recognized (Muslims, Orthodox Christians, Humanist organizations)'.[45] Spread across the Belgian population, this costs about €3 per capita.

Local Establishments

Church councils (*fabriques d'églises*) receive money from the regions (approximately €7.9 million per year) and municipalities (approximately €100 million per year). The basis for this is anchored in Article 6, § 1, VIII, 6° of the Law of 8 August 1980 on institutional reforms. Spread across the Belgian population, the cost is about €10 per capita.

As has been mentioned, this funding is based on historical grounds, with Belgium perpetuating such a mechanism via the Law of 30 December 1809 on local establishments.[46]

It is important to underline that 'buildings dedicated 1. to religious services (such as churches, cathedrals, mosques, temples) and to presbyteries and 2. to supporting Humanism are free from property tax'.[47] It is worth noting that non-recognized religions *may also* benefit from this specific tax exemption.

---

42 Husson (n 5) 150.
43 ibid.
44 ibid.
45 ibid.
46 Caroline Sägesser, 'Les rapports entre l'Eglise et l'Etat au XIXe siècle: l'application de la Constitution de 1831' in Brigitte Basdevant-Gaudemet et al. (eds), *Le droit ecclésiastique en Europe et à ses marges (XVIII–XXe siècles)*, Symposium of Research Center Droit et Sociétés Religieuses, Université de Paris-Sud, 12–13 octobre 2007 (Peeters 2009) 38.
47 Husson (n 5) 153.

Other Kinds of Funding

Several other types of funding can be identified.

Religious *radio and TV broadcasters* receive money from the French, Dutch and German communities – because of their legal competence in related matters. Currently, only Anglicanism and Islam do not benefit from this system.[48] Furthermore, 'in all three communities, airtime is allocated to religious and Humanist groups'.[49]

As far as *education* is concerned, the French and Flemish communities pay the salaries of teachers performing their duties in classes of religion and ethics. Those salaries were estimated at €290 million in 2000, 'of which 19.5 per cent are going to non-confessional ethics' teachers and 68.2 per cent to teachers of Catholic religion'.[50] Spread across the Belgian population, this costs about €30 per capita. But, as already said, it is unusual in Belgium to include the education budget in the debate on funding religions.

Particular Tax Regime

Belgian Law organizes a special tax regime for goods and services of a religious nature. Here are several examples to illustrate this reality.

Firstly, religious communities – recognized or not – are exempt from property tax (*Code d'impôt sur les revenus*, Article 12).

Secondly, bodies with a religious aim are exempt from value-added tax (VAT) with regard to the services they provide and the goods they supply (*Code de la taxe sur la valeur ajoutée*, Article 44, § 2, 11°). This means that religious activities, such as marriages, baptisms, funerals, and religious ceremonies in general,[51] are exempt from VAT.

Thirdly, goods used for a community's religious activities cannot be seized by State authority (*Code judiciaire*, Article 1408, § 1, 4°).

Global Evolution (2001–2008)

Between 2001 and 2008, the Catholic faith continued to be allocated a relatively high proportion of salaries in the Belgian State budget for *salaries* for religions and philosophies, but decreased from 84.1 per cent to 76.6 per cent. If we compare this to other kinds of support (mainly local buildings or churches), the drop is not so sharp – from 94 per cent to 89.2 per cent. The explanation is trivial: the falling number of priests has no influence on the number of buildings and churches to

---

48   Hasquin (n 2) 102.
49   Husson (n 5) 153.
50   ibid.
51   Frans Vanistendael, 'Financiering van religie' (2012) *Recht, Religie, Samenleving* 11.

Table 3.3   Public financing for recognized denominations in Belgium – synthetic distribution

Total million €		Global Support (2001 and 2008)	Catholic	Protestant	Anglican	Jewish	Orthodox	Islamic	Humanist
		%	%	%	%	%	%	%	%
Salaries	2001	91.5	84.1	2.7	0.27	0.66	0.93	0.66	10.7
	2008	**106.0**	**76.6**	**4.1**	**0.37**	**0.8**	**1.2**	**4.1**	**12.5**
Other aid	2001	192	94	1.5	0.08	0.27	0.24	0.1	4
	2008	**178.4**	**89.2**	**1.7**	**0.08**	**0.17**	**0.8**	**1.5**	**7.0**

maintain. Moreover, older and less populated local Catholic communities have stable (or even increasing) fixed costs. This fact is very often pointed out in the political debate, especially by the municipalities, which have to partially contribute to building maintenance.

Another comparison between State support for Secular Humanism and Islam shows that the relative share allocated to Secular Humanism since 2002 has been increasing more rapidly than that of Islam since 1974. A first explanation is already clear – the difference in criteria for recognition of local communities: with no minimal number of members being requested from Secular Humanists, it is easier for this organization to receive growing support without any discussion about a potential growth in concrete member numbers. A second explanation relates to the difficulties Muslim communities have in organizing themselves so as to be able to select a unique representative as requested by the State, thereby enabling them to file applications for recognition of local communities.

Must the Belgian System be Reformed?

The Belgian Church–State regime – in effect since 1831, with the only major difference being the admission of non-confessional organizations in 1993 – has never really been disputed. Apart from a tough political controversy in 1865 on the monitoring of local budgets, no important political debates had taken place before 1999. As mentioned above, after the recognition of Secular Humanism, political discussions were mainly devoted to the more objective issue of distribution between the different communities. To resolve that problem, a number of proposals were introduced to Parliament and some working groups were invited by the Minister of Justice to suggest some reforms.

It is also important to analyse the emergence of new questions and new issues, as far as religion is concerned.

Reform Proposals by Members of Parliament

Some authors and members of the Belgian Parliament have criticized the regime concerned with the funding of religious and non-confessional organizations. They have formulated some proposals to reform this regime, but none has ever been followed up by the legislator.

The most important of those proposals can be summarized as follows:

Proposal to transform the regime into a secular state
In recent years, several proposals were introduced to insert the principle of secularity (*laïcité*) into the Belgian Constitution.[52] Those proposals seemed to be inspired by

---

52 Proposition de déclaration de révision de l'article 1er de la Constitution, en vue d'y inscrire le principe de la laïcité de l'Etat fédéral, Doc. parl., Sénat, sess. ord. 2008–2009,

the French Republican regime. In France, there is indeed a clear separation between Church and State. Article 1 of the French Constitution states that 'France shall be an indivisible, *secular*, democratic and social republic', but it is amazing that even these principled propositions were not aimed at ending the funding systems of religious and non-confessional organizations, but only at discouraging any mechanism of reasonable accommodation, particularly in favour of Islam.

Transforming the Belgian regime into such a secular State seems to be contrary to Belgium's aim: the Belgian State is characterized by neutrality, by mutual independence between Church and State and cannot be assimilated to the regime of the French Republic.

Proposal to create a 'philosophically dedicated tax'
At the end of 1998, some members of the Senate proposed that taxpayers would indicate in their tax form what religion or non-confessional organizations of their choice they wanted the State to subsidize using a part of the taxes they pay. Such a system would be inspired by the 'philosophically dedicated tax' – also called 'tax assignment' – in place in Italy and Spain.

This proposal was never adopted, probably for two main reasons (pointed out during the political debates). Firstly, it denies the principle of 'the right to respect for private and family life' (Constitution, Article 22), because believers would have to reveal their beliefs in a file which would be read by the public administration. Secondly, this proposition would be problematic for people who do not want to fund any religion or non-confessional organization.

Proposal to organize a specific and regular referendum
Some other proposals were inspired by the Secular Humanist Central Council and were aimed at organizing a kind of legal referendum to ask each citizen which religions or non-confessional organizations the State should fund. Every five years, the referendum results would have directly determined the funding allocation for each organization.

In Belgium, such a method is not allowed by the Constitution. Article 33 of the Belgian Constitution forbids using any plebiscite at regional or federal level, stating that 'all the powers emanate from the Constitution'. It is only authorized at local level (provinces and municipalities). No revision of the Constitution has ever been proposed to repeal this prohibition.

Proposals of reform by expert workgroups
Two successive Ministers of Justice appointed their own expert workgroups in 2005 and 2008 in order to proceed with an overall scientific analysis of the funding system.

No. 4–782/1, and Proposition de déclaration de révision de l'article 1er de la Constitution, en vue d'y inscrire le principe de la laïcité de l'Etat fédéral, Doc. parl., Sénat, sess. ord. 2006–2007, no. 3–2134/1.

The first workgroup: *The mission of the first workgroup (2005) was to establish the main principles and weaknesses of the funding system. The final report recommended continuing the system, but also eliminating all forms of discrimination through greater transparency of recognition criteria and legal controls* Besides a number of technical improvements, two main issues were addressed by the report:[53] (a) how to impose additional duties on subsidized churches – in terms of democratic training for ministers, internal programmes on non-discrimination and churches' greater loyalty to human rights (and especially due process in internal procedures); (b) how to reconcile these new requirements with the constitutional and international guarantees of Church autonomy. The report considered that a specific public funding programme could justify specific duties being imposed on subsidized churches, both in terms of special training and in terms of respecting due process requirements.

The report also suggested new methodology in order to improve the fairness of funding each religion and non-confessional organization: conducting a sociological survey of the level of religiosity and religious practice of the population. This proposal was different from the previous proposals on mechanical computation of individual wishes of taxpayers or voters. The new objectivity test would not be based on individual wishes, but on actual practices and religiosity. The State would be required to organize such a survey through objective and anonymous inter-university research, conducted every five or ten years and, afterwards, take the results into account when allocating funds. This survey would have no direct or mechanical effects on the budget allocation, but should be taken into account by the Government through specifically justifying and explaining the reasons for increasing or decreasing relative allocations for each religion or non-confessional organization.

The second workgroup: *The mission of the second workgroup, appointed by another Minister of Justice, was to review and to implement the report of the first workgroup and to propose concrete solutions to improve the system* Published in February 2011, the report by this inter-university workgroup recommended that the legislator create a special procedure to recognize new religions.[54] First, there would be a largely open procedure of *registration*, and then a successive procedure of *recognition*, opening the door to some State support. This step-by-step procedure would bring transparency to religions and non-confessional organizations and to

---

53   Marie-Françoise Rigaux et al., *Le financement par l'Etat fédéral des ministres des cultes et des délégués du Conseil central laïc*, Rapport de la Commission des Sages à la demande de la Ministre de la Justice Laurette Onkelinx (2006).

54   Léon-Louis Christians et al., *Rapport du groupe de travail interuniversitaire chargé de la réforme de la législation sur les cultes et sur les organisations philosophiques non confessionnelles au nom du Ministre de la Justice Stefaan De Clerck* (2011) <http://belgianlawreligion.unblog.fr/2012/04/05/rapport-sur-le-regime-des-cultes/> accessed 15 August 2014.

the public. This workgroup has also proposed some adaptations of Articles 19, 21, 24 and 181 of the Belgian Constitution to make them more precise in respect of conflicts between human rights, such as Church autonomy *versus* due process.

Besides a number of technical improvements, the main principles included in the first report have been accepted. The second report confirmed regular inter-university sociological surveys as a better tool for improving the objectivity and transparency of the system. The scope of this survey was more precisely defined in order to combine different kinds of approaches: items should address three types of questions: (a) on individual beliefs and belonging – 'How do you identify yourself? As a member of a religion, a world view, or nothing at all?' (b) On Church attendance and concrete contact with religious or non-confessional spiritual counselling services – 'Do you do this in practice?' (c) On individual wishes for the allocation of public funding – 'Which world view should be supported by the State?'[55]

The proposal to limit the effects of the surveys to only *indirect* effects was also confirmed: the Government would only have to take into account and justify its decisions by discussing the results of the survey. To implement the objectivity of this procedure, the second report suggested the creation of a new inter-denominational advisory board whose mission would be to prepare a first, thoughtful analysis of the survey results and to put forward some advice to the Government about the objectivity and normative consequences of these surveys. The composition of this advisory board would include church and non-confessional representatives, civil servants, university professors and international experts. This board would have to work by consensus and not through a formal decision-making procedure.

Another proposal suggested by the first workgroup has also been retained and improved. Up to now, for each recognized local community, the number and level of salaries is determined by the recognition decision (for example, one curate and three vicars). The system is not very flexible. Both reports suggested that religious authorities might be allowed to manage local human resources more autonomously. Moreover, it is suggested that, in the Belgian Ecclesiastical Salaries Act, descriptors for different religious functions should be modified: up to now, the religious vocabulary used to describe each religious function was inscribed in the law itself (bishop, priest, rabbi, imam, and so on). The proposal is to limit the law to the indication of anonymous scales (A1, B2…).

---

55   For the Belgian political philosophers, Leni Franken et al., 'Is Active State Support for Religions and Worldviews Compatible with the Liberal Idea of State Neutrality? A Critical Analysis of the Belgian Case' (2012) *Journal of Church and State*, first published online 25 April 2012, the proposed survey should, besides the three questions mentioned above, 'contain another more fundamental question: "Do you think worldviews should be supported by Government?" This question is needed because the State's choice for a system of active support for worldviews is already a non-neutral choice. Therefore, citizens should also be able to decide whether they actually are in favour of such a system or not. A neutral, liberal state can only support specific options if civil society is in favour of support'.

A last important point from a non-discriminatory perspective was to address the legal status of religious or non-confessional duties of ministers and delegates paid for by the State. Up to now, delegates of non-confessional organizations were appointed as employees on a contractual basis, while religious ministers were always considered as holding a '*sui generis*' public office. The second workgroup's report finally suggested that labour law would presumably be applied, but only if religious authorities refrained from choosing an alternative solution and another way to guarantee minimal social rights for their ministers or delegates.

New Religious Issues

As underlined by many authors, 'globally, despite the fact that Belgium has long been a predominantly religious Catholic country, the system has proven able to adapt itself by recognizing "new" religions, Humanism and recently Buddhism'.[56]

However, new issues concerning the funding of religious and non-confessional organizations have recently come to light. Nowadays,

> it seems that any current policy regarding religious and non-confessional communities should include debate on public order questions (which may concern some religious communities as well as new religious movements and sects), uneven availability of resources among communities, fair treatment of religious and/or philosophical communities, demands from the population in terms of religious/moral assistance, women's status as ministers of religion and the large, crucial and difficult question of equality.[57]

It is also striking to see that the status of women (for example, Catholic parish assistant) remains worse than the status of the priests. Still based on the nineteenth-century figure of the Catholic priest (man), Belgian legislation needs to be adapted to principles of non-discrimination.

Recognizing Humanist organizations also raises unresolved questions. Many difficulties are due to the attempt to address 'specific questions of comparability with religious communities, the latter already having differences in practices among them'.[58]

While Economist Jean-François Husson underlines that 'financial instrument analysis and evaluation, *ex ante* and *ex post*, appears crucial in getting a balanced, legitimate and efficient system',[59] social recognition issues, perhaps apparently more symbolic, seem to be decisive for tomorrow. If public policies on funding religions continue to reinforce the conditions for entry into the system, the use of private funding will expand, with new, even greater problems.

---

56   Husson (n 5) 162. See also Franken et al. (n 55) 19.
57   Husson (n 5) 162.
58   ibid.
59   ibid.

List of References

Christians LL, 'Le financement des cultes en droit belge: bilan et perspectives' (2006) *Quaderni di diritto e politica ecclesiastica*

—— 'Les tensions du régime des cultes dans la Constitution belge: l'actualité des débats du Congrès national de 1830' in B Basdevant et al., *Le droit ecclésiastique en Europe et à ses marges (XVIII–XXe siècles)* (Peeters 2009) 159–77

Christians LL et al., *Rapport du groupe de travail interuniversitaire chargé de la réforme de la législation sur les cultes et sur les organisations philosophiques non confessionnelles au nom du Ministre de la Justice Stefaan De Clerck* (2011) <http://belgianlawreligion.unblog.fr/2012/04/05/rapport-sur-le-regime-des-cultes/> accessed 15 August 2014

De Pooter P, *De rechtspositie van de erkende erediensten en levensbeschouwingen in Staat en maatschappij* (Larcier 2003)

Delpérée F et al., 'Les aspects constitutionnels, budgétaires et fiscaux du financement des cultes' (2001) 61, 4 *Les Annales de Droit de Louvain*

Delville J-P, 'Le financement des cultes en Belgique: approche historique' in J-F Husson (ed.), *Le financement des cultes et de la laïcité: comparaisons internationales et perspectives* (Editions namuroises 2005)

Franken L et al., 'Is Active State Support for Religions and Worldviews Compatible with the Liberal Idea of State Neutrality? A Critical Analysis of the Belgian Case' (2012) *Journal of Church and State*, first published online 25 April

Hasquin H, 'Is Belgium a *laïque* State?' in F De Beaufort et al. (eds), *Separation of Church and State in Europe* (European Liberal Forum 2008)

Husson J-F, 'New policies with old instruments? Financing religious and philosophical communities in Belgium' in M Moravcikova et al. (eds), *Financing of Churches and Religious Societies in the 21st Century* (Institute for Church–State Relations 2010)

Huyttens E, *Discussions du Congrès national de Belgique*, tome I (Société typographique belge 1834)

Rigaux MF et al., *Le financement par l'Etat fédéral des ministres des cultes et des délégués du Conseil central laïc*, Rapport de la Commission des Sages à la demande de la Ministre de la Justice Laurette Onkelinx (2006)

Sägesser C et al., 'La reconnaissance et le financement de la laïcité organisée' (2002) 1756 *Courrier hebdomadaire du CRISP*

Sägesser C, 'Les rapports entre l'Eglise et l'Etat au XIXe siècle: l'application de la Constitution de 1831' in B Basdevant-Gaudemet et al., *Le droit ecclésiastique en Europe et à ses marges (XVIIIe–XXe siècles)* Symposium of Research Center Droit et Sociétés Religieuses, Université de Paris-Sud, 12–13 octobre 2007 (Peeters 2009)

Schreiber J-P et al. (eds), *175 ans de financement des cultes en Belgique* (Academia Bruylant 2009)

Simon AVJM, 'Le Saint-Siège et l'Union Catholico-Libérale (1828–1846)' (1962) 34 *Bulletin de l'Institut Historique Belge de Rome* 595–615

Torfs R, 'Church and State in France, Belgium, and the Netherlands: Unexpected Similarities and Hidden Differences' (1996) *Brigham Young University Law Review*

Vandevivere P, 'Du culte et du clergé sous l'empire de la constitution belge' (1851) *Belgique judiciaire*, tome 9, 1265

Vanistendael F, 'Financiering van religie' (2012) *Recht, Religie, Samenleving*

Van Overloop I, *Exposé des motifs de la Constitution belge* (H. Goemaere 1864), tome 4, 106

Wagnon H, 'Le concordat de 1801–1827 et la Belgique indépendante' in *L'Eglise et l'Etat à l'époque contemporaine – Mélanges dédiés à la mémoire de Mgr Aloïs Simon* (Facultés universitaires Saint-Louis 1975)

Wattier S, 'Le financement des cultes au XXIe siècle: faut-il réviser l'article 181 de la Constitution?' (2011) *Revue Belge de Droit Constitutionnel*

Chapter 4

Public Funding of Religions: the Situation in France

Pierre-Henri Prélot

The Law of 9 December 1905 on the separation of Church and State prohibits all forms of public funding for religions in France. Article 2 strictly states that 'the Republic neither recognises, nor pays nor subsidises any faith' and that 'accordingly, with effect from 1 January following the enactment of this law, all expenditure relating to the exercising of worship shall be removed from the budgets of the State, the *départements* and *communes*'. One can observe in the wording of Article 2 that the concepts of recognition and public funding are closely associated. Throughout the nineteenth century, in fact, public recognition of faiths primarily implied payment by the State for ministers of the Catholic, Reformed and Lutheran faiths, as well as the Jewish faith from 1831. Although sociologically in the majority, Catholicism ceased, from the Revolution of 1789, being the national religion of France, except between 1814 and 1830 during the period of the Restoration.

Of course, once public funding for religion has been forbidden, nothing should be able to be added to what has just been said. Moreover, the times in which we live are marked both by increased religious pluralism and a demand for equality that is increasingly exaggerated, with the result that such a ban benefits from a strong presumption of relevance, because as long as you are giving nothing to no-one, you are giving exactly the same thing to everyone.

But religions are societal institutions and prayer is not their only reason to exist – far from it. Religious activity also consists in teaching, caring for one's fellow man, helping others through charity; it may have an objective based around tourism or leisure (organizing a Scout camp or youth days); it is also expressed through art and creation and, finally, its materiality may consist of retail activities. Whether we welcome or deplore it, this is a reality which it is impossible for a State to prevent. To the extent that the public authority is entitled to financially support such activities, when they have a secular character, and it does not hesitate to do so, because of their social utility, then there is a form of *discrimination* (Part I) in refusing to support them when they are conducted by a religious group.

Furthermore, if the ban on public funding for religious groups is a rule enshrined in the Law of separation, the symbolic force of which is well-known in the French republican tradition, still it only ever appears in one law and has not been enshrined as an integral component of the constitutional principle of secularity. On 16 March 2005, the Council of State issued an important ruling[1] in which it very clearly stated that 'the constitutional principle of secularity … does not, by itself, forbid granting, in the public interest and under the conditions defined by law, certain subsidies for activities or equipment on which religions depend' and that particularly in parts of France in which the 1905 Law had not been introduced (Alsace-Moselle, Overseas Territories), such subsidies are not prohibited in principle. This means that the ban on public funding of religious activities in Article 2 of the 1905 Law may be subject to *statutory exceptions* (Part II), and indeed several texts allow one-off public funding for faiths.[2] It also means that Article 2 itself may, on an *ad hoc* basis, be suspended, modified or eliminated altogether by a simple law. This was, moreover, the main question asked at the Machelon Commission established in 2005 by Nicolas Sarkozy, then Minister of the Interior.

Discrimination Based on the (Non-)Financing of Religions

The issue of funding discrimination is a major challenge relating to the legal regime for faiths in France. Discrimination to which a religion can be subject, can be of two types: discrimination towards religion (religious discrimination) on the one hand, and discrimination towards a specific religious group (discrimination between religions) on the other.

Discriminating Financially against Religions

Talking about discriminating against religions means that some financial support is granted to non-religious activities or institutions and that religious activities or institutions are refused such public support, even if they all meet the conditions for it to be granted. At the outset and for a long time thereafter, the ban on public funding of religious activities was understood primarily to relate to the institution: no public money for religious institutions. Such an understanding seems openly discriminatory in the light of the fact that, as mentioned above, religions also engage in secular activities. This traditional understanding of financial separation by institution, as expressed in the letter of Article 2 of the 1905 Law,[3] nowadays tends to be replaced by an understanding that relates rather to the nature of the activity supported and this, too, is taken into consideration by Article 2 of the 1905

---

1   *Ministre de l'Outre-Mer*, no. 265560 (CE, 16 March 2005).

2   For example, the Debré Law of 31 December 1959 organizing the financing of private schools, which in France are overwhelmingly Catholic.

3   Article 2 stipulates that the Republic does not recognize or subsidize any religion, nor does it pay the ministers of any religion.

Law.[4] It can be summarized as follows: no public money to finance activities of a religious nature, even those that may be conducted by non-religious institutions.[5]

In a decision dated 21 December 2010,[6] the Bordeaux Administrative Court of Appeal cancelled the subsidies awarded by the Limousin Regional Council for organizing the seven-yearly processions called *ostensions*, a traditional festival in honour of the saints of the region, held every seven years in Dorat, a village in the Limousin region, during which the relics of saints – as symbols of the fight against ergotism – are presented and honoured by the faithful. These processions, which originated in the early eleventh century, involve a traditional procession with the marching of hooded penitents and a Eucharist. It is a highly important cultural and tourist event, attracting visitors from all over Europe, and, despite the considerable economic and tourist interest aroused by the *ostensions*, the Administrative Court of Appeal confirmed the cancellation of subsidies granted by the Regional Council to two *communes* organizing the event, on the grounds of its religious character. By applying so strictly such an activity-based criterion, the administrative court is, of course, not discriminating between religious and non-religious institutions, since, as we can see, it is a grant from one local authority to another, from the Regional Council to two *communes*, which is thereby cancelled in the name of secularity. But there still remains the possibility of discriminating between religious and non-religious activities. Why indeed should such a tourist event – including a religious parade or ceremony of worship – be denied any subsidy, whereas if the event had been purely secular, public funding would have been allowed? The difficulty in France is that an understanding of the religious is far too essentialist; it is not social or cultural enough. The five decisions of 19 July 2011 by the Council of State, which will be presented at the end of this chapter, undoubtedly mark a definitive evolution in public funding for religions.

Discrimination Between Religions

Discrimination may also arise between religions, when they are treated differently by public authorities, without legitimate justification. Often, such discrimination results from the law itself and is not intentional. But even if the discrimination were considered indirect, it does exist nevertheless. In 1905, it was decided to allow public authorities (essentially the *communes* for churches and the State for cathedrals) ownership of the religious buildings that had been nationalized in 1789. These buildings were kept free of charge for the use of the Catholic Church and have remained assigned exclusively to worship. The Law of separation originally provided that the faith to which the buildings are assigned should bear the cost

---

4   Article 2 removes from public budgets 'all expenses relating to religious practice'.

5   Conversely, the weakening of the 'institutional' criterion implies that religions can more easily benefit from public support for their secular activities.

6   *Commune du Dorat*, no. 10BX00634 (CCA Bordeaux, 21 December 2010).

of repairs to them. But, from 1908,[7] the owner authorities have been allowed to fund this work, and that is what they do today most of the time. This power, given to local authorities to finance the repair of legally assigned places of worship of which they were owners, was extended in 1942 to buildings belonging to religious associations, but it is fairly rare for the *communes* to assume the costs of repair for places of worship which they do not own, apart from in the case of buildings classified as historical monuments.

In other words, the Catholic Church can practise worship in churches maintained for it by the *communes*, while, at the same time, Protestant and Jewish owners have, most of the time, to assume themselves the burden of repairs to their temples and synagogues. As for Muslims, except for the special case of the Paris mosque – the construction of which was financed by the State in the 1920s as a tribute to African soldiers who had fallen in the First World War – it is their responsibility to fully fund the construction of their mosques. Indeed, prior to repairing a place of worship, it must be built, and there is no legal provision in France allowing direct public support for building places of worship, which means that it must be financed from private funds. Of course, efforts have been made. Since 1962, *communes* are authorized to guarantee loans to finance the construction of places of worship. Moreover, resorting to emphyteutic leases can now help at least partially in the construction of mosques. The measure consists in a *commune* renting land to a religious association for a term of 99 years (emphyteutic lease), ensuring its long-term use. The lease is granted for a nominal fee (sometimes one Euro per year). The association then builds at its expense the religious building on the leased land and it can use it during the term of the lease. This option of the so-called 'cardinal's building sites' – which amounts to the town hall providing virtually free of charge land for construction – has been practised since the 1930s and has allowed for the construction of new churches in the suburbs of large cities. This measure was secured in law in 2006,[8] so as to protect the construction of mosques against legal action of any kind.

Support for the construction of mosques has indeed been challenged systematically before the courts on the grounds that, by allowing the use of land for a merely symbolic rent, the balance of contractual services was not being respected and the principle banning State subsidies for religious activities was thereby being violated. The administrative courts and appeal courts have pronounced contradictory decisions on the matter. But the Council of State, in a landmark ruling by the General Assembly on 19 July 2011,[9] decided to end the uncertainty, stipulating that the emphyteutic leases for the construction of places of worship constituted a statutory exception to Article 2 of the Law of 1905,

---

7   Law of 13 April 1908.
8   Order of 21 April 2006, Article L.1311–2 of the General Code of Local Authorities.
9   No. 320796 (CE Ass., 19 July 2011). This decision is part of a set of five important decisions made on the same day by the General Assembly and which are mentioned later under II) B).

expressly provided for since 2006 by the General Code on Local Authorities, with the result that the low rent did not affect the legal validity of the arrangement. This is undoubtedly a fundamental decision, inspired by a well-understood desire for rebalancing in the public treatment of religions, and which must be understood as encouraging the *communes* to support the construction of mosques.

Exceptions to the Ban on Public Funding of Faiths

There are many exemptions to the ban on publicly financing religions. Article 2 of the 1905 Law already provided an exemption for chaplaincy services 'designed to ensure the free exercise of religion in public institutions such as schools, colleges, hospitals, asylums and prisons'. If a rule as important as the prohibition against subsidizing religious organizations was accompanied by an exemption in its very wording, this clearly means that it has never been an absolute (constitutional) rule and it may have other exceptions than just that one. Examples abound: since 1908, public authorities can, as mentioned above, take on the cost of repairing places of worship under their ownership; in 1921, the French Parliament approved a loan of 500,000 francs for the construction of a grand mosque in Paris; in 1959, Catholic private schools became part of the State education service and, as such, state-funded; since 1962, *communes* can guarantee loans for financing places of worship; most recently, in the above-mentioned decision of 19 July 2011, the Council of State considered that emphyteutic leases for the construction of places of worship also constituted an exemption from Article 2 of the 1905 Law.

Considering the number of texts authorizing the public financing of religions, one may wonder whether it is actually the ban that constitutes the exception and the authorization the rule. To try to answer this question, one must first understand the functioning of the ban on public funding of religious organizations within the French context. The first function is one of unification and centralization. The second is one of privatizing religion.

Unity and Centralization

Even for a religion as centralized as Catholicism may be, religious life is community-based, therefore local. A typical French village is also a parish with its church opposite the town hall, with a mayor and formerly its priest. At the time of separation, the Republicans thought that, going beyond abolishing the budget for religious affairs, a general ban was essential to avoid local agreements. It was necessary to prevent some *communes* continuing to pay the salary of the priest after the State had renounced on it.[10] Moreover, Republicans especially did not want

---

10   It is to be noted that in many *communes*, the priest is in charge of looking after places of worship and for this task he typically receives payment, the amount of which is capped by decree.

the conflict between the Republic and the Church to degenerate into a multitude of local wars. At the turn of the twentieth century, the ban on local funding was certainly based on a strict standpoint of civil peace. But today the situation is very different. Decentralization has increased considerably, especially since the 1980s, and today the general ban is a form of denial of self-administration and local democracy. Also, today the *communes* subsidize all kinds of social activities, such as theatre, music, cinema, sport, the practice of pottery or bookbinding, and so on, which they did not a century ago, and, finally, the only activity for which funding is prohibited is religious activity. When a *commune* plans to finance a religion today, it does not do so for ideological or religious reasons most of the time, but by starting from an assumption of neutrality, considering a specific local interest or the need to integrate a part of the population into the community. Public neutrality – or what the Germans call the *Identifikationsverbot* – prohibiting a public body from identifying with a religion through preferential treatment of the latter, does not necessarily imply a systematic ban on any public funding.

The Privatization of Worship

The ban on any public funding of religious groups, in 1905, was also a direct result of a 'privatization' of religions, which were ceasing to be recognized, organized and supported by the State and were thus reduced to purely private activities devoid of any collective benefit. The public authority is only authorized to financially support activities that are in the public interest. To the extent that religions are solely related to the private interests of individuals, they cannot therefore be subsidized. Many people in France believe that secularity is synonymous with the privatization of religious convictions.

Such a conflict between, on one hand, the public interest represented by the State and local authorities and, on the other hand, the purely private interest represented by religions, is nowadays clearly being called into question. In its ruling of 2005, *Department of Overseas Territories*, in the introduction, the Council of State highlighted that the condition of the legality of subsidizing a faith in the parts of France in which Article 2 does not apply, depends on the contribution of this faith to a public interest that is distinct, strictly speaking, from the religious interest. As it happens, the presbytery of Tahiti, the reconstruction of which was funded in part from public funds, was home to many educational and social activities and served as a shelter for refugees during hurricanes.

The solution arrived at following this decision by the Council of State, *Minister for Overseas Territories*, applies in those places where the 1905 Law was not introduced. But, by extension, one is led to wonder to what extent the existence of a local, public interest is not such as to justify subsidizing a religious organization, including under the regime of separation, since it is not the activity of worship as such that is being supported, but the interest it represents for the public authority. Four out of the five decisions by the General Assembly relating to public funding of religious groups and pronounced by the Council of State on

19 July 2011, provide clarification on this point. In a case involving the *commune* of Trélazé,[11] the Council of State approved the purchase by a *commune* of an organ and its installation in the communal church assigned to worship, provided that, in accordance with an agreement concluded with the religious beneficiary, the organ could be used at its convenience by the owner 'in the context of its cultural and educational policy', 'so as, in particular, to develop teaching of the arts and to organise cultural events in the public, communal interest'. Such a solution was inconceivable before then, and besides, the Administrative Court of Appeal had rejected the arrangement put in place by the *commune* in agreement with the religious authorities. In another case decided upon the same day – the National Federation for Free-thinking and Social Action of the Rhône (*Fédération nationale de la libre pensée et de l'action sociale du Rhône*)[12] – the Council of State approved a grant to finance the construction of a lift designed to allow access for disabled people to the basilica of Lyon Fourvière from the square. The Council of State in this case based its judgement on the fact that the equipment installed was in the local public interest, 'in particular linked to the importance of the building for cultural outreach or for the development of tourism and the local economy and that it (the equipment) was not intended for worship'. It also stressed 'that the fact that such equipment or facility is, furthermore, likely to benefit those who participate in worship, would not, when the conditions listed above are met, affect the legality of the decision of the local authority'.

The Council of State also referred to the notion of local public interest to justify the development of a town hall to serve as temporary slaughterhouse for the feast of *Eid el Kebir*. The latter case is interesting because the Council of State stresses that the public facility in question is designed exclusively – which was not the case in the two previous matters – to 'allow for undertaking practices of a ritual nature relating to free religious practice'. As for the public interest that such funding achieves, it is not, as before, confined to achieving a purely secular aim (cultural or educational policy, culture and tourism), but 'to the need for worship to be exercised in a manner consistent with the requirements of public order, particularly public health'. In other words, the proper conduct of worship, in the absence of the practice itself, does in itself constitute a public interest, which implies the deployment by the public authority of means (including financial) facilitating it. It is significant here that the solution was found for Islam, for which critical infrastructures are lacking. Finally, in a last decision by the General Assembly on the same day,[13] the Council of State also approved the construction of a multi-purpose room and its use by the Muslim community for practising worship, underlining the fact that a *commune* may rightly 'authorise, in accordance with the principle of neutrality toward religion and the principle of equality, the use of premises belonging to it for the practice of worship by an association, when

---

11   No. 308544.
12   No. 308817.
13   *Commune de Montpellier*, no. 313518 (CE Ass, 19 July 1919).

the financial terms of this authorisation exclude any generosity, and consequently, any help to a religion'. The Council of State added for the benefit of recalcitrant *communes* that shelter beneath the principle of secularity 'that a *commune* may not deny a request for use of such premises on the sole grounds that this request is made by an association for the purpose of practising a religion'. But besides premises not being made available for worship free of charge, the Council of State said that this should remain solely on an *ad hoc* basis and that a *commune* cannot extend the system of legal assignment in the 1905 Law through a mechanism of conventional assignment for the benefit of religions. So, it explains that 'local authorities may not, without disregarding the aforementioned provisions of the Law of 9 December 1905, decide that a premises they own will be made available exclusively and for the long-term to an association for the practice of worship and thus constitute a building of worship'.

With the decisions of July 2011, the whole idea of Article 2 of the 1905 Law, set out according to a principle of strict separation – both institutional and activity-based – is called into question in a way that is probably irreparable. Henceforth, local authorities are invited to consider the public interest represented by the religious activity when supporting it. Beyond the financial aspect of the issue, it is a great, symbolic victory for religions, emerging in some way from a long banishment – with religious activity being regarded until now as excluding any possibility of contributing to the public interest and the common good. In a more *ad hoc* way, public support for the establishment of the (currently unsatisfactory) infrastructures necessary for a dignified practising of Islam is being encouraged by a Council of State that Gabriel le Bras had described in his time as 'regulator of parish life' and which has now become the main 'regulator of religious life', while direct intervention by the lawmaker, more than a century after the separation, remains tinged by suspicion.

List of References

Gueydan J, 'Fiscalité et religions, le droit applicable en France' Thèse droit (Strasbourg 1990)

Machelon JP (dir.), 'Les relations des cultes avec les pouvoirs publics: travaux de la commission de réflexion juridique' Rapport au ministre de l'Intérieur (La documentation française 2006)

Messner F, Prélot PH and Woehrling JM, *Traité de droit français des religions*, 2nd edition (Lexis-Nexis 2013)

Prélot PH, 'Les transformations coutumières de la loi de 1905' in *Mélanges en l'honneur de Francis Messner* (P.U.S. 2014) 527–48

Chapter 5

Public Funding of Faiths According to Local Law in Alsace-Moselle

Francis Messner

Unlike most other Member States of the European Union, France is characterized by the existence of a plurality of statutes and religious regimes marked by their asymmetrical uniqueness: the regime of separation (Law of 9 December 1905), local law on faiths in Alsace-Moselle (Law of 18 Germinal Year X), local law on faiths in the overseas *département* of Guiana (Order of 27 August 1828) and, lastly, local law in the Overseas Territories (amended Decree-Law of 16 January 1939).

Each of these systems includes a specific mode for funding religious activities and institutions. Institutions – religious personnel and activities – receive statutory funding from public authorities according to local laws in French Guiana and Alsace-Moselle. In the Overseas Territories, they can be funded on a voluntary basis, but subject to certain conditions. Paying salaries and public subsidies for faiths is, however, prohibited by Article 2 of the Law of 9 December 1905, which does tolerate a number of exceptions. Indeed, the 1905 Law authorizes salaries for chaplains in closed settings: public hospitals, prisons and the army. The principle of freedom of worship enshrined in Article 1 of the Law of 9 December 1905 takes precedence over the principle banning salaries for faiths. Furthermore, the 1905 Law authorizes maintenance of buildings used for worship that belong to the *communes*, as well as those belonging to religious associations.

Under Article 1 of the Constitution of 4 October 1958, 'France shall be a … secular … Republic. It shall ensure the equality of all citizens before the law, without distinction of … religion. It shall respect all beliefs'. The Constitutional Council, in a Decision of 21 February 2013 (No. 2012-297 QPC), considered that

> the principle of secularism is one of the rights and freedoms guaranteed by the Constitution; that it follows that the State must be neutral; that it also follows that the Republic does not recognize any religion; that the principle of secularism requires in particular that all beliefs be respected, the equality of all citizens before the law without distinction based on religion also be respected, and that the Republic guarantee the free exercise of religion; that it implies that it shall not subsidize any religion.

It adds, however, that

the Constitution did not however call into question any specific legislative or regulatory provisions on the organization of certain religions, including in particular the remuneration of religious ministers.

This decision guarantees maintenance of local laws and specifically Alsatian local law on faiths and its funding mechanisms, but prohibits remuneration of ministers of worship in general law, except, it seems, for religious officers serving believers contained in closed environments (hospitals, prisons or the army), without however banning subsidies, some of which are enshrined in the Law of 9 December 1905. The Constitutional Council chose to shed light on the historical models existing in France, leaving however, a few uncertainties that will have to be clarified by case law.

In local law on faiths in Alsace-Moselle, funding religious activities, institutions and personnel is characterized by the state's duty to pay ministers of the four recognized religions whose posts were provided for in the state budget and the obligation for *communes* to balance the budgets of public local or parish institutions (Israelite consistories, Catholic *fabriques*, presbyteral councils of the Reformed Church and the Church of the Augsburg Confession), when they are in deficit.

In the absence of a legal ban on subsidizing religions (the Law of 9 December 1905 and more specifically Article 2, was not introduced in the *départements* of the Rhine and Moselle), local authorities and, where appropriate, the State can financially support faiths, whether they are statutory (recognized) – involving non-mandatory subsidies paid on top of mandatory grants – or non-statutory (not recognized), organized under private law.

The principles governing historical evolution in public funding of religions in local law of Alsace-Moselle will be discussed first of all and complemented by a presentation of current law and emerging practices.

Historical Developments

This thematic presentation focuses on the emergence of the principle of compensation, which is at the origin of state funding for religious denominations. It also includes a presentation of the religious policies of the Second German Reich in relation to paying ministers of recognized religions and funding a faculty of Catholic theology within the German Imperial University, designed to 'germanize' religious leaders. The issue of repealing local law on faiths has repeatedly been raised since the return of Alsace-Lorraine to France in 1918.

The Emergence of the Theory of Compensation

Under the *Ancien Régime*, the Catholic Church (religion of the kingdom) was funded by the heritage it owned and by income from tithes. Following the French

Revolution, tithes of any kind and fees of a similar nature were abolished by order of the Constituent Assembly of 4–11 August 1789 and, a few months later, all ecclesiastical property was put at the disposal of the nation in accordance with Article 1 of the Decree of 2 November 1789. These legal texts put an end to the financial autonomy of the Catholic Church and its quasi-monopoly on education[1] and charity. They were to result in the theory of 'compensation' still referred to today, the first premises of which were written into the Decree of 2 November 1789: all Church property was put at the disposal of the Nation, which was responsible for providing in a fitting manner for the expenses of worship, remuneration for ministers and relief of the poor, which would in future be dependent on the *communes* and their charitable offices and no longer on parishes. The Civil Constitution of the Clergy passed on 12 July 1790 enacted the principle of compensation. The 'useful' Catholic clergy (bishops, priests, vicars) was employed by the State, while other clerics (collegiate and general chapters) were no longer part of the organization of faiths. But a Decree of 18 September 1794 removed the obligation to pay the constitutional clergy and introduced a first separation that would be reinforced by the Decree of 21 February 1795. Subsequently, in the context of religious pacification under the regime of the Consulate, the obligation to pay bishops and priests was enshrined in the Convention of Messidor (Concordat 15 July 1801), then extended to Protestant religions (Reformed Church and Church of the Augsburg Confession: Lutherans) by the Law of 18 Germinal Year X (1802). Subsidies for faiths were awarded some time later to the Jewish faith by the Law of 8 February 1831, and to the Muslim faith solely in the *départements* of Algeria at the end of the nineteenth century.

At the beginning of the nineteenth century, maintenance of buildings which were in their entirety, at least for the Catholic Church, the property of *communes* or the State, as well as support for the costs of local or parish worship, fell exclusively to religious institutions established by the Law of 18 Germinal Year X: *fabriques* for the Church Catholic and consistories for the two Protestant Churches. From 1809, the *commune* intervened on a secondary level, in accordance with the Decree of 30 December 1809 on the *fabriques* of the Catholic Church. This provision was later extended to other recognized religions, namely those whose ministers were employed by the State, for the sake of equality under the Law of 18 July 1837.

The theory of compensation – the State paying the salaries of the Catholic faith in exchange for the secularization of Church assets, as favoured by Catholic jurists – was challenged by the doctrine. Théophile Ducrocq, Professor at the Law Faculty in Paris, stated in a new edition of his *Course in Administrative Law* in 1888, during the first phase of the separation of Church and State, that '[i]ntroducing the budgets of the faiths into the budget of the State has no more the character of a

---

1 The rise of regalism had certainly already eroded the powers of the Gallican Church under the *Ancien Régime*.

national debt than does the budget of the Protestant faith'.[2] The Professor of Law points to one of the weaknesses in the argumentation. The assets of the Catholic faith were indeed secularized, but Protestant denominations deprived of their status and assets under the *Ancien Régime* were equally being subsidized.

The Decree of 23 June 1803 granted a salary of 3,000 francs to Parisian pastors who were 'married and men of letters'. First class Catholic priests who did not belong to this category – being single and briefly trained in the seminaries of the era – received half that amount. Moreover, pastors of the Augsburg Confession of Alsace and Montbéliard, whose property ownership had not been guaranteed by international treaty – the Treaty of Westphalia of 1648 – were not secularized by the Laws of the Revolution, thanks to the intervention of a Lutheran, Alsatian minister in the Constituent Assembly, *Député* Koch. This situation constituted an obstacle to unconditional support for these pastors. They would finally be paid at least in part by the State under the terms of an Order of 28 July 1819, fixing salaries for Protestant ministers across the kingdom.

However, Jewish ministers of religion, while organized by the State (chief rabbis, rabbis and officiating ministers) were considered to be poorly integrated into French society and were not paid by the State in the early nineteenth century. According to the terms of a Decree of 17 March 1808, payment of remuneration to the Chief Rabbi of the General Consistory, chief rabbis in the consistories, rabbis and officiating ministers and the expenses of worship were funded by a 'religious tax'. This contribution was divided among the members of the Jewish community in each *département* consistory. The role of dividing up the money fell to the consistory and was enforced by the prefect. Debt recovery was undertaken by the recipients of the direct contributions. During the Consulate, the First Empire and the Second Restoration, Jewish citizens could not resign from their faith. Every citizen had to be affiliated with a religion. But belonging to a recognized Christian religion had no financial consequences. Ministers of the Jewish faith were ultimately provided for by the state following the July Revolution in 1831.[3] The reasons given were those of equality and especially maintenance of religious harmony. According to Count Portalis, rapporteur of the draft bill, 'the public salary of ministers of religion is granted more in the interests of the State than in the interests of the faith itself'.[4]

The annexation of the *départements* of the Rhine and Moselle (Alsace-Lorraine) by the Second German Reich did not put an end to the theory of compensation. On the contrary, debate flared up in the 1900s on salaries of ministers of the four recognized religions of the *Reichsland Elsaß-Lothringen.* They were characterized by their great modesty compared to those paid to the clergy by the other federated

2   Théophile Ducrocq, *Cours de droit administratif et de législation française*, vol. 3 (Berger-Levrault 1888) 465.

3   Law of 8 February 1831.

4   Quoted in Henry Lucien-Brun, *Etude historique sur la condition des israélites en France depuis 1789* (Imprimerie P. Legendre 1900) 135.

states of the Second Reich. The Government of Alsace-Lorraine imagined at first a solution inspired by practices in the kingdoms, principalities, duchies and grand duchies of the Second Reich by proposing the establishment of a church tax. But creation of this tax, which could only be justified for the Protestant and Jewish faiths whose assets had not been secularized, if 'compensation' was assumed, encountered stiff opposition from Catholic authorities whose assets had been secularized. The debate dissolved into an unlikely battle of numbers involving those *pro* and *contra*. The Bishop of Strasbourg, Monseigneur Fritzen, in his letter to the Government on the low salaries of the Catholic clergy in 1907, stressed the compensatory nature of these payments, while pointing out the services rendered by the Catholic religion to the population.[5] The Catholic hierarchy of the time defended in unison both the theory of compensation and that of the services rendered, which corresponded to the German doctrine of the time.

The rationale for different bodies funding recognized religions is not confined to one sole argument. Stances adopted in the nineteenth century evolved in relation to power shifts, transformations of the sociopolitical context and representations of general interest. But in every case, it was the State interest that prevailed. The desire to improve the financial situation of active and retired ministers and the creation of a faculty of Catholic theology are a good illustration of this.

Improved Funding for Recognized Religions during the Second German Reich

Salaries and retirement pensions
The issue of improving salaries had been partially settled for solely Protestant pastors through the creation of a religious tax on natural persons of Protestant confession (local Law of 6 July 1901). This tax did not cover all the expenses of worship. It was designed to complement salaries and to provide a solution for Protestant ministers wishing to retire for reasons of old age or illness. The religious tax was used to fund any complements to the salary, as well as disability and retirement pensions for Lutheran and Reformed ministers. This solution was finally abandoned in favour of continuing in the spirit of the system of recognized religions, all expenses of worship being the responsibility of the public authorities. The passing of a local Law of 15 November 1909 on salaries and pensions for ministers of the four recognized religions finally put an end to the debate. The purpose of the law was threefold.

The first implicit aim was political and highly symbolic. The 1909 Law sought to confirm the status of faiths in the *Reichsland* of *Elsass-Lothringen*, while conversely in France the Law of 9 December 1905 banned State and public authorities recognizing and paying salaries to faiths. The 'Republic of the Republicans' had, even before the passing of the Law of December 1905, chipped

---

5   Adolf Fritzen, *Gehaltslage des Katholischen Pfarrers in E.L und im übrigen Deutschland* (F.X. Le Roux, n.d.), p. 3–4. See also Justus, *Elsass–lothringische Zeitfragen. Kultusaus-gaben und Paritat. Separatabdruck aus dem 'Elsässer'* (Strasbourg 1908) 13–26.

away at the budget for faiths and abolished the allowance paid to cardinals (Law of 23 December 1880) and salaries for canons (Law of 22 March 1885). Salaries of archbishops were reduced by one quarter and those of bishops by one third following the Law of 22 December 1879, so as to return to the sum originally fixed by the Convention of Messidor. Finally, the municipal Law of 5 April 1884[6] limited *communes'* intervention in cases where local or parish establishments of the four recognized religions (*fabriques*, presbyteral councils, consistories) had insufficient revenues to pay for major repairs to buildings assigned to 'the public service of worship': churches, temples, synagogues and lodgings for priests, pastors and rabbis and, in the absence of lodgings, payment of an allowance.

The second objective was to raise salaries for all ministers of the recognized faiths and to remunerate the administrative staff of the religious authorities. Pastors whose wages at the end of their career hit the first class ceiling of 2,560 marks would, from 1909, receive 4,400 marks at the end of their career, while second class priests moved from 1,560 marks to 2,600 marks by the end of their career. Note, however, that their Prussian colleagues received 3,200 marks. This salary increase was intended to align the remuneration of ministers of recognized faiths with that paid to clergymen of other States of the *Reich*.

Thirdly and finally, Article 10 of the Law of 15 November 1909 grants a pension to ministers of the four recognized religions, 'when, after at least ten years of service, they subsequently become permanently unable to exercise their ministry as a result of disability or impairment of their physical or intellectual faculties and for this reason are given early retirement'. At the time, pensions were paid to ministers who were ill or frail and thereby incapacitated, while guaranteeing the freedom of churches and religions: 'The ecclesiastical ministry is of the Church and it is the Church which must decide when he should retire'.[7] Under the terms of Article 10 of the Law of 1909, retirement was pronounced by the authority which was competent for deciding on the dismissal of the minister of worship, i.e. the competent religious authorities of each denomination. From 1909, ministers of religion benefited from the same advantages as imperial officials, whose pension was fixed by an 1873 Law.

All these measures were designed to accelerate the integration of ministers from Alsace-Moselle by treating them in the same way as their colleagues from the other States of the *Reich* (salaries) and as other German state officials or public agents (pensions).

Funding a faculty of Catholic theology in Strasbourg
Following the restoration of the faiths in 1802, public authorities, anxious to control the training of ministers of recognized religions, created seminaries and academies of Protestant and Catholic theology. In the minds of public authorities,

---

6   Article 136.

7   Abbé Winterer, as quoted by Jean Schlick (ed.), *Le régime actuel des pensions de retraite des ministres du culte en Eglises et Etat en Alsace et en Moselle* (Cerdic 1979) 160.

ministers from recognized religions, especially those called upon to exercise important responsibilities (bishops, vicars general, cantonal priests) should receive training similar to that of other leaders of the nation. Theology therefore figured logically among the subjects taught at the French Imperial University of the early nineteenth century. It served the State and trained its leaders. The Faculties of Catholic and Protestant theology were created for this purpose. The Imperial University was created by Decree of 17 March 1808, Article 8 of which states that '[t]here will be as many faculties of theology as metropolitan churches, there will be one in Strasbourg and one in Geneva for the Reformed religion'. Catholic theology faculties were also created in the public universities of Paris, Aix, Bordeaux, Lyon, Rouen and Toulouse. They were abolished in 1885.

The Faculties of Protestant theology, created in Montauban in 1809 and in Strasbourg in 1819 – the latter was transferred to Paris in 1877 and this time a new German Faculty was born in Strasbourg – were abolished somewhat later by the Law of 9 December 1905, Article 2 of which prohibits the subsidizing of faiths and thereby funding for training ministers of religion. This difference in treatment is explained by the existence of legal texts in principle obliging Protestant pastors to hold a degree in theology to perform their duties and receive their pay from the State.

In Alsace, Strasbourg University (Protestant) was established as a '*Haute Ecole*' in 1538 and included a faculty of theology. Abolished by the Laws of the Revolution, an academy for the training of pastors was formed in 1802 (Organic Articles of the Protestant faiths, Law of 18 Germinal Year X). The Faculty of Protestant Theology created within the Imperial University in 1818 included three professors and was supplemented by two more some years later. They also taught at the academy, which had become a seminary. Professors at both establishments were integrated into the German University in Strasbourg, which ended the dual purpose and therefore the dual funding of the university (state)/seminary (St. Thomas Foundation).

The new German University in Strasbourg (*Kaiser Wilhelm Universität*) did not, however, include a faculty of Catholic theology, as Strasbourg was not a metropolitan see. Its creation was positively desired by the German Government, but the Bishop of Strasbourg and the Holy See were, like much of the Alsatian clergy, in principle opposed to the creation of such an establishment. Public authority control over the sacred sciences, perceived as limiting Church freedom, possible contact between seminarists with secular students of science, the risk of witnessing a modernist theology emerge, the formation of a cultivated clergy – culture carries within it the seeds of insubordination – and finally, the imposition of the German model for training the clergy, all constituted so many disincentives for Rome, the episcopate and the local clergy.

The German Government had meanwhile decided to fund the establishment and operation of this new faculty. The prestige of the Imperial University, the desire to turn the page of the *Kulturkampf* and erase the image of an anti-Catholic

Germany and, finally, the desire to germanize the clergy were all arguments in favour of creating a faculty of Catholic theology in Strasbourg.

The central argument was undoubtedly that of the will to germanize the clergy and integrate them, in the broadest sense of the term, into the Second Reich. The German administration was convinced that the Grand Seminary of Strasbourg, where the French language continued to be cultivated, only took limited interest in the German political culture and tradition in its courses. But the Catholic Alsatian clergy, several members of which had been elected as ministers in the *Reichstag*, exerted great influence over people. Moreover, public authorities were calling for a peaceful society by reducing tensions between religions. Yet, tolerance is only possible when the intellectual level of the population guided by the clergy is high. The Faculty of Catholic Theology might contribute to this. The intellectual level of the Grand Seminary professors, few of whom had degrees, was judged to be insufficient. Initially set at six, the number of Catholic theology teaching posts created and funded by the Second Reich rose to ten in the convention signed between the German Government and the Holy See in 1902.[8] The German Government decided to fund the creation and costs of a faculty of Catholic theology despite reluctance by the authorities of this religion for sociopolitical reasons: assimilation of the Catholic clergy into the ecclesiastical system of the German Empire, keeping religious peace through the integration of Catholic thought into German national culture and finally heightening the prestige of the Imperial University. In principle, a fully-fledged university in Germany had a faculty of Catholic theology and a faculty of Protestant theology.

On the occasion of the return of Alsace and Moselle to France in November 1918, the question of the maintenance and therefore funding of theological faculties in the university arose once more. While the two Protestant Churches sought firmly to safeguard the Faculty of Protestant theology in the new French university, the Holy See and the Bishop of Strasbourg did not object to the closure of the Faculty of Catholic Theology, which in the event of it continuing, might be reserved for a clerical elite and not for all the seminarists.

First of all, the French Government derived its inspiration quite logically from the model forged by the Laws of secularization and separation (1879–1905) and concluded with the establishment of a university without theology faculties. Such was, among others, the position of the Conference of Alsace-Lorraine from 1915. But this stance did not stand up to the test of reality. In the absence of a public faculty, the priestly elite could be trained in Switzerland, or worse, in Germany. So, finally, the faculties of theology were maintained. The Faculty of Catholic Theology had the aim of becoming a centre of high Catholic and French culture, in the words of politicians.[9] In this case too, the ideology only had reduced impact.

---

8   Bernard Le Léannec, 'L'enseignement supérieur' in Schlick (n 7) 301 *et seq.*

9   Ulrike Rother, *Die theologischen Fakultäten der Universität Strassburg* (Schöningh 2000) 322 *et seq.*

Pragmatism prevailed. What mattered was the integration of Alsace-Moselle into French society. The training of ministers of religion at any price was one means.

The Recurrent Issue of Removing Funding from the Regime of Recognized Religions

Called into question during changes of sovereignty

The abolition of the regime of recognized religions, which was on the agenda in Alsace-Moselle in the early twentieth century, was applied for the first time to Alsace-Moselle by the Nazi Government after the *de facto* annexation of Alsace-Lorraine by the German Third Reich. Advocated under the Fourth Republic in the hope of unifying the regime of faiths in France and tentatively put forward in the joint programme of the Left in 1972, its abolition was once more on the cards during the 2012 presidential campaign.

The local law on faiths was kept alive after the disannexation of 1918 by the Law of 17 October 1919 and Article 7 of the Law of 1 June 1924. But, from 17 June 1924, following the victory of the left-wing coalition, Herriot, President of the Council of Ministers, announced in his inaugural speech to the Chamber the introduction of so-called secular laws in the *départements* of the Rhine and Moselle – laws on secularization passed in the late nineteenth century – as well as the Law of Separation of 9 December 1905. The application of these provisions governing the general regime would have led to the abolition of funding to pay for ministers of religion, maintenance of religious buildings by the *communes* and remuneration for teachers of religious education in schools and public education establishments, as well as in the two theological faculties. People in Alsace and Moselle, flanked by denominational associations, reacted very strongly. Nearly 500,000 people marched through towns in Alsace and Moselle. The project was abandoned and subsequent governments have shown great caution in this area. The Council of State, consulted by the Government, also removed any ambiguity on the legal front by declaring in a notice dated 24 January 1925 that the Concordat regime resulting from the Law of 18 Germinal Year X and, as a result, the funding of religious personnel and institutions was still in force in Alsace-Moselle.

However, following the defeat of 1940, Alsace and Moselle were annexed *de facto* to the German Third Reich. No international act ratified this conquest. German laws and regulations of the time were introduced *en masse* on this occasion. In religious matters, the Concordat of 1801 and the Convention of 1902 establishing a faculty of Catholic theology were unilaterally denounced, without preventing the 1933 German Concordat from being applied in these three *départements*. All texts that applied to recognized religions were repealed by the Order of 28 October 1940 for Alsace and by a similar order for Lorraine. The repeal of the local law on faiths led to important changes in the functioning of Catholic, Lutheran and Reformed Churches. Their institutions lost their status in public law. They formed associations and were required to be self-funding in accordance with an Order of 2 August 1940 for Alsace. This text provided for new methods of funding religious organizations and came into force in 1941. Members of the three aforementioned Christian Churches who had reached adult age were subject to payment of a membership fee. If they refused, they had to resign from their churches. But even during this period, local law continued to be applied and recognized religions funded. In fact, teachers at the faculties of theology and ministers of religion who had withdrawn to the unoccupied zone were remunerated by the Vichy Government and, on 25 August 1943, the Council for the Affairs of Alsace-Lorraine, based in Algiers, expressed its opinion that the Concordat texts had not ceased to be in effect. The solution of maintaining the repeal decided upon by the Nazis was rejected following the liberation. Article 3 of the Order of 15 September 1944 re-establishing republican law maintained local law: 'The legislation in force in the *départements* of the Lower Rhine, Upper Rhine and Moselle as of 16 June 1940 remains the only one to apply and is provisionally maintained in force'. Under the terms of the 1944 Order, the system of recognized religions and its funding were now explicitly to be part of the republican legal system.

Attempts to unify the local regime with the general regime
From 1952 to 1957, the majority centre-right French Government started negotiations with the Holy See in order to create a legal framework for future peaceful relations between the State and the Catholic Church. The 'concord without concordat' proposed by the Pinay Government sought to find a solution to fund private schools, to determine a unique status for all religious buildings and to revitalize the process of recognition of religious congregations. In return, local law on the faiths in Alsace-Moselle, and thereby their funding and remuneration, would be repealed in favour of a regime applicable throughout mainland France. Negotiations led by Robert Lecourt, jurist and member of the MRP (Christian Democrat), finally broke down in 1957. The abolition of 'Concordat legislation', rejected by religious authorities in Alsace-Moselle, was the main reason for this failure. It should be noted that the Debré Law of 1959 – two years after the end of the Lecourt negotiations – established funding mechanisms for private schools and that the procedure for recognizing congregations was to resume in the 1970s, without local law in Alsace-Moselle being abolished in return.

Several decades later, the joint government programme drawn up by the Communist Party and the Socialist Party in 1972 advocated that 'the benefits of secular laws will be extended to the entire territory (including Alsace-Moselle)'. But despite nationalizing private schools, the joint programme did not explicitly abolish funding for religious personnel, buildings and activities. Following the victory of the Left in 1981, the Socialist Minister, Bockel, from Mulhouse favoured the creation of the Institute of Local Law in Alsace-Moselle and thereby reinforced study and knowledge of local law on the faiths. Finally, in the election of 2012, presidential candidate François Hollande undertook in his proposal 46 to include the fundamental principles of the Law of 1905 on secularity in the Constitution, by inserting into Article 1 a second paragraph worded as follows: 'the Republic guarantees freedom of conscience, guarantees the free exercise of religion and respects the separation of the Churches and the State in accordance with the first title of the 1905 Law, subject to the special rules applicable in Alsace and Moselle'. Here again, the funding of statutory and recognized religions in the three *départements* was not called into question.

Current Law on Funding for Statutory or Recognized Religions

In Alsace-Moselle local law, the State (via the Ministry of the Interior) and the *communes* are required to fund statutory religions. They can also, without this constituting an obligation, subsidize statutory and non-statutory religions.

Funding Statutory Religions

The funding of statutory religions takes place on two levels. It includes the state's duty to pay a salary and invalidity and retirement pensions to ministers from the four statutory religions and employees of the secretariats of the higher religious authorities whose posts figure in the budget of the Ministry of the Interior, as well as to maintain diocesan buildings (episcopal residences, seminaries and cathedrals) of the Catholic faith. *Communes* and their clusters are responsible for providing lodgings for ministers of worship or for paying a lodging allowance and for balancing the budgets of local or parish public institutions (Israelite consistories, Catholic *fabriques*, presbyteral councils of the Union of Protestant Churches in Alsace and Lorraine), when they are in deficit.

Funding from the Ministry of the Interior: remunerating ministers of religion and maintaining diocesan buildings

Almost the entire budget of the Ministry of the Interior (€54.6 million in 2011) is allocated to salaries and allowances. Allowances are paid to ministers of worship reading mass in several Catholic or Protestant parishes or rabbinical districts and include social contributions and benefits. A total of 1,393 posts were paid for by the State in 2011 and the number has been constant for several years. It includes ministers of religion (religious authorities, priests, officiating priests, vicars, pastors and rabbis), laypersons entrusted with a pastoral mission by the Catholic Church (paid for by vacant posts of ministers of worship) and employees of the secretariats of the higher religious authorities. The Minister of the Interior also pays operating grants to faiths, which include an endowment to pay officiating ministers of the Jewish faith (€1,305,600) and grants for maintaining diocesan buildings, including grand seminaries and episcopal residences in Strasbourg and Metz (€660,000 in 2011). Cathedrals are taken care of by the Ministry of Culture as part of national heritage.

One budget item that cuts across the ministries concerned envisages in 2011 a sum of €15.1 million to pay for pensions in Alsace-Lorraine. This comprises pensions for ministers of worship, as well as survivors' pensions paid to spouses.

Ministers from the four statutory faiths[10] (Catholic, Reformed, Lutheran, Jewish) occupying positions included in the budget of the Ministry of the Interior are paid as part of a hierarchical classification of ranks and posts modelled on that in force for state officials. Salaries vary from single to triple, depending on the post occupied.

Other ministries also pay salaries and grants to statutory religions under local law in Alsace-Moselle. The Ministry of National Education pays temporary teachers of religion in primary schools, permanent and temporary teachers of religion in secondary schools, as well as professors and lecturers in theology faculties in Strasbourg (Catholic and Protestant) and Metz (Catholic) and temporary teachers of religion at the University Teacher Training Institute of Strasbourg University. Lastly, some personnel are, under common law, remunerated by the Department of Justice – prison chaplains – and the Ministry of Defence – army chaplains. Chaplains in public hospitals receive payment from the hospital administration under local law, without there being substantial differences between local and general law.

Funding the costs of local or parish worship: obligations of public institutions
Operating and investment expenses of Catholic and Protestant parishes, as well as of rabbinical districts dependent on Israelite consistories, are funded by the public establishments of the faiths concerned: *fabriques* for the Catholic Church, parishes or presbyteral councils for the Reformed and Lutherans, consistories for the Jewish faith. This expenditure includes the costs necessary for celebrating worship, salaries and costs of personnel employed by the institution (sexton, organist, maintenance personnel), improvement, maintenance and repair work, major repairs and, where applicable, reconstruction of buildings of worship and lodging for ministers of religion (mainly Catholic and Protestant rectories) and insurance of goods and people, including covering liability risks.

Revenues from public institutions of worship are made up of interests from their own assets, donations and bequests, collections and offerings received during religious acts and manual donations by the faithful. Unlike other public establishments, public religious institutions in the three *départements* of eastern France are self-funding and are not directly funded by the state or local authorities. Expenditure for local or parish worship is therefore charged to members of the parish.

Funding the costs of local or parish worship: obligations of communes
Communes are subject to an obligation: that of providing lodgings for parish ministers of the four statutory religions and, failing that, to pay a housing allowance.[11] This direct charge for the *communes* is combined with a subsidiary obligation that

---

10   In fact, since assembling the Reformed (EPRAL) and the Lutherans (EPCAAL) in a federation (UEPAL), one could mention only three statutory religions.
11   General Local Authorities Code, Article L 2543-3.

provides a security net enabling continuity of religious public services: the duty of balancing the budgets of public institutions of religions, should the latter be in deficit. The obligation to balance the budgets of public institutions is enshrined in Article L 2543-3 3 of the General Local Authorities Code: 'In case of insufficient income from the *fabriques*, presbyteral councils and consistories, as evidenced by their accounts and budgets, the costs of worship of religions whose ministers are employed by the State are required to be included in the budget of the *communes*'.[12]

The procedure for applying for grants from the *communes* is laid down in Articles 93, 94 and 102 of the Decree of 30 December 1809, as amended. The deliberative assembly of the establishment of worship concerned adopts the budget, highlighting its inadequate resources, and submits it to the higher religious authority. It is then forwarded to the *commune* for submission to the municipal council. In case of dispute, such as refusal by the council to balance the accounts of the public institution, 'any person interested in taking action' may instigate legal action at the Regional Chamber of Accounts. If it considers the complaint to be receivable, it will then decide on the binding nature for the *commune* of the envisaged expenditure. If the Regional Chamber of Accounts considers the request made by the public religious institution to be justified, it issues a formal demand for such expenditure to be included in the *commune*'s budget. Should the local authority refuse, the Chamber will ask the prefect to make an automatic entry. The decision by the prefect and the Chamber may be appealed in the administrative court.

Funding Non-Statutory Religions

In Alsace-Moselle, where the Law of 9 December 1905 has not been introduced, *communes*, *départements* and *régions* have the option of paying subsidies to faiths that have not been officially recognized in respect of their jurisdiction and the principle of speciality. Building a place of worship for an unrecognized faith may correspond to a need felt by the inhabitants of the *commune* and thus constitutes general interest under the provisions of Article L 2541-12 10 of the General Local Authorities Code. In this case, the *commune* may legally participate in its funding via a grant, by providing premises or use of premises free of charge.[13]

Non-statutory faiths reunite all religious groupings other than the four statutory faiths and are required to exist in law in order to receive government subsidies. The status of association registered under local law with an aim that is exclusively religious is widely used by such groups. The payment of subsidies to associations representing members of faiths must, in the absence of legal texts, be subject to conditions required for obtaining tax exemptions. These faiths must be well-known, adhere to commonly shared values and be minded to integrate into society. One

---

12 Communities of *communes* and urban area communities (CGCT, Article L 5812-1 and L 5814-1) may exercise such authority in lieu of member *communes*.

13 Ministerial response, no. 18172 [14.07.2003] *JOAN* Q 5666.

example is the City of Strasbourg, which provides a budget allocation, a portion of which is donated to religious associations. It also supported the construction of a mosque by providing the association responsible for the construction with land and it pays a grant of up to 10 per cent of the construction cost.

Non-statutory religions, in particular Islam, already fall under local law: the possibility of publicly subsidizing non-statutory faiths as a result of the Law of 1905 not being introduced and organization within the framework of a registered association. However, conferring on them a special status as for Catholic, Protestant and Jewish faiths seems problematic. The Constitutional Council states in its *Somodia* Decision of 5 August 2011 that, if local law is protected by a basic principle recognized in the Laws of the Republic, its extension is excluded, because these 'particular provisions can only be adapted to the extent that differences in treatment are not increased and that their scope is not extended'. For Jean Marie Woehrling, President of the Institute of Local Law, this decision does not crystallize local law and new provisions can be applied, as long as they are not contrary to the principle of equality, which does not mean uniformity. Differences in legislation would be possible on a regional level, provided that they are justified by special circumstances.

Conclusion

This investigation into developments in the law on funding religions and their justification allows several hypotheses to be put forward.

The first concerns the great stability of the system put in place. The method of funding religions is difficult to change or else to abolish, as evidenced by the creation of *ad hoc* religious taxes for Jewish (1808) and Protestant (1901) faiths. These were perceived as discriminatory by minority faiths and as unfair by Catholics. The abolition of public funding has never been seriously considered, except by the Nazi regime known for its brutality and contempt of the peoples it conquered. The financial gain would not have been commensurate with the political cost. Rather than chipping away or removing altogether, the tendency is to improve or maintain the *status quo.*

But funding recognized religions is based neither on theological considerations, nor even on the theory of compensation, which is sometimes politely referred to by the administration. Political arguments are the sole drivers to justify maintaining and improving the system of recognized religions. As much in 1870 as in 1919, it was not the done thing to upset people by abolishing the regime of faiths in existence. Moreover, German and French Governments used this instrument in order to accelerate the integration of populations. The Faculty of Catholic Theology created in 1902 to germanize an influential clergy was transformed after 1919 into an institution capable of disseminating French culture.

Integration also means that the status of clerics in the *Reichsland Elsass-Lothringen* was not to be inferior to that prevailing in the kingdoms, grand duchies and principalities of the Second Reich. The local Law of November 1909 aimed to make up for this delay by demonstrating a favourable policy towards religions, while conversely the Catholics of 'Old France' struggled to recover from the 'separation' and quarrels about inventories.

In this subtle game, broad principles carry scarcely any weight. The Law of 9 December 1905 would coexist, less than two decades after its passing, alongside the Law of Germinal Year X, which would be maintained in Alsace-Moselle in 1919.

List of References

Ducrocq T, *Cours de droit administratif et de législation française*, vol. 3 (Berger-Levrault 1888)

Fritzen A, *Gehaltslage des Katholischen Pfarrers in E.L und im übrigen Deutschland* (F.X. Le Roux)

Justus, *Elsass–lothringische Zeitfragen. Kultusaus-gaben und Paritat.* Separatabdruck aus dem 'Elsässer' (Strasbourg 1908)

Le Léannec B, 'L'enseignement supérieur' in Schlick, J. (ed.) *Le régime actuel des pensions de retraite des ministres du culte en Eglises et Etat en Alsace et en Moselle* (Cerdic 1979)

Lucien-Brun H, *Etude historique sur la condition des israélites en France depuis 1789* (Imprimerie P. Legendre 1900)

Rother U, *Die theologischen Fakultäten der Universität Strassburg* (Schöningh 2000)

Schlick J (ed.), *Le régime actuel des pensions de retraite des ministres du culte en Eglises et Etat en Alsace et en Moselle* (Cerdic 1979)

Chapter 6

Funding of Religious Activities in France 1790–1905

Jeanne-Marie Tuffery-Andrieu

The issue of funding in France arose in the Frankish period. At that time the Church had vast wealth resulting from pious bequests and donations. It very quickly emerged as the most important property owner in the kingdom. So, during the Merovingian period, kings did not hesitate to confiscate some of these ecclesiastical properties to use them for the benefit of their followers. In return, on the one hand it granted immunity to the Church, which exempted church property from public services. Church lands, in principle, were subject to direct taxation, but the certificate of immunity contained a provision that, in most cases, gave the taxes to the beneficiary. On the other hand, the king granted the Church the ability to levy a tax: the tithe. Initially, this practice was based on writings in the Bible. In the seventh century, councils began to proclaim the religious obligation of it, and failure to comply was likely to result in sanctions. Finally, a series of capitularies imposed on subjects the legal obligation to pay the tithe.

The tithe was a proportional fee charged in kind on certain income, including the main fruits of the earth. Its rate was in principle 10 per cent, but it varied according to the province. It was collected in kind at harvest time and was very often less than the one tenth due. Established in compensation for the royal confiscations, the tithe's main purpose was to maintain the clergy. The tithe belonged to the parish priest. In practice, individuals and cathedral chapters appropriated a large portion of the tithe, leaving the priest the bare minimum.

During the Middle Ages, this system was maintained, and supplemented by that of the *droit de régale*, which constituted a serious attack on the heritage of the Church. The king safeguarded the worldly goods of a bishopric, while the seat was vacant, to prevent usurpation and he received the revenue from the benefice.

From the sixteenth century onwards, the Church, one of the orders of the Nation, could be called upon to pay its share of the public costs of the kingdom. The Contract of Poissy, in 1561, established a new practice, by which the clergy agreed to pay a tax, called the free gift (don gratuit).

In terms of funding for faiths, the kingdom of France appeared very reserved, especially as the importance of Church property rapidly aroused the keen interest of the laity: the enfeoffed tithes, the *régale*, even the doctrines of secularization were little by little to lead to the undermining of a system that had, however, made the Catholic religion one of the largest contributors to the financing of public expenditure.

The Establishment of a New Funding System (1790–1801)

The Civil Constitution of the Clergy in 1790 and the Decrees of Separation of Church and State in 1795 brought about a new policy in terms of funding religion.

The Civil Constitution of the Clergy (12 July 1790)

The French Revolution tried to impose the authority of the State over the Church by means of the Civil Constitution of the Clergy. This constitution was proclaimed on 12 July 1790. Previously, the National Assembly had already begun to intervene in the Church of France: religious property had been confiscated and monks 'invited' to leave their monasteries. Religious property came under state ownership and the State assumed responsibility for the maintenance of the clergy and places of worship. Although the need for money was the economic reason for such measures, which allowed the majority of monasteries to be sold off as 'national property', thereby raising money, the desire to put the Church under state tutelage was a very real one. The Civil Constitution of the Clergy was aimed at organizing a 'national' religion in a France open to religious freedom. Recalling the importance of religion in city life, the Assembly wished to organize the national Church to make it mainly a source of public morality and no longer the foundation of politics. This approach was linked to the demystification of royal power, which had come no longer to be considered as a 'divine right'. As the national religion, the Church of France, reorganized by the Civil Constitution of the Clergy, saw its Gallicanism intensify and its organization thrown into disarray: dioceses were reworked along the lines of the French *départemental* divisions, bishops had to be elected, priests too. The hierarchy was modelled on the political system and the temporal authority of the Pope was very much weakened. From 1792, the State could not meet its financial commitments towards constitutional bishops and priests. Indeed, from Year II, pensions and salaries were late, then the expenses of worship themselves ceased to be regularly provided for. After Thermidor, the sworn clergy claimed the arrears, but the state of the finances did not allow the State to satisfy their demands. Protests led the Government to study the problem of separation in financial terms and the Finance Committee entrusted Cambon with preparing a report which concluded by stopping all payments. In addition, this situation of insolvency led a number of bishops of the constitutional clergy to demand the separation of Church and State and consequently to establish the principle of freedom of worship.

Separation of Church and State

From 1795, the Government implemented a policy of State neutrality in religious matters.

Articles 352 and 354 of a Decree of 3 Ventôse Year III, incorporated into the Constitution of the Year III, state that: 'The law does not recognise religious vows or any commitment contrary to the natural rights of man'; '[n]o person may be prevented from practising, in accordance with the laws, the religion he has chosen; no-one can be forced to contribute to the expenses of worship. The Republic does not employ any one of them'. As a result of this provision, the State was no longer to fund any religion whatsoever.

The Funding Regime of Recognized Religions (1801–1905)

The Law of 18 Germinal Year X established a system for funding the recognized (Catholic, Protestant and Jewish) religions.

The Catholic Faith

By restoring the legal existence of the Catholic faith and making it a public service, the legislator of Year X ensured it would receive an endowment. This endowment included movable and immovable property and financial allowances.

The immovable endowment
The endowment for immovables consisted of buildings dedicated to religious worship or to housing ministers.

Under Article 12 of the Concordat, all metropolitan churches, cathedrals, parochial and other non-alienated churches necessary for worship had to be put at the disposition of the bishops. The extent of the terms of this transfer was specified by Article 75 of the Law of 18 Germinal Year X. Of the churches covered by the Concordat, metropolitan and cathedral churches remained the property of the State and parish churches were considered in law to be the property of the *communes* (see opinion of the Council of State of 3 Nivôse and 2 Pluviôse Year XIII). Many former churches that had not been alienated during the Revolution were not included in being restored to religious worship; a Decree of 30 May 1806 assigned full ownership of them to the *fabriques*[1] of the parish in the circumscription in which they were located. When the restored churches were later established as parishes, branches or parochial chapels, they became communal property in exchange for the commitment of the *commune* to provide for the expenses of worship and the maintenance of churches in the event of the *fabriques* having

---

1   The *fabrique* consisted of churchwardens charged with the maintenance of the fabric of the churches of the parish [Translator's note].

insufficient resources (see opinion of the Council of State of 12 February 1841). As for the churches built since the Concordat, they belonged to the legal person, State, *commune* or *fabrique* which built them, or to which they had been given or bequeathed.

If the *communes* were owners of parish churches, the church councils (*fabriques*) had, however, a special right over these buildings, which has similarities to usufruct. This right allowed them to resist by all legal means usurpations which might threaten these churches and, notably, to bring an action *in rem* to enforce their claim. They might act alone or jointly with the *commune* that owned them; they might even defend their right of usufruct against attacks from the *commune* itself.

The *communes* which owned the churches were also owners of their dependencies, and, in particular, of the movables that were joined to and incorporated in these buildings, notably at the time of their restoration, or those that had since been installed more permanently, such as, for example, statues placed in the niches. As for goods that had preserved their status as movables, the *communes* were only owners of those located in the churches at the moment when they were restored to the faith and of any placed there since.

Officially consecrated churches belonged to the public domain. The churches designated for worship in implementation of the Concordat could be closed down, no matter what the bishop thought of this. A decree was necessary in each case. As long as churches retained their purpose, they were inalienable and could not be the object of either an easement nor a right of joint ownership. They were imprescriptible. Among the movables adorning churches, those classified as being of artistic or historic interest and which belonged to the State were equally inalienable and imprescriptible (Law of 30 March 1887).

The episcopal palaces belonged to the State. This applied to buildings that the Government had, since the Concordat, restored to their former purpose, or other state-owned buildings it had made available to archbishops and bishops. The bishop as beneficiary of the use resided in the palace. The palaces were furnished by the State. The composition of the furniture is determined by the order of 7 April 1819.

The State owned the buildings used for the grand seminaries. It even remained so after the Decree of 9 April 1811, which conceded ownership of the buildings used for state education to the *communes*.

The presbytery was the house used for accommodating parish or officiating priests (*desservants*). Under the terms of Article 72 of the Law of 18 Germinal Year X, the presbyteries and adjoining gardens that had not been alienated had to be returned to the parish priests and officiating priests (*desservants*) in succursal parishes. In the absence of such presbyteries, municipal councils were authorized to provide them with accommodation and a garden.

In principle, presbyteries during the Concordat were the property of the *communes*. Those built or acquired by the *communes* after the Concordat, those given or bequeathed, also belonged to the *communes*. Some presbyteries could also be the property of the church councils (*fabriques*). Such difficulties as might arise between the *communes* and the church councils (*fabriques*) relating to the ownership of presbyteries were within the competence of the judicial courts.

The parish priests and officiating priests (*desservants*) had the right of usufruct of the presbytery that they occupied. This right was not the same in every case. When the presbytery belonged to the *commune*, it acquired a special right *sui generis* which was not clearly defined and which was neither the right of usufruct, nor the right to housing as defined by the Civil Code. This was nonetheless a true usufruct that could be cited before judicial or administrative courts, in opposing either third parties or the *commune* itself, as a result of acts that would be likely to infringe this right (see Article 72 of the Law of 18 Germinal Year X and Article 92 of the Decree of 30 December 1809). Case law decided that the priest's usufruct of the presbytery could not go so far as to allow him to object to the *commune* decorating the exterior walls of the presbytery or using these walls to affix laws and other official notices (see Jurisdictional Court, 15 December 1883, D.P. 83, 3, 57). The priest's right of usufruct included in counterpart certain charges – rental repairs as well as repairs arising from damage for which he was responsible.

The usufruct of the parish priest or officiating priest (*desservant*) ended with the termination of his duties. The mayor of the *commune* could petition the court to be placed in possession of the presbytery without awaiting the appointment of the successor. The *communes*, as owners of the presbyteries, did not have the right to evict the priest while he was in office under any circumstances; an eviction could not be ordered by the administrative authority.

If the building was to be allocated a different purpose, this change could not be made by deliberation of the municipal council, even if approved by the prefect, regardless of the date on which the assignment of the presbytery was decided. A decree was necessary in all cases. Complete closure could only be authorized in order for the *communes* to provide adequate housing to dispossessed officiating priests (*desservants*).

The legislation on religious cults in Year X imposed no obligation on the church councils (*fabriques*) or the *communes* to provide housing for vicars. However, former vicarages that, following the Law of Germinal Year X and in execution of the order of 7 Ventôse Year XI, had been restored by the *communes* to their former purpose, have today to be considered as communal property and immovables of the Concordat.

Endowment for movables

Regardless of the immovables which were necessary for religious worship and for accommodating ministers, the Catholic worship incurred multiple expenses arising from personnel and equipment which were provided for through a combination of the State, public institutions and *communes*.

Among the expenses of the Catholic worship that the State bore, some were related to the Concordat, others not. In Article 14 of the Convention of 26 Messidor Year IX (Concordat), the State was only liable to the Holy See for providing bishops and priests with an adequate salary. It mentioned that the State was not compelled to provide endowments for the chapters or seminaries. All other expenses that the State bore after that period were therefore more akin to gracious endowments that it could withdraw at any time. This distinction – between salaries that are linked to the Concordat and allowances that are not – was established by the Law of 29 December 1883.

Clergymen were only entitled to their salaries from the day they moved in (order of 4 September 1820). These salaries were payable quarterly. The clergyman who did not exercise *de facto* in the *commune* to which he was assigned could not obtain his salary (Law of 23 April 1884, Article 8). In the event of removal of the post holder in case of illness or misconduct, a part of his salary was payable to his replacement (Decree of 17 November 1811). Finally, salaries could be suspended using an administrative procedure.

The State was to bear the costs of materials, including: certain annuities for transferring some episcopal palaces; loans for the maintenance of movables in bishoprics and for providing diocesan offices; special loans for completion and rehabilitation of certain cathedrals. Finally, the State provided assistance to *communes*, acting on proposals by general councils, for maintenance or construction works for their churches and presbyteries (Law of 10 August 1871, Article 68).

It was the church councils (*fabriques*), as public institutions, which, with the various resources available to them, paid the largest part of faith-related expenditure. How they operated is not directly part of the question being addressed here.

Since the Law of 5 April 1884, *communes* were no longer required – as they had been under the influence of the Decree of 30 December 1809 and the Law of 18 July 1837 – to compensate in general for any lack of resources within the church councils (*fabriques*). Their obligations were reduced to two kinds of expenses: the rental allowance for the parish or officiating priest (*desservant*) and any major repairs to be made to buildings of worship. And this charge was only subsidiary, insofar as it fell to the *commune* only if the *fabrique* could not pay it.

When the *fabrique* claimed that its resources were insufficient to provide either housing allowances or major repairs, and it called upon the finances of the *commune*, if the *commune* refused to allocate the subsidy, it was decided upon by a decree issued on the basis of a report by the Ministries of the Interior and of Religious Affairs (Law of 5 April 1884, Articles 136 § 11 and 12). According to this decree, the Head of State decided whether the expenditure was, under the circumstances, an obligation for the *commune*: his decision could be referred to the Council of State, either by the *fabrique* or the *commune*, according to the case. But the proportion of the amount charged to the *commune* could not be dealt with by litigation (Council of State, 9 August 1889, D.P. 91, 3, 29).

According to administrative case law, the resources of the *fabrique* were deemed insufficient when its ordinary revenue did not allow it to bear the expense. The resources available are only the excess income over expenditure; rights to annuity did not therefore form part of the property of the *fabrique*. This establishment could not be forced to dispose of its capital before calling for assistance from the *commune*.

When two or more *communes* joined together to worship and formed a single parish, the obligations relating to the housing allowance and major repairs were divided between the *communes* of the joint parishes. This apportionment took place according to the following rules: in the case of housing allowance, it was the prefect who did the apportionment (Decree of 25 March 1852). In the case of major repairs, it was the General Council [*Conseil Général*] that intervened (Law of 10 August 1871, Article 46). Legislation prior to 1905 did not prescribe the principles of the apportionment: *communes* could define these principles by freely debated agreement. Failing agreement, the General Council or the prefect determined them at their discretion. The decisions taken by them in this regard did not, moreover, preclude each *commune* from challenging its obligation in relation to the *fabrique* and they therefore could not be attacked for abuse of power.

The expenses indicated above were the only binding ones. The costs of rebuilding a church were thereby not binding. But *communes* were free to vote appropriations for the worship expenses. So when a *commune* applied to erect a parish chapel, it had to undertake to pay the salary of the chaplain. Despite this commitment, it was no longer free to enter these appropriations in its budget. Should it decide to remove them, the chapel would be closed, if the *fabrique* did not have sufficient resources by itself to provide for religious worship.

The *départements* were not committed to any mandatory spending on religious activities, but they were free to vote subsidies for diocesan or parish work.

Protestant Faiths

The costs of the Protestant worship, like those of the Catholic faith, were shared between the State, public institutions and the *communes*. The State's share, except for some relief for pastors and widows, the maintenance of the Faculty of Theology and Protestant seminaries and some endowments for the upkeep of churches, was comprised exclusively of pastors' salaries. The latter are divided into three classes, not counting the pastors of Paris. The provisions concerning the salaries of Catholic ministers of religion also applied to them, except for the difference that income from curial property and gifts that pastors received were deducted from the salary that the State was to pay them (Law of 18 Germinal Year X, Article 7). The majority of the expenses of the Protestant services were covered by public establishments of worship, the presbyterial councils and consistories, and for the Lutheran Church, the presbyterial councils, consistories and individual synods. The Decree of 27 March 1893 reorganized the budgets and accounts of the presbyterial councils, whose accounting, since the Law of 26 January 1892, was subject to the same rules of public accounting and, in principle, to the same regime as the *fabriques*. The duties of the certifying officer were entrusted to the president of the presbyterial council, the duty of accountant, sometimes to the treasurer, sometimes to a special receiver, sometimes to the collector of direct taxes. In the

Church of the Augsburg Confession, the accountant was always a parish receiver selected and appointed from outside the presbyterial council (Law of 1 August 1879, Article 10).

Where there existed property or undivided rights common to several presbyterial councils of the same church consistory, the consistory directly exercised the powers of the presbyterial council to administer this property and establish the budget of their revenues and expenses. If such undivided ownership existed between presbyterial councils from different consistories, the administration of property and the consequential budgetary allocations were undertaken by a delegation, whose composition was determined by the Minister of Religious Affairs and which included representatives in equal numbers from the ecclesiastical bodies concerned (Decree of 27 March 1893, Articles 34 and 35).

As to the obligations of the *communes*, they were the same as for the Catholic faith, and the same provisions applied to them. Thus, *communes* were only required to pay a housing allowance to pastors, if presbyteries justified their lack of adequate resources.

The Jewish Faith

Since the Law of 8 February 1831, Ministers of Religion would receive a salary from the State. The rules on salaries are the same as for ministers of other religions. Most of the church-related expenses were borne by the budgets of consistories and communities (Decree of 27 March 1893, Article 4). The obligations of the *communes* were the same as for the Protestant faiths.

List of References

Basdevant-Gaudemet B, *Le jeu concordataire dans la France du XIXème s.*, (PUF 1988)
—— *Histoire du droit canonique et des institutions de l'Eglise* (Economica 2013)
Basdevant-Gaudemet B and Messner F (eds), *Les origines historiques du statut des confessions religieuses dans les pays de l'Union européenne* (PUF 1999)
Dalloz, *Répertoire pratique* (Dalloz 1912) (see 'Cultes')
Delsol X, Garay A and Tawil E, *Droit des cultes, personnes, activités biens et structures* (Dalloz 2005)
Husson JF (ed.), *Le financement des cultes et de la laïcité* (Les éditions namuroises 2006)
Lafon J, *Les prêtres, les fidèles et l'Etat. Le ménage à trois du XIXème siècle* (Beauchesne 1987)
Messner F, *Le financement des Eglises. Le système des cultes reconnus* (CERDIC 1983)
—— *Régime des cultes. Financement et patrimoine* (Jurisclasseur Alsace-Moselle 2004) fasc. 233

—— (ed.), *Dictionnaire Du Droit Des Religions* (CNRS 2011) (see 'Financement Des Cultes')

Messner F, Prelot PH and Woehrling JM, *Traité de droit français des religions*, 2nd edn (Litec 2013)

Minnerath R, *L'Eglise catholique face aux Etats* (Cerf 2012)

Szramckiewicz R and Bouineau J, *Histoire des institutions 1750–1914* (Litec 1998)

Chapter 7

Church Tax, Subsidies and State Aid – Church Funding in Germany

Heinrich de Wall

The Current Situation: Sources of Church Funding in Germany

The German System of Church Funding

The German system of church funding[1] is not dependent on one single source, but consists of a mixed system. Churches receive money in various ways, the most important source being church taxation, which in Germany cannot be described as public funding; instead, it is a system of funding based on churches' own resources. Before examining the current situation and difficulties pertaining to the various systems of funding, an approximate overview of sources of church income in Germany will be provided. The figures are based on the Protestant Church in the year 2005.[2] In this particular year, the income of the Protestant Church amounted to around €10 billion. Proportionally, and as regards the method of funding, there is little difference, however, between Protestant and Catholic churches.

The sources of the Church's income in Germany can be divided into four groups:

1. *The Church's own resources*: these include Church Tax (€4 billion) and membership fees, donations (€266 million), as well as income from the Church's own assets (property, company shares and so on: €1.7 billion).
2. *State subsidies*: based on laws, contracts or special grants, as specified in Article 138 § 1 of the Weimar Constitution. These consist of contributions made on the basis of historical, legal entitlements, which were being paid out as early as 1919 (€232 million).
3. *State or third party contributions* in return for services or payments by the Church (€2 billion). For example, the parents of a child who attends a church kindergarten have to pay fees to allow him or her to go there. These fees do not cover the kindergarten's expenses. A second example is that, in

---

1 For a short outline in English, see Gerhard Robbers, 'State and Church in Germany' in G Robbers, *State and Church in the European Union* (Nomos 2005) 89–90.

2 Evangelische Kirche in Deutschland (EKD), *Zahlen und Fakten zum kirchlichen Leben* [Figures and facts about Church activities] (2011) <http://www.ekd.de/download/broschuere_2011_mit_Links.pdf> accessed 18 October, 37.

German law, the State is obliged to finance the cost of religious instruction at state schools, which includes teachers' salaries. If a priest teaches religion, the Church, which pays his stipend, is reimbursed by the State.

4. *State aid* for church activities that benefit the community, for example, a nursery or hospital building. The State also provides financial support for the same purpose to secular institutions such as the German Red Cross. From a German legal point of view, it would therefore be seen as a breach of the Principle of Equality, if churches were not to receive similar aid (€1.8 billion in state and private aid).

We also have to take into consideration that many church activities are not carried out by Catholic dioceses or by Evangelical territorial churches or parishes. There is a wide range of organizations which are legally independent of the Church within the umbrella structures of the respective churches' charitable bodies, and these see themselves and their activities as part of the Church and its vocation and are at the same time acknowledged by the Church. Most 'church' hospitals and nursing homes are run by such legally independent bodies. In Germany, there are two significant umbrella organizations in this domain: the Catholic *Caritas* and the Protestant *Diakonie*. Both are subdivided into charitable organizations with 450,000 employees in each Church. These independent bodies also receive contributions and state aid in accordance with points 3 and 4.

Church Tax

According to Article 137 § 6 of the Weimar Constitution (WRV) taken together with Article 140 of the German '*Grundgesetz*' (GG – Basic Law), religious societies that are corporations under public law are entitled to levy taxes using the civil taxation lists. Consequently, Protestant and Catholic churches in Germany and some other religious communities (for example Jewish communities) have the constitutional right to fund their activities through taxation.[3] It goes without saying, however, that only members of the respective denomination may be asked to make tax contributions to the Church, a matter seen in Germany as corresponding to the principle of religious freedom. Consequently, a church tax may not be imposed on corporate bodies, unlike, for instance, in Switzerland. Church Tax is nothing other than a membership contribution, but one charged not in the usual manner, but rather as taxation. The main factor that distinguishes it from the membership fee for a private society is that a church may use administrative enforcement to collect its tax, whereas a society must take legal action against members who are not

---

3 For details, see Felix Hammer, *Rechtsfragen der Kirchensteuer* (Mohr 2002); Heiner Marré, 'Das kirchliche Besteuerungsrecht' in Joseph Listl et al. (eds), *Handbuch des Staatskirchenrechts der Bundesrepublik Deutschland*, vol. 1, 2nd edn (Duncker Humblot 1994) 1109–47; Peter Unruh, *Religionsverfassungsrecht* (Nomos 2009) 181–9; Axel Von Campenhausen et al., *Staatskirchenrecht* (C.H. Beck 2006) 226–38.

willing to pay their fees voluntarily. This slight, but highly significant, difference guarantees a reliable and steady flow of funds and, as the figures show, Church Tax is by far the most important source of income for the Church. Church Tax is levied as a share of state income tax, and comprises 9 per cent of income tax in most of Germany's *Länder*, 8 per cent elsewhere.

Although Article 137 § 6 of the WRV states that churches may consult the civil tax lists and, on this basis levy their own taxes, state tax laws and agreements between Churches and the State have actually given rise to a different procedure. The bulk of the Church Tax is in fact collected and administered by the state tax authorities. As long as church taxes are levied along with income tax, employers simply transfer employees' tax contributions directly to the tax office. In this way, private employers are also included in the Church Tax collection procedure, regardless of whatever denomination they belong to. A Catholic employer, for instance, is obliged to collect Protestant employees' Church Tax and transfer it to the tax office, which in turn passes it on to the respective church.

This system saves the need to set up tax authorities within the churches themselves. Thanks to digital technology, the procedure is straightforward, because it is easy to calculate Church Tax payments. At the same time, the State is not required to keep civil tax lists. These lists, specified in Article 137 § 6 of the WRV, do not in fact exist. They would have to be introduced specifically for the Church Tax.

The state system of Church Tax collection through tax offices does not in fact mean that the Church Tax constitutes public funding of churches. For one thing, tax payments come from church members, not from the State. Also, a percentage of church income, between two and four per cent, is paid to the State for administration of the Church Tax. Thus, the State provides a service for the churches and is rewarded accordingly by them.

In the area of taxation, it must be said that churches frequently profit from tax benefits. For one thing, they themselves are exempt from a whole range of taxes, especially from corporation tax. Also, Church Tax contributions made by a church member are special payments which can be deducted from the latter's income tax. In other words, one is not obliged to pay income tax on the sum one pays as Church Tax. Similarly, donations to other welfare organizations are supported. This of course leads to considerable benefits. Nonetheless, over the last few years and decades, many people have left the Church precisely as a consequence of the Church Tax. This becomes particularly apparent whenever the State increases taxes, which in turn leads to a significant drop in church membership. In spite of this, however, income from Church Tax has almost always been increasing, mainly because of Germany's economic performance, from which churches profit too.

State Subsidies

Only state subsidies based on special grants or historic entitlements from before 1919 constitute direct funding of the church by the State.[4] Although they constitute quite a considerable sum, namely around €460 million a year for both churches, the proportion of total church income they represent, about 2–3 per cent, is relatively low. However, these state subsidies have continually been criticized in public. One of the arguments is that these payments, which partly go back to the secularization process at the beginning of the nineteenth century or even earlier, have lost their purpose after 200 years. The law is clear, though, because according to Article 136 § 1 of the WRV, state subsidies have to be redeemed. The State has not yet carried out this redemption and is therefore obliged to continue the payments.

State Aid and State Contributions

As with other organizations, churches can receive state aid for causes that are in the public interest, providing that they account for their activities. This involves submitting evidence and they may be subject to auditing by state authorities. The problem with this procedure is of course that, when evidence is sought about how these state grants are spent, it means the entire church budget is being monitored and checked. The churches have indeed to submit appropriate evidence, as specified in all applicable laws, which at the same time limits their right to determine their budget themselves (Article 137 § 3 of the WRV), but the right to self-determination may only be limited as far as is absolutely necessary. The consequence is that limits are also placed on state audits, although it is difficult to determine the extent to which this actually happens. The matter is, of course, made less controversial by the fact that many of the subsidized charitable projects are carried out by providers who are themselves independent charitable organizations under the umbrella of the Protestant *Diakonie* or the Catholic *Caritas*. If these independent organizations receive subsidies, the audit is carried out on the basis of *their* budgets and not those of the churches.

With regard to state aid, but also state contributions to church projects, especially charitable ones, there is further controversy. The level of subsidies or contributions is naturally determined according to principles of economic viability. A church hospital is expected to operate just as efficiently as a secular one. The same applies to the likes of church nursing homes. Without these principles of economy common to secular institutions and also applied to church bodies, these institutions would not be viable. However, the regulations may occasionally place severe restrictions on church schemes. For instance, in the care industry, the

---

4   For details, see Michael Droege, *Staatsleistungen an Religionsgemeinschaften im säkularen Kultur- und Sozialstaat* (Duncker und Humblot 2004) 156–256, and Heiner de Wall, 'Staatsleistungen – ewige Rente?' in Rosemarie Will (ed.), *Die Privilegien der Kirchen und das Grundgesetz* (Humanistische Union 2011).

attention an elderly or disabled person is thought to require is specified right down to the minute. It is, however, church institutions in particular which emphasize the importance of devotion towards individuals and the need to devote time to their needs. It is an intrinsic principle of humanity in nursing not only to fulfil patients' physical needs, but also to give them the attention they require. Unfortunately, state nursing budgets frequently fail to take these issues into account.

Examples

The training of church ministers in Germany is divided into two parts: a first period of approximately five years of theology studies, usually at state universities, and, secondly, training in the practical aspects of the profession which is organized by the churches themselves. There is no state funding for this second part.

The faculties of theology at state universities are state institutions and therefore funded by the State. This is usually how the training of students is provided: students have to pay for their maintenance and the State pays for the institutions – schools and universities. As the *Bundesverfassungsgericht* has recently decided, the State is free to consider theology as a discipline which should be part of universities and therefore faculties of theology at state universities are not forbidden by the Constitution. As Germany's Basic Law guarantees the right to a free choice of job for everyone, and as the training for jobs which require academic standards is provided by state universities for all professions, there is no reason why theology should be excluded from this model. The funding of faculties of theology therefore cannot be considered to be a privilege of the churches and it is not state funding of churches.

Remuneration of ministers (and of other employees) is a matter for the churches themselves. There is no state funding especially for this purpose. However, some of the 'public subsidies on the basis of a law, contract or special entitlement' as guaranteed by Article 138 of the Weimar Constitution were granted for the purpose of clerics' alimentation. These subsidies are, however, not paid to the ministers directly, but to the Church. Usually, as mentioned above, an overall amount, covering all the different historically based subsidies, has been agreed upon by Churches and State. Only the Bavarian concordat still specifies payments for the purpose of the remuneration of individual bishops or other church officials.

The construction and maintenance of church buildings is a matter for the respective owner, the Church. There is no special state funding of church buildings in Germany, unless the obligation to maintain a church building is based on a special historical entitlement as it is guaranteed by Article 138 of the Weimar Constitution. On such a basis, the State has (or has had) to maintain quite a large number of church buildings, including important and famous churches. In some cases, Church and State have agreed on annual payments instead of the obligation to maintain church buildings.

Not only the State, but also local communities, have to maintain church buildings in numerous cases, again due to historical commitments. There is discussion whether obligations of the local communities are guaranteed by Article 138 of the Weimar Constitution. But attempts by some local communities to rid themselves of their obligations on the basis of the *clausula rebus sic stantibus* have been rejected by the German administrative courts.

Today, apart from those historical entitlements, in general there is no state funding for the construction and maintenance of church buildings. However, for the construction of buildings for special purposes – for example, kindergartens, hospitals, retirement homes – state aid may be granted.

Financing media of a religious nature: there is a great number of newspapers and magazines of a religious nature. They are usually edited by persons or organizations with close links to the Church. The churches have their own institutions to support these media and give financial and other aid for this purpose. There is no state funding of such media.

The major radio and television networks in Germany – public or private – have to offer time slots to broadcast church programmes, such as Sunday services on TV or radio. Private networks have to be reimbursed by the churches for the costs of these time slots.

The Historical Background of Church Funding in Germany

Church Funding in Early Modern Times

The German system of church funding results from two main lines of historical development of the country: firstly, the long process of separation of State and Church during which the State frequently expropriated and 'secularized' church property and, secondly, the development of the modern economy, during which the importance of real estate as a source of income declined, whereas the population was growing and, along with it, numbers of churchgoers.[5]

In early modern times, churches in Germany derived their income from different sources, the most important of which was church property, especially its real estate. This was almost the same all over Europe. An important part of the income came from dues connected with land which belonged to the Church or where the Church had at least the right to ask for these dues. Different varieties of tithes are among these estate-based sources of income. Secondly, monasteries and several other ecclesiastical institutions tended to generate an important part of their income through their own agricultural or other commercial enterprises, such as breweries, vineyards or pharmacies. Rural parish priests were also frequently endowed with their own fields which they could either let or work themselves.

---

5   For an outline of the history of church funding in Germany, see Heiner de Wall et al., 'Germany: Constitutional Complexity and Confessional Diversity' in Keith Robbins (ed.), *The Dynamics of religious Reform in Northern Europe, 1780–1920, Political and Legal Perspectives*, vol. 1 (Leuven University Press 2011) 181–8.

Thirdly, a minor source of income came from fees for specific services rendered by the priest to the parish, particularly for marriages and burials (*Stolgebühren*), reading special masses, ringing the bells on specific occasions or for providing pews. These fees mainly contributed towards the income of the parish priest and other staff. Fourthly, a major source, particularly for the charitable work, came from pious foundations. Finally, there were the offerings collected during services or on other occasions.

Reformation and Secularization

The split between Christian confessions and churches, which resulted from the Reformation, also led to deep conflict concerning the property of the church. Negotiations on the peace treaty of Augsburg in 1555 were, to a considerable extent, also negotiations about church property and church funding. In particular, the question had to be resolved whether secularization of monasteries, foundations and other ecclesiastical institutions should be annulled or justified. The decision was made in favour of the latter.

This heralded the sweeping secularization of church property during the time of the Reformation, especially in the Protestant territories which continued during the sixteenth and seventeenth centuries. So, Protestant churches in particular lost a considerable part of what could have been their property, if the assets of the Church had been left to them. As part of this process, however, also tasks and functions which were traditionally performed by the Church were now taken over by the secular government, e.g. in the area of schooling. It has therefore been argued that the secularization of church property in the Protestant German territories after the Reformation was rather a consequence of a secularization of tasks than a way to enrich the princes or the State.

Secularization of church properties, for example, by dissolving monasteries etc., remained on the agenda throughout the early modern age, especially during the Age of Enlightenment.

The Great Secularization of 1803 and its Effects

The political and cultural changes brought about by the French Revolution and Napoleonic rule also resulted in far-reaching political reforms in Germany. The reforms of the legal position of the Catholic Church were brought into effect by the *Reichsdeputationshauptschluss* (Principal Decree of the Imperial Deputation) of 1803. Its aim was to compensate those German princes allied to Napoleon for their losses to France on the west bank of the Rhine. To provide this compensation, the prince-bishoprics were secularized and the rights to rule over them were transferred to the secular princes. Prince-bishops and abbots lost both their territories and their positions as imperial princes. Rights and entitlements which applied to their lands were transferred to the new territorial lords who were also permitted to expropriate church property in their territories, except for the assets of the local parishes. As a result of the secularization of former church territories, more than 2.4 out of about 20 million Germans were made subjects of new territorial lords and came under new government.

These transfers meant that the Catholic Church lost a major part of its wealth in Germany and with that the basis of its maintenance – which the Protestant churches had already partly lost in the sixteenth and seventeenth centuries. Although the princes were ordered to compensate the Church for some of its losses, such compensation was made only reluctantly and was by no means adequate. Nevertheless, it formed the basis of a complex system of payments by the various German States to the Church.

The legal foundation and the reasons for such payments and compensation were quite complex. For instance, according to the *Reichsdeputationshauptschluss*, cathedral chapters had to be bestowed with real estate in order to secure their maintenance as compensation for the secularization. Instead of fulfilling this obligation, the States preferred annual payments of subsidies. A second example: many monasteries were secularized at the beginning of the eighteenth centuries. Parish churches were incorporated into many of them, so that the monasteries had to care for the pastoral needs of the parish and pay for the maintenance of the parish priest and the parish church. When the State took over the assets of the monastery, these obligations passed over to the government. These are only two examples of a great number of reasons and legal foundations underlying state funding of churches. And it is easy to understand why details and the amounts to be paid were subject to much discussion and legal dispute. In order to arrive at a set of reasonable terms, it was preferable for both sides to settle the details of these payments by compromise and fair agreement. During the nineteenth and twentieth centuries, a large number of contracts and bills were to arise as a result of this situation.

But there were far more reasons for providing state funding of churches in the nineteenth century. In the 1800s, step by step Churches and State were separated. Some sources of state funding can be considered to be consequences of this process. The Protestant consistories, for example, were state agencies. They were turned into church agencies during the nineteenth century in many German States. The State was still, however, held responsible for the expenses of the consistories. So, the state buildings in which the consistories resided were (and still are in some cases) left for the church authorities to use. The churches, likewise, were funded for the expenses incurred by their officials via annual payments *für Zwecke des Kirchenregiments* (for the purpose of church administration). The idea of equality of religions and confessions also played a role in the funding of the churches. In Bavaria, for example, the State was obliged to pay for maintenance for Roman Catholic bishops and other high-ranking clerics. So, in a similar way, the Bavarian State paid (and still pays) for the maintenance of Protestant church officials.

The 'Guarantee' of State Subsidies in the Weimar Constitution and the Basic Law

In the 1919 Weimar Constitutional Assembly, State–Church relations and funding for churches was a major issue. Some left-wing politicians and parties assumed that the churches should be kept totally out of the public sphere. However, they were not successful. The so-called *Weimarer Kulturkompromiß* (Weimar cultural compromise) is a compromise between this concept and a restoration of the *status quo ante*. Article 138 of the Weimar Constitution, which deals with the question of church property and funding, is in itself a compromise between claims to stop all state subsidies, on the one hand, and the wish for everything to be as it was before, on the other hand. The Weimar solution was to stop state subsidies and so to separate State and Church in the financial domain, but, in exchange, to compensate churches by giving them assets to secure their income.[6]

According to Article 140 of Germany's Basic Law, this article is still in force. Until now, the second part of this compromise – compensation for churches – could not be achieved due to the reluctance of the legislator to ratify the law on the principles of compensation. Thus, the first part (the end of state funding) has not been achieved. So, in effect, the public funding of churches on the basis of these historical entitlements is continuing more than 90 years after the compromise.

New Ways to Fund Churches – the Church Tax

Throughout the nineteenth century, church funding remained an important political issue. The church maintenance system had to be changed, not only as a result of the secularization of church property, but also because the traditional sources of income had become less and less effective. The growing population and other social developments, such as rapid urbanization and industrialization changed the needs of the faithful and the tasks of the churches and resulted in higher funding requirements too. The states, which to a certain degree accepted their responsibility for the funding of the churches, were themselves notoriously short of money and unable to meet the demands of the churches. Additional fundraising from church members, first on an irregular and local, then on a continuing and general basis, became inevitable. This was true for all the German States, which, over the course of the nineteenth century, all gradually introduced an additional, income-related Church Tax.[7] First attempts to do so had already been made in some minor states in Northern Germany in the late 1820s and 1830s. Country upon country followed their example, Prussia and Hesse in 1875, Württemberg in 1887, Baden in 1888 and Bavaria in 1908 granted traditional churches and other religious associations

---

6   Article 138 of the Weimar Constitution reads as follows: '1. Rights of religious societies to public subsidies on the basis of a law, contract or special grant shall be redeemed by legislation of the *Länder*. The principles governing such redemption shall be established by the Reich … '.

7   Hammer (n 3) 3–78.

recognized as public corporations the right to impose occasional taxation. However, there were clear state restrictions concerning the level of taxation and the State had the right to decide whether it was necessary at all.

The Weimar Republic finally incorporated the rights of all religious associations recognized as public corporations to tax their members according to the specific tax regulations of the individual States (*Länder*). This paragraph of the Weimar Constitution (§ 137) was adopted into the Basic Law of the Federal Republic and is still valid today. The Church Tax, as it is in effect today, a percentage (8 per cent or 9 per cent) of the income tax of church members and collected by the states' tax office, was established in all parts of Germany only during the second half of the twentieth century.

The Church Tax was introduced in order to have churchgoers bear the costs of the churches, not the Government. Historically, the Church Tax is a milestone along the path of separation of Church and State.

Legal, Political and Social Challenges

As the German system is a mixed one, in which church funding takes place in a multitude of ways, the social and political challenges are equally varied, depending on the mode of funding. A central part of the system and of debate too, is the most significant source of income – the Church Tax – which is characteristic of the German system. A recurring issue in this context is also that of state subsidies which are based on historical entitlements. A less common topic of debate is the other sources of church funding, i.e. state aid and contributions in return for church services. Despite the fact that state aid for activities that are beneficial to the community is not only given to the Church, but also to non-church organizations with similar programmes, this issue hardly ever features in fundamental criticism, although details of the matter are occasionally discussed. One legal challenge targets the compatibility of such subsidies with EU regulations on state aid, but Articles 107–9 of the Treaty on the Functioning of the European Union, which are applicable to 'any aid granted by a Member State or through state resources in any form whatsoever which distorts or threatens to distort competition by favouring certain undertakings' (Article 107), usually do not rule out aid for social purposes.

A further challenge is the integration of new religious communities, which were not originally part of the German system, the main one being the Islamic community, to which around four million people in Germany belong. However, Muslims are not very closely organized and stable communities with large membership numbers are only just beginning to establish themselves. The integration of these into the Church Tax system will not become an issue until they have expanded further and become more stable. Of course, state aid to Islamic groups is only likely if the latter's activities prove beneficial to the community. In this case, there is no question that they would, indeed, be just as eligible for benefits as the aforementioned organizations, enjoying the same conditions and the same scale of funding.

Issues Relating to Church Taxation

The Church Tax has continually been subject not only to political, but also to legal, criticism. It has also been contested in the law courts. However, Germany's Church Tax, which is established in the Constitution of the Federal Republic – the Basic Law – was proclaimed to be constitutional by Germany's Federal Constitutional Court. In particular, the employers' role in the levying of church taxes was seen not to be a breach of religious liberty, but as support for the State in its responsibility to retain a functional taxation system for churches.[8] The European Court of Human Rights (ECHR) only recently asserted that compelling employees to report to the fiscal authorities, whether they belong to a tax-levying religious denomination or not, was in accordance with the principle of religious freedom stipulated in Article 9 of the ECHR. Although the Court conceded that it affected individual freedom of religion, it was within the limits placed on religious freedom in Article 9 § 2 of the ECHR, because it was an established constituent part of German federal law and was justified according to federal policy on church taxation.[9] However, only one chamber has passed judgement on this matter; a complaint before the Grand Chamber is pending.

The political aspects of Church Tax are regularly subject to criticism. One of these is that a special sum is demanded of church members who are not in gainful employment and whose spouses are not members of a church. Because these church members have no income of their own, the spouse without church membership is expected to pay the sum for them. However, the courts ruled that this charge, like the membership fee in sports clubs, is part of the obligation that the breadwinning spouse is expected to comply with, and that it was therefore acceptable. Cases like these are proof of the fact that the German legal system and taxation regulations are complex. For this reason, solutions constantly have to be found to benefit the Church. What at first sight may seem to be an unfair advantage is, when closely examined, a necessary measure to safeguard churches' fundamental, constitutional rights.

Many people criticize not only specific details, but the Church Tax system as a whole. According to some surveys, a majority of the German population would vote for the abolition of the system. This leads to the question whether this is possible or realistic. As to the legal situation, it must be pointed out that the right of churches to levy taxes is guaranteed in Article 140 of the Basic Law in conjunction with Article 137 § 6 of the WRV. To change this, a constitutional majority of two-thirds in the *Bundestag*, or lower house, and two-thirds in the *Bundesrat*,

---

8   [1966] *BVerfGE* 19, 240.

9   *Wasmuth v Germany*, no. 12884/03 (ECHR 17 February 2011) <http://cmiskp.echr. coe.int> accessed 18 October 2011.

or assembly of the *Länder*, is required. In view of the present constellation in Parliament, this is unlikely. The abolition of the Church Tax system could not simply be treated as an isolated case, but would in fact lead to a fundamental debate on the relationship between Church and State, a matter which is unlikely to come about, because the two large catch-all parties – the CDU/CSU and SPD – are both advocates of the current system. Even among the Greens – a party whose attitude towards the German State–Church partnership was originally a sceptical one – there are now a large number of supporters of the system, partly because the Greens see much common ground with the churches and vice-versa. The liberal FDP tended to disagree with the system as stipulated by the Basic Law, but this attitude has largely given way to a general feeling of sympathy. And even though the party *Die Linken* remains opposed to the idea, a change to the *status quo* is not the party's highest priority.

What is not specifically covered in the Constitution is the particular manner for collecting the Church Tax – as a direct deduction from wages – and the administration of this tax by state tax offices. However, since this procedure is very straightforward and effective – allowing the State to make a small profit – and is legal and still constitutional, there is currently no serious political will to change matters.

One social challenge for the system of church taxation is the demographic situation, which is linked to, but not synonymous with, evolutions in church membership. For years now, numbers have been dropping, as has the proportion of church members in Germany as a whole. This is partly due to the significant number of people who have left the church. A more relevant factor is the low birth rate in Germany, which is accompanied by a falling baptism rate. By 2030, membership of the Protestant churches is expected to fall from 25 million to only 17 million.[10] The Roman Catholic forecast, though less pessimistic, is not a lot more hopeful. Admittedly, even though numbers have been dropping for decades now, there has not yet been a significant drop in capital from church taxation, but the reason for this is, as already mentioned, a flourishing German economy, of which the churches are a part. Nevertheless, we can forecast that a continuous drop in members will eventually lead to a significant downward trend in income from tax. Since the demand for clergy and other church employees is linked to the number of members, certain cutbacks can be expected here, too. As the church becomes less influential, it will consequently require less money, but activities will have to be curtailed and structures rationalized.

---

10   Evangelische Kirche in Deutschland (EKD), *Kirche der Freiheit. Perspektiven für die evangelische Kirche im 21. Jahrhundert' – Impulspapier* (2006) <http://www.kirche-im-aufbruch.ekd.de/images/kirche-der-freiheit.pdf> accessed 18 October 2011, 21.

State Subsidies and their Redemption

As we have shown, state benefits only constitute a small proportion of churches' budgets, but at the same time they are becoming a political issue. Criticizing these contributions is a typical holiday 'silly season' topic. But even here, the constitutional position is clear-cut and there is no obvious majority trend to alter the situation. Because of the Constitution, occasional calls from humanist organizations to put a stop to state contributions are likely to be of no consequence.

One special case is that the Constitution, in its wording, has over the past 90 years demanded a redemption of the contributions, in other words the regular payments are to be substituted by a one-off sum with which churches can make up for their former revenue. This constitutional mandate has not yet been executed, so the state's contributions continue to be paid. At present, there are no signs that this will change, and there does not seem to be any political will to redeem state benefits, nor are the churches themselves drawing attention to the matter. According to the Basic Law, this would mean having to pass a federal law. It is true that there are occasionally mutual agreements within the *Länder* to redeem the odd state contribution, but a comprehensive redemption would no doubt be far too costly. It is estimated that the amount due would be 20 to 25 times higher than the annual sum of about €450 million, in other words between €9 and €11.5 billion. In view of the sum spent over the last few years to tackle the financial crisis, this is a relatively low figure, but at the moment it would impose a severe strain on public budgets.

Benefits and Drawbacks of Church Funding in Germany

The German Church Tax system has proved beneficial to the churches. What used to be a supplement to a budget that did not draw enough revenue from other sources has since become the churches' most significant source of income.

In its present state, the Church Tax guarantees a regular and predictable flow of revenue. Apart from the fact that German tax legislation is highly complicated, which has, as a result, led to complex individual regulations in the church taxation field, the basic structure is straightforward. The assessment and levying of taxes is uncomplicated and saves the churches from having to create their own large Church Tax administration bodies. As an independent source of revenue, Church Tax secures churches' independence, both from the toil of constant fundraising drives and the ensuing danger of dependence on major donors or on the State. Because of its own reliable revenue, the Church is not forced to play the role of supplicant of the State and the Church Tax allows German churches to carry out comprehensive activities that reach the public.

From the churches' point of view, the Church Tax is, by and large, socially just. The reason for this is that taxpayer productivity is the main criterion governing state income tax. The Church can benefit from this fair regulation, but, as previous examples show, there are occasional difficulties. The Church Tax is partly dependent on state income tax policies, and not all state tax measures are in the church's interest. If, as has for example been done in the past, tax benefits are used to subsidize shipbuilding, the church earns less in tax, meaning that it, too, is indirectly supporting the shipbuilding industry. Similarly, if capital gains tax is lowered, this automatically affects church income as well. Complex regulations are often implemented to partly counteract these practices.

Within the German system, the Church Tax has proved its worth as a source of Church revenue. Nevertheless, it is unlikely that the example set by Germany would work in other countries, where the situation is very different.

As far as state aid to churches for charitable work is concerned, the same doubts can be voiced in opposition to any form of state aid. The danger is always that, when market principles are thrown overboard, an undesirable bandwagon effect can emerge.

State aid can also automatically lead to activities that are not actually required, which is why it is generally argued that such payments are unwise and superfluous.

This is, however, not specifically a church problem. We must also bear in mind that most church activities are social ones and that people who benefit from such actions are often unable to pay a reasonable market price for what they receive. Subsidies of this nature are undoubtedly justified.

Prospects for Reform?

Irrespective of the aforementioned criticism, experts do not consider it necessary to change the present system. Such a step would mean a reform of the Basic Law, a measure which, as explained, is dependent on a large majority vote. A further argument against change is the prohibitive cost and effort it would necessitate and it would mean completely restructuring churches' revenue streams – specifically, the manner in which Church Tax is levied. If we look at the figures for other countries, where there is only a voluntary church taxation system and where Church Tax is calculated, but the actual payment is a non-mandatory one, we must cast doubts on the effectiveness of an alternative system's ability to achieve a similar quality of church funding and reliable church activity.

The same is true of the discussion some time ago to base the German church taxation system on the Italian *otto-per-mille* system. It is exemplary to some in Germany, because it prevents people who leave the Church from acquitting themselves completely of their duty to pay the tax. Under the ruling, one is expected to dedicate a certain percentage of one's income tax to social causes, which include church causes. This probably stops people from leaving a Church merely to save money, a practice common in Germany. However, this system can be criticized in Germany as being fundamentally unconstitutional. For one thing, the levying of church taxation is guaranteed by the Basic Law, and cannot simply be altered via an *otto-per-mille* system, which would mean a constitutional change. Furthermore, the duty to pay the tax is linked to church membership and is thus a membership fee. The obligation to pay a sum to a social cause, as stipulated in the *otto-per-mille* system, and from which the churches too would benefit, could in Germany prove to be a breach of religious freedom and of the State's neutral stance in matters of faith and conscience. Besides, a regulation of this kind can by no means guarantee the level of revenue that churches receive at present by way of the Church Tax. The *otto-per-mille* would have to be replaced by something closer to an *otto-per-cento* in Germany, and it is highly unlikely that the State and taxpayers who do not belong to a church would agree with such a ruling.

In the last few years, demands to introduce a system of this nature have become less frequent. Public opinion is, however, unpredictable and, to prevent a sudden change from taking place, it is necessary to convince people of the objective legitimacy of the system. If the churches themselves doubt it, a rapid change might emerge. Just recently, during his visit to Germany, the Pope demanded that the Catholic Church abandon its privileges. It is very unclear if this very vague statement is aimed at the system of church funding. Nevertheless, discussion of this issue did take place. Although it would be wise to consider alternatives, it does not look at present as if voluntary donations or similar arrangements would be as effective as the current German system.

List of References

BverfGE, *Entscheidungen des Bundesverfassungsgerichts* (Mohr)

De Wall H, 'Staatsleistungen – ewige Rente?' in R Will (ed.) *Die Privilegien der Kirchen und das Grundgesetz* (Humanistische Union 2011)

De Wall H et al., 'Germany: Constitutional Complexity and Confessional Diversity' in K Robbins (ed.) *The Dynamics of religious Reform in Northern Europe, 1780–1920, Political and Legal Perspectives* vol. 1 (Leuven University Press 2011)

Droege M, *Staatsleistungen an Religionsgemeinschaften im säkularen Kultur- und Sozialstaat* (Duncker und Humblot 2004)

Evangelische Kirche in Deutschland (EKD), *Kirche der Freiheit. Perspektiven für die evangelische Kirche im 21. Jahrhundert – Impulspapier* (2006) <http://www.kirche-im-aufbruch.ekd.de/images/kirche-der-freiheit.pdf> accessed 18 October 2011

Evangelische Kirche in Deutschland (EKD), *Zahlen und Fakten zum kirchlichen Leben* (2011) <http://www.ekd.de/download/broschuere_2011_mit_Links.pdf> accessed 18 October 2011

Hammer F, *Rechtsfragen der Kirchensteuer* (Mohr 2002)

Marré H, 'Das kirchliche Besteuerungsrecht' in J Listl et al. (eds), *Handbuch des Staatskirchenrechts der Bundesrepublik Deutschland* vol. 1, 2nd edn (Duncker Humblot 1994)

Robbers G, 'State and Church in Germany' in G Robbers (ed.) *State and Church in the European Union* (Nomos 2005)
Unruh P, *Religionsverfassungsrecht* (Nomos 2009)
Von Campenhausen A et al., *Staatskirchenrecht* (C.H. Beck 2006)

Chapter 8

A Long Historical Path towards Transparency, Accountability and Good Governance: On Financing Religions in Denmark

Lisbet Christoffersen

The central message in this contribution to the book on financing religion in the future Europe is that no matter which type of financing – and no matter whether the economic foundation for religion in Europe is public, private or a combination – the most central need is to secure transparency in the religious economies combined with accountability in regard to the use of the money collected and good governance in regard to the leadership of the religious communities. Religious communities are led by human beings and in these powerful institutions – as in all other powerful contexts – there is a necessity to take stakeholders' needs for information on economy and leadership into account. This necessity is a central challenge in the legal regime regarding the economy of faith communities – the majority Church as well as minority religions – in Denmark and thus a central message from this contribution, which deals with historical background for the current regime as well as challenges for the future relevant for a broader European context.

The chapter takes its starting point in an introduction to the legal relations between State, *folkekirke*[1] and minority religions in Denmark as well as to the question about legal personality. This is done even though legal status of religious communities is not the subject of the volume. However, the question regarding State financing is closely linked to an understanding of these legal relations between the State and the religious communities in the country. Against this background, the first part of the chapter explains how the State currently supports religious

---

1   As has become normal among Danish scholars when writing about the Danish majority Church (Evangelical-Lutheran, in which 78 per cent of Danes are members, according to the Constitution Article 4 supported by the State 'as such', that is as majority Church and as Evangelical-Lutheran, I also use the term *folkekirke* instead of trying to translate this term. See for a longer explanation on different possible translations Lisbet Christoffersen, 'State, Church and Religion in Denmark at the beginning of the 21st Century' in L Christoffersen et al. (eds), *Law & Religion in the 21st Century – Nordic Perspectives* (DJØF Publishing 2010) 145 *et seq.*

communities directly and indirectly. The second part explains the historical roots and background; the third informs about current challenges to this situation and the more theoretical fourth part reflects on possible tracks for the future. Finally, in the fifth part, a more detailed consideration is given to Transparency, Accountability and Good Governance as general requirements to religious communities in a European context in the twenty-first century, be they privately or publicly legally organized and sponsored.

Legal Status of Religious Communities in Denmark – an Introduction to the Question on how Religious Communities are Financed

Normally, there is a close link between the owner's rights and responsibilities and an obligation to pay for establishing and maintaining what is owned. The clarity on ownership is normally linked to an even more obvious clarity in regard to legal personality. Seen from a private law perspective, the normal approach is that an institution is owned by somebody or at least self-owned and as such also self-sufficient as regards maintenance and economic funding. Such an approach also seems to be the clear background for this volume, based on the idea that religious organizations are by nature independently owned, either by being self-governing and funded through decisions from the board or by being privately owned.[2]

Such clarity is however not the case when it comes to Danish churches, especially in regard to the *folkekirke*. It is therefore relevant to open a discussion of possible economic relations between State, Church and Religion by briefly introducing the problems concerning ownership.

Minority churches and minority religious organizations in Denmark are normally legal subjects under private law. They might be organized as associations, based on a yearly or regular assembly, where the members on the basis of established statutes decide who runs the association through common elections. This is for example the case for the Baptist churches in Denmark.

A religious organization can however also be organized as a private foundation (charity) or a self-governing body, in which case the statutes decide how the governing body is elected, who the possible members of such a body are and how

---

2   A couple of years ago, when travelling in the United States, I saw an advertisement board outside a house. It announced the function of the house we went past: 'Mr. Hansens Church'. I commented on this (for me very surprising) idea that a church could be privately owned, to some American colleagues – for whom of course it was as surprising that a church might not be privately owned. In my traditional European understanding, however, a Church is always an institution meant for the purpose of a collective (eventually having individuals hired as employees), never something based on which a private individual could earn his or her fortune. Whether this institution is covered under private law or public law is a different question – but never individual private ownership in a European understanding of Churches.

they are elected, without, however, involving any laity or members in any elections. In some of the religious independent bodies, the norm is that the governing body itself elects new members, for example every second year in order to secure the identity; or the norm can be that the bishop appoints members of the body (as is the case in the Catholic Church in Denmark). There are many such independent bodies in Denmark and normally their statutes or regulations are approved of by a governmental institution according to the Act on Charities and other Independent Bodies, chapter 4.

Religious organizations are however explicitly exempted from the law. It directly states that 'self-governing institutions in relation to the *folkekirke*, religious organizations and educational bodies are excepted from the law, as long as they do not deal with other tasks than their main purpose'.[3] Consequently, religious organizations can be established and can run their practice under the constitutional freedom of religion without any governmental approval of by-laws, practice, economical dispositions and so on, which also means that in general there is no control on behalf of the individual involved that the organizations actually are run in accordance with their idealistic objective.

Religious communities can however wish for public approval of their status as religious communities. This entails legal advantages such as civil status of marriages performed by pastors (imams, rabbis, etc.) within the religious community; easy access to residence permits for missionaries; and the possibility for the private individual, who wishes to support the organization economically, to withdraw the money spent on the organization in his or her personal income tax. For the organization this approval involves a requirement to inform tax authorities about received funding from private individuals and on how this part of the organization's budget is used.

Professor Tamm has suggested that 'the informality of Danish law' generally leads to a lack of requirement of any specific official recognition for the establishment of legal personality for religious communities.[4] However, this informality is based on a positive political decision in the Act on Charities to leave religious communities, in contrast to other self-governing institutions or charities, without any sort of State intervention, as much as possible. One of the central questions in this chapter is whether this has proven to be a wise decision.

In contrast to the legal status of other religious communities that are legal subjects outside the law and outside any sort of public control except for the

---

3 Fondslovens § 1, stk. 2: Loven omfatter ikke ... 3) Folkekirkens selvejende institutioner, trossamfund og godkendte uddannelsesinstitutioner, såfremt fonden ikke udover sit hovedformål varetager andre opgaver.

4 Ditlev Tamm, 'Religious Entities as Legal Persons – Denmark' in Lars Friedner (ed.) *Churches and Other Religious Organizations as Legal Persons: Proceedings of the 17th Meeting of the European Consortium for Church and State Research* (Peeters Publishers 2007) 61.

individual money received by private funders, the *folkekirke* as such is not a legal subject and it is fully controlled by law and by State administration.

However, the *folkekirke* comprises approximately 2,350 local church buildings, many of them based in an ecclesiastical centre containing also a rectory (here meaning the parish buildings plus land, in the countryside in the form of a free-hold farm), a cemetery surrounding the church building with other buildings on the cemetery and also very often a church hall functioning as community centre either in one of the former farm buildings in the rectory or newly built nearby – and here we find legal subjects:[5] the church building is a self-governing body with its own legal personality, and so is the rectory. However, both the church building and the rectory are, together with the cemetery (including relevant buildings) and a possible church hall/community centre, governed by the local congregation council. These ecclesiastical centres are no doubt basically public law entities, even though scientific analysis differs when it comes to whether or not the State is then the owner. Dübeck argues against,[6] whereas Stenbæk[7] does not (anymore) see any distinction between the Church and the State, legally speaking.[8]

A common distinction between a body (the Church) that needs economic support and another body (the State) that supports economically is thus not a well-chosen example for the Danish situation.

There are also theological explanations for the differences in both the United States and Europe between a group of churches where it is possible to distinguish between a legal subject, the Church, that might get economic support from the State, and the State as such and the Scandinavian model, where this distinction is not as easy to picture. A consequence of and later on a central dimension of the theological changes, called the Lutheran Reformation was that the Church should no longer be based on its own independent parallel legal system, but should be governed under the (common) law of the land. The civic constitutions in the nineteenth century accordingly introduced the establishment of and distinction between legislative, executive and judiciary as the relevant governing bodies of the land and thus also for churches and religious communities. It is only hesitantly that Nordic theory is about to accept a return of the concept of *Church autonomy* and only as long as the authorities of the collective freedom of religion accept and support individual freedoms and rights, not only as exit rights but also within their

---

    5   See Lisbet Christoffersen, 'From Cultural to Religious Arguments in the Use of Buildings: On Danish Funding of Religious Heritage' in Anne Fornerod (ed.) *Funding Religious Heritage* (Ashgate 2013).

    6   Inger Dübeck, 'Kirchenfinanzierung der nordischen Länder' (2002) 47, 2 *Zeitschrift für Evangelisches Kirchenrecht* 369–93.

    7   Jørgen Stenbæk, 'Folkekirkens ejendomsforhold og økonomi – historisk belyst' [the *folkekirke* – Legal Status and Economy, analysed historically], (2003) *Kirkehistoriske Samlinger* 123–48.

    8   I turn to the historical background for which parts of the Church are legal subjects and which are not, in this chapter.

own organizations. Tamm could thus still in 2007 with no reservation regarding collective freedom of religion or for example ministerial exemptions argue that religious entities have a general 'duty to observe law and order'.[9] That discussion is not as easy now.[10] On the contrary the general picture in countries where the Catholic Church, the Orthodox Church or the Reformed Churches are the majority (as well as a pluralist country such as Germany) seems in contrast to be based on a legal distinction between the churches as legal subject on the one hand and the State on the other. The same seems to be the case for American *wall of separation*-understanding. That is why I underline this basic question about legal subjectivity so much in the introduction to this chapter. The hope is to possibly obtain what Kierkegaard saw as essential: to meet the reader where he or she is and explain the different world from that point of view: not only does history matter, as we will see further down; so, too, do confessional traditions.[11]

Financing the *Folkekirke* and other Religious Communities in Denmark – the Law

Financing of the Folkekirke

The main financial source for the *Folkekirke* is church taxes, paid by the members and levied together with taxes for State and Municipality. The yearly budget in 2012 was around 7.7 billion DKK (a little more than €1 billion) for the entire *folkekirke*. The income from church taxes cover nearly 7 billion DKK of this entire budget, of which 5.8 billion are disposed of in the local church committees and deanery committees. This part of the budget is used for the maintenance of local buildings and for locally employed staff (organists, people employed on church property, etc.). The national budget of the *folkekirke* is 1.05 billion, financed originating from the church taxes and disposed of on national level, supplied by 750 million DKK (€100 million yearly), paid by the State and financed over the common State taxes, paid by all Danes. The State thus directly supports the *folkekirke* economically with 1/8 of the entire yearly budget.

There is also a huge indirect financial support from the State to the *folkekirke* already in the fact that the church taxes are levied by the public tax authorities.

---

9 Tamm (n 4) 66.

10 See for the question of legal consequences of the concept of *Church autonomy* in Lisbet Christoffersen, 'Church Autonomy in Nordic Law' in Christoffersen et al. (eds) (n 1) 563–92.

11 Lisbet Christoffersen, 'Religious Entitites as Legal Persons – Northern Europe (Nordic and Baltic Countries)' in Lars Friedner (ed.) *Churches and Other Religious Organizations as Legal Persons: Proceedings of the 17th Meeting of the European Consortium for Church and State Research* (Peeters Publishers 2007) 17 *et seq.*

This support is decided in parliamentary law[12] and it of course gives the *folkekirke* a huge budgetary security.

The local church taxes are not only disposed of, but also decided by the local church committee and approved of by committees at deanery level. (The deaneries, of which there are 104 within the *folkekirke*, are a regional level within each diocese. The deaneries are led by a dean together with a democratically elected deanery committee.) All local expenses, except the salary for the local priests, deans, etc. are covered by the local church taxes, added to by minor income from former church land, now rented out for farming. It is compulsory for church committees to rent the farmland out[13] and they are now also supported in selling off former farm land as well as rectories no longer in use – each local church committee must keep one rectory, whereas they can decide whether they want to offer rectories for further priests (in which case it is compulsory for the priest to live there). The income from selling off land and rectories is to be delivered to the diocese which disposes of this revenue by distributing it to local church communities to be used when there is a need to renew buildings locally and as support for building new churches.[14] However, this revenue is not to be used in order to lower the local church tax.

It is the local church committee that manages the church building, the rectory, the cemetery and other local buildings and the church committee is obliged by law and legislative regulation to keep the buildings and cemeteries in good order.[15] This means that members of the church locally – being 50 per cent of the population as in some areas of Copenhagen or 95 per cent as in some areas in Jutland – are obliged to finance the keeping and maintenance of the local church buildings to a good standard. The recent restoration of *Our Savior's Church* in Copenhagen could be mentioned as an example. This church is visited by a good number of tourists every year, due to the attraction of walking up the staircase on the outer curve of the steeple (reaching a height of nearly 100m).[16] Even though that is the case, then the restoration running up to nearly 100 million DKK was paid for by the Copenhagen members of the church.

The sum of 1.8 billion DKK of the entire budget for the Danish *folkekirke* is disposed of on a national level. Of this amount 750 million DKK are paid through

---

12 *Bekendtgørelse af lov om folkekirkens Økonomi*, LBK no. 753 of 25/06/2013 [Act on the Economy within the *folkekirke*].

13 *Bekendtgørelse om præsteembedernes faste ejendomme*, BEKG no. 411 of 03/05/2006 [Regulation on the real estate belonging to the Rectory].

14 *Bekendtgørelse om bestyrelse af kirke- og præsteembedskapitalen*, BEKG no. 1367 of 05/12/2010 [Regulation on the Governance of funds for Church Buildings, etc.].

15 *Bekendtgørelse af lov om bestyrelse og brug af folkekirkens kirker mm*, LBK no. 796 of 24/06/2013 [Act on Governance of Church Buildings within the *folkekirke*].

16 According to the Church homepage <http://www.vorfrelserskirke.dk/taarnet# Restaurering%201991–1996> Jules Vernes was in Copenhagen in 1881 and wrote about a visit to the tower in his book *De Rotterdam à Copenhague*.

State taxes and 1.05 are, directly translated, named *national church taxes*.[17] There is no democratically elected committee (general assembly or synod or anything like that) on a national level in the Danish *folkekirke*. The income from the national church tax and how the money shall be disposed of is thus decided solely by the Minister of Gender Equality and Ecclesiastical Affairs, a member of the Government. As part of the national budget for the State he also proposes the amount of money necessary for the State to pay as support for the *folkekirke*. This proposed budget for the State support is decided by the parliament or the parliamentary committee for financial affairs.

The Minister of Gender Equality and Ecclesiastical Affairs, who because of the law has to decide on and dispose of the national church taxes, decided some years ago following heavy criticism of the lack of democracy in making these decisions to appoint a consultative committee on budget affairs. This committee is made up of representatives from the bishops, from the administrative authorities on diocesan level, from the Ministry of Gender Equality and Ecclesiastical Affairs and from an organization of all local church committees.[18] It is however still the Minister solely who decides the entire budget on a national level.

The national economy within the *folkekirke* is used to pay the salaries of the bishops and for the administration (funded solely through the subsidiaries from the State budget); salaries of the church ministers, of which the funding is shared between State support (40 per cent) and national church taxes (60 per cent); national educational institutions for further education of church ministers, musicians and others; and compensation accounts used to minimize the size of the local church taxes in areas with fewer inhabitants and thus a lower level of church taxes and also more church buildings, very often from the Middle Ages.[19]

The dioceses within the *folkekirke* are funded through the national funding of the salaries for the bishop and the administrative staff. The cathedrals are funded as other churches through local church tax from the church members living in that council where the cathedral is situated. Ecclesiastical initiatives can be taken by the bishop under advice from newly established diocesan councils consisting of lay members and church ministers elected by the members of church councils in the diocese. Such ecclesiastical initiatives are financed through a percentage of the local church taxes. The dioceses are thus the institution where the local and the national dimension of the *folkekirke* meet.

---

17   *Landskirkeskat.*

18   *Bekendtgørelse om budget og regnskabsvæsen for fællesfonden*, BKG no. 813 af 26/06/2013 [Regulation on budget for the common/national economy within the *folkekirke*]; Pernille Esdahl, 'Kirkeministerens økonomiske særkompetencer', *Kirkeretsantologi – dansk kirkeret i europæiske belysning*, no. Dansk pers: Selskab for Kirkeret (2004) 448–68.

19   *Notat om Folkekirkens fælles økonomi* [Note on the common (national) dimensions of the Financial Structure within the *folkekirke*], written by Mr Jørgen Engmark, Ministry of Gender Equality and Church Affairs for the Government Committee on Governance Structure, 25 September 2012, published May 2013.

Funding of Other Religious Communities

All other religious communities in Denmark are solely privately funded. There is no direct State support for religious communities other than the *folkekirke*. And there is no knowledge about the entire economy within the religious communities in Denmark. They are only obliged to inform tax authorities on one part of their economy, namely the economy funded by private individuals. How religious communities get their money to run their organizations – if they receive funding from abroad; if they receive funding from private individuals that do not want to have their support published; if they receive funding from owning land or other sources – is thus not public knowledge in Denmark.

Private individuals who support a religious community under application automatically have their personal taxes reduced with the amount of money given to the religious community.[20] The general requirements for ideal organizations are among others that they have more than 300 members paying membership fees or more than 100 people paying gifts to them every year. They must also prove an income of more than 150,000 DKK per year or a fortune of the same size and be present in an area covering no less than 40,000 people. It is also in general required that the organization is independent from those who started the organization and that at least one member of the governing committee represents interests outside the organization as such.

These requirements that are meant to prove that the ideal organization has a basis in the population as such are not binding for religious organizations.[21] They must just prove that they are religious organizations. The tax authorities are expected to check this with the Ministry of Justice (which has the competence to approve that an organization is a religious organization on application from the organization as such). Within the Ministry of Justice the general requirement is among others that there are more than 50 members at the time of approval. It is currently being debated whether this requirement is also binding for the tax authorities or whether the tax authorities have no right to require a minimum number of members.[22]

The easy access to a reduction of personal taxes when supporting religious organizations is of course an indirect support from the State. The support however goes to the individual religious person and only after another indirect transaction to the religious community who, on the other hand, has the administrative obligation

---

20   This is also the case for other ideal organizations such as the Red Cross or The Danish Society for Nature Conservation and a huge group of other organizations; see Act on State Taxes §§ 8A and 12.

21   *Bekendtgørelse om godkendelse m.v. af bl.a. religiøse organisationer efter ligningslovens § 8A og 12, stk 3*, BEK no. 837 of 06/08/2008 [Regulation on Approval of among others religious organizations to receive private funding based on tax deduction].

22   This information comes from Mr Ebbe Holm, who as lawyer for the Danish Baptist Churches has taken legal action against the tax authorities on this matter.

to inform the tax authorities of the money received from a private individual on the basis of these rules.

Another, slightly more, nevertheless still indirect, State support to religious communities is that they are not obliged to pay VAT, which the *fokekirke* is obliged to do, even though part of the budget is based on so-called church taxes, levied by the tax authorities. Religious communities are also not obliged to pay property taxes.

A religious organization that offers educational activities for adults has the possibility of applying for economic support from the local municipality for such activities. It is also possible to require room in public institutions owned by the local municipality for such activities.[23] It is however a condition that the educational activities should not take the form of religious preaching.[24] It is thus not possible, according to these rules, to get any economic support for the religious dimension of activities within a religious community.

Lack of Equality in Regard to State Support

It follows from the previous overview that there is a lack of equality regarding economic support from the State to the *folkekirke* on the one hand, and to other religious communities in Denmark on the other. The *folkekirke* is both directly funded through the State budget and indirectly supported through the use of tax authorities to levy church taxes. These possibilities are not open to other religious communities. However, other religious communities are not obliged to pay VAT and their supporters can get tax exemptions for their payments to religious communities, possibilities that are not open to (members of) the *folkekirke*.

These differences have to do with the differences in regard to legal subjectivity and ownership – and there are of course historical explanations that will be outlined in the next part of this chapter.

Historical Path Dependency

Christianity came to Denmark before these islands were given this name, that is, during the Viking Age. Archaeological finds from old graveyards, for example outside Aalborg in Northern Jutland, show that Christianity came in around 700 from Ireland, as is the case also in Sweden, where Birka and Sigtuna in mid-Sweden

---

23 *Bekendtgørelse af lov om støtte til folkeoplysende voksenundervisning mv (folkeoplysningsloven)*, LBK no. 854 of 11/07/2011 [Law on public support to educational activities for adults], chapter 6.

24 *Bekendtgørelse om støtte til folkeoplysende voksenundervisning og frivilligt folkeoplysende foreningsarbejde*, BEK no. 1251 of 12/12/2011, [Regulation on Economical Support to Educational Activities for Adults], § 5, stk. 2.

outside current Stockholm were meeting places, not only commercially, but also between different types of religion, including different types of Christianity.

Historical sources point to Sankt *Ansgars* as the person who brought Christianity to Denmark from the South, where he was archbishop of Bremen. His arrival, along with the building of churches, among others in Ribe on the south-western side of Jutland, is dated to 824; in 934 King Gorm on his Runic Stones in Jelling names the country Denmark and finally King Harald Bluetooth on his major runic stone raised a little later also in Jelling claims that he is the one who baptized the Danes. The content of this proclamation is that Christianity from then on became the Danish State religion.

The first Danish churches were built out of wood and only their foundations remain. From the twelfth century, however, churches built of brick made at the monasteries are visible in the Danish landscape – they still stand there as a visible sign of the old Christian heritage of the country.

Nobody however knows who built the churches. The initiative may have been taken and the churches financed by local farmers or noblemen on a collective basis; individual noblemen also built churches in relation to their manor houses, not only in the Middle Ages, but also during early modern times and many of these churches also still exist; and finally also the king, the cities and the monasteries took the initiative in raising churches.

The ownership of church buildings and rectories at a local level has of course been subject to conflicts; more central in Danish history were however the conflicts between bishops and the king regarding ownership of land given to the bishop or the church and the monasteries. These conflicts were however solved over the centuries and by the Reformation there was no doubt that all church land belonged to the Church as legal bodies that were independent from the king, the cities or the local villages. The Church's fortune consisted of the *fabrica ecclesia* (meant for the church building) and *mensa presbyterii* (for financing the local church minister). Also the cathedrals as well as the University of Copenhagen (1479) managed their own basic support through *fabrica* and *mensa episcopalis*.[25]

The local *mensa* and *fabrica* were governed by local church wardens and the bishop or a private person functioned as protector or *jus patronatus*. The patron was obliged to keep the church in good order and well maintained, and on the other had could use the income; this was however not seen as ownership.

The local churches and church ministers were financed through tithes combined with the economic results of farming in the rectory. In addition to tithes, the bishops also received economic support from church land and the king too received tithes, that is, one third of the tithes each to the local church, the bishop and the king. Churches and monasteries were not obliged to pay taxes. The church

---

25   Dübeck (n 6); Lisbet Christoffersen, 'The financing of Religious Communities in Denmark' in Brigitte Basdevant-Gaudemet et al. (eds), *The Financing of Religious Communities in the European Union* (Peeters 2009) 129–36.

ministers also received payment related to rites such as baptism, marriage, etc. and they also received yearly payments related to holidays.

As part of the Reformation in Denmark in 1536 the king took over church land belonging to the bishops and the dioceses as well as the monasteries. Originally the idea was that bishops were not necessary anymore; they were soon re-installed, but now paid a salary by the king since they were seen as the king's superintendents supervising the Church and the local church ministers on behalf of the king.

The local churches were however still self-sufficient and independent legal bodies and the church ministers had their – very different – outcome from the local tithes and the result of the farming of the rectory.

A further contribution to the discussion about financing of the churches was that the King started to see himself as having the right to the local tithes which he could therefore also sell to local *patronates* who were then obliged to keep the church buildings in good order under the surveillance of local church wardens. The rectories were however kept for the use of the local church minister as well as the tithes.

The question about ownership to land and revenue, governed as 'belonging to the Church' was discussed in the collegium, formulating the Civic Constitution in 1849.[26] A proposal to formulate an article in the Constitution, saying that all church land could only be used for ecclesiastical purposes, was rejected. Among the central arguments were that the Church is not an independent body parallel to the State as is the case in a Catholic context, and that financially (and legally) speaking the Church is only to be seen as a governmental part of the State.

The system that was established from the Reformation and onwards was thus still supported, meaning that the State paid for the bishops' salaries and also received the bishops' and kings' tithes; that the church buildings very often were under the patronage of a private individual who, under surveillance of church wardens, received the tithes and was obliged to maintain the church building; and that the rectories together with tithes were the economic foundation for the church ministers. In the middle of the nineteenth century, the Danish *folkekirke* (introduced as a concept in the Constitution of 1849) was thus to be regarded as being funded by a combination of private and public finances.

This changed in the twentieth century. Among other legislative initiatives the most central was the decision of 1919 to forcefully sell off local church property in order to establish small self-sufficient farms on the land, offered by the State to people in the countryside who had previously not had the possibility of owning their own land to live on. The tithes were dissolved and the revenue collected in a fund that was meant to finance the local church ministers' needs. The aim was to reduce the threat of impoverishment of many people in the countryside; the result

---

26   Jørgen Stenbæk, 'Hvad forstaas ved den evangelisk-lutherske Kirke? Om Henning Matzens statskirkelige folkekirkeforståelse' *Festskrift til Hans Gammeltoft-Hansen* (Djøf 2004).

was however also an impoverishment of the church ministers who no longer had tithes or enough property to live on.

Thus the State after the Second World War took on responsibility for church ministers' salaries. This was seen as a welfare state obligation; should the State still support the Church (which was an obligation according to the constitution) then that should be on decent conditions; laws on church taxes to supply the financing of salaries for church ministers were already decided as early as before the dissolution of tithes in 1919; from 1958, however, the State took on full responsibility for covering what was not covered through church taxes.

The historical background for the full State payment of bishops' salaries is thus historical, stemming back from the expropriation of church property in 1536. The explanation for the State giving economic support to the Church, covering 40 per cent of salaries of church ministers is also historical, based on the dissolution of tithes and the expropriation of church property in 1919 and so are the concepts 'Church tax' for the local church community and 'national Church taxes' [*landskirkeskat*], taken in through the tax authorities.

Historical Background for the Lack of Economic Support to Other Religious Communities

There is no doubt that the change from the Norse gods to Christianity marked a period of religious pluralism in Denmark. However, this happened 1,500 years ago. Since then, Christianity in one form or another was the majority religion and questions regarding freedom of religion only arose again after the split within Christianity, called the Reformation. As a result of the religious wars, the Peace of Westphalia meant religious absolutism also in Denmark; here it was given a legal basis in *Danske Lov* [Danish Law] from 1683, which states that it is the king's obligation to ensure all the people living in the country follow the one, pure and true dogma, namely Lutheran Christianity. Being given this obligation legally also means that it was the king's prerogative to dispense with the rule and so he did. Already in 1685, the recently built town of Fredericia [directly translated as 'peace city'] on the east coast of Jutland was opened to 'foreign believers', meaning people from abroad who were allowed to keep their religious tradition even though they had settled in Denmark. Thus Fredericia had a Jewish, a Catholic and a Calvinist minority. Also in Copenhagen, a Calvinist church was built (to support Danish queens from a Calvinist background) and later in the eighteenth century a Catholic church was built in Copenhagen at the Austrian embassy.

The tolerance towards accepting 'foreign believers' and acknowledging their access to their own religious buildings was however not seen as basis for any State support to these religious minorities and Danes were not allowed to convert to any of these religions. On the contrary – as long as they were seen as 'foreigners', then they were also expected to pay for their religious services on their own, eventually on support from their 'homelands' (that is, for the Calvinist and the Catholic congregations; the Jewish congregation was tolerated as long as it paid for itself).

Citizenship regulations were introduced in 1776 and here, for example, the Jewish minority was still perceived of as foreign, that is, not Danish.

This changed during the Enlightenment, that is, before the civil constitution of 1849. The Jewish congregation was given Danish citizenship in 1813; the members were however obliged to follow Danish law, also in regard to family law; a sort of confirmation was introduced, but apart from that the Jewish congregation as such was upheld also under Danish citizenship; in general it was still financed by the members themselves. This was also the case when the synagogue in Copenhagen after the burning of Copenhagen in the late eighteenth century was rebuilt in the first half of the nineteenth century.

When freedom of religion with the constitution of 1849 took over from tolerance combined with religious monopoly, the main idea was to give both the majority Church (the *folkekirke*) and other religious communities freedom from State interference and independent legal structures. The State should still be obliged to support the *folkekirke*; however, this support was basically seen as non-economic except for the salaries for the bishops, because the local parishes were, as we have seen, self-sufficient, economically speaking. Therefore there was of course absolutely no suggestion that the State should start to support other religious communities, not because they were seen as more privately and independently owned than the parishes within the *folkekirke*, since they were also self-supporting and the private–public distinction was not the central analytical tool; also the self-supporting *folkekirke*-parishes were seen as public even though they were paid for by the members only. No, the central argument was that freedom of religion for religious communities outside the *folkekirke* includes an economic independence from the State. This has been the main norm in Danish religio-politics ever since, not only from the side of the State, but also from the side of the religious communities.

What changed was thus the welfare state support to the parish economy within the *folkekirke*, that is, that the church ministers as other academically educated professionals in the welfare state became civil servants and changed from an economy based on benefit in kind into an economy based on cash payments. The same change was not introduced for church ministers within the religious communities outside the *folkekirke*.

Thus, the legal differences between economic State support to the *folkekirke* and the total lack of direct economic support from the State to the other religious communities and consequently freedom of religion without any equality between faith communities in Denmark is based on a historical path dependency having its roots in the time of the Reformation and supplemented during Absolutism, Enlightenment, nineteenth-century freedom of religion, twentieth-century change of economy from in kind to in cash, and from local church responsibility to welfare state support to the *folkekirke*. The question is how far these explanations of the system are still efficient as social, legal and political support in the globalized twenty-first century.

Challenges in the Twenty-First Century

Four Challenges

At the turn of the twenty-first century, the age-old Danish system of financing religious communities has given rise to several challenges, argued in political, public, religious and theoretical contexts. The following part of this chapter gives voice to some of these considerations, but also to some of the political and legal answers to the challenges. Subsequently, in the final parts of the chapter, I reassume the situation by pointing to some elements of good practice that might pave the way to the future.

Lack of equality

Denmark was among the European States that negotiated the European Convention of Human Rights (ECHR). The question about the lack of equality between the *folkekirke* and other religious communities as well as the State support to the *folkekirke* was of course on the agenda in relation to ECHR Articles 9 and 14. The existence of the State Church was however accepted by the other parties behind the European Convention of Human Rights. Arguments were several: Denmark had had total freedom of religion since 1849 (whereas Norway had to change the 1814 Constitution and delete the prohibition against Jesuits trying to enter the kingdom, which they did in the 1960s in order to be able to ratify the European Convention of Human Rights). Denmark also did not, as was the case in Sweden until the 1990s, have a system where children were automatically born into the majority church; baptism (e.g. a religious ceremony) had always been the precondition for membership, meaning that it had been possible for more than 100 years to live in Denmark without being a member of any religious community.

As the Danish 1849 Constitution was changed in 1953, introducing articles that made it possible for Denmark to become a member of the *North Atlantic Treaty Organization*, the Council of Europe (and to sign the European Convention of Human Rights with the Court competences) and the European Union, nobody thus used the chance to establish ground for further equality between religious communities, since all State authorities and legal experts believed that the age-old system of freedom without equality, also in regard to State support to the *folkekirke* vs other religious communities, was undisputed.

Changed religious practice

The age-old habit of baptizing all children, unless the family was a member of another faith community than the *folkekirke*, was however problematized after 1968 with a new generation that found that they as parents should not decide such matters for their children. Consequently, a new group of citizens did not become members of any religious community. In the same period the secularization of Danish society reached its peak, problematizing the role of the *folkekirke* in Danish society. In addition the central spokesmen for the *folkekirke* now problematized the fact that the State through its economic contribution to the Church was paying for the public preaching of a religion – should not the State be religious-neutral and would it not be better if the State paid for maintenance of medieval churches and for public functions as a public authority, such as deciding whether and how a body could be buried, ran the debate.

Church registers and services from the folkekirke to the State
The church ministers in the *folkekirke* still uphold some public functions that were their responsibility in the Middle Ages; most central among them is that the parish registers are still the public register for all Danes, except in the southern part of Jutland (formerly North Schleswig, which was under German authority from 1864–1920). Here the German system was upheld and all civil registration was organized under the municipality. The church registers thus in mainland Denmark function as the civil registration system for birth, names, baptism, confirmation, marriage, death and burial. At the same time some of the religious functions automatically also include civil functions (for example, baptism is at the same time the naming of a child; marriage is at the same time a civil registration of a marriage, and so on), and church ministers are the public authority to decide on funerals for all deceased Danes.

This system could have been changed a couple of times over the past centuries. On 2 April 1968 the State of Denmark thus introduced a civil registration system where each individual was given a number in a combination of the day, month and year of birth and four added individual numbers. This system paved the way for, among others, payment of personal taxes via the employer before the salary is paid to the employee (before 'tax-by-source' as it is called, the individual received his full salary and was obliged to pay taxes personally on a quarterly basis, which of course led to problems for many people). In 1968 it had of course been possible to move responsibility for the public registration from the churches to the local councils. The existing system where the church ministers were responsible for registration was however seen as the cheapest system and pragmatically it was decided that the church books that had functioned perfectly since the Middle Ages should be upheld and that the church ministers should carry out the registration of all Danes; it thus follows from the law on registration of birth and death (L 225/1968, still in force) that all birth and death registration shall be done through the church books.

In principle, the system is still the same. Several (pragmatic) changes due to digitalization now, however, lead to slightly changed analysis. During the 1990s the Church Register was changed from being handwritten to a digital system, called *The New Church Book*;[27] from 1998 the digitalization was used to combine the hospital registration with the church book, meaning that the midwives were obliged to complete a parallel registration of birth (L235/1997); the parents were however also still obliged to inform the Church Register, that is, the local church

---

27   Den Ny Kirkebog.

minister within the *folkekirke* about the birth of their child. This changed in 2010, where a new change of law based on further technological advancements meant that midwives have the main responsibility for the registration of births (and parents, only if a midwife was not present at the birth) and in the same law, doctors responsible for certifying cause of death are now responsible for formally informing the Church Register of a death (L 249/2010). Now, citizens are no longer obliged to register births and deaths, as this is done by professionals within the health care system. As for the naming of newborns, citizens now have the possibility to simply register a name on a website[28] which in itself implies that a decision on baptism has become more of a technicality and less a traditional way that children are given names. Moreover, the technical changes in the system has led to a distinction between the public citizen register and the register related only to the *folkekirke*, meaning that registration of religious acts (baptism – and thus membership of the church, confirmation, etc.) take place in one part of the electronic register, whereas the civil dimensions are dealt with in another part of the register.

This electronic version of the civil register in Denmark, based on the church books, is paid for by the members of the *folkekirke* through the national church tax that in a period in the late 1990s had a huge budgetary problem, due to these changes. Also because of this, many argue that it is not the State that supports the churches. The churches, is it argued, support the State even more with this civil registration, but also with the maintaining of cemeteries and the registration of births and deaths as such.

New focus on religious minorities
The fourth debate, which was opened in the last decades of the twentieth century, was based on globalization. During only a couple of decades in the late twentieth century, the number of Muslim believers in Denmark grew from less than 5,000 to more than 250,000, that is, from less than one per thousand to around five per cent. Many Muslims came as labour immigrants from Turkey or the former Yugoslavia; others came as refugees; and many came maybe precisely because they had suffered from the consequences of a too tight relation between religion and State. This influx, together also with a major influx of Catholics (especially from South America and South-East Asia) as well as many very old Christian groups (such as various Middle Eastern churches) and new Christian groups (such as Evangelical and Pentecostal traditions from different African countries) have made the religious minorities in Denmark much more visible. This has of course been a debate of its own, not least related to the Cartoons-crisis,[29] but it has also sparked a debate on the one hand on whether or not the State and the *folkekirke* are

---

28   www.borger.dk
29   Lisbet Christoffersen, 'The Danish Cartoons Crisis Revisited' in W Cole Durham et al. (eds), *Islam and Political-Cultural Europe* (Ashgate 2012) 217–28.

too intertwined,[30] and on the other hand, whether the conditions for non-*folkekirke* communities in Denmark are actually as good as everyone believed: is it enough to have freedom without any of the economic advantages that are related to the position of the *folkekirke*?

Many both old and new churches outside the *folkekirke* and other faith communities have started to problematize this situation of freedom without equality.

A Leading Verdict

Individual members of the Baptist Church as well as of the Catholic Church in Denmark thus decided to file a case against the State for discrimination against them because of the economic support from the State to the *folkekirke*, utilized for salaries for church ministers, that is, for preaching the content of a religion; and because of the compulsory registration of all newborn children in a system that basically was organized and driven by the *folkekirke*, which they saw as a result of a lack of distinction between the State and a religious community and as discrimination against their freedom of religion.

The Supreme Court of Denmark decided on the case in 2007.[31] The Supreme Court rejected all arguments from the side of the members of minority churches. As for the economic support from the State to the *folkekirke*, the court argued[32] that there is no direct link between the individual who pays taxes and the use of the general tax revenue for the support of the church. The freedom of religion for the individual could thus not be touched by this State tax support. Apart from that, the court argued that part of the church budget is used for common society functions, such as civil registration and authority concerning funerals as well as the maintenance of cemeteries. Also this is not problematized in regard to the combined prohibition to discriminate in religious matters in ECHR Articles 14 and 9.

The Supreme Court further argued that when the Church keeps the civil registration through the Church Register, then the church ministers are authorized to maintain a common administrative task under public law; there is no religious dimension linked to this registration; and certificates (e.g. birth certificates) can be delivered with or without the name *den danske folkekirke* (interchangeable for members and non-members) on the certificate. The court thus did not find any conflict with the ECHR Articles 14 and 9. Since the same rule applies to all, the court also did not find any lack of compliance with CCPR Articles 2, 18 and 26.

---

30 Lisbet Christoffersen, 'Intertwinement. A new concept for understanding religion-law-relations' (2006) 19, 2 *Nordic Journal of Religion and Society*.

31 U2008.342H, which means that the verdict was published in the weekly journal publishing court cases in 2008 on page 342. H indicates that the decision is from *højesteret:* Supreme Court.

32 With reference to *Darby vs Sweden,* Case no 11581/85.The Supreme Court did not include ECtHR-cases in the verdict.

Legally speaking, the Danish Supreme Court has thus found the entire system not only acceptable, but in accordance with statutory law, the Danish Constitution and all relevant international obligations.

Theoretical Challenges and Political Responses

It should however be noticed that while the before mentioned court case found its way to the Supreme Court, the legislation – as referred to in the previous part of the chapter – concerning how birth and death registration should proceed, was slightly changed on the basis of new technological solutions and with the clear goal of establishing clear walls of separation between the civic part of the system and the ecclesiastical part of the system.

Also in the same way, theoretical and further political subtle changes are intertwining in a rather pragmatic way.

It is thus obvious that the Danish situation with no clear legal and financial distinction between State and the *folkekirke* has given rise to several critical analytical approaches over the years. On the other hand, it is also obvious that the Danish situation – even though it does not contain much equality – is ripe with freedom in a country where the absolutely clear majority is still related to the national church. And, as should perhaps be mentioned even more, it is also the case that the individual freedom not only of religion as such, but also from religious interference in everyday matters, moral interference, etc. based on legal rights for religious communities is very low in Denmark. This has also led very young Danish political scientists to suggest that there might be arguments for keeping close relations, also economic ones, between the State and the majority church, as long as the rights and possibilities of the minority churches and religious communities are not infringed. These political scientists talk about *soft secularism*[33] in a context of *secular religious establishment.*[34]

Even though there is this theoretical acceptance of some sort of intertwinement between State and religion, voices are also heard about the problematics of the situation. In the sociological report for *religare,*[35] we thus quite surprisingly found that the majority of interviewees argued for a change in relations between the State and both the *folkekirke* and also other religious communities. Even though the

---

33   HB Dabelsteen, 'Staten, folkekirken og dansk sekularisme' in L Christoffersen et al. (eds), *Fremtidens danske religionsmodel* (Anis 2012) 339–55.

34   Sune Lægaard, 'Secular Religious establishment: Is institutional religious establishment compatible with political secularism?' Paper for panel on Secularism and Religious Establishment in Multicultural Societies: The Normative Challenges of Religious Governance, at the 63rd Political Studies Association Annual International Conference, 25–27 March 2013, City Hall, Cardiff (forthcoming).

35   Niels Valdemar Vinding et al., *Danish Regulation of Religion. State of Affairs and Qualitative Reflections* (Centre for European Islamic Thought, Faculty of Theology, University of Copenhagen 2012) 9–235. See also <www.religareproject.eu>

directions in these wishes for change were not clear in our interviews,[36] what was clear was a general understanding that these changes should not come through a court decision in Denmark and especially not from Europe and or out of political decisions from Europe: this is a matter for the Danes to decide.

There is thus a rising tendency to regard the situation as problematic if the State is too much intertwined, at least economically, with the majority church, especially if the minority religious communities are raising their voice against the system – and there is a rising support to find political definitions of what is problematic as well as national political solutions.

One of the very active partners behind this rising tendency is the National Council of Churches in Denmark, consisting of not only minority churches, but also leading members of the *folkekirke* leadership.[37] The council has during some years had a committee to analyse how the existing very high level of freedom for religious communities could possibly be combined with a higher level of equal conditions, both economically and legally.[38] The main approach has been that nothing should be taken from the *folkekirke*, although something may be given to the other religious communities.

In 2013, this committee sent a paper for discussion to all the member churches in the National Council for Churches.[39] The paper to be discussed wanted to pinpoint different possibilities of giving the churches (and other religious communities) outside the *folkekirke* clearer legal and economic conditions. One suggestion was that members of registered faith communities should have the possibility to pay their contributions to their own religious community via the tax system. It was thus suggested that the concept of a *church tax*, i.e. where the State tax system is used for taxing members of a faith community, should be a possibility for all religious communities that fulfil certain conditions. Another suggestion was that State contributions to the maintenance of religious buildings that are deemed to be historical heritage should be divided equally between the *folkekirke* and other religious communities.[40]

None of these suggestions have yet been discussed politically, but they have been discussed at length at a level just below the Parliament and the Government.[41]

---

36   Vinding et al. (n 35) 121–2.

37   The Dean at the Cathedral of Copenhagen is thus the chair of the council: <http://www.danskekirkersraad.dk/>

38   National Council of Churches in Denemark: <http://www.danskekirkersraad.dk/arbejdsomraader/frihed-og-lige-vilkaar/>

39   See *diskussionsoplæg 2013*.

40   See further in Christoffersen (n 5).

41   Topics regarding equal treatment of religious communities in Denmark were thus discussed on the *folkemødet på Bornholm* (National Political Public meeting on Bornholm in June 2013) in several settings; it was on the agenda in *dansk selskab for kirkeret* (the National association for Ecclesiastical Law) in 2012 and again in September 2013; these topics are discussed in the national council of churches, in organizations such as *folkekirke og religionsmøde* and in the Interchurch council.

The same has for a while been the case regarding the *folkekirke*. Even though the abovementioned Supreme Court verdict supported the current regime totally, the general feeling was that merely the fact that this case came up shows that something has to be done, however politically. This is among the arguments behind the government appointment of a committee in 2012 to analyse (among others) how the national budget for the *folkekirke* should be constructed in the future and how economic relations between Church and State should proceed. A note of May 2013 was sent out for public debate before the committee was to conclude its work in the first months of 2014.

Transparency, Accountability and Good Governance

It is thus possible that some of the problematic dimensions of the age-old financial system between the State, the *folkekirke* and other religious communities are to be changed in the near future. The risk, on the other hand, is that the debate may become so principled that nothing really happens. Instead of running this risk, one very pragmatic route forward could be to find and follow some of the good practices that already exist within or without the field of economic support for faith communities.

It has in Denmark been common to compare the *folkekirke* with a chess club: why should the State interfere so much? This is however anything but a chess club. A relevant answer to that might be that it is rather unusual to find a chess club – or any other club – where nearly 80 per cent of the country's inhabitants are members. There are however other huge organizations, with which it is relevant to compare not only the *folkekirke*, but also other faith communities, be they big or small. These are another type of organization, collecting money in order to function without necessarily having a clear democratic basis, and which keep the organization accountable and secure good governance via an annual general meeting.

These organizations – with or without democratic basis – have recently formed a professional association, called the Professional Association of Fundraising Organizations.[42] As part of its function, this umbrella organization has formulated ethical guidelines for fundraising organizations. The guidelines are binding for all members of the organization, among which are many religious organizations, such as the Catholic Church in Denmark. Central concepts in these guidelines are *respect* for the individual giving money to a fundraising organization, and *transparency* and *good governance* on the side of the organization, concerning goals, leadership and economy in the organization as well as concerning the results of concrete fundraising activities.

---

42 Indsamlingsorganisationernes brancheorganisation, ISOBRO, member of the *European Fundraising Association:* <http://www.isobro.dk/index.php?id=254>

In Denmark, fundraising activities as such are not regulated, except when it comes to concrete public collections of money. A public committee has proposed a new and more general legislation in the field.[43] According to ISOBRO, the main proposals concern a general regulation forcing all fundraising organizations to follow such general principles.[44] The government has however not yet proposed a law in parliament and it is unclear whether the delay is due to practical reasons,[45] or based on more principled arguments.

A general law concerning fundraising organizations would also cover religious communities, unless they – once again – were exempted from the law as is the case for the law on funds and charities.

It is of course not clear what the best way forward is for religious communities outside the *folkekirke* in regard to clarity about funding, public financing and legal relations with the State. It is also not clear – yet – what the best way forward is in regard to the existing intertwinement of State and the *folkekirke*, also economically. From this perspective, this chapter has been written in the middle of the process.

There is however – for this author – no doubt that all religious communities would gain much greater legitimacy if their way of dealing with finances was much clearer. It is good that many of them follow ethical rules on the basis of general responsibility; those who don't follow the same rules might however be those that really need to do so.

While waiting for more principled solutions, my suggestion would thus be to focus much more on rules concerning transparency, accountability and good governance for religious communities.[46]

List of References

Basdevant-Gaudemet B et al. (eds), *The Financing of Religious Communities in the European Union* (Peeters 2009)
Christoffersen L, 'Intertwinement. A new concept for understanding religion-law-relations', (2006) 19, 2 *Nordic Journal of Religion and Society*

---

43 *Betænkning om indsamlinger Betænkning no. 1532 Kapitel 6.*

44 ISOBRO Betænkning om Indsamlingslov Moms – Informationsmøde 11. april 2012 – Diakonissestiftelsen – Generalsekretær Robert Hinnerskov – Sekretariatschef Mette Holm.

45 Henrik Hoffmann-Hansen (2013), 'Kirkelige og humanitære organisationer får alligevel ikke nye regler for deres indsamlingsvirksomhed i å' *Kristeligt-Dagblad*, 23 February 2013: <http://www.kristeligt-dagblad.dk/artikel/500140:Danmark--Regeringen -udskyder-ny-lov-om-indsamlinger>

46 Lisbet Christoffersen, 'Transparency, Good Governance and Accountability – tre af Tiedemanns etiske grundprincipper', in Bredholt, Nik et al. (eds), *E-festskrift. Erling Tiedemann 80 år* (2012) spec. 37–45, <http://www.erling.tiedemann.dk/efestskrift1–3d. pdf>; Christoffersen, Lisbet (2013).

——— 'Religious Entitites as Legal Persons – Northern Europe (Nordic and Baltic Countries)' in L Friedner (ed.), *Churches and Other Religious Organisations as Legal Persons: Proceedings of the 17th Meeting of the European Consortium for Church and State Research* (Peeters Publishers 2007)

——— 'The financing of Religious Communities in Denmark' in B Basdevant-Gaudemet et al. (eds), *The Financing of Religious Communities in the European Union* (Peeters 2009)

———'Church Autonomy in Nordic Law' in L Christoffersen et al. (eds), *Law & Religion in the 21st Century – Nordic Perspectives* (DJØF Publishing 2010)

——— 'Et religionsretligt problem og forslag til løsning. Om finansiering af religiøse bygninger I Danmark' in C Henrichsen et al. (eds), *Ret, informatik og Samfund. Festskrift til Peter Blume* (DJØF forlag 2010)

——— 'State, Church and Religion in Denmark at the beginning of the 21st Century' in L Christoffersen et al. (eds), *Law & Religion in the 21st Century – Nordic Perspectives* (Copenhagen: DJØF Publishing 2010)

——— 'Religion and State: Recognition of Islam and Related Legislation' in N Jorgen (ed.), *Islam in Denmark. The Challenge of Diversity* (Lanham/NY/Toronto/Plymouth: Lexington Books 2012)

——— 'The Danish Cartoons Crisis Revisited' in WC Durham et al. (eds), *Islam and Political-Cultural Europe* (Ashgate 2012)

——— 'Transparency, Good Governance and Accountability – tre af Tiedemanns etiske grundprincipper' in N Bredholt et al. (eds), *E-festskrift. Erling Tiedemann 80 år* (2012)

——— 'From Cultural to Religious Arguments in the Use of Buildings: On Danish Funding of Religious Heritage' in A Fornerod (ed.) *Funding Religious Heritage* (Ashgate 2013)

——— 'Some considerations on Transparency, Accountability and Good Governance in the Church', Editorial, News from the RELIGARE project (CNRS 2013)

Dabelsteen HB, 'Folkekirkeligehed. Dansk sekularismes blinde plet', (2011) 44, 199 *I Kritik*

——— 'Staten, folkekirken og dansk sekularisme' in L Christoffersen et al. (eds), *Fremtidens danske religionsmodel* (Anis 2012)

Debatoplæg fra udvalget om en mere sammenhængende og moderne styringsstruktur for folkekirken, May 2013 <http://miliki.dk/kirke/folkekirken/folkekirkens-styringsstruktur/>

Diskussionsgrundlag for Danske Kirkers Råds medlemskirker ved deres drøftelse af 'de fra Folkekirken afvigende trossamfunds forhold, deadline 1 August 2013,<http://www.danskekirkersraad.dk/fileadmin/user/filer/dokumenter/DKR_Dokumenter/130410_Diskussionsoplaeg_til_DKRs_medlemskirker_vedr_____69_fra__Frihed_og_lige_Vilkaar__april_2013.pdf>

Dübeck I, 'Kirchenfinanzierung der nordischen Länder' (2002) 47, 2 *Zeitschrift für Evangelisches Kirchenrecht*

Esdahl P, 'Kirkeministerens økonomiske særkompetencer', *Kirkeretsantologi – dansk kirkereti europæiske belysning*, no. Dansk pers: Selskab for Kirkeret (2004)

Friedner L (ed.), *Churches and other Religious Organisations as Legal Persons* (Peeters 2007)

Indsamlingsetiske retsningslinier, ISOBRO 2004, <http://www.isobro.dk/file admin/filer/Etik/retningslinierdela.pdf>

Justitsministeriets notat af 10. August 2009 om forholdet mellem understøttelsespligten I grundlovens § 4 og en omlægning af statens økonomiske støtte til folkekirken til et bloktilskud, Betænkning 1511/2009, 135–51

Lægaard S, 'Unequal recognition, misrecognition and injustice: the case of religious minorities in Denmark' (2012) 12, 2 *Ethnicities* (Sage Journals)

—— 'Secular Religious establishment: Is institutional religious establishment compatible with political secularism?' Paper for panel on Secularism and Religious Establishment in Multicultural Societies: The Normative Challenges of Religious Governance, at the 63rd Political Studies Association Annual International Conference, 25–27 March 2013, City Hall, Cardiff (forthcoming)

Notat om Folkekirkens fælles økonomi, written by Mr Jørgen Engmark, Ministry of Gender Equality and Church Affairs for the Government Committee on Governance Structure, 25 September 2012, published May 2013; <http:// miliki.dk/fileadmin/share/Styringsstruktur/Notat_faelles_oekonomi.pdf>

Notater om kirkeskat som kildeskat for trossamfund udenfor folkekirken <http:// www.katolsk.dk/814/>

Stenbæk J, 'Folkekirkens ejendomsforhold og økonomi – historisk belyst' in *Kirkehistoriske Samlinger* (2003)

—— 'Hvad forstaas ved den evangelisk-lutherske Kirke? Om Henning Matzens statskirkelige folkekirkeforståelse' *Festskrift til Hans Gammeltoft-Hansen* (Djøf 2004)

Tamm D, 'Religious Entities as Legal Persons – Denmark' in L Friedner (ed.) *Churches and Other Religious Organizations as Legal Persons: Proceedings of the 17th Meeting of the European Consortium for Church and State Research* (Leuven: Peeters Publishers 2007)

Vinding, NV et al., *Danish Regulation of Religion. State of Affairs and Qualitative Reflections* (Centre for European Islamic Thought, Faculty of Theology, University of Copenhagen 2012)

Chapter 9

Public Funding of Religious Groups in Italy

Vincenzo Pacillo

Church Funding from 1861 to 1928

When Victor Emmanuel II was proclaimed King of Italy on 17 March 1861, the Savoyard set of rules determining the financial relationship between the State and the Catholic Church was based on Law no. 878 of 29 May 1855 (the so-called 'Rattazzi law'). This followed several plebiscites which declared the annexation of Lombardy, the Duchy of Parma, the Duchy of Modena, the Grand Duchy of Tuscany, the Kingdom of the Two Sicilies, Romagna, Marche and Umbria by the Kingdom of Sardinia (name given to the Savoyard State after 1720, when the House of Savoy received the crown of Sardinia and thereafter annexed the isle to their possessions). In the spirit of the Kulturkampf that characterized a number of Western European legal systems during that period, the Rattazzi Law served to abolish many Catholic Church institutions considered useless, because they were not dedicated to preaching, to education or to assisting the infirm.[1] The Rattazzi Law also created a public institution called *cassa ecclesiastica* or clerical treasury, which was provided with its own budget and was independent from State finances. This institution was called upon to manage the patrimony of abolished clerical institutions, in order to fund not only the maintenance cheques for the ex-members of these institutes, but also support for some Catholic priests and bishops who were being inadequately supported by the charity system.[2]

Furthermore, in the Kingdom of Sardinia, the Catholic Church was not the only religion to obtain economic subsistence from the State: the House of Savoy in fact decided to offer a financial contribution to the Waldensian Board, which was fixed at 6,462.30 ITL by Royal Decree of 29 April 1843.[3] According to the law on Jewish communities of 1857, Jews who had already lived in the kingdom for more

---

1 Francesco Scaduto, *Diritto ecclesiastico vigente in Italia*, I (Bocca 1892) 19.

2 Arturo Carlo Jemolo, 'Il "partito cattolico" piemontese nel 1855 e la legge sarda soppressiva delle comunità religiose', *Il Risorgimento italiano*, XI–XII (1918–1919), (Stralcio da periodico,) 1–52.

3 Emilio Friedberg, *Trattato del Diritto ecclesiastico cattolico ed evangelico*, edizione italiana riveduta in collaborazione con l'autore dall'Avv. Francesco Ruffini (Bocca 1893) 151.

than one year were obliged to pay an annual sum – as a kind of obligatory tax – to the territorial Jewish Community to which they belonged.[4]

The provisions of the Rattazzi Law were progressively extended, first to Umbria (Decree of the Royal Commissioner no. 105 of 29 October 1860), then to Marche (Decree of the Royal Commissioner no. 705 of 3 January 1861), then to the Neapolitan Provinces (Lieutenant's Decree no. 251 of 17 February 1861),[5] and finally to the entire territory of the Kingdom of Italy in Law no. 99 of 7 July 1866.[6] The entire ecclesiastical politics of the newborn Kingdom of Italy were, furthermore, a development of those adopted during the Kingdom of Sardinia, which, since the 1840s, had been based on two objectives:

a) The status of all citizens should not encounter any differentiation based on the religion they practised and the Italian legal system had to be inspired by the principles of freedom of conscience (even with remarkable limitations)[7] and equality, irrespective of the credo practised: it is true that Article 1 of the Albertine Statute proclaimed that 'the Roman, Catholic, Apostolic religion is the only State religion', but *de facto* this norm had no other meaning than to prescribe that, if a public institution had ordered to perform a religious function, this function had to be performed in accordance with the liturgy of the Roman, Catholic, Apostolic Church.[8] Besides, Piedmontese ecclesiastical legislation during and after the statute totally confirmed the will of the Piedmontese legislator to guarantee – even with some limitations linked in particular to the manifestation of personal ideas on religious matters – freedom of conscience and the principle of equality without distinction of belief.

---

4   Mario Piacentini, *I culti ammessi nello Stato italiano* (Ulrico Hoepli 1934) § 44.

5   Romeo Astorri, 'Leggi eversive, soppressioni delle corporazioni religiose e beni culturali' in Gemini, Fiorenza (ed), *La memoria silenziosa. Formazione, tutela e status giuridico degli archivi monastici nei monumenti nazionali* ; atti del convegno, Veroli, Abbazia di Casamari 6 – 7 novembre 1998, Ferentino, Palazzo comunale 8 novembre 1998 (Roma 2000) 42 *et seq*.

6   Carlo Calisse, *Diritto ecclesiastico* (Barbèra 1893) 237.

7   Enrico Vitali states that, in Piedmont, freedom of conscience – understood as a licence to express one's personal religious persuasion in acts, words and documents – remained subordinated to respect for all the laws intended to sentence all attacks and offences directed at the State religion, including articles 164–5 of the Criminal code of 1839 and articles 16–18 of the Press edict. Vitali means that the juridical scene of the Savoyard Kingdom concerning ecclesiastical matters after the concession of the statute was based on tolerance in a strict sense; afterwards, this was interpreted as admission, without proclamation, of freedom of conscience and faith (limited to the Waldensians and the Jews); this was because tolerance had to be understood as 'the repudiation of intolerance, the permission to practice one's own faith'. See Enrico Vitali), *Vilipendio della religione dello Stato – Contributo all'interpretazione dell'art. 402 del Codice penale* (CEDAM 1964).

8   Arturo Carlo Jemolo, 'La natura e la portata dell'art.1 dello Statuto' (1913) *Rivista di diritto pubblico*, p. 253 *et seq*.

Here it will be sufficient to remember the so-called 'measures of equalization',[9] aimed at obtaining the civil emancipation of the Waldensians and the Jews:[10] on 18 February 1848 – realizing that the reasons for the restrictions on the civil liberties of the Waldensians and the Jews had ceased – a letters patent was issued, which declared that the Waldensians were authorized to possess all civil and political rights that belonged to the subjects of the kingdom, that they could attend the schools of any order and level (including universities) and obtain academic degrees. Note also the Royal Resolution of 29 March 1848, which recognized Jews' ability to enjoy civil rights and the right to obtain academic degrees; a few days later, a decree issued by Prince Eugene of Savoy Carignano, Lieutenant of the Kingdom, admitted Jews to military service; with regard to all religions, there was a fundamental provision contained in Article 1 of the Election Law of 17 March 1848; it states: 'Admitting citizens to exercise their voting rights does not take into account the special orders concerning the civil or political rights to which somebody could be subjected because of the faith he practises'. Finally, Law No. 735 of 19 June 1848 'intending to eliminate all doubts about the civil and political capacity of those citizens who do not practise the Catholic Religion',[11] ruled that differences of religion could not imply any discrimination either in applying civil and political rights, nor in access to public or military offices.

b) The legislation had to lead to the elimination of ecclesiastical mortmain and of some privileges that the Catholic Church enjoyed: in particular, we have to remember here the Laws of Sardinia/Piedmont no. 777 of 25 August 1848, which abolished the 'Company of Jesus' and the corporation of the 'Society of the Sacred Heart of Jesus' (which had managed to deprive their members of the right to assembly); Law no. 1013 of 9 April 1850, which provided for the abolition

---

9 Isacco Rignano, *Della uguaglianza civile e della libertà dei culti* (Franc. Vigo 1868) 6.

10 Jews especially, who had been put on an equal footing with Catholics during the French occupation before the measures cited here, suffered major limitations in the use of civil and political rights: the letters patent of 1 March 1816 obliged Jews to sell, within a limit of five years, buildings bought during the French occupation; furthermore, they forbade leaving the ghetto during the night, they reaffirmed the ancient ban (formulated by Carl Emmanuel in 1770) on accessing universities, community offices, government offices, civil and also military offices. The Waldensians, who had been present since the sixteenth century in the Piedmontese territory and who, after being massacred subsequent to an attempt at insurrection in 1655, obtained, through the Treaty of Pinerolo, permission to practise their own faith freely within the limits of their valleys, and during the nineteenth century enjoyed definitely better conditions than the Jews, but with limitations of a certain importance: they were in fact allowed to freely choose their domicile, taking into consideration special requests from those who wanted to live in the capital city, yet they could not possess real estate. In other words, as Rignano states (n 9), 'nearly total negation of the civil rights to the Jews, very imperfect and limited participation as for the Protestants, of this kind was therefore, in a word, the condition of non-Catholics in the subalpine Kingdom in 1847'.

11 Preamble to the draft bill.

of the privilege of the ecclesiastical forum; and no. 1037 of 5 June 1850 that introduced the obligation for civil and clerical institutions to obtain governmental authorization before acquiring property, inheritances and suchlike. These laws were passed in order to counteract the phenomenon of so-called 'ecclesiastical mortmain', which was destructive to the economy of the Kingdom.[12] In the middle of the nineteenth century, Piedmontese ecclesiastical politics were not immune to a good portion of anticlerical regalism based on formerly Protestant fundament: the doctrine espoused by Giovanni Nepomuceno Nuytz, Professor of Ecclesiastical Law at the University of Turin during these tormented years had probably more influence on Piedmontese ecclesiastical politics than Cavour's separatism,[13] which was to be expressed in its entirety by Earl Camillo Benso only in his discourse of 27 March 1861.[14]

The 'Cassa ecclesiastica' system had been based upon the so-called historical continuity between the ecclesiastical politics of the Kingdom of Sardinia and those of the Kingdom of Italy and founded on the principle that, if the State had to distribute funds for clerical expenses, it would be able to do this using only funds of ecclesiastical origin and not by taking money from tax revenues.[15] It was confirmed and consolidated by Law no. 3036 of 7 June 1866 and Law no. 3848 of 15 August 1867. With these measures, inability to possess real estate was sanctioned for all moral ecclesiastical institutions, except the parishes: only the buildings used for worship, Episcopal buildings and the seminary buildings were excluded from being transferred to State property.

In particular, Law no. 3548/1867 provides for the suppression of all those religious institutions which the State considered superfluous to people's religious lives, sparing only seminaries, cathedrals, parishes, '*fabbricerie*' and dioceses.

---

12   Antonio Scialoja, 'La Chiesa, lo Stato e la liquidazione dell'Asse ecclesiastico' (1867) serie I, 5 *Nuova Antologia* 741–64.

13   Vittorio Gorresio sustains the thesis of a non-negligible influence of Nuytz on Piedmontese ecclesiastical politics. Vottorio Gorresio, *Risorgimento scomunicato* (Parenti 1958).

14   According to Pietro Piovani, 'the point of view of Cavour, comprehended in part by collaborators ... (executors of a letter of difficult comprehension, defectively intended) does not perfectly coincide with the formulations of either classical liberalism or Catholic or para-Catholic liberalism. Not close to the regalism-inspired suggestions ..., distant from deistic yearnings, sceptical about the possibilities of the strictly juridical or generically spiritualistic arrangements, and always misunderstood by all supporters of the ethical state (Hegelian or not), Cavour believes in the church, in its future in freedom. The church, in order to exist, has to be free'. Pietro Piovani, 'Da un temporalismo all'altro' in *Un secolo da Porta Pia* (Guida editore 1970) 317 *et seq*. Besides, also the writings of two authors very close to the ideas of Cavour like Pier Carlo Boggio and Marco Minghetti, were published only several years after the 'leggi eversive' (revolutionary anti-clerical laws), as recalled by Arturo Carlo Jemolo, *Chiesa e Stato in Italia dall'unificazione ai giorni nostri*, XII rist. of 'editio minor' (1955, 1996) 9 *et seq*.

15   Calisse (n 6) 234 *et seq*.

Law no. 3036/1866 deprived all orders, corporations, regular religious congregations, conservatories and retreats of clerical character and implying life in community, of their juridical personality (and therefore of their patrimonial capacity). The properties of these suppressed institutions were confiscated by the State; furthermore, it sanctioned the duty to sign in the public debt register a revenue of five per cent in favour of a new institution – the Church Fund, which for all purposes replaced the '*Cassa ecclesiastica*' of the Kingdom of Sardinia.[16]

One of the Church Fund's duties was to pay – but only within the limit of available capital – an extra amount in the form of cheques, given to parish priests whose annual income was less than 800 ITL: this integration was called '*supplemento di congrua*'. Nevertheless, the Church Fund was burdened with other charges, which were considered – from a political and juridical point of view – to be priorities compared with those deriving from the duty to pay the most destitute clerics: so, the supplementary cheques were paid out only from 1887 onwards.

The main doctrine[17] remarks that these supplementary cheques assumed the form of financial aid; we cannot consider them remuneration for the cleric's spiritual activity, but rather a concession – not seizable – in order to assure his subsistence. This implied the impossibility of arguing that the Italian clergy was employed by the State, which intervened only for supporting purposes to ensure some citizens a decent existence.

If such statements led the reader to think of a 'light' intervention by the Kingdom of Italy in Catholic Church funding – instead of an intervention based on a series of discriminatory acts of dispossession, evidently opposed to religious freedom – this occurred so as not to undervalue other normative instructions which were designed in part against a rather different backdrop.

First of all, we have to recall Article 237 of the Law of 20 March 1865, Annexe 'A' (law on communal and regional administration), initially a transitory norm, then extended until 1931 when it finally became permanent in Royal Decree 1175/1931, which burdens the communes with the necessary expenses for the conservation of public places of worship.[18] I would also like to bring to mind some instructions contained in Law no. 214 of 13 May 1871 (the so-called *legge*

---

16   19,235 moral institutions preserved and subjected to the transference of their real estate determined by Law of 7 July 1866; 2,184 religious corporations were suppressed by the same law; 43,579 moral institutes suppressed by the Law of 15 August 1867. The revenue from the three groups of institutions verified and subject to mortmain tax was: 25,618,894.46 ITL, 14,675,150.27 ITL and 18,429,942.61 ITL. Altogether the possessions incorporated in the State came from 64,998 institutions and had a revenue of 58,723,987.34 ITL. Gaetano Zingali, *I rapporti finanziari tra Stato e Chiesa e il trattamento fiscale agli enti di culto* (Vallardi 1943) 38.

17   Vicenzo Del Giudice, *Manuale di diritto ecclesiastico*, 10th edn (Giuffrè 1964) 302.

18   Arturo Carlo Jemolo, *Lezioni di Diritto ecclesiastico*, 5th edn (Giuffrè 1979) 471.

delle guarentigie), for example, Article 4, which assigned an annual endowment of 3,255,000 ITL to the Holy See as indemnity for loss of income caused by the cessation of its temporal power:[19] it is important to note that the Apostolic See did not accept, and therefore never cashed in, this revenue and that the amount so accumulated and not received was imputed as justification for the much more conspicuous governmental donation – one more time in favour of the Holy See – contemplated by the financial convention annexed to the Lateran Treaty dated 11 February 1929 (to which we will return later).

It is evident that such measures were born out of the will to attenuate an exclusively 'negative' vision of Catholic religious freedom, providing the 'Church' institution a series of economic instruments designed to facilitate the exercise of the faculties resulting from this freedom. In fact, it is well-known that the liberal state saw the rights of freedom mostly as indispensable instruments to assure the satisfaction of a subjective legal position of the single entity by non-interference of public powers: hence, the idea that the realization of the interest protected by the law had to be carried out exclusively by the duty of abstention.

By means of the aforesaid financial norms, the Kingdom of Italy seemed to be approaching a juridical and political theory which considered the possibility of concretely guaranteeing the right of religious freedom only if government financial initiatives existed for faiths within its territory; this theory would come to dominate after 1948.

Such initiatives became a kind of indirect funding in legislation from 1871 to 1929, and were concretized in a series of fiscal privileges, such as the exemption of the Catholic Church and its institutions (even those without legal status) from certain taxes, or such as the possibility – for institutions or individuals connected to the Catholic Church – to pay dues and taxes in reduced proportions compared with other categories of subjects.

So, exempted from the ordinary dues were churches, sacristies, belfries, all buildings assigned to worship for recognized faiths (Law no. 3682 of 1 March 1886, Article 17) and also the ecclesiastical benefits enjoyed by the clerics entitled to receive the supplementary cheques (Decree no. 78 of 5 February 1922); also, these benefits were subtracted from the mortmain fee (Royal Decree no. 3271, dated 30 December 1923); furthermore, the Church Fund paid the supplementary cheques as a gross sum to the priests, without any tax deducted (Law no. 191, 4 June 1899; Royal Decree no. 910 of 2 July 1922).

Church Funding from 1929 to the Racial Laws

There is no doubt that 1929 represented a turning point in the financial relationship between the Kingdom of Italy and the Catholic Church: the composition of the 'Roman Question' cost the State an enormous financial sacrifice, which completely

---

19   Zingali (n 16) 50.

cancelled out the idea – long contemplated by Italian Liberals – that public powers could distribute sums for Church expenses using only funds of clerical origins, leaving tax revenues untouched.

In reality – also because of relevant enhancements to supplementary cheques for priests, which increased from 1,000 ITL (Law Decree no. 396, 17 March 1918) to 3,500 ITL stated in Royal Decree no. 364 of 31 March 1925 – the expenses supported by the Church Fund had already been out of control for several years and the biggest charges 'deriving from these measures were burdened on the State'.[20]

The Lateran Accords represented the culmination of fascist church politics, which considered protection of religions to be in the public interest, being seen as institutions and social-ethical powers necessary for civilization and the State; this consideration is based on the predominant role assigned by the fascist ideology to the phenomenon of the religious tradition and its incidence on the population.

The State saw the Catholic religion as a fundamental instrument to serve its ethical purposes and to provide widespread acceptance based on the influence that the clerical hierarchy had over the masses; the Catholic religion was considered capable of playing a fundamental role in the moral development of both individual and society.

In this way, religion declined from expression of individual spirituality into mere *instrumentum regni*: therefore, religion obtained special protection, based on the political role given to it in the creation of the system.[21] A system that sacrificed – by strengthening the instructions of Article 1 of the Albertine Statute and by a solid normative complex designed to repress the freedom of dissenting or non-Catholics – individual religious freedom on the altar of the Catholic Church's 'clerical freedom', totally neglecting the religious interests of individuals or protecting them within the limits that coincide with the institution's interest. Just respecting this strictly political option, the fascist State embraced within its entire ecclesiastical legislation a rigid principle of confession – in the sense of Catholic confession.

The fascist religious ideology did not hesitate to redefine the financial relationship between State and Catholic Church in a largely favourable manner for the latter. Among the measures implemented by the Kingdom of Italy, which mainly improved the economic and financial situation of the Church of Rome, we may recall:

a) Annex IV of the tractate established between the Holy See and Italy on 11 February 1929, entitled 'Convenzione finanziaria' (Law no. 810 of 27 May 1929). This agreement obliged Italy to pay the Holy See the sum of 750 million ITL and to transfer one billion ITL in five per cent shares. In exchange, the Vatican declared the Roman Question to be definitely closed. Now in possession

---

20   Besides, Royal Decree no. 164 of 2 February 1922 extends the right to obtain supplementary cheques from the State also to other clerical categories, like vicars, chaplains, curates and bishops. Zingali (n 16) 45.

21   Vitali (n 7) 63.

of a huge quantity of cash, the Vatican had to deal with the problem of investing profitably. To do so, Pope Pius XI established on 7 June 1929 the Holy See's Special Administration and called upon engineer Bernardino Nogara to run the Vatican's financial institution.

b) The agreement of 11 February 1929, which was 'intended to regulate the conditions of religion and church in Italy'. Articles 25, 26 and 29/h confirmed:

1. The Italian State renouncing the 'Regio Patronato' – a sovereign prerogative – on significant and small benefices. At the time of stipulation, 92 patronage seats existed, but economic consequences resulted only in renouncing the rights attached to the seats related to clerical institutions situated in provinces which already belonged to the Kingdom of the Two Sicilies;
2. The abolition of regalia on significant and small benefices. The regalia right authorized the King to administer vacant benefices and to handle freely the so-called 'interjected fruits', which meant the yields from benefices that had matured during the vacant period;
3. The abolition of the so-called 'pensionable third part', which meant the Italian King's right to dispose of a third part of the income of the dioceses, the prelacies and of some patronage benefices located in certain provinces formerly belonging to the Kingdom of the Two Sicilies, in order to assign – with the Pope's consent – a pension to certain people selected by the sovereign;
4. The abolition of the so-called 'extraordinary tax of 30 per cent' on the patrimony of 'non- suppressed' ecclesiastical institutions, introduced by Law no. 3848 of 15 August 1867;
5. The abolition of the so-called 'concourse share', which meant the 'withdrawal of part of the income of preserved clerical institutions' (in particular, the wealthier ones) 'granted by the State in favour of other religious offices'[22] (in particular, the needier ones), introduced by Article 31, Law no. 3036 of 7 July 1866;
6. The complete fiscal equalization of religious groups to align them with beneficence or instruction organizations;
7. The non-applicability of the tax upon the professions, the licence tax (introduced by Royal Decree no. 2538 of 18 November 1923) and every other similar due, to the clergy for the exercise of their priestly function, public intervention to sustain the Catholic Clergy.[23] Article 30 of the agreement confirms the will to 'remedy income deficiencies of the clerical benefices by using cheques to confer amounts equal to the real value fixed by current laws', reinforcing the will to ensure priests and clerics identified

---

22   Hence, the Court of Cassation's verdict of 9 January 1903, cited by Zingali, (n 16) 73.

23   Vicenzo Del Giudice, *Corso di Diritto ecclesiastico*, 4th edn (A. Giuffre 1939) 322 *et seq.*

in Royal Decrees no. 227 and no. 228 of 29 January 1931[24] received congruous and decent personal sustenance in cases of insufficient benefice revenue. The funds for this financial intervention were found thanks to specific allocations of the State budget, because the capacity of the Church Fund as well as of the fund for religion and beneficence of the city of Rome was insufficient.

While the agreement undeniably reinforced the economic and financial condition of the Italian Catholic Church, fascist legislation remained almost silent on the other religions. The Waldensians continued to receive the annual sum of 6,462.30 ITL fixed by Royal Decree of 29 April 1843,[25] while Royal Decree no. 1731 of 30 October 1930 confirmed that Jews were part of the system of self-funding which was legal, according to the procedure of obligatory contribution. Besides, we should notice that Royal Decree no. 1731 of 30 October 1930 (followed by the execution rules included in Royal Decree no. 1561 of 19 November 1931) contained a series of instructions to regulate in all-embracing manner the juridical status of Italian Hebraism; this law also created an organization – the Union of Hebraic Communities – to which all the Jewish communities in the Kingdom were obliged to belong, as well as pay an annual due. The legal status of religious minorities came crashing down in 1938 with the passing of the racial laws: these put significant limitations on property rights of Italian Jews and introduced a regime of spoliation (see Royal Law Decree no. 1728 of 17 November 1938 and Royal Decree no. 126 of 9 February 1939).

Furthermore, we have to remember that Royal Decree no. 383 of 3 March 1934 confirmed the burdening – if necessary – of the communes with expenses related to the preservation of all public places of worship.

The Early Constitutional Era

The promulgation of the Constitutional Charter of 1948 delineated – in relation to religious freedom – a series of principles absolutely antithetical to those which had inspired fascist ecclesiastical ideology. In effect, the Italian Constitution explicitly guarantees: equality for all citizens without distinction of religion (Article 3); distinction of the temporal order from the spiritual order (Article 7, I); equal freedom of all religions (Article 8, I); the right to organize themselves according to their own statutes (Article 8, II); the provision of agreed legislation to regulate the relationship between State and non-Catholic confessions (Article 8, III); and finally, freedom to profess one's own religious belief, to promote it, to worship in public and in private (Article 19).

---

24 Or rather vicars, chaplains, autonomous curates, members of cathedral chapters, simple clergymen, bishops.
25 Friedberg (n 3) 173.

Article 2 of the Constitution allowed the entire Italian ecclesiastical law to be constructed, referring to individual rights as well as to collective rights, because man cannot call himself free if there is no guarantee of his freedom to express his personality also through the social groups he belongs to.[26] Throughout Article 2 of the Constitution, Ecclesiastical Law became a real '*legislatio libertatis*' with the duty of protecting the free expression of members' religious beliefs. This theoretical premise was succeeded by the thought that religious freedom was to be guaranteed not only 'negatively', through eliminating obstacles, but also 'positively', through the duty for the public powers to create concrete protective instruments and to allow their effective fruition; in this way, in addition to the usual classical-liberal meaning of right to religious freedom ('negative'), the possibility arose to invoke State intervention ('positive'), allowing the complete execution of the faculties deriving from Article 19 of the Constitution.[27] This interpretation was in clear contrast to current legislation concerning support for religions, which contemplated economic support almost exclusively for the Catholic Church, since it was a confession founded on the principles and dogma of the 'State Religion' and therefore privileged compared to the others.

Furthermore, we have to point out that the years between 1948 and 1957 characterized our Republic as a true 'clerical regime',[28] where the *confessionismo di costume* pushed doctrine as well as jurisprudence to concentrate on Article 7 of the Constitution, contemplating a kind of free zone for those norms: among them was the confirmation of the financial obligations sanctioned by the Lateran Treaty (including supplementary cheques for clergymen).

At the time of the promulgation of the Italian Constitution, the system of funding the Catholic Church was based on several instruments:

a) The Constitution had not changed the Lateran Concordat of 1929, which – under the provision of Article 7, paragraph 2 of the Fundamental Charter – had even acquired the status of 'super primary' source.

By virtue of this option, Article 30 of the Concordat – under which the State had undertaken to compensate for deficiencies in ecclesiastical benefices, if they did not secure the clergy a decent livelihood – continued to be valid. Several measures adopted after 1948 were necessary to ensure the Catholic clergy the

---

26 Luigi De Luca, *Diritto ecclesiastico ed esperienza giuridica* (Giuffrè 1970); Enrico Vitali, 'Legislatio libertatis e prospettazioni sociologiche nella recente dottrina ecclesiasticistica' (1980) 90, I *Il Diritto ecclesiastico* 24–66.

27 Giuseppe Casuscelli, 'Pluralismo confessionale e organizzazione dei culti acattolici. Contributo all'interpretazione sistematica del primo e secondo comma dell'art. 8 della Costituzione' in Alessandro Anastasi et al., *Scritti in onore di Salvatore Pugliatti*, III (Giuffrè 1978) 235–313.

28 Piero Calamandrei, *Innesto confessionale, in Scritti e discorsi politici*, I, 1 (La Nuova Italia 1966) 315–16.

so-called 'additional stipend' paid in order to make income from an ecclesiastical life more decent.[29]

In this regard it should be noted that the Catholic priest had the subjective right to receive this additional amount if the income derived from the benefice was less than a figure determined by law and deemed necessary to sustain a decent life.

In addition to this amount, a cheque equal to 15 per cent of the stipend was granted to parish priests to cover the expenses needed for the maintenance of holy buildings and for the general expenses of worship. The right to receive the 'additional stipend' was not only a prerogative of parish priests, but also of other clerics with an ecclesiastical office: among them, vicars and chaplains (but, in this case, the stipend was equal to four-sevenths of that applicable to the parish priest), archbishops, bishops, prelates and abbots with full episcopal jurisdiction. This, of course, meant a growing demand on the State budget and ended by further weakening the stated link between confiscated assets from the subversive legislation of the nineteenth century and the need to provide for the needs of the Catholic clergy.[30]

b) Each year the Minister of Labour allocated a variable financial contribution towards social security. Further subsidies were often added to this contribution for the restoration or reconstruction of Catholic parish churches and canonical houses still linked to the Catholic faith. The Constitution had not even changed Article 91, Letter I of the '*Testo Unico*' of 3 March 1934, no. 383, which made municipalities bear the necessary expenditure to preserve buildings intended for public worship, if there were no other means to do so. Without a doubt, Catholic parish churches were part of this category. There was much discussion whether the law could also apply to buildings of worship other than Catholic ones. Part of the doctrine observed that, whereas we should give the expression 'public worship' the meaning of 'worship practised by an indefinite and indeterminable part of the population', only Waldensian temples could enjoy the benefits under the legislation of 1934, since the other places of worship were deemed essential to the religious needs of certain groups because of their very small and precise numerical relevance.

Others interpreted the term 'public worship' as worship to which anyone could have access and this significantly increased – of course – the number of groups which could benefit from the legislation of 1934. However, it is clear that funding systems in place in the aftermath of the promulgation of the Constitution were in evident contradiction with the provision of Article 8 § 1 of the Constitution, since the need to ensure equal freedom for all religious denominations – in a welfare state system which intervened with economic measures in support of the confessional

29 Jemolo (n 18) 472–4.
30 Vicenzo Del Giudice, *Manuale di Diritto ecclesiastico*, 8th edn (Milano 1955) 302–4.

needs of citizens – cannot be guaranteed without the full participation of non-Catholic denominations in the funding systems and maintenance of worship.[31]

Denominations other than the Catholics were still excluded from the public contribution system: the Waldensians did not lose the right to the annual contribution of 6,462.30 ITL as established by Royal Decree of 29 April 1843, but the amount – not having been re-assessed – was not significant from an economic standpoint. Jewish communities continued to be self-sustaining through the contribution due from those who belonged to them, in view of the fiscal power accorded to them by Articles 24 *et seq.* of Royal Decree No. 1731 of 30 October 1930, while other religious groups were completely excluded from any State contribution.

The tendency to draw all possible conclusions on what was considered the renewed *confessionismo* of the State, ended up influencing other financial measures: among these, we may recall Law no. 222 of 18 December 1952, which allowed eight billion ITL to be spent on completing or constructing Catholic churches or living quarters for parish priests.

The Agreement of 15 November 1984 and Law no. 222 of 1985

The excessive nature of this contributory system began when the Catholic Church started to rethink the conditions for paying and supporting the clergy.

As is common knowledge, this was the result of the Second Vatican Council's decree *Presbyterorum Ordinis*, point no. 20 of which contemplated the end of the benefice system in favour of the introduction of diocesan or inter-diocesan institutions with the task of administering ecclesiastical goods in accordance with principles of equality and distributing wealth among the various parishes and dioceses. By implementing the principles of the Council, Canon no. 1274 of the Code of Canon Law in force effectively sanctioned the creation of these institutions to support the clergy.[32]

Under the agreement between the State and the Catholic Church of 15 November 1984 (Law no. 206 of 1985) the Italian Republic has completely redesigned its participation in maintaining the Catholic clergy and more generally in providing financial support for the worshipping needs of Italian Catholics.

Firstly, the Italian legal system has granted civil legal status to the central institute for the sustenance of the clergy and to the different diocesan institutions (Article 22 of Law 222/1985): the function of the diocesan institutions is to ensure – with the possible contribution of the central institute – that the clergy performing services for their respective dioceses enjoy a reasonable and decent

---

31   On this debate, see Del Giudice (n 30) 332–3.

32   Jean-Pierre Schouppe, *Diritto patrimoniale canonico* (Giuffrè 2008) 130 *et seq.*; Giorgio Feliciani, 'Sostentamento del clero' in *Enciclopedia del Diritto*, vol. 43 (Giuffrè 1990) 122 *et seq.*

livelihood.[33] The Italian Episcopal Conference determines the amount which must be paid to the various diocesan clerics.

Secondly, the institutes have their own assets, consisting not only of property formerly belonging to the benefices (now defunct), but also of annual payments of money by the State, which had pledged to pay the Italian Bishops' Conference a sum equal to eight per thousand of the tax on the personal income (IRPEF) of those who have expressed their will, in an official document, to allocate that amount to the Catholic Church. To tell the truth, the Italian Bishops' Conference also receives a contribution equal to eight per thousand of the tax on the income of individuals who have not, in the aforementioned official document, expressed an option, but this contribution is shared between the various bodies, allowing them to benefit from this system of funding (and soon we will see which they are) in direct proportion to the choices expressed.[34]

It is noteworthy that not all revenue from the so-called eight per thousand is intended to support the clergy. It is for the Italian Bishops' Conference to decide, on the basis of data acquired from the central institute for the livelihood of the clergy, if providing the latter with money is necessary to ensure clerics the payment of the cheque (Article 41 of Law 222 of 1985). The remaining part of the capital paid by the State is used by the CEI autonomously; it ensures the functioning of the diocesan offices and charitable actions in favour of the national community or third world countries (Article 48, Law 222 of 1985).[35]

The CEI has to send to the Ministry of the Interior an annual report summarizing the actual utilization of the funds received: this report should then be forwarded to the Ministry of Economy – accompanied by an explanatory memorandum – and published in the gazette of the Episcopal Conference. It should also be noted that taxpayers can offer the Catholic Church voluntary donations in cash, too. These voluntary donations – up to a sum of €1,032.91 – can be deducted from taxable IRPEF.

This 'Copernican revolution' of the Catholic Church funding system deserves some reflection.

a) It has gone from a system in which the State directly provided salaries for the Catholic clergy (the benefice system – especially towards the end of its validity – gave rise to such inequalities, that some parishes were able to guarantee a decent livelihood for their own clergy only thanks to almost entire support from the State) to a system in which the State is limited to providing – within the limits of the willingness of the

---

33   Giorgio Feliciani, 'Gli istituti per il sostentamento del clero nella nuova normativa della CEI' (1985) 36 *Aggiornamenti sociali* 687–96.

34   Pierluigi Consorti, *La remunerazione del clero* (G. Giappichelli 2000) 46 *et seq.*

35   Giorgio Feliciani, 'L'applicazione della legge 20 maggio 1985, no. 222. Gli esiti di una ricerca' (2006) 117 *Il diritto ecclesiastico* 455–61.

taxpayers – financial contributions which are then freely administered by the ecclesiastical authority;[36]

b) The system of 'eight per thousand' can in no way be defined as a system of 'facilitated self-funding', or even less can it be compared to a tax on worship, at least as it exists in Switzerland and Germany. If, in fact, in these countries the economic sacrifice rests with the faithful, and the State is limited to ensure the collection of the tax, in Italy the economic sacrifice is paid by the State budget;[37]

c) The system of 'eight per thousand' represents a form of 'imperfect fiscal democracy': since, although it provides – in principle – that each taxpayer can choose whether the State should fund the Catholic Church, the aforesaid system also proposes an allocation of the sums resulting from choices that are not expressed, which in fact ensures revenues to the major confessions well above those that would be derived from the opinions expressed. In this regard, it should be noted that unexpressed choices account for 50 per cent of the statements, and that over 80 per cent of the choices expressed are in favour of the Catholic Church.

In any case, another innovation of huge significance of the 'eight per thousand' system is – as we shall see below – the possibility for some non-Catholic denominations to participate in the allocation of funds intended by the State to fund the religious needs of the population. In the document – which offers individual taxpayers the possibility of exercising an option on the allocation of their 'eight per thousand' – *the Catholic Church contributes alongside religious denominations that have signed an agreement with the State which should convey on its own the choices of those who, for ideological or non-membership reasons, do not want to guarantee funding to any of the groups that have concluded agreements with public authorities.* The State will use the sum received through 'eight per thousand' for special measures, to combat world hunger, natural disasters, to assist refugees and preserve cultural heritage.

So, minority groups are entitled to fully participate in government funding and this will certainly ensure a greater and fuller implementation of Article 8 § 1 of the Constitution: in fact, the possibility of minority religious groups competing alongside the Catholic Church for the allocation of government grants intended directly and primarily to support religious freedom unquestionably creates an embodiment of that equality in the freedom that the Constituent Fathers meant to secure.

It should also be noted that the possibility for the State to participate in the allocation of 'eight per thousand' fully ensures respect of the principle of

36   Nicola Fiorita, *Remunerazione e previdenza dei ministri di culto* (Giuffré 2003) 68 *et seq.*

37   Nicola Fiorita, 'L'autofinanziamento agevolato: critica di una definizione' (1997) 108 *Il diritto ecclesiastico* 518–34.

secularism, even though – in the opinion of part of the doctrine – this will happen only if the authorities decide to use the sum collected exclusively for secular purposes (those avoiding using it to restore religious buildings as was the case – as we shall see – after 2005).[38]

The Public Funding of Religious Minority Groups

Regarding the funding of religious minorities, the general rule – of separatist inspiration – is still one of 'nothing from the State' under Law no. 1159 of 1929 – which governs the relationship between the State and religious denominations that have not signed agreements with the State subsequently approved in law – the funding is the responsibility of the respective believers.

It should be pointed out that – regarding the religious minorities which have entered into agreements with the State approved in law (the Waldensian Church, Assemblies of God, Adventist Church, Jewish Communities, Christian Baptist Union, Evangelical Lutheran Church in Italy) – the legal system foresees public support implemented through the system of the 'eight per thousand'.

Law 516 of 1988 and Law 517 of the same year stipulate that taxpayers can choose to allocate the Adventist Church and to the Assemblies of God in Italy the share of 'eight per thousand' of IRPEF: Law 637 of 1996 decided to allocate solely to the Adventist Church – when no other choice has been expressed by the taxpayer – a portion of the amounts not allocated, in proportion to the choices expressed in favour of that church.

Later, even the Waldensian Church (Law 409/1993) and the Evangelical Lutheran Church in Italy (CELI) (Article 27 of Law 520/1995) decided to take advantage of public funding for their social, health, humanitarian and cultural actions: both of these groups – in the case of no choices being expressed by the taxpayer – receive a share of the sums not allocated in proportion to the choices expressed in support of those churches.

Taxpayers may also – besides the allocation to the religious denominations of the eight per thousand of IRPEF – make voluntary donations of money to the same bodies, which – up to a sum of €1,032.91 – can be deducted from taxable IRPEF.

A somewhat different system has been designed for Jewish communities, which are funded primarily by the contribution charged to the members under Article 34 *et seq.* of its statutes. That contribution is deductible from taxable IRPEF of individual taxpayers.

Any dispute about the amount of the contribution is a matter for an arbitration committee or, alternatively, if the dispute cannot be resolved in that context, for the standard judicial authority.

---

38 Ingrid Pistolesi, 'La quota dell'otto per mille di competenza statale: un'ulteriore forma di finanziamento (diretto) per la Chiesa cattolica?' (2006) 1 *Quaderni di Diritto e Politica ecclesiastica* 163–82.

In addition, with effect from the 1996 tax year, the Union of Italian Jewish Communities has been competing for allocations of the 'eight per thousand' share of IRPEF.

In the case of decisions that are not expressed, the Union participates in the allotment of the share not allocated in proportion to the decisions expressed in favour of Jewish communities.

Each year, all non-Catholic religious groups that have entered into an agreement with the State must submit a report to the Ministry of Interior on the effective use of the sums received from individual donors and from the State as its share of 'eight per thousand': this record – accompanied by a report – has then to be forwarded to the Ministry of Economy.

Other Contributions

To public funding through 'eight per thousand' and voluntary deductible donations, has to be added a series of tax concessions enjoyed by all religious denominations which have drafted agreements, arrangements or accords approved by law, and another set of contributions directly or indirectly related to the confessional world. These contributions include: the salaries of teachers of Catholic religion in public (State) schools (which are fully paid by the State under DPR – Presidential Decree- 399/1988 and Law 186/2003), the salaries of Catholic military chaplains (also included in the public budget in accordance with Law 512/1961), financial aid to private schools (often run by religious bodies) under Law 62/2000, funding for the construction of places of worship (arranged in various regional laws).

As to tax concessions, we may firstly recall Article 6 of the DPR no. 601/1973, which introduces a reduction of 50 per cent on corporate income tax (IRPEG) for a number of organizations and institutions.

Among them there are also the institutions whose purpose is assimilated by law for the purposes of charity and education, then also the bodies belonging to religious institutions that have entered into an agreement with the State and have obtained the recognition of their legal status.

With Circular no. 91 of 19 July 2005, the Revenue Agency has also clarified the extent of this concession, noting that it can apply only if there are two requirements: one subjective and one objective.

The institution concerned must be listed within the categories in Article 6 of DPR 601/1973, but also engaged in an activity which the legislator seeks to encourage, and this is the objective requirement. It follows that the ecclesiastical body is still subject to full payment of IRPEG, when engaging in activities other than those of religion and worship, including business or profit-making activities.

A further tax concession for denominational institutions concerns local council property tax (ICI) established by Legislative Decree no. 504 of 30 December 1992. The total tax exemption is provided for – among others – buildings used exclusively for practising worship, those used by so-called 'non-commercial organizations' exclusively dedicated to 'relief, social security, educational, receptive, cultural, recreational and sporting' activities and for 'religious activities and worship' in Article 16a of the Law of 20 May 1985, no. 222. To obtain the concession, a subjective element is therefore necessary (the use of the property by 'non-commercial entities', including 'legally recognized', ecclesiastical ones) and an objective element (the use of the building exclusively for the purposes listed, being socially relevant and non-profit making. The norm, and especially its implementation, is not free of uncertainties and clarification has repeatedly been sought by the legislator and case law. Among these, we may recall the Circular of the Ministry of Economy no. 2/2009, which pointed out that the ICI exemption can be applied only in cases where the aforementioned activities 'have not only a commercial nature' (see Article 7 § 2-bis, DL [Legislative Decree] 203/2005, as reformulated by Article 39, DL 223/2006, later Law 248/2006); therefore, for the purpose of entitlement to exemption, it is necessary that the activities carried out in the buildings for which the ICI exemption must be approved – should be carried out to meet the needs of social relevance which are not always provided by public structures and which are outside the sphere of action of private business operators.[39]

We should also recall the so-called 'national law on parish youth clubs' (Law 206/2003), which establishes the recognition and encouragement by the State of educational and social duties that are performed in local communities through the activities of parish youth clubs. This recognition ensures that the loss of income by the municipalities resulting from the ICI exemption on the building of oratories will be covered entirely by the State.[40] This facility – which is in addition to funds provided directly for the oratories at regional level – seems to be an excess of interventionism.

A new form of tax concession was introduced by Article 14 of the Law of 14 May 2005 no. 80. This new provision is intended to encourage the activities of organizations that make up the so-called 'third sector' and establishes that

> liberalities in money or in nature paid by natural persons or by entities subject to the income tax of societies in favour of non-profit organizations of social utility ... are deductible from the total income of the donor within 10 per cent of the total declared income, and in any case within a maximum of €70,000 per year.

With the subsequent circular no. 39 of 19 August 2005, the Revenue Agency has indicated that – among those persons who can receive tax-deductible donations – there are also the so-called partial NPOs, or 'ecclesiastical bodies of religious denominations with which the State has signed pacts, agreements or accords ... to

---

39   Nicola Fiorita, 'Prime riflessioni sulla politica ecclesiastica degli ultimi anni: enti ecclesiastici e agevolazioni fiscali' (2006) 2 *Diritto pubblico* 441–66.

40   Maria Luisa Lo. Giacco, 'La legge sugli oratori tra funzione sociale e libertà religiosa' (2004) 115 *Il diritto ecclesiastico* 144–59.

the extent of performing the activities listed in Article 10 § 1, Legislative Decree no. 460 of 1997'. To receive the financial contribution, the organization concerned shall ensure the keeping of complete accounting and analytical records, in order to ensure sufficient transparency of the activity.[41]

The discriminations made by the legislator are obvious, even in this case; in fact, once again, all entities of groups that have not concluded an agreement with the State are excluded by those who are eligible for the donation. This is a differentiation hopelessly affecting equal freedom of religious groups.

More recently, another facility that is part of Article 1 § 337 of Law no. 226 of 2005 was introduced and it provides the possibility for individual taxpayers to allocate their 'five per thousand' of the amount due as tax on personal income tax in favour of particular people and the pursuit of specific objectives identified by the norm itself.

Among the agencies that may be recipients of such contributions figure also ecclesiastical entities, if they are non-profit organizations under the Legislative Decree no. 460 of 1997, or because they operate in one of the fields of activities planned for non-profit organizations and they have to be part of the list specifically set up by the Revenue Agency.

The justification for such facilities has been identified in the transition from welfare state to welfare community.[42] This transition leads to the lightening of the tax burden, to the support of processes of privatization of public enterprises and to the replacement of private enterprise by the State in a number of areas of high social relevance traditionally reserved for the State itself. This replacement obviously entails a lightening of government spending and greater efficiency in theory, but also an obligation on the State to promote and support the private action involved: the direct intervention of the latter in the traditional operational areas of entities at issue would, in fact, lead to much greater expenditure by the welfare state, far more than the minor revenues resulting from the granting of concessions and tax exemptions.

Concluding Remarks

The Italian model – at least in our opinion – is a good starting point if we want to create an 'ideal type' of the funding system of worship. It enables in fact, an effective expression of 'tax democracy', ensuring all taxpayers have the right to choose whether to allocate a proportion of income tax to a church and also the right to choose to which denomination to allocate this sum.

In addition, it manages to provide support to churches without bearing too much upon the State budget: the high proportion of atheists, agnostics and those

---

41   Antonio Fuccillo, *Dare etico* (G. Giappichelli 2008) 97 *et seq*.

42   Maria Cristina Folliero, *Enti religiosi e non profit tra welfare state e welfare community. La transizione* (G. Giappichelli 2002).

who in any case feel they have to allocate money to religious denominations is – at least theoretically – able to reduce in acceptable terms the economic sacrifice of the nation.

However, it is clear that the Italian model requires many corrections, especially if we intend to bring back funding to churches under the motto of so-called 'sustainable development' and if we intend to justify its existence on the basis of the character of social utility that religious denominations can (and should) fulfil today in a new welfare state, characterized by the principle of subsidiarity and by the central role of local authorities.[43]

First, a real tax democracy which respects the right of religious freedom is established only if all faiths recognized as such are eligible for allocation of public funding. The distinction made by the Italian system, where only the groups that have entered into an agreement with the State then approved in law, may be admitted to the system of 'eight per thousand', was not only unacceptably discriminating between faiths 'without agreement' and groups which see their relationships with the State governed by law on the basis of accords, but it has distorted the original function intended by the 'Constituent Fathers (*Padri costituenti*)' for the instrument provided in the third paragraph of Article 8 of the Fundamental Law. In fact, in practice, agreement serves primarily as an instrument of emancipation from the law on recognized faiths of fascist origin, and as a technique for access to 'eight per thousand'. This is demonstrated by the fact that this happened in general by concluding 'photocopy' agreements modelled on the first of the agreements (the one with the Waldensians), which have subverted the original meaning of Article 8 of the Constitution, intended to protect the individual agreements governing the specific identities of all denominations, which cannot be protected by common law.

Secondly, the using of the share of the taxable income allocated to the State for purposes that are not entirely secular is not compatible with a real tax democracy which respects the right to religious freedom: here we should not forget what was decided by the third Berlusconi government (DPC published in the Official Gazette of 26 January 2005), under which a large proportion of funds allocated by the citizens of the State had been designed to fund the restoration of property and buildings of historical and artistic value of the Catholic Church (about €10 million, 10 per cent of the total 100 million of the State's share).[44]

---

43   Antonio Spadaro, 'Laicità e confessioni religiose: dalle etiche collettive (laiche e religiose) alla 'meta-etica' pubblica (costituzionale)', in Associazione Italiana dei Costituzionalisti, *Annuario 2007. Problemi pratici della laicità agli inizi del XXI secolo* (CEDAM 2008) 140 *et seq.*

44   Emilio Vitali, 'Il modello di finanziamento italiano: considerazioni del discussant' (2006) 117 *Il diritto ecclesiastico* 462–8.

List of References

Astorri R, 'Leggi eversive, soppressioni delle corporazioni religiose e beni culturali' in F Gemini (ed.), *La memoria silenziosa. Formazione, tutela e status giuridico degli archivi monastici nei monumenti nazionali* ; atti del convegno, Veroli, Abbazia di Casamari 6–7 novembre 1998, Ferentino, Palazzo comunale 8 novembre 1998 (Roma 2000)

Calamandrei P, *Innesto confessionale, in Scritti e discorsi politici*, I, 1 (La Nuova Italia 1966)

Calisse C, *Diritto ecclesiastico* (Barbèra 1893)

Casuscelli G, 'Pluralismo confessionale e organizzazione dei culti acattolici. Contributo all'interpretazione sistematica del primo e secondo comma dell'art. 8 della Costituzione' in A Alessandro et al., *Scritti in onore di Salvatore Pugliatti*, III (Giuffrè 1978) 235–313

Consorti P, *La remunerazione del clero* (G. Giappichelli 2000)

De Luca L, *Diritto ecclesiastico ed esperienza giuridica* (Giuffrè 1970)

Del Giudice V, *Corso di Diritto ecclesiastico*, 4th edn (Giuffrè 1939)

—— *Manuale di Diritto ecclesiastico*, 8th edn (Giuffrè 1955)

—— *Manuale di diritto ecclesiastico*, 10th edn (Giuffrè 1964)

Feliciani G, 'Gli istituti per il sostentamento del clero nella nuova normativa della CEI' (1985) 36 *Aggiornamenti sociali*

—— 'Sostentamento del clero' *Enciclopedia del Diritto* vol. 43 (Giuffrè 1990)

—— 'L'applicazione della legge 20 maggio 1985, no. 222. Gli esiti di una ricerca' (2006) 117 *Il diritto ecclesiastico*

Fiorita N, 'L'autofinanziamento agevolato: critica di una definizione' (1997) 108 *Il diritto ecclesiastico*

—— *Remunerazione e previdenza dei ministri di culto* (Giuffré 2003)

—— 'Prime riflessioni sulla politica ecclesiastica degli ultimi anni: enti ecclesiastici e agevolazioni fiscali' (2006) 2 *Diritto pubblico*

Folliero MC, *Enti religiosi e non profit tra welfare state e welfare community. La transizione* (G. Giappichelli 2002)

Friedberg E, *Trattato del Diritto ecclesiastico cattolico ed evangelico*, edizione italiana riveduta in collaborazione con l'autore dall'Avv. Francesco Ruffini (Bocca 1893)

Fuccillo A, *Dare etico* (G. Giappichelli 2008)

Giacco MLL, 'La legge sugli oratori tra funzione sociale e libertà religiosa' (2004) 115 *Il diritto ecclesiastico*

Gorresio V, *Risorgimento scomunicato* (Parenti 1958)

Jemolo AC, 'La natura e la portata dell'art.1 dello Statuto' (1913) *Rivista di diritto pubblico*

—— 'Il 'partito cattolico' piemontese nel 1855 e la legge sarda soppressiva delle comunità religiose' in *Il Risorgimento italiano*, XI–XII (1918–1919) (Stralcio da periodico)

—— *Chiesa e Stato in Italia dall'unificazione ai giorni nostri* XII rist. of 'editio minor' (1955, 1996)

—— *Lezioni di Diritto ecclesiastico*, 5th edn (Giuffrè 1979)

Piacentini M, *I culti ammessi nello Stato italiano* (Ulrico Hoepli 1934)

Piovani P, 'Da un temporalismo all'altro' *Un secolo da Porta Pia* (Guida editore 1970)

Pistolesi I, 'La quota dell'otto per mille di competenza statale: un'ulteriore forma di finanziamento (diretto) per la Chiesa cattolica?'(2006) 1 *Quaderni di Diritto e Politica ecclesiastica*

Rignano I, *Della uguaglianza civile e della libertà dei culti* (Franc. Vigo 1868)

Scaduto F, *Diritto ecclesiastico vigente in Italia*, I (Bocca 1892)

Schouppe J-P, *Diritto patrimoniale canonico* (Giuffrè 2008)

Scialoja A, 'La Chiesa, lo Stato e la liquidazione dell'Asse ecclesiastico'(1867) serie I, 5 *Nuova Antologia*

Spadaro A, 'Laicità e confessioni religiose: dalle etiche collettive (laiche e religiose) alla 'meta-etica' pubblica (costituzionale)' in Associazione Italiana dei Costituzionalisti, *Annuario 2007. Problemi pratici della laicità agli inizi del XXI secolo* (CEDAM 2008)

Vitali E, *Vilipendio della religione dello Stato – Contributo all'interpretazione dell'art. 402 del Codice penale* (CEDAM 1964)

—— 'Legislatio libertatis e prospettazioni sociologiche nella recente dottrina ecclesiasticistica' (1980) 90, I *Il Diritto ecclesiastico*

—— 'Il modello di finanziamento italiano: considerazioni del discussant' (2006) 117 *Il diritto ecclesiastico*

Zingali G, *I rapporti finanziari tra Stato e Chiesa e il trattamento fiscale agli enti di culto* (Vallardi 1943)

Chapter 10

Paying the Piper? Public Funding and Supervision of Religion in a Secularized Society (United Kingdom)

Frank Cranmer

Introduction: the Current Situation of Religion in the United Kingdom[1]

Early results from the 2011 United Kingdom Census[2] – which, for the second time included an optional question on respondents' religious affiliations – revealed that about nine per cent of the population of England and Wales belongs to a non-Christian religious community. Christianity was the major religious presence with 33.2 million people (59.3 per cent of the population: down from 41 million in 2001). The second largest group was the 14.1 million people, roughly one in four, who professed no religion whatsoever. Next came 2.7 million Muslims (4.8 per cent: a rise from three per cent in 2001), some 800,000 Hindus, over 400,000 Sikhs, some 260,000 Jews and some 250,000 Buddhists. Seven per cent of respondents chose not to answer the question.[3]

---

1   Javier García Oliva and Russell Sandberg commented very helpfully – as always – on a very early draft of this chapter but bear no responsibility whatsoever for the result. The currency conversion rate is £1 = €1.16.

2   Office of National Statistics, *Religion in England and Wales 2011*. Published online 11 December 2012 <http://www.ons.gov.uk/ons/dcp171776_290510.pdf> accessed 27 February 2013.

3   Office of National Statistics (n 2). In Northern Ireland a question about religion has been asked since 1861. The question in the 2011 Census distinguished between the major Christian denominations and, of those who answered, out of a population of 1.81 million 85 per cent were Christians of one sort or another: 41 per cent were Roman Catholic, 19 per cent members of the Presbyterian Church in Ireland, 14 per cent from the Church of Ireland and 3 per cent Methodists. A further six per cent belonged to other Christian denominations and a mere 0.8 per cent to non-Christian religions, while 17 per cent either professed no religion at all or declined to answer. Northern Ireland Statistics and Research Agency, *Census 2011: Key Statistics for Northern Ireland,* Table KS211NI. Published online 11 December 2012 <http://www.nisra.gov.uk/Census/key_report_2011.pdf> accessed 27 February 2013.

At the time of writing only preliminary census data was available for Scotland.

Paradoxically, the United Kingdom is becoming at once both increasingly multi-faith and, at least so far as its nominally Christian majority is concerned, increasingly secularized. *Laïcité* is not a concept that translates happily into English and there is no parallel to the strict constitutional separation between religion and the State that pertains in France or Turkey; nevertheless, traditional Christianity attracts fewer adherents with every passing year – the phenomenon that Grace Davie identified as 'believing without belonging'.[4] At the same time, the Muslim population, with much the lowest age-profile of the major faith communities, is increasing. A recent American study suggests that the Muslim population of the United Kingdom as a whole will rise from an estimated 2,869,000 in 2010 (which is broadly in line with the England and Wales 2011 Census data) to 5,567,000 by 2030.[5]

Furthermore, though the Church of England and the Church of Scotland enjoy a particular legal status that differs both from that of other Christian denominations and faith communities and from each other, in recent years 'religion' has increasingly come to be seen by government as a private matter for the individual believer.

This situation is to some extent reinforced by the classic doctrine on individual freedom of action and public interference in private activities expounded by Lord Donaldson MR in *Attorney-General v Guardian Newspapers Ltd (no.2)*:[6] 'the starting point of our domestic law is that every citizen has a right to do what he likes, unless restrained by the common law ... or by statute'.

Perhaps surprisingly, therefore, unlike many other members of the Council of Europe, the United Kingdom does not have any system of preferential or compulsory registration of faith communities[7] as a necessary precondition of their being allowed to practise their religions. As we shall see, there are statutory provisions that enable faith communities and congregations to register as charities for other reasons that are largely financial; but the practice of religion *per se* is unregulated except for the need to comply with the general law. Moreover, unless they are forced into a corner – for example by the recent spate of disputes about religious dress, mostly but not exclusively in the context of regulations on school

---

4   Grace Davie, *Religion in Britain since 1945: Believing Without Belonging* (Blackwell Publishers 1994).

5   Pew Forum, *The Future of the Global Muslim Population: Projections for 2010–2030.* Published online 27 January 2011 <http://pewforum.org/The-Future-of-the-Global-Muslim-Population.aspx> accessed 27 February 2013.

6   *Attorney-General v Guardian Newspapers Ltd (no.2)* [1990] 1 AC 109.

7   As, for example, do Austria and, in a more extreme form, Moldova: see *Religionsgemeinschaft der Zeugen Jehovas & Ors v Austria* [2008] ECtHR 762; *Verein der Freunde der Christengemeinschaft & Ors v Austria* [2009] ECtHR 353 and *Masaev v Moldova* [2009] ECtHR 774. For a discussion of the current situation on registration of religion in Europe, see Norman Doe, *Law and Religion in Europe: a comparative introduction* (OUP 2011) 94–6.

uniform[8] – judges are showing an increasing reluctance to involve themselves to any great extent in matters of religion, taking the view that, except in very particular circumstances, such as actions in relation to property held on trust,[9] religion is not their concern and they are in any case ill-equipped to adjudicate on matters touching on religious belief.[10] Perhaps the most trenchant expression of current judicial thinking on the relationship between law and religion was that made by Laws LJ, *obiter*, in *McFarlane v Relate Avon Ltd*:[11]

---

8   See *R (on the application of Begum) v Headteacher and Governors of Denbigh High School* [2006] UKHL 15 (refusal to permit Muslim schoolgirl to wear the long *jilbab* coat); *Azmi v Kirklees MBC* [2007] UKEAT/0009/07/30003 (refusal of school to allow Muslim support worker to wear *niqab* veil in classroom); *R (on the application of Playfoot (A Child)) v Millais School Governing Body* [2007] EWHC Admin 1698 (refusal to allow Christian girl to wear 'purity ring' in order to manifest belief in premarital chastity); *R (on the application of X) v Y School* [2007] EWHC 298 (Admin) (refusal to allow Muslim schoolgirl to wear *niqab* veil); *R (on the application of Watkins-Singh) v The Governing Body of Aberdare Girls' High School* [2008] EWHC (Admin) 1865 (wearing the Sikh *kara* bangle at school); *Noah v Desrosiers t/a Wedge* [2008] ET/2201867/07 (Muslim hairstylist insisting on wearing headscarf at all times) and *Eweida and Ors v United Kingdom* [2013] ECtHR 37 (refusal to allow Christian employees to wear visible cross or crucifix with uniforms).

9   See, for example, *Free Church of Scotland (Continuing) v General Assembly of the Free Church of Scotland* [2005] CSOH 46, in which the Lord Ordinary (Lady Paton) had to decide whether, by splitting off from the Free Church of Scotland in 2000, the Free Church of Scotland (Continuing) had forfeited its entitlement to any of the property and assets held in trust for the Church from which it had split: she concluded that neither party had departed from the fundamental tenets of the undivided Free Church, nor had either party forfeited its entitlement to the trust property and assets.

10   See, for example, *Blake v Associated Newspapers Ltd* [2003] EWHC 1960 (QB) (action for defamation stayed because, were it to proceed, it would involve the court in 'substantive doctrinal questions including the canon law of the Catholic Apostolic Churches [and] questions of ecclesiastic procedure' which were not justiciable (at para 33)); *HH Sant Baba Jeet Singh Ji Maharaj v Eastern Media Group Limited & Anor* [2010] EWHC 1294 (QB) (action for defamation stayed because of 'the well-known principle of English law to the effect that the courts will not attempt to rule upon doctrinal issues or intervene in the regulation or governance of religious groups' (at para 5)); *Shergill v Purewal & Anor* [2010] EWHC 3610 (QB) (action for defamation stayed because the pleadings inevitably raised 'doctrinal issues relating to the Sikh religion and its traditions' and it was impossible to circumvent 'the insuperable obstacle placed in the way of a fair trial of the action by the fact that the court is bound to abstain from determining questions which lie at the heart of the case' (at para 35)) and *Khaira & Ors v Shergill & Ors* [2012] EWCA Civ 983 and *Shergill v Khaira & Ors* [2012] EWCA Civ 1582 (dispute about the trusteeship and governance of two Sikh *gurdwaras*: in the second the appeal was dismissed because 'we do not think that this dispute is justiciable in the English courts': *per* Mummery LJ at 6).

11   [2010] EWCA Civ B1: *McFarlane* was one of the conjoined cases in the *Eweida* appeal in Strasbourg.

The promulgation of law for the protection of a position held purely on religious grounds cannot ... be justified. It is irrational, as preferring the subjective over the objective. But it is also divisive, capricious and arbitrary. We do not live in a society where all the people share uniform religious beliefs. The precepts of any one religion – any belief system – cannot, by force of their religious origins, sound any louder in the general law than the precepts of any other. If they did, those out in the cold would be less than citizens; and our Constitution would be on the way to a theocracy, which is of necessity autocratic. The law of a theocracy is dictated without option to the people, not made by their judges and governments. The individual conscience is free to accept such dictated law; *but the State, if its people are to be free, has the burdensome duty of thinking for itself.*[12]

The Historical Context

Any discussion of 'religion' in the United Kingdom cannot ignore the fact that the United Kingdom comprises three separate legal jurisdictions – England and Wales, Scotland and Northern Ireland – and the precise position both in legal and religious terms differs slightly between them. The Church of England is the church established by law in England and the Church of Scotland is the church established by law in Scotland and, though many of the other churches in the United Kingdom also have a statutory basis,[13] in legal and constitutional terms the Church of England and the Church of Scotland are *sui generis*. There is no establishment of religion in Wales or Northern Ireland.

At the Reformations,[14] the Church of England (which originally included within its jurisdictional boundaries what is now the Church in Wales), the Church of Ireland and the (Reformed) Church of Scotland were financed by a combination of their own land-holdings, the donations and legacies of the faithful and the obligation

---

12 At para. 24: emphasis added. For detailed analyses of *McFarlane* see R Sandberg, 'Laws and Religion: Unravelling *McFarlane v Relate Avon Limited*' (2010) 12, 3 *Ecclesiastical Law Journal* 361–70; and F Cranmer, 'Beating People Is Wrong: *Campbell and Cosans, Williamson* and their Aftermath' in M Hunter-Henin (ed), *Law, Religious Freedoms and Education in Europe* (Ashgate 2012).

13 For example, under the Methodist Church Union Act 1929 and Methodist Church Act 1976 and the United Reformed Church Acts 1972, 1981 and 2000. These were private acts promoted by the churches in question; part of the reason for promoting them was to ensure that there could be no challenge on doctrinal grounds to the future use of assets held on trust.

14 'Reformations' in the plural because the process in Scotland was different from that in England, Wales and Ireland – Scotland then being a separate State with its own Crown, Parliament and legal system.

on parishioners to pay tithes (in Scotland, 'teinds') which persisted, albeit in a somewhat attenuated form, until well into the twentieth century.[15] Subsequently:

- the Church of England retained its land-holdings: its current investments in United Kingdom and overseas company shares, private equity and gilts, urban and rural property and holdings in overseas managed property funds are worth some €6 billion;
- the Church of Ireland was disestablished and disendowed by the Irish Church Act 1869;
- the Church in Wales was disestablished by the Welsh Church Act 1914 – the operation of which was left in abeyance until the end of the First World War – and largely disendowed when disestablishment came in 1920; and
- the Church of Scotland retained its historical endowments.

That is the formal position in relation to resources which are now the property of the Churches, but which might once have been regarded in some sense as 'public money' because they derived originally from public endowments. But, more generally, tensions exist between the principle of the free organization of charities (which include religious communities) and the need for them to account for the proper use of public funds.

The Status of Religious Bodies

As indicated above, in the absence of any comprehensive system of registration, religious organizations are, generally speaking, charities: all three of the modern territorial statutes include 'the advancement of religion' for the public benefit in the list of activities that are regarded as charitable[16] and, in so doing, give statutory recognition to the third 'head of charity' enunciated by Lord Macnaghten in *Pemsel*: 'trusts for the advancement of religion'.[17]

Depending on their place of operation, charities are ultimately accountable for their activities to the Charity Commission for England and Wales (CCEW), to the Office of the Scottish Charity Regulator (OSCR) or to the Charity Commission for

---

15 In Wales, for example, there was a tithe distraint sale at Gwersyllt Old Hall Farm, Wrexham, as late as 1933: see Carol Twinch, *Tithe War 1918–1939: The Countryside in Revolt* (Media Associates 2001).

16 S. 7(2)(c) Charities and Trustee Investment (Scotland) Act 2005; s. 3(1)(c) Charities Act 2011 (which consolidated the earlier legislation for England and Wales) and s. 2(2)(c) Charities Act (Northern Ireland) 2008. Many Irish Churches and charities are all-Ireland institutions and in the Republic 3(1)(b) of the Charities Act 2009 makes similar provision.

17 *Income Tax Special Purpose Commissioners v Pemsel* [1891] AC 531 at 583.

Northern Ireland (CCNI).[18] Subject to certain exceptions, charities must register with the appropriate regulator;[19] they must maintain proper accounts in accordance with the Statement of Recommended Practice (SORP) for Charities and they must adhere to the general law of trusts operating in the three jurisdictions. However, very small charities do not have to register while, under the provisions of the Charities (Exception from Registration) Regulations 1996 as amended by the Charities (Exception from Registration) (Amendment) Regulations 2012, certain churches in England and Wales continue to be excepted from the duty to register with the CCEW until 31 March 2014.[20]

That said, however, it is not necessarily the case that a religious body will automatically be a charity. The best-known example of a religious organization that is not is the Church of Scientology, which the Charity Commission refused to register on the grounds, *inter alia*, that Scientology was not a religion for the purposes of English charity law and that, even if it were so, its public benefit could not merely be presumed, given its relative newness and the public and judicial concern expressed about its activities.[21] More recently, the Commission refused to register the Gnostic Centre on the grounds that it did not provide public benefit by advancing education (*not*, it should be noted, by advancing religion) but merely encouraged a particular viewpoint based on the teachings and beliefs of Gnosticism.[22] The Commission has, however, registered the Druid Network,[23] which describes itself in its constitution as 'an ancient pagan religion ... based on the reverential, sacred and honourable relationship between the people and the land ... [and] the spiritual interaction between an individual and the spirits of nature'.[24]

18　In the Republic of Ireland, plans to establish the Charities Regulatory Authority provided for by Part 2 of the Charities Act 2009 were abandoned on grounds of cost.

19　At the time of writing, registration was not yet fully in force in Northern Ireland.

20　The churches specified under the 1996 Regulations are churches within the meaning of section 2 of the Baptist and Congregational Trusts Act 1951, churches affiliated to the Fellowship of Independent Evangelical Churches, the Unitarian and Free Christian Churches, the Presbyterian Church of Wales, the Church of England, the Church in Wales, the Methodist Church, the Religious Society of Friends (Quakers) and the United Reformed Church.

21　*Church of Scientology (England and Wales), Re* [1999] Charity Commn (17 November 1999) and see also *R v Registrar General ex parte Segerdal & Anor* [1970] 3 WLR 479 CA (about an application from the Church of Scientology to register a chapel as a place of public religious worship – which would have exempted it from local property taxes). At the time of writing, the judgement in *Segerdal* was likely to be challenged in an appeal against a refusal to permit a religious marriage in a Church of Scientology chapel: *Hodkin & Ors, R (on the application of) v Registrar General of Births, Deaths and Marriages* [2012] EWHC 3635 (Admin).

22　*Gnostic Centre, Re* [2009] Charity Commn (16 December 2009).

23　*Druid Network, Re* [2010] Charity Commn (21 September 2010).

24　*Druid Network, Re* [2010] Annex 2.

Registration as a charity, therefore, depends ultimately on a value judgment by the appropriate regulator – and one might well ask what particular theological expertise the various regulators bring to that task.

Control of Public Funds

Increasingly, charities are undertaking to provide social and community services under contracts with local and central government and there is considerable concern within the charity sector that what has come to be called 'the contract culture' might erode their independence. A report by the CCEW in 2007, *Stand and Deliver*, concluded that:

> public service delivery is having an impact upon the independence and governance of charities. It would be of concern to the Commission if these findings translated into:
>
> a charity carrying out activities or services outside its objects or powers in order to gain funding;
>
> a public authority exercising control over a charity's decision-making processes in such a way that the trustees were prevented from acting solely in the charity's interests: or
>
> insufficient involvement by a charity's trustees in decisions about what activities the charity should undertake.

Potentially, this could impact on religious organizations: not because they are 'religious' but because they are major providers of social services. For example, in England and Wales the Salvation Army is almost certainly the biggest single provider of social services outside central and local government: in London alone it operates two residential detoxification services, a day-care centre for children, seven residential 'lifehouses', two non-residential centres for the homeless and two residential homes for elderly people. Similarly, the social services arm of the Church of Scotland, CrossReach, employs more than 2,000 staff in various forms of social care and its total expenditure in 2011 was some £110/€128 million. The Kirk itself provides very little of CrossReach's resources: most of its income comes from local authorities contracts, from donations and from legacies.[25]

Inevitably, tensions will sometimes arise between the principle of the free organization of religion and the legitimate interest of central and local government in the proper use of public funds and the extent of the margin of appreciation

---

25 Church of Scotland, *CrossReach: what we do*. Published online 2009 <http://www.crossreach.org.uk/what-we-do> accessed 27 February 2013.

to be accorded to religious communities in that respect is both delicate and complex. A recent example of those tensions has been the degree to which religious communities may offer publicly funded services in accordance with their theological convictions, even where those convictions conflict with the general law, and this has been brought into very sharp focus by two recent cases involving provision of adoption services.

The Equality Act (Sexual Orientation) Regulations 2007 included an obligation on adoption agencies not to discriminate on grounds of sexual orientation and, in January 2007, the then government decided that there could be no exemptions for faith-based adoption agencies that were publicly funded. At the time, there were 30 voluntary adoption agencies in England, every one of which derived its income from fees from local authorities for each suitable adoptive family that it found. Faith-based adoption agencies were given a period of grace until 31 December 2008 to change their practices where they conflicted with the sexual orientation obligation; but Catholic Care, an adoption agency based in Leeds, attempted to circumvent the 2007 Regulations by asking the Charity Commission if it could change its charitable objects to state that '[t]he Charity shall only provide adoption services to heterosexuals and such services to heterosexuals will only be provided in accordance with the tenets of the [Roman Catholic] Church'. The Commission refused consent.

The 2007 Regulations were repealed and their content subsumed into the Equality Act 2010. Under section 193 of the 2010 Act it is permissible to restrict the provision of benefits to persons who share a protected characteristic (of which, by virtue of section 4, religion or belief is one), if the person acts in pursuance of a charitable instrument and if the provision of the benefits is a proportionate means of achieving a legitimate aim or for the purpose of preventing or compensating for a disadvantage linked to the protected characteristic. Catholic Care tried to take advantage of this provision and the resulting litigation has been a long-running saga with several appeals both to what was then the Charity Tribunal and to the High Court. Judgment in the most recent appeal was handed down in November 2012[26] and Catholic Care was unsuccessful yet again.

Most recently, the focus has moved to Scotland, where the Office of the Scottish Charity Regulator told St Margaret's Children and Family Care Society, a Glasgow-based Roman Catholic adoption agency, that it had failed the charity test under section 7 of the Charities and Trustee Investment (Scotland) Act 2005, because it gives preference as prospective parents to couples who have been married for two years or more and, in effect, discriminates against unmarried and same-sex couples.[27] The Scottish Government has expressed some concern about

---

26 *Catholic Care (Diocese of Leeds) v Charity Commission for England and Wales* [2012] CA/2010/0007 UKUT (Tax & Chancery).

27 Office of the Scottish Charity Regulator: Report under section 33 of the Charities and Trustee Investment (Scotland) Act 2005: St Margaret's Children and Family Care Society SC028551 (Dundee 2013).

the regulator's decision and, at the time of writing, the matter was subject to further discussions between the charity, the regulator and Scottish Government officials.[28]

During his State Visit to the United Kingdom in September 2010, Pope Benedict XVI addressed both Houses of Parliament and, in the course of his speech,[29] made what looked remarkably like a veiled reference to Catholic Care:

> I am convinced that ... there are many areas in which the Church and the public authorities can work together for the good of citizens ... For such cooperation to be possible, religious bodies – including institutions linked to the Catholic Church – need to be free to act in accordance with their own principles and specific convictions based upon the faith and the official teaching of the Church. In this way, such basic rights as religious freedom, freedom of conscience and freedom of association are guaranteed.

But how to reconcile the freedom of religious bodies 'to act in accordance with their own principles' with the legitimate public interest in equality and non-discrimination – especially where the charity relies on public funding – remains an extremely difficult and sensitive issue.

Are Certain Religions Subject to Greater Controls than Others?

As we have seen, in the United Kingdom the practice of religion is, generally speaking, a private law matter. Unlike the situation in some European States, where registration is either compulsory or only avoidable at the cost of extreme inconvenience, there is no obligation on any religious group to register with local or central government. Therefore, if people choose to practise a religion in private and do not offend the general law while doing so, they will simply not engage with government or with the common law in any of the three jurisdictions.

There is one major exception to this: the General Synod of the Church of England has power to enact primary legislation ('Measures') which is then subject to affirmative resolution of both Houses of Parliament[30] and to promulgate and amend its own canons. In one sense, that might look like 'greater control' by the State but, in another, it could equally be regarded as an enormous privilege. Uniquely among Church governing bodies in England, it is possible for the General Synod of the Church of England to enact legislation which can amend or even

---

28   Daniel Lombard, 'Scottish government pledges to help Catholic adoption agency' (11 February 2013) *Third Sector*.

29   Joseph Alois Ratzinger, *Speech to both Houses of Parliament*. Published online 18 September 2010 <http://www.thepapalvisit.org.uk/Replay-the-Visit/Speeches/Speeches-17-September/Pope-Benedict-s-address-to-Politicians-Diplomats-Academics-and-Business-Leaders> accessed 27 February 2013.

30   Church of England Assembly (Powers) Act 1919.

repeal statute law: for example, the Church of England (Worship and Doctrine) Measure 1974 repealed the remaining live provisions of the Acts of Uniformity 1548 and 1558 and the whole of the Act of Uniformity 1662 except for sections 10 and 15.

Where religious groups start to come under more general 'control' is when they seek privileges that confer particular financial or administrative benefits: either registration under the Places of Worship Registration Act 1855[31] and the concomitant exemption from paying local property taxes ('non-domestic rates') or recognition as charities under the relevant territorial statute and the tax benefits that flow from that recognition.

If, however, a religious group does neither of these, it can nevertheless operate totally undisturbed – though it has been suggested that in England and Wales it may be possible to set up a charity unwittingly, without a positive intention to do so, and thereby become subject to charity law.[32] Moreover, until recently, the CCEW was making great efforts to persuade non-Christian groups – particularly, though not exclusively, Muslim ones – to register as charities: partly because it would be in their financial interest to do so, but partly also because the Commission was worried that some unregistered groups were not complying with proper accounting standards. However, as we have seen, not all religious organizations – whatever their self-understanding – will be recognized by the regulators as fulfilling the necessary criteria for registration as a charity.

More controversially, after the 2005 London bombings the previous government started a programme called 'Prevent' as part of its counter-terrorism strategy. Prevent was largely about social cohesion projects, such as sports clubs and multicultural events, and public funding was some €150 million in 2008–9; but critics complained that almost all the money went to the Muslim community and that, in highlighting Islam, the programme was merely fostering insecurity among the Muslim population and doing as much harm as good. In its report on the Prevent programme, the House of Commons Communities and Local Government Committee (2010 paragraph 40) concluded that its approach might be

---

31   Registration is not possible for places of *private* worship or places where 'worship' as defined in common law does not take place. For a refusal to accept an application for registration on the grounds that what took place within the building was not 'worship' see *R v Registrar General ex parte Segerdal & Anor* [1970] 3 WLR 479 CA and note 18 above. For a refusal to accept an application for registration on the grounds that the building was private rather than public, see *Gallagher (Valuation Officer) v Church of Jesus Christ of Latter-day Saints* [2008] UKHL 56. *Gallagher* is currently being appealed to the European Court of Human Rights.

32   The argument is as follows: provided that a body has a constitution that is in valid charitable form, it will be a charity *ipso facto*, irrespective of the intentions of the settlors. The trustees will then be under a statutory duty to register it as a charity unless it falls into one of those classes of charity that are not currently required to register: 'exempt' charities, smaller 'excepted' charities and any charity in England and Wales with an annual income of £5,000/€5,800 or less.

counter-productive: 'We cannot ignore the volume of evidence we have seen and heard which demonstrates a continuing lack of trust of the [Prevent] programme amongst those delivering and receiving services.'

Possibly as a result of that criticism, in November 2010 the new Home Secretary, Theresa May, announced a review of the strategy for preventing violent extremism,[33] following which the strategy[34] was refocused with three objectives:

- to respond to the ideological challenge of terrorism and the threat from those who promote it;
- to prevent people from being drawn into terrorism and to ensure that they are given appropriate advice and support; and
- to work with sectors and institutions where there are risks of radicalization that need to be addressed.

Looked at in strictly legal, human rights terms, it is (or it certainly should be) impossible under the terms of the Human Rights Act 1998 for any government to treat one religious group differently from all the others;[35] and many of the difficulties of successive United Kingdom governments of all political persuasions in dealing with 'religion' have been driven by a fear of Islamic extremism – which has in turn led them to impose a more rigorous regime than previously on faith communities generally in relation, for example, to visa requirements for ministers of religion coming from outside the European Economic Area and Switzerland to work in the United Kingdom. The current Immigration Rules include two special categories for ministers of religion and those engaged in religious activity.

Tax Exemptions and Financial Support for Religious Activities and Institutions

Charitable Tax Reliefs

In the United Kingdom there is no direct automatic funding of religious communities *qua* religious communities. Insofar as faith communities benefit

---

33   HM Government, *Review of Counter-Terrorism and Security Powers: Review Findings and Recommendations* (Cm 8004) (TSO 2011).

34   Home Office, *Prevent strategy 2011.* Published online 7 June 2011 <http://www.homeoffice.gov.uk/publications/counter-terrorism/prevent/prevent-strategy> accessed 26 February 2013.

35   That is to say, in terms of such matters as freedom of speech and of assembly. The State is not precluded from giving particular recognition to a particular church: see *Darby v Sweden* (Application no. 11581/85) [1989] ECommHR (9 May 1989): [1990] ECtHR (23 October 1990).

from public financial support they do so as charities. Charities generally, religious or not, receive certain tax benefits not available to non-charitable bodies:

- charities are exempt from income and capital gains taxes;
- bequests to charities do not count towards the overall inheritance tax liability of the testator's estate;
- they enjoy certain specific VAT reliefs;
- they benefit from a considerable degree of relief from non-domestic rates;
- under the Gift Aid scheme, charities may reclaim the standard rate of tax on donations paid by donors who are prepared to make a formal declaration that they are taxpayers; and
- from April 2013, provided they fulfil some fairly basic criteria, they will be able to claim a 'Gift Aid-like' repayment of tax at the standard rate on cash donations up to an annual limit of £5,000: a maximum of £1,250/€1,450 per charity.[36]

Gift Aid, Accounting Obligations and the 'Fit and Proper Person' Test

One of the two most important sources of State support for charities generally is the Gift Aid scheme, under which a charity can reclaim from government the standard rate income tax paid by donors on the money that they have donated: 25 pence in the pound. Total Gift Aid repayments to all charities in 2011–12 were roughly £1/€1.2 billion and it is thought that some 20 per cent of the total repayments went to religious charities – in an average year about 10 per cent of Gift Aid repayments go to the Church of England alone.

The Court of Justice of the EU ruled in *Stauffer*[37] and *Persche*[38] that territorial restrictions on tax incentives for charitable giving contravened the provisions of the EU Treaty on the free movement of capital and, as a result, the previous government made provision in Schedule 6 to the Finance Act 2010 for Gift Aid claims by not-for-profit organizations established in the European Economic Area and in Switzerland. Any charitable body is obliged to keep proper accounts, any organization (whether charitable or not) receiving public money must account to the funding body for how the money has been spent and, more generally, charity trustees are under the common law obligation to act prudently and to operate within their charity's objects. That said, however, both HM Treasury and HM Revenue & Customs (HMRC) are deeply suspicious of the credentials and motives of certain foreign charities and not-for-profit organizations and under the terms of the schedule, in order to qualify as charitable for tax purposes, a trust wishing to

---

36   The scheme is, in fact, very complex: the above is merely a summary.

37   *Centro di Musicologia Walter Stauffer v Finanzamt München für Korperschaften* [2006] ECJ C–386/04.

38   *Hein Persche v Finanzamt Lüdenscheid* [2008] ECJ C–318/07.

reclaim tax – whether situated in the United Kingdom or outside it – must now satisfy three tests:

- that it is subject to the charity jurisdiction of a relevant United Kingdom court or of a court in the territory where it is registered;
- that it is registered in accordance with the appropriate domestic legislation; and
- that it is managed by 'fit and proper persons'.[39]

This last provision is a potential problem for United Kingdom charities. It is entirely foreseeable that a trust that has been properly registered as a charity or not-for-profit foundation with the appropriate regulator could still fail the 'fit and proper person' test, because HMRC does not regard its management as 'fit and proper'. For example, in the Church of England each parochial church council is a charitable trust in its own right and the members of the council *pro tem* are the trustees *ex officiis*. So if one of them were declared bankrupt (and therefore, presumably, no longer a 'fit and proper person') and continued to be a member of the council, would that mean that the council would no longer be able to make Gift Aid claims? And what of an independent congregation that has not established a separate trust and in which all the members are therefore trustees by default? Officials from HMRC have stated publicly that they intend to regulate the test with a light touch: but only time will tell how this will work out in practice and perhaps a religious charity and HMRC could one day find themselves in dispute.

Property Taxes and Places of Public Worship

As noted above, under the terms of the Places of Worship Registration Act 1855, as amended, a place of *public* worship in England and Wales certified as such by the Superintendent Registrar in the district where it is situated is wholly exempt from paying non-domestic rates. Churches belonging to the Church of England and the Church in Wales are also exempt from non-domestic rates – but exemption in their case is automatic and they are not required to register under the Act. No place of worship is *obliged* to register but it will not benefit from the exemption if it does not do so. In Scotland, churches and other places of worship are entered in the Valuation Roll for non-domestic rates but are wholly exempt from payment.[40] In addition, under the terms of the Local Government Finance Act 1988, other buildings occupied by charities for their charitable purposes qualify for a mandatory 80 per cent reduction in non-domestic rates and local authorities have discretion under the Act not to levy the remaining 20 per cent. The cost of

---

39   Finance Act 2010 Schedule 6 Part 1.

40   Scottish Government, *Non Domestic Rates – A Guide* Section 2.2. Published online December 2004 <http://www.scotland.gov.uk/Publications/2004/12/20460/49146> accessed 27 February 2013.

this to public funds is impossible to quantify – not least on account of the fact that, given their automatic exemption, places of worship belonging to the Church of England and the Church in Wales do not appear in the valuation lists *at all*. Some very rough indication may be derived from the position in Scotland, however, as the following example suggests.

Hamilton is a small burgh to the south-west of Glasgow with a population of 48,546 as recorded in the 2001 Census: its postcode district is ML3. A search of the current Valuation Roll (last updated in 2010) revealed that there were 27 places of worship in ML3 with a total valuation of £575,950 (some €668,000). The current non-domestic rate poundage payable as a proportion of rateable value in Scotland is 45p: on that basis, the exemption for places of worship in Hamilton is worth some £260,000/€301,600: an average of £9,630/€11,100 for each building or 5.3 pence per head of population.

Peter Brierley calculates that there are some 50,000 places of worship in the United Kingdom.[41] Scaled up from the (very small) sample from Hamilton, the non-business rates foregone would amount to some £480/€557 million. Even at a very conservative average annual rateable value of £2,000, the global amount of revenue foregone would be some £45/€52 million.[42] The further benefit of the 80 per cent reduction in non-domestic rates on other charitable buildings that belong to religious communities is simply impossible to quantify.

VAT and Buildings for 'Charitable Purposes'

Where a charity constructs or acquires by sale or by long lease a building that is to be used for a 'relevant charitable purpose' (that is, a building occupied by a charity other than in the course of business, as a village hall, or to provide social or recreational facilities for a local community) the construction or acquisition of the building is zero-rated for VAT.[43] In order to qualify, the building must be wholly used for charitable purposes: in practice, a *de minimis* non-charitable use of five per cent of the building's floor-area is permitted. A church would be zero-rated in almost all conceivable circumstances; but the *de minimis* threshold might come into play where the building was mixed-use: for example, a worship space with a café or book-shop attached.[44]

---

41   Peter Brierley, *Major UK Religious Trends, 2010 to 2020* (Peter Brierley Consultants 2011).

42   In reality, the annual rateable value of some of the larger churches in Scotland is considerably more than that: for example, £76,200/€88,400 for the High Kirk of St Giles and £62,800/€72,800 for St Mary's Cathedral, Palmerston Place – both in Edinburgh – and £20,000/€23,200 for St Andrew's Cathedral, Inverness.

43   HM Revenue & Customs 2008.

44   For a recent rating and valuation case on the issue of 'charitable use' of a church building, see *Ebury (Valuation Officer) v Church Council of the Central Methodist Church* [2009] 138 (LC) LT Case no. RA/33/2007 (17 July 2009).

In addition, until 31 October 2012, alterations to *all* listed buildings, whether owned by charities or in private hands, were zero-rated for VAT – while repairs were not. With VAT at 20 per cent, the zero rate on alterations was extremely important where, for example, the congregation of a large church decided to turn one of its transepts into a community meeting-place and install a kitchen area and lavatories. However, in the 2012 Budget, the Chancellor of the Exchequer announced the abolition of the zero rate on alterations. His ostensible reasoning was twofold: that the zero rate created a perverse incentive to alter a building rather than repair it and that it gave wealthy private owners of secular listed buildings what amounted to an unfair tax break.

It should be said that the Chancellor's perverse incentive argument was and is extremely thin: the installation of lavatories, for example, is not an alternative to repairing a leaking roof. As to the argument about 'fairness', whatever one's opinion of private owners being able to install basement swimming-pools without paying VAT, the knock-on effect of the change on charities and church buildings was simply disregarded. As we shall see, a temporary compromise was reached for listed places of worship; but the wider financial effects of the change on religious organizations have yet to be felt.

Support for Church Buildings and the Listed Places of Worship Grant Scheme

Government funding for the built heritage has come under considerable pressure as a result of recent spending cuts. The Heritage Lottery Fund estimated in 2011 that the annual reduction on overall public spending on heritage projects of all kinds (not just religious heritage projects) as a result of the Coalition Government's Comprehensive Spending Review would amount to some £650–675/€695–680 million.[45]

The various publicly financed heritage bodies give limited repair and refurbishment grants for places of worship of major cultural importance – *but that is because of their heritage value, not because they are 'religious'*. Between 1990 and 2009, English Heritage gave some £52/€60 million to fund conservation work at English cathedrals with the bulk going to the Church of England. Alex Glanville, Head of Property Services at the Church in Wales (which cares for 29 per cent of Welsh Grade I listed buildings) estimates that, in recent years, Cadw[46] has provided £500,000/€580,000 annually – but only to 'outstanding buildings'.[47]

A major general source of funding for the ecclesiastical built heritage has been the Listed Places of Worship Grant Scheme, introduced by the then Chancellor

45 House of Commons Culture, Media and Sport Committee, *Third Report of Session 2010–12: Funding of the Arts and Heritage* (TSO 2011) para. 159.

46 The Welsh counterpart of English Heritage: the name, pronounced 'Ca-doo' means 'to keep'.

47 Alex Glanville, 'The View from the Church in Wales' *Building Conservation* (2011).

of the Exchequer, Gordon Brown, in March 2001, initially as an interim scheme until 31 March 2011. Under the scheme, places of worship 'listed' by government as being of architectural and/or historical importance benefit from the refund of the difference between five per cent and the actual amount spent on VAT on eligible repairs and maintenance. Work done by Paul Walker[48] suggests that there are about 14,500 listed places of worship in the United Kingdom, of which about 85 per cent are in the care of the Church of England. Moreover, almost half of all listed buildings in the highest categories across the United Kingdom – Grade I in England and Wales and Grade A in Scotland and Northern Ireland – are places of worship.[49] The scope of the rebate was extended in March 2004 to cover the full amount of VAT levied on eligible works carried out on and after 1 April 2004 and the Department for Culture, Media and Sport calculated that, between 1 April 2001 and 30 June 2010, some £112/€130 million was refunded under the scheme.

The scheme as devised was in accordance with EU law because it provided matching *grants* rather than applying an unauthorized reduced rate of VAT – which would have been contrary to the Sixth VAT Directive.[50] However, the previous government wanted to make the scheme permanent and proposed to the European Commission that the Directive should be extended to permit a reduced rate specifically for repairs to listed places of worship. In spite of strong pressure from HM Treasury, however, the proposal was rejected at the meeting of the EU Finance Ministers (ECOFIN) in March 2009.

In addition to the rebuff from ECOFIN, the continuation of the scheme was called into question as a result of the Comprehensive Spending Review undertaken by the Coalition Government in the wake of the international financial crisis of 2007–2008 and, from January 2011, repairs to organs, pews, bells and clocks and – crucially – professional fees became ineligible for grants under the scheme. However, after considerable pressure from churches and heritage bodies, the government agreed to continue the scheme in its revised form until 31 March 2015 and to refund VAT at the increased rate of 20 per cent that came into effect from 1 January 2011 – but with quarterly fixed budgets rather than a rolling matching grant and subject to an annual ceiling on the total grants of some £12/€13.9 million. In the transition between the old eligibility criteria and the new it was likely that around £24/€27.9 million would eventually be paid in relation to claims for the 2010–11 financial year – around £10 million more than was expected.[51]

---

48   Paul Walker, 'Snapshot survey of listed churches' (2006) 98 March/April *Church Building*.

49   Jonathan Taylor, 'Protected Buildings: A Brief Guide to the Legislation' (2012) *Building Conservation* 26–7.

50   Council Directive 77/388/EEC of 17 May 1977 on the harmonization of the laws of the Member States relating to turnover taxes – Common system of value-added tax: uniform basis of assessment.

51   Department for Culture, Media and Sport, *Listed Places of Worship Grant Scheme.* Published online 2010 <http://www.lpwscheme.org.uk/> accessed 27 February 2013.

The loss of the zero rate of VAT on alterations to listed buildings, already mentioned, then brought the scope of the Listed Places of Worship Grant Scheme into question yet again and after long and hard negotiations by the Church of England, it was agreed that the scheme would be extended to include alterations as well as repairs and that the Treasury would make available an extra £30/€34.8 million to the scheme in each financial year for the remainder of the present Parliament – which is scheduled to end in 2015. Currently, therefore, the total available annual grant under the scheme is £42/€48.7 million.

It was thought that £30/€34.8 million represented fair compensation for the additional VAT; however, the decision has been criticized on the grounds that the concession applies only to listed *places of worship* and not to other listed buildings such as schools, colleges and parsonage houses in the care of religious communities. Moreover, the change has introduced a large degree of uncertainty into future funding arrangements. The new funding commitment is for the present Parliament only: nor could it be otherwise, since no government can bind its successors. Finally, the decision to revoke the zero rate is irrevocable since, under EU VAT law, once a reduced rate of VAT has been abolished, it cannot be reinstated except with the unanimous agreement of the individual member States – and it is inconceivable that such agreement would ever be forthcoming.

Training of Religious Leaders and State Support[52]

In the United Kingdom, the study of theology and religion is an academic activity like any other and, historically, universities have been given the same level of funding for theological students as for any other subject in the humanities. Though a handful of professorial chairs – four at Oxford and one at Durham – are annexed to cathedral canonries and therefore, in principle, open only to Anglicans,[53] the overwhelming majority of university teaching posts in theology are open to those of all faiths and none; profession of any kind of faith is not regarded as a necessary condition for the serious academic study of religion. If there has been any government support for training religious leaders, it has been by virtue of the fact that the vast majority of potential clergy in full-time training study theology

---

52   Some of this material appeared as 'La Présence Religieuse dans l'Enseignement Supérieur au Royaume-Uni' in Anne Fornerod (ed), *Assistance spirituelle dans les services publics* (Presses Universitaires 2012). I am indebted to The Revd Dr Stephen Heap, the Church of England's National Adviser on Higher Education, for his perceptive and helpful comments on an early draft of the material on ministerial training.

53   Though until recently the Oxford Chair in Ecclesiastical History was held by a lay Roman Catholic, Professor Henry Mayr-Harting, who duly took his turn with the other Residentiary Canons of the Cathedral to officiate at Matins and Evensong in the Cathedral. The Dean of the Cathedral is also the Head of House of Christ Church and must therefore be an Anglican priest.

at public universities alongside secular students – and their fees (like everyone else's) have been heavily subsidized.

But all that has changed. The Westminster Government decided to increase the current limit on university tuition fees in England to £9,000/€10,440 for 2012–13 and all the most selective institutions (including Oxford, Cambridge and Durham: three of the biggest theology departments in England) opted to charge the maximum permissible fee. That in itself made the academic study of theology vastly more expensive and, to make matters worse, the government also decided that, in England, teaching for all arts, humanities and social science subjects would no longer be publicly funded, resulting in severe funding cuts for university departments of theology and religious studies. When combined with the possibility that fewer people will want to study religion when they could choose something more obviously marketable like law, accountancy or business studies, the recent changes have raised a fundamental question: will theology and religious studies survive in England as a widely studied academic discipline?

So far as the churches are concerned, the rise in tuition fees is making the most selective institutions vastly more expensive and training costs for full-time students reading first degrees in theology have risen dramatically.[54] Moreover, in 2007, the then government decided – as part of its general desire to widen access to higher education – to concentrate financial support at the institutional level on first-time students and to withdraw funding from Higher Education institutions in respect of students pursuing 'equivalent or lower qualifications' (ELQs) to those that they already hold. Unfortunately for the churches, many ordinands begin training in their thirties or even later and a high proportion has already graduated in other disciplines. Figures from their ministerial training divisions indicate that, in early 2008, about 75 per cent of Church of England trainees held qualifications equivalent to or higher than those for which they were studying at theological college, while for the Methodist Church the figure was approximately 40 per cent. The churches argued that if the universities were to lose funding for ordinands pursuing ELQs in theology and had to increase their tuition fees, they in turn would have to contain their own training costs, either by restricting the number of training places or by making other economies which would lower academic standards. For the Church of England alone, the estimate of the total cost of the changes for 2011 was £1.55/€1.8 million.[55] The Churches also pointed out that the policy seemed to be at odds with the previous government's avowed desire, in the interests of social cohesion, to see better educated faith leaders.[56]

---

54   G James and D Eastwood, *ELQs and the Churches' Ministerial Training – A Review* (published online 2008).

55   Church of England Ministry Division, *A Review of Models and Funding of Pre-Ordination Training in the light of the Proposed Changes to HE Funding*: summary paper circulated to the General Synod – GS 1836/2011 (General Synod 2011).

56   Higher Education Funding Council for England, *Withdrawal of funding for equivalent or lower qualifications (ELQs) Consultation on implementation*. Published

In the wider context, the previous government commissioned an independent review 'to examine, with the communities, how to build the capacity of Islamic seminaries, learning from other faith communities as well as from experience overseas'. Among the themes identified in the report were:

- the need for the integration of theory and practice;
- proper academic accreditation of training courses;
- development and expansion of existing courses in Islamic pastoral care and counselling; and
- continuing professional development of Islamic faith leaders.

The authors of the study concluded that[57]

> Government has a key role to play in supporting the developments and improvements which providers of Muslim faith leadership training seek ... and in facilitating closer partnerships and relationships between Muslim institutions and publicly-funded institutions.

Whether this will be taken forward by the present government remains to be seen.

Chaplaincy

Chaplaincy in Higher Education

Higher education chaplaincy is largely a matter for the individual churches and the individual universities and its extent and nature vary widely between institutions, because the institutions themselves vary so widely. Almost every college of Oxford, Cambridge and Durham has a chaplain of its own and because, under their statutes, almost all of them are Anglican, their chaplains are normally Anglicans also.

Chaplaincy in a modern provincial university will most likely be provided by the various denominations themselves: there will probably be full or part-time Roman Catholic, Church of England and Free Church chaplains funded by their denominations and supplemented by unpaid chaplaincy from the other local faith communities. In addition, some universities have historic arrangements with particular denominations to provide a chaplain and in many cases the costs of such an appointment are shared, so that the chaplain's stipend might be paid by

---

online September 2007 <http://www.hefce.ac.uk/pubs/hefce/2007/07_27/07_27.pdf> accessed 27 February 2013.

57 Department for Communities and Local Government, *The Training and Development of Muslim Faith Leaders: Current Practice and Future Possibilities* (Communities and Local Government Publications 2010).

the university and housing provided by the denomination in question. In some cases, the chaplaincy building itself is provided by the university and in others by a particular church: in the case of the University of Birmingham, for example, the chaplaincy building is provided by the Cadbury Trust – an independent charity established by the leading Quaker family in the city. A number of universities, mainly those established after 1992, employ a chaplain themselves and do so regardless of denominational allegiance. Such posts are fully funded by the university and accountability is to the university except insofar as chaplains are answerable to their own denominational authorities in matters of doctrine and purely ecclesiastical discipline. Increasingly, higher education institutions also appoint Jewish and Muslim chaplains.

Chaplaincy in the Armed Forces

The three armed services provide chaplaincy services for members of the armed forces at public expense. The total cost of chaplaincy services to the United Kingdom armed forces in 2006 was some £30/€34.8 million.[58] At a recent meeting of the Ecclesiastical Law Society the then Chaplain General to the Army confirmed informally that expenditure on military chaplaincy in 2010 was some £35/€40.6 million. Military chaplains are almost exclusively Christian, but they come from all the major denominations.

Health Care Chaplaincy

National Health Service Primary Care Trusts are responsible for providing chaplains in hospitals. The salaries and pensions of full-time chaplains are paid from the public purse, while part-time chaplains are paid fees from the NHS for the chaplaincy work that they undertake.

The government itself appears not to have any information about expenditure on hospital chaplaincy – on the grounds that chaplains are not employed centrally; but the Hospital Chaplaincies Council reported that at the beginning of 2010 there were some 425 full-time and approximately 3,000 part-time chaplains employed by the NHS.[59] On that basis, and assuming a median stipend of £30,000, the cost of *whole-time* hospital chaplaincy services in the United Kingdom must be of the order of £12/€13.9 million.

58   HC Deb (2005–06) 449 24 July 2006 c768W.

59   Hospital Chaplaincies Council, *Health Care Chaplaincy and The Church of England: A Review of the work of the Hospital Chaplaincies Council* (National Church Institutions 2010).

Prison Chaplaincy

By statute, every prison in England and Wales has a chaplain who in England must be a priest of the Church of England and in Wales a priest of the Church in Wales.[60] Other Christian denominations and other faiths also provide chaplaincy services but only the Anglican chaplain is a statutory official.

Overall, there are some 350 directly employed chaplains in the Prison Service in England and Wales: the remainder are part-time chaplains paid by the hour. A request under the Freedom of Information Act 2000 by a member of the British Humanist Association elicited the information that annual expenditure on directly employed chaplains was about £10.3 million/(€12m2).

In Scotland, under section 3 (General superintendence of prisons) of the Prisons (Scotland) Act 1989, each prison must have a chaplain who is a minister or a licentiate of the Church of Scotland. In addition, under section 9 the religious denomination of each prisoner must be recorded on reception and there is an obligation to provide prison ministers for prisoners belonging to other denominations and faiths. The chaplaincy service is delivered to the terms of an Agreement between the Scottish Prison Service, the Church of Scotland and the Roman Catholic Church in Scotland. Policy is made by the Prison Chaplaincy Steering Group, whose members are drawn from a variety of faith communities and from Scottish Prison Service senior management.

'Schools with a Religious Character'

There are approximately 6,750 maintained 'schools with a religious character'[61] in England and Wales out of a total of around 20,000 maintained schools (Department for Education 2012). They are usually either 'voluntary aided' (VA) schools (which are maintained schools in which the government pays the running costs but the governing body must usually pay at least 10 per cent of the costs of any capital work) or 'voluntary controlled' (VC) schools (which are fully funded).

---

60   Prison Act 1952 S. 7 for the Church of England; also, S. 53(4) requires that references to the Church of England must be construed as applying equally to the Church in Wales. The latter may appear somewhat anachronistic, given that the Prison Act was enacted some 30 years after disestablishment. But chaplaincy was introduced by the Gaols Act 1823, the provisions of which were incorporated into subsequent legislation. The Prison Act 1952 was '[a]n Act to consolidate certain enactments relating to prisons and other institutions for offenders and related matters with corrections and improvements made under the Consolidation of Enactments (Procedure) Act 1949' and merely restated the law current at the time rather than amending it. Disestablishment notwithstanding, the 1952 Act did not, therefore, disturb the arrangement under which the Church in Wales provided the statutory chaplains to Welsh prisons.

61   More popularly (but inaccurately) known as 'faith schools': see School Standards and Framework Act 1998 schedule 19 paras 3 & 4.

In the case of a VA school, admissions policy is determined and administered by the school's governors in consultation with the local education authority[62] and other relevant schools in the area, whereas in a VA school the admissions policy is usually determined and administered by the local education authority alone. Crucially, a school designated as having 'a religious character' can lawfully restrict entry based on religion or belief.[63]

It can be (and frequently is) argued that VA and VC schools do not involve public support for religion at all. If such schools did not exist, their pupils would still have to be educated and the vast majority would no doubt attend local authority maintained schools at public expense. The Catholic Education Service for England and Wales sets out the argument like this:[64]

> All taxpayers contribute to the cost of the nation's schools, Catholic taxpayers no less than any other taxpayer. The suggestion, therefore, that Catholic schools are being unfairly funded by taxpayers is entirely fallacious. The Catholic community actually pays *more* for its schools as 10 per cent of the capital expenditure has to be provided from the Catholic community, whereas ... other maintained schools ... receive 100 per cent funding. In addition to their taxes, the Catholic community provides in excess of a further £20 million per annum to its schools for capital expenditure. It should be remembered that 30 per cent of pupils in Catholic schools are not Catholic and this is therefore a contribution that could be viewed as to the good of society.

The Church of England and the Church in Wales could reasonably advance similar arguments. In many rural areas, the local church primary school is simply 'the village school' and, in any case, the religious test for admission to church schools is often either minimal or non-existent – and there are Church of England VA schools in which 90 per cent or more of the pupils are Muslim. A report on education of Muslim children noted that church schools were the second largest provider of education for Muslims and that, where they have the choice,[65]

> many Muslim parents choose to send their children to Christian or other faith schools, whether voluntary-aided or voluntary controlled, instead of choosing the more secular community schools. In some cases, the reason is simply that

---

62   For a recent case on the validity of a VA school's admission policy see *E, R (on the application of) v Governing Body of JFS & Anor* [2009] UKSC 15. For an analysis, see Franck Cranmer, 'Who is a Jew? Jewish Faith Schools and the Race Relations Act 1976' (2010) 164 *Law & Justice* 75–80.

63   For a full discussion of such schools see Russell Sandberg, *Law and Religion* (Cambridge University Press 2011) 160–68.

64   Oona Stannard, *The Funding of Catholic schools.* Published online October 2007 <http://www.cesew.org.uk/standard.asp?id=6104> accessed 9 August 2011.

65   Open Society Institute, *British Muslims and Education* (2005) 122.

there are more single-sex schools available in the church school sector, and many Muslim parents favour such provision. In other cases, it may be because a school with a religious ethos, even a non-Muslim one, is considered preferable, so long as no attempt is made to convert the children. It may also be because Christian schools often have a good academic reputation, and because the moral guidance they provide is rooted in religion.

Conclusions

So How Much Does It All Cost?

It is extraordinarily difficult even to make an informed guess at the value of public financial support for religion in the United Kingdom: partly because some of the payments are for services supplied under contract in return for payment by local or central government (such as the provision of places in care-homes run by religious organizations), partly because some clergy (such as hospital chaplains) are engaged not by central or local government, but by third parties such as NHS Primary Care Trusts, and principally because it is not in any case clear precisely what constitutes 'public financial support'.

More generally, on 2 December 2010 in reply to a Written Question in the House of Lords from Lord Beecham about the impact on charities of the impending 2.5 per cent increase in VAT, Lord Sassoon, the Commercial Secretary to the Treasury, gave the following estimate of tax benefits for charities: 'The charity sector benefits from over £3 billion a year in specific tax reliefs, including nearly £1 billion in gift aid and over £150 million in respect of specific VAT zero rates ...'.[66]

Assuming that one-fifth of that £3 billion goes to faith groups and religious charities (which would be consistent with the proportion of Gift Aid repayments that goes to them), the annual reliefs would be worth some £600/€695 million. When taken with other forms of support for which we have reasonably reliable estimates and scaling up where necessary to take account of the populations of Scotland and Northern Ireland, an extremely impressionistic figure for public subsidies to 'religion' for the financial year 2011–12 might look something like this:

---

66   HL Deb (2010–11) cWA476.

Table 10.1   Estimated public subsidies to 'religion' for 2011–2012

	£m	€m
Hospital chaplaincy	£12.00	€ 13.90
Listed Places of Worship Grant Scheme	£42.00	€ 48.70
Military chaplaincy	£35.00	€ 40.50
Prison chaplaincy	£11.60	€ 13.46
Charity tax reliefs generally (mainly Gift Aid)	£600.00	€ 695.00
Non-domestic rates foregone	£45.00	€ 52.00
Total	**£745.60**	**€ 863.56**

That includes an extremely hypothetical sum for non-domestic rate relief (but, given that there are about 50,000 places of worship in the United Kingdom, even on a very conservative calculation of average rateable value, the total relief is unlikely to be much below €500 million and could be considerably higher than that). On that basis, *the annual total public subsidy for 'religion' across the United Kingdom as a whole might be of the order of* £750/€870 *million* – but that is only about £11.86/€13.76 per head of population or about £24.50/€28.40 from each of the 30.5 million people who pay income tax. The principal item left out of account is public funding of faith schools but, as already suggested, that can be seen as a repayment for services rather than as a subsidy.

But these figures are, of course, purely impressionistic: no more than a reasonably intelligent guesstimate. The honest answer to the question, 'what is the overall cost to public funds of support for religion?' is '*we simply do not know*'. We have no reliable figures, because HM Treasury and HMRC make no distinction between religious and secular charities when collecting their data (and, realistically, it would be verging on impropriety were they to do so); nor is there any reliable information available on the amount of rating income forgone under the concession for places of worship.

Socio-Political Challenges: Can Public Financial Support for 'Religion' be Justified?

In an increasingly secularized Europe, public financial support for religion is becoming increasingly controversial. In a recent report, the National Secular Society (NSS) estimated that NHS Trusts in England spent £29/€33.65 million to provide hospital chaplaincy services in 2009–10. The NSS argues that[67] 'if churches, mosques and temples wish to have representation in hospitals to visit those patients who want some religious support whilst in hospital, they should do it at their own expense'.

Similarly, the Accord Coalition (whose Chair is Rabbi Dr Jonathan Romain) has for some time argued against religious tests for admission to publicly funded schools with a religious character. Romain and his associates[68] do not take any position 'on the desirability or undesirability of state-funded faith schools *per se* ... ' but wish to see a system in which 'admissions and recruitment policies in all state-funded schools [are] free from discrimination on grounds of religion or belief'. In short, they argue that such schools are both selective in terms of social class and divisive in terms of community cohesion – and the experience of Northern Ireland would certainly tend to support the second of those contentions.

State support for faith schools is the extreme case. As to state support more generally, very little of it is overtly about 'religion'. As noted above, religious charities are supported not because they are religious but because they are *charities*. Listed places of worship are supported because they are of architectural and townscape merit – and that support recognizes the fact that, if society generally wishes to maintain its historic buildings, it cannot depend on dwindling religious communities to do that job for it.

There is also an entirely secular economic case for supporting the ecclesiastical built heritage. As the Prime Minister pointed out in a keynote speech on 12 August 2010,[69] tourism is the United Kingdom's third highest export earner after chemicals and financial services. One of the things that tourists come to the United Kingdom to see is its historic buildings and townscapes – and the ecclesiastical built heritage is an important part of that. As we have seen, the Church of England alone has some 16,000 listed buildings, 4,000 of which are listed at the highest grade. Of the 25 current UNESCO World Heritage Sites in the United Kingdom, six[70] include major ecclesiastical buildings in current use. Without the funds that flow from the Listed Places of Worship Grant Scheme and Gift Aid, many of these would be at even greater risk than they are at present.

---

67 National Secular Society, *Costing the Heavens: Chaplaincy Services in English NHS Provider Trusts 2009/10.* Published online 28 February 2011 <http://www.secularism.org.uk/uploads/nss-chaplaincy-report-2011.pdf> accessed 27 February 2013.

68 Accord Coalition, *About Us*. Published online 18 August 2010 <http://accordcoalition.org.uk/about-us> accessed 27 February 2013.

69 David Cameron, *PM's Speech on Tourism*. Published online 12 August 2010 <http://www.number10.gov.uk/news/pms-speech-on-tourism> accessed 27 February 2013.

70 Canterbury Cathedral, St Augustine's Abbey and St Martin's Church; the City of Bath (which includes Bath Abbey); Durham Castle and Cathedral: the Old and New Towns of Edinburgh (which include the High Kirk of St Giles and St Mary's Episcopal Cathedral); and the Palace of Westminster, Westminster Abbey and St Margaret's Church. One of the major buildings in a seventh, Saltaire Village, is a Grade I listed URC church.

Perhaps because the United Kingdom is neither an avowedly secular State nor – the special position of the Church of England and the Church of Scotland notwithstanding – an avowedly confessional one, faith communities and secular society seem to coexist with very little friction. Government recognizes the contribution that religion can make in areas such as support for social services and, more generally, to social cohesion, while most of the mainstream denominations try as far as possible to integrate their activities into wider society. Nevertheless, there remains a degree of tension between the self-understanding of faith communities and the perceptions of at least some adherents of liberal secularism.

Almost all the major world faiths assume that, rather than being a solitary, individual path, religion is practised *in community*; moreover, many faiths assume that, in order to be part of the worshipping community, adherents must abide by a particular body of teachings or holy book. But precisely because the United Kingdom is neither a confessional State nor a merely secular one, from the perspective of the secular authorities, as suggested earlier, religious practice is regarded as a matter for the individual, subject always to the guarantee of the right to manifest under Article 9 ECHR and to the general law. Where disagreements may arise is when the religious obligations of an individual or a faith community come into conflict with a particular policy pursued by the secular authorities in the interests of what they perceive as 'the greater good' – and to that clash of interests there is no easy answer.

As to the funding of religion, there are inevitable tensions between the needs of religious communities for increasingly scarce resources in order to maintain their buildings and their social services and their understandable desire to maintain their independence from government. Additional challenges come from those, such as the National Secular Society, who have principled and fundamental objections to public subsidy for something that many of them would regard as suspicious at best and positively dangerous at worst and from the more general demand from civil society for financial support from a seriously depleted public purse. The result is that, in matters of religion, even if it were tempted to try to call the tune, the government could not conceivably afford to pay the piper.

List of References

Accord Coalition, *About Us*. Published online 18 August 2010 <http://acco rdcoalition.org.uk/about-us> accessed 9 August 2011

Brierley P, *Major UK Religious Trends, 2010 to 2020* (Peter Brierley Consultants 2011)

Cameron D, *PM's Speech on Tourism*. Published online 12 August 2010 <http://www.number10.gov.uk/news/pms-speech-on-tourism> accessed 26 February 2013

Church of England Ministry Division, *A Review of Models and Funding of Pre-Ordination Training in the light of the Proposed Changes to HE Funding*:

summary paper circulated to the General Synod – GS 1836/2011 (General Synod 2011)

Church of Scotland, *CrossReach: what we do*. Published online 2009 <http:// www.crossreach.org.uk/what-we-do> accessed 26 February 2013

Cranmer F, 'Who is a Jew? Jewish Faith Schools and the Race Relations Act 1976' (2010) 164 *Law & Justice*

—— 'Beating People Is Wrong: *Campbell and Cosans, Williamson* and their Aftermath' in M Hunter-Henin, *Law, Religious Freedoms and Education in Europe* (Ashgate 2012)

Davie G, *Religion in Britain since 1945: Believing Without Belonging* (Blackwell Publishers 1994)

Department for Communities and Local Government, *The Training and Development of Muslim Faith Leaders: Current Practice and Future Possibilities* (Communities and Local Government Publications 2010)

Department for Culture, Media and Sport, *Listed Places of Worship Grant Scheme*. Published online in 2010 <http://www.lpwscheme.org.uk/> accessed 26 February 2013

Doe N, *Law and Religion in Europe: a comparative introduction* (OUP 2011)

Fornerod A (ed.), *Assistance spirituelle dans les services publics* (Presses Universitaires 2012)

Glanville A, 'The View from the Church in Wales' (2011) *Building Conservation*

Higher Education Funding Council for England, *Withdrawal of Funding for Equivalent or Lower Qualifications (ELQs) Consultation on Implementation*. Published online September 2007 <http://www.hefce.ac.uk/pubs/hefce/2007 /07_27/07_27.pdf> accessed 26 February 2013

HM Government, *Review of Counter-Terrorism and Security Powers: Review Findings and Recommendations* (Cm 8004) (TSO 2011)

Home Office, *Prevent strategy 2011*. Published online 7 June 2011 <http://www. homeoffice.gov.uk/publications/counter-terrorism/prevent/prevent-strategy> accessed 26 February 2013

Hospital Chaplaincies Council, *Health Care Chaplaincy and The Church of England: A Review of the work of the Hospital Chaplaincies Council* (National Church Institutions 2010)

House of Commons Culture, Media and Sport Committee, *Third Report of Session 2010–12: Funding of the Arts and Heritage* (TSO 2011)

James G and Eastwood D, *ELQs and the Churches' Ministerial Training – A Review* (published online 2008) <http://www.hefce.ac.uk/media/ hefce/content/whatwedo/learningandteaching/howwefundlt/equivalentorlo werqualifications/ELQinterimreport.PDF>

Lombard D, 'Scottish government pledges to help Catholic adoption agency' (11 February 2013) *Third Sector*

National Secular Society, *Costing the heavens: Chaplaincy services in English NHS Provider Trusts 2009/10*. Published online 28 February 2011 <http://

www.secularism.org.uk/uploads/nss-chaplaincy-report-2011.pdf> accessed 26 February 2013

Northern Ireland Statistics and Research Agency, *Census 2011: Key Statistics for Northern Ireland,* Table KS211NI. Published online 11 December 2012 <http://www.nisra.gov.uk/Census/key_report_2011.pdf> accessed 27 February 2013

Office of National Statistics, *Religion in England and Wales 2011.* Published online 11 December 2012 <http://www.ons.gov.uk/ons/dcp171776_290510. pdf> accessed 26 February 2013

Open Society Institute, *British Muslims and Education* (2005) 122

Pew Forum, *The Future of the Global Muslim Population: Projections for 2010–2030.* Published online 27 January 2011 <http://pewforum.org/The-Future-of-the-Global-Muslim-Population.aspx> accessed 26 February 2013

Ratzinger JA, *Speech to both Houses of Parliament.* Published online 18 September 2010 <http://www.thepapalvisit.org.uk/Replay-the-Visit/Speeches/Speeches-17-September/Pope-Benedict-s-address-to-Politicians-Diplomats-Academics-and-Business-Leaders> accessed 26 February 2013

Sandberg R, 'Laws and Religion: Unravelling *McFarlane v Relate Avon Limited*' (2010) 12, 3 *Ecclesiastical Law Journal* 361–70

—— *Law and Religion* (Cambridge University Press 2011)

Scottish Government, *Non Domestic Rates – A Guide* Section 2.2. Published online December 2004 <http://www.scotland.gov.uk/Publications/2004/12/20460/49146> accessed 26 February 2013

Stannard O, *The Funding of Catholic schools.* Published online October 2007 <http://www.cesew.org.uk/standard.asp?id=6104> accessed 9 August 2011

Taylor J, 'Protected Buildings: A Brief Guide to the Legislation' (2012) *Building Conservation*

Twinch C, *Tithe War 1918–1939: The Countryside in Revolt* (Media Associates 2001)

Walker P, 'Snapshot Survey of Listed Churches' (2006) 98 March/April *Church Building*

Chapter 11

Differential, Disguised and Deterritorialized: State Funding of Religion in Turkey

Zana Çitak, Aykan Erdemir and Tuğba Tanyeri-Erdemir

The emergence of the current system of state funding of religious institutions and services in Turkey has been gradual and piecemeal.[1] This process has been shaped both by the legacy of the former Ottoman system and the radical break from it, namely the creation of the secular Turkish Republic. In other words, continuities and ruptures with the past have merged to bring forth an eclectic regime of state funding of religious institutions and services in Turkey's case.

The current regime can be best described as a patchwork of practices, laws, by-laws, regulations, and institutional arrangements; decentralized and diffused across different institutions, actors and services have been bundled together and disguised within many subcategories. The funding system cannot be disaggregated, so it is very hard to track and measure and is consequently difficult to hold to account. It is characterized by unequal, differentiated and often discriminatory treatment of different religious groups. In Turkey, religious communities do not have a distinct legal personality, which restricts freedom of religion and association. As such, the current regime of state funding of religion in Turkey cannot necessarily be understood as 'state support' for religion. That means, in some cases, state funding might have the objective of assimilating individuals who do not adhere to the orthodoxy and orthopraxy advocated by the Sunni-Hanefite majority. Therefore, state funding does not necessarily mean 'support' for all religions, and often ends up being a liability for individuals who do not conform to the state-endorsed version of Sunni-Hanefite Islam.

Moreover, the current funding regime has an important transnational dimension. The Turkish State organizes and funds mosque associations and religious services outside Turkey, particularly in countries with sizeable Turkish expatriate populations. To sum up, the three main characteristics of the current funding regime are: its patchwork character, the differential treatment of different religious groups and the transnational dimension.

---

1   Zana Çitak would like to thank the Kroc Institute for International Peace Studies at University of Notre Dame, which provided support for a Visiting Fellowship in autumn 2011, during which this chapter was written.

Patchwork

Various actors, processes and legal frameworks have been involved in state funding of religion in Turkey, which should mainly be understood as funding of Sunni-Hanefite Islam. The defining characteristics of the variety of funds available for religious functions and services are that they come from a multitude of different channels and sources and are embedded in the budgets of state institutions in multiple ways, making it almost impossible to disaggregate them. To start with the actors, major funds are channelled through the budgets of state institutions, including the Directorate of Religious Affairs (*Diyanet İşleri Başkanlığı*, henceforth: Diyanet), the Ministry of Education, the Ministry of Culture, the Ministry of Foreign Affairs, the Directorate General of Endowments (*Vakıflar Genel Müdürlüğü*), Turkish Radio and Television (TRT), the Prime Minister's Office and state universities. Furthermore, they are under the regulation of – and subject to – a wide range of laws, by-laws, and regulations.[2] They have emerged over time as part of a series of unconnected arrangements.

The Diyanet – which is the leading actor in the current regime of state funding of religion – therefore provides salaries for imams, preachers and other religious personnel and is in charge of the administration and maintenance of mosques. At the same time, since 1965, it has been given the task of 'enlightening the public about religion',[3] which has meant a wider range of activities for the Diyanet, such as conferences, seminars, Koranic courses, religious publications as well as helplines (*Çağrı Merkezi Sistemi*) established at the Office of Religious Inquiries (*Dini Soruları Cevaplandırma Bürosu*) and family counselling offices (*aile irşad büroları*). The Ministry of Education is another significant institution which funds religion through both religious vocational schools called İmam-Hatip Liseleri (imam and preacher high schools) and providing compulsory courses in religion (*Din Kültürü ve Ahlâk Bilgisi Dersleri*). It also pays the salaries of the Turkish language teachers in minority schools.

---

2   The Diyanet itself, until the recent changes in law, has been described as a 'legal oddity' by observers, as it existed for a long time without a technically legal basis. The 1975 Law reorganizing the Diyanet was never ratified, and since 'a previous law does not come into effect automatically', Article 633 of the 1965 Law on the Diyanet could not provide a legal basis for the Diyanet either: see İştar Gözaydın, 'A Religious Administration to Secure Secularism: The Presidency of Religious Affairs of the Republic of Turkey' (2006) 11, 1 *Marburg Journal of Religion* 3–5. This legal vacuum under which Diyanet has functioned was recently filled with the passing of Law no. 6002 of 1 July 2010 (www.diyanet.gov.tr), which broadly extended the scope of the mission and activities of the Diyanet: see Thijl Sunier et al., *Diyanet: The Turkish Directorate for Religious Affairs in a Changing Environment* (VU University Amsterdam and Utrecht University 2011) 48–50; Mine Yıldırım, 'TURKEY: The Diyanet – The Elephant in Turkey's Religious Freedom Room?'(2011) *FORUM 18 News Service*, 4 May <http://www.forum18.org>

3   İştar Gözaydın, '*Diyanet* and Politics' (2008) 98, 2–3 *The Muslim World* 220.

A large number of almost exclusively historical sites, which were once operating as bases for religious foundations, are registered under the Directorate General of Endowments, an institution linked to the Prime Minister's Office. Former dervish lodges and religious complexes are included in the registry of the Directorate General of Endowments. It is responsible for restoration and renovation of these sites. In some cases, the Directorate can rent out these buildings and their attached lands to other institutions. Sometimes, the sites can be operated by the Ministry of Culture. The Directorate can also provide free or subsidized land and buildings for religious activities and services. Local governments also provide discretionary assistance for maintenance and repair of religious sites.[4] The Prime Minister's Office has allegedly undocumented discretionary funding for religious events and projects through the Discretionary Fund (*Örtülü Ödenek*), which cannot be tracked or documented.

Imams sent to Europe by the Diyanet are funded through a special funding agency under the control of the Ministry of Foreign Affairs: the Fund for Advertising Turkish Cultural Heritage Abroad (*Yurtdışında Türk Kültür Varlığını Tanıtma Fonu*).[5] The TRT broadcasts religious programmes during Ramadan as well as on special religious days, in line with Sunni-Hanefite teaching, with no broadcasting time allocated to other religions and belief systems. Recent Law No. 6002 of 1 July 2010 has given the Diyanet the possibility to open up its own radio and television channel, with national radio and TV frequencies to be provided free of charge through the RTÜK (The High Agency for Radio and Television).[6] The State has also established theology faculties in many state universities.[7]

Differential Treatment

There are basically two main sources of the differential treatment in state funding of religion in Turkey: firstly, the existence of the Diyanet as an administrative organ to manage all places of prayer and to pay imams' salaries and, secondly, the absence of legal entity status for religious communities.

The very institution of the Diyanet has been at the source of the differential and discriminatory treatment *vis-à-vis* different religious groups in Turkey. The Diyanet was 'originally conceived as a mere administrative branch of the

---

4 The 2010 Activity Report of the Diyanet mentions that steps have been taken to have the municipalities take care of the cleaning of mosques. Diyanet İşleri Başkanlığı, *Raporu* (2010) 37.

5 Zana Çitak, 'Between 'Turkish Islam' and 'French Islam': The Role of the Diyanet' in Conseil Français du Culte Musulman (2010) 36, 4 *Journal of Ethnic and Migration Studies*, 622.

6 Yıldırım (n 2) 3.

7 Mehmet Ali Gökaçtı, *Türkiye'de Din Eğitimi ve İmam-Hatipler* (İletişim Yayınları 2005) 250–73.

government with no sacred significance attached to it'[8] and 'the founding Kemalist elite created an institution with a very weak status and prestige within the new national State'.[9] However, over time, the Diyanet's budget and the number of civil servants employed[10] have grown and solidified into a solely Sunni-Hanefite institution; there was a failed attempt in 1963 to establish an office for the faiths (*mezhepler dairesi*), which would have transformed this institution into a more inclusive one.[11] It is this exclusively Sunni-Hanefite dimension of the Diyanet that constitutes the basis of the differential treatment of the current state funding regime in Turkey.

With five departments, 106,275 employees, a considerable budget (2,287,177,581 TL or approximately €1 billion)[12] higher than that of some government ministries[13] and the wide range of functions noted above, the Diyanet today enjoys 'massive institutional and financial status'.[14] All of these functions are paid for by the taxes collected from all Turkish citizens – Sunni-Muslim, non-Sunni-Muslim and non-Muslim, practising or non-practising alike. In a situation where only the Sunni Muslim community benefits from the services provided by the Diyanet, with all other religious communities receiving no funding from the State and having to finance their religious services by themselves, the result is, as Yıldırım notes, 'paying twice'.[15] The Lausanne Treaty of 1923 defined only Jewish, Greek Orthodox and Armenian communities as 'minorities', with the accompanying privileges of funding their own religious services and the right to open their own schools. However, this does not lift the burden of having to pay taxes that are also used by the Diyanet. Other non-Muslim communities such as the Syriac Christians, Keldanis and Nestorians are not, however, covered by the Lausanne Treaty.[16] As for non-Sunni Muslims such as the Caferis or other heterodox belief communities, such as Alevis and Baha'is or non-practising Muslims, Jehovah's Witnesses or atheists, there is simply no way for them to avoid paying taxes for the Diyanet's services, which can be defined as theologically Sunni-Hanefite.

---

8   Gözaydın (n 3) 218.
9   İsmail Kara, *Cumhuriyet Türkiyesi'nde Bir Mesele Olarak İslam* (Dergâh Yayınları 2008) 62–3.
10   Diyanet İşleri Başkanlığı (n 4) 15.
11   Gözaydın (n 3) 6.
12   Diyanet İşleri Başkanlığı (n 4) 28.
13   It is interesting to note that the Diyanet's 2010 Activity Report itself admits that 'it does enjoy a considerable share of the state budget in comparison with other public institutions'. Nevertheless, the report adds that, since 94.56 per cent of its budget goes towards staff salaries, there is a need to increase the budget available for other expenses. Diyanet İşleri Başkanlığı (n 4) 63, 29.
14   Yıldırım (n 2) 2.
15   Yıldırım (n 2) 3.
16   Baskın Oran, *Küreselleşme ve Azınlıklar* (İmaj Yayınevi 2000).

This discriminatory treatment is based on – and results in – a hierarchical relationship among citizens of different faiths, with Sunni-Hanefite believers at the top. In this sense, it is incompatible with secularism, since the State is not neutral in respect to different religious communities and belief systems, and since there is a *de facto* hierarchy among citizens. Moreover, the State, most conveniently through the Diyanet, finds itself in a position to define what religion is or what can be defined as Islam.

Thus, demands by the Alevis to have their '*cemevis*' recognized as 'places of worship' have been consistently rejected by the State, based on the argument that Alevis do not constitute a different religious community, but just a different interpretation of Islam and hence, *cemevis* cannot be considered as places of worship, since they are only cultural centres. The continuous denial of a separate Alevi identity by the Diyanet is based on the perception of religious diversity as division and, therefore, as a threat to national unity, which it has been put in charge of 'promoting and consolidating' according to Article 136 of the 1982 Constitution.[17] In a recent report, the Diyanet indeed explicitly defines 'efforts and initiatives to make ideas and interpretations within Islam into separate religions' as a 'threat' to itself.[18]

The absence of the right to have a legal personality is, in turn, another source of differential treatment of religions in Turkey within the current regime of state funding for religion. No religious community has direct status as a legal entity.[19] For non-Muslim minorities, besides recognizing the rights of equality and non-discrimination and religious freedom, the Lausanne Treaty also envisaged group-specific rights such as opening their own mother-tongue schools. Articles 39–42 of the Treaty also allowed for the establishment, management and control of religious foundations, as well as the preservation of the existing ones.[20] But, in 1936, the State fixed the number of properties owned by religious foundations. Properties obtained after 1936 were either confiscated, or, based on a Court of Appeal (*Yargıtay*) ruling in 1974, returned to their original owners. If the original owner had died and left no heir, then the property was transferred to the Directorate General of Endowments or to the Treasury. The ruling also made it impossible for non-Muslim minorities to obtain new property after 1974.[21] In other words, not only was the basic right of religious freedom violated, but the fundamental

---

17   Gözaydın (n 3) 223.
18   Diyanet İşleri Başkanlığı (n 4) 62.
19   Yıldırım (n 2) 2.
20   Hale Akay, 'Uygulamada Laiklik: Devlet-Din Ekseninde Özgürlükler, Hizmetler ve Finansman' (2011) 120 *Toplum ve Bilim* 30; and Ahmet İçduygu et al., 'Turkish Minority Rights Regime: Between Difference and Equality' (2006) 42, 3 *Middle Eastern Studies* 453–4.
21   Akay (n 20) 30–31, and İçduygu et al. (n 20) 462.

blood supply necessary for the survival of rapidly shrinking non-Muslim religious communities was also cut off.[22]

This situation was remedied to a limited extent through reform packages in 2002 and 2003, which opened the way for non-Muslim communities to obtain, manage and register their properties; however, enjoyment of this right was made conditional upon obtaining permission from the Council of Ministers to acquire properties. Moreover, the Directorate General of Endowments could use their discretion, as regards foundations' boards of trustees, which violated the autonomy of the latter to a great extent.[23] A new amendment to the Law on Foundations in 2008 returned all confiscated properties except for those which had been returned to the original owners.[24] Besides the fact that these exemptions deprived the Greek Orthodox community, in particular, of significant properties, the Law on Foundations No. 5737 and its accompanying statute did not completely remove the possibility of confiscation.[25] At the same time, it introduced the principle of international 'reciprocity' (*milletlerarası mütekabiliyet*) (Article 2) for the implementation of the law in general, and for the establishment of foundations by foreigners (Article 4) (www.tusev.org.tr). The latest improvement to the Law of Foundations took place in August 2011, through the inclusion of a provision in a set of governmental decrees (also known popularly as 'Torba Yasa') that included several other changes in other unrelated areas. Accordingly, not only will confiscated properties of non-Muslim community foundations be returned, cash compensation will be paid for those properties which had been confiscated and then sold to a third party (www.tusev.org.tr).[26]

The absence of legal personality status for religious communities equally affects non-Muslim communities that are not defined as minorities within the Lausanne framework.[27] The Syriac Christian community in Turkey, for example, has no possibility of opening up its own schools.[28] Recently, these non-Muslim communities have begun to establish foundations and associations. Nevertheless, there are many limitations, as the Turkish Civil Law (Article 101) does not allow for the establishment of foundations and associations 'to support an ethnic group or a religious community' and 'discriminating against members based on language,

---

22   Etyen Mahçupyan, *Türkiye'de Gayrimüslim Cemaatlerin Sorunları ve Vatandaş Olamama Durumu* Üzerine, Ekonomik ve Sosyal Etüdler Vakfı (TESEV 2004) June, no. 1 <http://www.tesev.org.tr/etkinlik/demokratiklesme_cemaatler.php>

23   Akay (n 20) 31, and İçduygu et al. (n 20) 463.

24   One must note that the new Law No. 5737 brought with it other improvements too, such as allowing foreigners to become members of the board of trustees and involved in activities in foreign countries; they could also accept donations from foreign donors, as well as domestic ones <www.tusev.org.tr>

25   Akay (n 20) 31.

26   651 sayılı KHK, *Resmi Gazete*, 27 August 2011, tarihli ve 28038 sayılı.

27   Akay (n 20) 32.

28   İçduygu et al. (n 20) 464.

ethnicity, colour, sect, family and class'.[29] In the same way, non-Sunni groups, such as the Alevis, have also increasingly established foundations and associations.[30]

In fact, the Diyanet itself is not recognized as a legal personality and therefore cannot own mosques or property; it only manages them. Individuals and public entities, such as municipalities, village mosque associations, and most commonly, the Diyanet Foundation, own mosques.[31] Obtaining a legal personality has been cited as one of the Diyanet's expectations for the future in its 2010 Activity Report.[32]

The differential treatment is manifested also in establishing places of worship, meeting the religious needs of the elderly, prison inmates and army personnel, in training clergy and in theology teaching. Protestants have had many difficulties in establishing places of worship, despite the positive changes in the law (İmar Kanunu) in the 2003 Reform Package, which facilitated the construction of places of worship, 'if permission is given by the highest administrative bureaucrat in a given district and if it conforms to the construction statute'.[33] Again, while the Diyanet provides religious personnel for public hospitals, prisons, social services and the army, this is not the case for members of other religious or belief communities or sects.[34] As for the teaching of theology, the Orthodox Seminary of Khalki (*Heybeliada Ruhban Okulu*) has remained closed since 1971, despite the fact that the Greek Orthodox community was given the right to train its own clergy by the Lausanne Treaty.[35]

---

29   Akay (n 20) 32. Mine Yıldırım argues that the Diyanet Foundation (Türkiye Diyanet Vakfı–TDV) 'constitutes an irregularity in the application of the law'. TDV is closely linked to the Diyanet: its aim, according to its website, is to assist and support the Directorate of Religious Affairs in its efforts to explain 'true Islam' as well as building mosques, opening hospitals for the poor and collecting and distributing the donations to the needy (Yıldırım (n 2) 2). Furthermore, the President of the Diyanet is also the head of TDV's board of trustees, see <www.diyanetvakfi.org.tr>. At the same time, the Diyanet admits that 'civil financial support' has been crucial for its activities (Diyanet İşleri Başkanlığı (n 4) 60). One can safely assume that it is largely TDV's support that is implied in that statement.

30   Akay (n 20) 32.

31   Yıldırım (n 2) 2.

32   Diyanet İşleri Başkanlığı (n 4) 63.

33   Akay (n 20) 32.

34   Akay (n 20) 33–7.

35   The Cyprus issue and the tension in Turkish–Greek relations in the 1960s and 1970s constituted the context for the closure of the Khalki Seminary. Alleged Greek imperialism over Turkey, as well as the state's fear that the opening of the Khalki might be perceived as an excuse for further strengthening imam-hatip schools could be seen as reasons that prevented its reopening. See Elçin Macar et al., *Heybeliada Ruhban Okulu'nun Geleceği* Üzerine *Tartışmalar ve* Öneriler (TESEV 2005).

Transnational Dimension

A peculiarity of the Turkish system of state funding for religion is the extension of funding beyond Turkey's borders. In fact, the Diyanet's transnationalism should be seen as an extension of its domestic mission and activities. To a great extent, the Diyanet replicates its domestic role and functions in other countries. Just as in Turkey, the Diyanet provides religious services, such as sending imams to mosques, organizing funerals and pilgrimages for Turkish Muslims. It also 'enlightens people about religion' through international conferences, publications, support for religious education institutions abroad and the provision of religious education in Turkey for foreign nationals through short and long-term courses and the theological training of clergy. At the same time, the Turkish State had similar motives behind its decision to extend the Diyanet's activities abroad: besides the realization that Turkish immigration to Europe was not a temporary phenomenon and that religious needs of these people should therefore be met, the State also wanted to counter other religious and political currents and networks that had become influential among the migrants and which the State deemed as dangerous to its own legitimacy and existence. Since the 1980s, the State has increasingly perceived Islam as the most important cement for national unity, by closely associating 'Turkishness' with 'Muslimness', a relationship that lies at the core of what came to be known as the 'Turkish–Islamic Synthesis', the unofficial ideology of the Turkish State since the early 1980s.[36]

The transnational dimension of state funding can be analysed across three geographical areas and three historical periods. The Diyanet began its activities in Europe to meet the religious needs of immigrants originating from Turkey during the late 1970s. After several temporary, *ad hoc* and non-systematic responses such as sending imams to Germany during Ramadan, the Diyanet finally established formal and permanent mechanisms through bilateral agreements with migrants' host countries in Europe. The first Consulate for Religious Services (*Din İşleri Müşavirliği*) was established in Germany in 1978. Starting in the early 1980s, the Diyanet began to establish its network of DİTİBs (*Diyanet İşleri Türk–İslam Birliği*), umbrella organizations for mosque associations linked to the Diyanet. In most cases, the chairman of the DİTİB is a Diyanet-appointed counsellor for religious services who is accredited to the Turkish diplomatic representation in a given country.[37] The Diyanet-linked associations today constitute the largest religious network in Europe and have also recently been established in Japan, the USA and Australia.[38] The Diyanet has, since 2006, also organized an 'International Theology Project' (*Uluslararası İlahiyat Projesi*) under the auspices of the

---

36   Zana Çitak, 'Religion, Ethnicity and Transnationalism: Turkish Islam in Belgium' (2011) 53, 2 *Journal of Church and State* 226.

37   Çitak (n 5) 622.

38   The number of counsellors and attachés for religious services stands at 42 and that of religious personnel abroad at 1,525, as of 2010. Diyanet İşleri Başkanlığı (n 4) 15.

Turkish Higher Education Council (*Yükseköğretim Kurulu–YÖK*) to have students come from several European countries to study theology at Ankara University and Marmara University's faculties of theology.[39]

Since the collapse of communist regimes in Eastern and Central Europe and the disintegration of the Soviet Union, the Diyanet has also become actively involved in the Eurasian region, extending from the Balkans to the Caucasus and Central Asia. Not only has it provided support for religious educational institutions, students from these regions have also been enrolled in imam-hatip high schools and faculties of theology both at undergraduate and graduate levels.[40] In Africa, recently intensified, bilateral, commercial relations since the early 2000s have led to the emergence of an interest in, and extension of, certain activities within this region.[41]

The transnational dimension of state funding for religion has therefore emerged almost as a natural extension of the Diyanet's mission and self-image. The perception that is taken for granted of the Diyanet and its mission and activities, also in other areas such as public broadcasting, have led to the emergence of the Diyanet's transnational network without any legal basis. Just as the institution itself had remained a legal anomaly from 1975 until the recent Law of 1 July 2010, its organization outside Turkey lacked any legal framework and was made possible only through by-laws, until the enactment of Law No. 5676 of 30 May 2007, almost 30 years later.[42] Importantly, today the Diyanet sees itself also as a 'global institution' with a 'global vision',[43] with a long and rich historical experience in providing religious services and 'enlightening' people about 'true Islam', at home and abroad.

Historical Background

The very question of state funding for religion in Turkey's case arose only with the establishment of the Republic in 1923 as a Nation-State, based on the legitimacy

---

39   Ali Dere, 'The PRA of Turkey: The Emergence, Evolution and Perception of its Religious Services Outside of Turkey' (2008) 98, 2–3 *The Muslim World* 298. In 2010–2011, 108 students were enrolled in Ankara and Marmara universities within the framework of the International Theology Project. Efforts to establish a Council for Religious Education Abroad, to assess the project and students, have almost been completed. Diyanet İşleri Başkanlığı (n 4) 47.

40   Dere (n 39) 298. Numbers enrolled in imam-hatip high schools: 496; in faculties of theology in 2010–2011, undergraduates: 681, Master's students: 137, PhD students: 65. Diyanet İşleri Başkanlığı (n 4) 46.

41   Dere (n 39) 298.

42   İştar Gözaydın, *Diyanet: Türkiye Cumhuriyeti'nde Dinin Tanzimi* (İletişim Yayınları 2009) 140.

43   Mehmet Aydın, 'Diyanet's Global Vision' (April 2008) 98, 2–3 *The Muslim World* 164–172, esp 164.

of Turkish nationalism. However, the current eclectic, diffused and differential system of state funding for religion in Turkey has been piecemeal and gradual and is defined as much through the legacy of the Ottoman system as it is a radical break from it. This dual nature of Turkish secularism combined with the framework provided by the Lausanne Treaty, has determined the present regime of state funding of religion in Turkey.

Turkish Secularism

Different mechanisms and legal arrangements are embedded in a specific understanding of State–Religion relations in Turkey. One particular interpretation of secularism in Turkey has not only given rise to specific legal arrangements, such as the existence of the Diyanet as an administrative branch of the government, but it has also led to a series of institutional practices and prerogatives, which have not necessarily been defined or organized in law.

While the Ottoman State was a rather idiosyncratic entity during its first three centuries, it started to derive its legitimacy to a great extent from Islam and, more specifically since the sixteenth century, from Sunni Islam, with the Ottoman conquest of the Arab Middle East and classical centres of Islamic learning, like Egypt. Hence the term *din u devlet* (Religion and State) was used to emphasize this identification of the Islamic character of the State. From the sixteenth century, the *ulema* increasingly became part of the state establishment; the *Şeyhülislam* as the highest religious authority came only third after the sultan and the grand vezir in the hierarchy of imperial authority,[44] and Shari'a constituted the source of legitimacy for all imperial decrees and laws, which had to be compatible with God's law. Until approximately the mid-nineteenth century, religion constituted the basis of individual identity within the framework of the 'millet system', 'which classified subject peoples first into Muslims and non-Muslims and, in turn, the latter were further divided into Greek Orthodox, Armenian Gregorian and Jewish communities'.[45] Thus, non-Muslims were taxed heavily and their religious services were provided with funds collected from their own congregations. Significantly, Muslim subjects of the empire were considered a monolithic and unitary entity, with a deliberate sectarian suppression of Shi'is, Alevis, Yezidis and Nusayris, who did not enjoy official recognition.

The new State, with the establishment of the Republic in 1923, was to be based on the principle of Turkish nationalism, understood within a framework of a greater project of civilization, that is, Westernization. The republican founders were heirs to the Ottoman reformist movement of the nineteenth century. However, having neither the romanticism of the Young Ottomans for Islam, nor the instrumentalism of the Young Turks, the reformism of the republican founders reflected an unequivocally critical attitude *vis-à-vis* Islam and was aimed at separating State

---

44   Kara (n 9) 62.
45   İçduygu et al. (n 20) 449.

and Religion. This understanding of secularism had three main characteristics: firstly, it embraced freedom of religion. However, this recognition of religious freedom was conditional on religion being a private matter only.[46] Secondly, and related to the first point, it aimed at removing religion from the public sphere. The result was to eradicate social and symbolic manifestations of Islam in society. That is why the secularizing reforms of the early republican period targeted dress and the alphabet, the calendar and the official days of rest. Thirdly, the secularism of the founding elite was aimed at separating Religion from the State, but not the State from Religion. Landmark laws aimed at separating Islam from the State, such as the abrogation of the Caliphate and the elimination of the madrasas and religious courts on 3 March 1924, the adoption of a secular civil law in 1926 and the Constitutional Amendment of 1928, removing all reference to Islam as the state religion, all reflected a deep distrust in religion and led to the establishment of a state-controlled and state-funded public service. The Diyanet was founded in March 1924, precisely to provide religious services, based on an understanding of religion consisting of worship only, and therefore, confined to one's home and mosque.[47] Hence, the Diyanet was established as an administrative branch of the State, responsible to the Prime Minister, with no sacred significance attached to it.[48] In charge of the administration of mosques and appointment of religious personnel, it bore little resemblance to the Ministry of Shari'a and Religious Endowments (Şeriye ve Evkaf Vekâleti),[49] which it superseded together with the Directorate General of Endowments, the latter as a separate institution from the Diyanet. Not only was the new institution significantly demoted in terms of prestige, it was withdrawn from many crucial areas of responsibility, such as education and the judiciary. Importantly, the Diyanet was not given responsibility to train the religious personnel whom it administered. Following the logic of control intrinsic to Turkish secularism, the Turkish State undertook religious education by assigning it to the Ministry of Education, which was tasked with opening the imam-hatip schools and a faculty of theology, as well as offering optional

---

46   Gözaydın (n 2) 2.

47   Zana Çitak, 'Laïcité et nationalisme: une comparaison entre la France et la Turquie' in Jean Baubérot and Michel Wievorka (eds), *De la séparation des Eglises et de l'Etat à l'avenir de la laïcité* (Editions de l'Aube 2005) 207–22.

48   Gözaydın (n 3) 218.

49   Statements by both former and present high Diyanet officials and the Diyanet's own publications contradict one another on this issue. On the one hand, some argue that the Diyanet is a new, republican institution. On the other hand, others claim it to be the successor of the *Şeriye ve Evkaf Vekâleti*, emphasizing historical continuity both in its mission and activities. Scholarly studies of State–Religion relations in Turkey most of the time tend to underline the continuity between the Ottoman Empire and the Turkish Republic in terms of the relationship between the state and the religious establishment. For more nuanced arguments on this topic, see Kara (n 9) and Amit Bein, *Ottoman Ulema Turkish Republic: Agents of Change and Guardians of Tradition* (Stanford University Press 2011).

religious instruction in state schools.[50] A state-funded and state-controlled religion was meant to shape Islam as an individualized set of beliefs and compatible with science and modernity. Through the religious instruction offered by the State and the granting of salaries to imams, the founders of modern Turkey wanted to create an 'enlightened Islam'. When judged impossible to control, the State banned those manifestations of Islam, such as religious brotherhoods and dervish lodges (1925).

Thus, traditional religious institutions such as the madrasas and religious courts, which had existed side by side with their secular counterparts, withered away under the Republic, thus creating a duality in the modernization process of the Ottoman Empire from the early nineteenth century onwards.[51] At the same time, it also abandoned the Young Turks' Islamic justification for secular reforms.[52] Disestablishing Islam has brought with it control over Islam. Despite their distrust in Islam, however, the founding elite were aware of the salience of Islam in society and hence, the perception that religious service is like a public service. The transition to the multi-party system in 1946 resulted in increasing use of Islam by political parties, ending the rigid secularism of the single party period.[53] This also paved the way for increasing visibility of religion in the public sphere, particularly as a result of religious brotherhoods establishing various links with political parties.[54] The reappearance of Islam in political and social life had various manifestations: the reintroduction of courses of religion into the school system (1949), the re-establishment (1951) and eventual rapid spread of imam-hatip schools in the 1960s, the emergence of political parties with overtly Islamist agendas and programmes in the late 1960s and 1970s.

In addition to these, one could also see a considerable expansion of the Diyanet from 1965 onwards. Not only did its budget increase,[55] but Article No. 633 of the 1961 Constitution defined its mission in a much broader manner than Article No. 429 of the 1924 Law, which had stipulated that the Diyanet 'was formed as part of the Republic for the implementation of all provisions concerning faith and worship aspects of the religion of Islam, and the administration of religious institutions'.[56] In this new climate – and as a reflection of a new mentality in the 1960s – the Diyanet assumed new duties of 'carrying out affairs related to the

50   Kara (n 9) 62–3.
51   Niyazi Berkes, *The Development of Secularism in Turkey*, with a new introduction by Feroz Ahmad (Hurst & Co. 1998).
52   Bein (n 49) 20.
53   A debate on the necessity of making more room for Islam began initially in the Republican People's Party circle, when some MPs proposed the reintroduction of religious education as an effective weapon in the fight against communism. See Dankwart A Rustow, 'Politics and Islam in Turkey, 1920–1955' in Richard N. Frye (ed.), *Islam and the West* (Mouton & Co. 1957) 93.
54   Sam Kaplan, *The Pedagogical State: Education and Politics of National Culture in post-1980 Turkey* (Stanford University Press 2006) 43.
55   Gözaydın (n 42) 222–3.
56   Gözaydın (n 3) 218.

moral foundations of Islam' and 'enlightening society about religion'. This could be considered as the beginning of the use of the Diyanet as an ideological tool by political powers up until the present, in addition to its original role as an instrument of control.[57]

The 1982 Constitution, which has remained unchanged until today, further expanded the Diyanet's mission (Article 136), by defining its goal as 'promoting and consolidating national solidarity and unity'.[58] The assignment of such a duty to the Diyanet manifests the Turkish–Islamic synthesis, which increasingly determined the ideology of post-1980, centre-right Turkish Governments, equating 'Turkishness' with Muslim identity. It is not a coincidence that this new goal of national solidarity and unity was to be achieved also among Turkish immigrant communities in Europe; thus began the transnational network and the activities of the Diyanet. The recent Law No. 6002 of 1 July 2010 further consolidates the Diyanet's activities 'outside the mosque',[59] by stipulating the opening of more family counselling offices and giving the Diyanet the possibility of opening up its own radio and television channels, as well as Diyanet Academies for internal training.[60] The same law also regulates career opportunities for Diyanet employees (Yasal Mevzuat, www.diyanet.gov.tr).

The Diyanet was originally established to provide a public service and to oversee and control those who provide that public service[61] for 'securing secularism'.[62] It was also conceived as a non-sectarian and non-political institution. In time, however, it has increasingly become an institution serving the religious needs of the Sunni population and promoting Islam. While the Diyanet insists that religious services are provided in a completely non-discriminatory way,[63] it is precisely this ignorance of the diversity within the Muslim population, as well as within the Sunni majority, that leads to discriminatory and differential practices, going explicitly against the Constitutional Provision of Equality (Article 10 of the 1982 Constitution) of all citizens regardless of religious affiliation, language, race, ethnicity, faith, political opinion or philosophy.[64] Thus, the Diyanet is suffering from internal contradictions stemming from its dual nature. On the one hand, it is controlling Islam, by preventing radicalism and promoting moderation and compatibility of Islam with democracy and modernity. On the other hand, despite the constitutional provision that it should stay out of politics, it has been,

---

57   Gözaydın (n 2) 3–4, and Gözaydın (n 42) 164–6.

58   Gözaydın (n 3) 223.

59   The 2010 Activity Report of the Diyanet refers to 'outside mosque' activities as one of the 'strengths' of the institution. Accordingly, these allow for enhanced access to larger sections of society. Diyanet İşleri Başkanlığı (n 4) 60.

60   Sunier et al. (n 2) 49.

61   Gözaydın (n 42) 274.

62   Gözaydın (n 2) 1.

63   Diyanet İşleri Başkanlığı (n 4) 26.

64   Gözaydın (n 42) 288.

as an institution inside the State with no autonomy, frequently used as a tool by all governments for various political goals.[65] Again, there is also contradiction between the Diyanet's role as a domestic instrument to secure secularism on the one hand, and its promotion of (Sunni) Islam by 'enlightening society about religion' on the other.[66] In fact, it is these very contradictions and dualities that have made the Diyanet a popular institution for governments of a variety of political persuasions.[67]

A similar set of contradictions and duality also characterizes state funding of religious education, through compulsory religious and moral instruction (*Din Kültürü ve Ahlâk Bilgisi Dersi*) and imam-hatip schools. On 3 March 1924, the same date as when the Caliphate was abrogated and the Diyanet was established, the Law on the Unification of Instruction (*Tevhid-i Tedrisat*) was passed, which abolished the madrasas and secularized and unified the education system, ending a century-long duality in the Ottoman educational system. While the aim of assigning the responsibility for religious instruction to the Ministry of Education was again to control religion and train 'enlightened religious personnel', the imam-hatip schools, particularly after the 1970s, came to constitute separate 'religious-track' schools,[68] creating a duality not dissimilar to the previous one. In the same way, Article 24 of the 1982 Constitution, which made religious instruction compulsory from the fourth grade in elementary to the end of the high school, is a manifestation of the 'Turkish–Islamic synthesis'.[69] While the declared aim of this course is to 'enlighten' students about 'true religion' for the sake of secularism, it has again served to promote Islam in general, and its Sunni variant in particular.

The Lausanne Framework

The Treaty of Lausanne was signed between the Ankara Government and the Allied Powers after the victory of the former in the War of Independence (1919–1922). It brought about international recognition of the sovereignty of the Ankara Government in Eastern Thrace and Anatolia. Among other things, the treaty provided protection for non-Muslim minorities, which were defined in practice narrowly along the lines of the traditional Ottoman, non-Muslim religious communities of Armenian Gregorians, Greek Orthodox and Jews. While the Republic brought with it equality of citizens, irrespective of language, race,

---

65 Gözaydın (n 2) 7.

66 Sunier et al. (n 2) 140. An example of promotion of Islam by the Diyanet is the huge billboards that have been recently installed for display around the country and which feature the pictures of a father and son, in which the little boy is quoted saying 'Yippee! I am going to the mosque!' ('*Yaşasın Camiye Gidiyorum*'). For further details on the 'Child and Mosque' campaign, please see the Diyanet's website <www.diyanet,gov.tr>

67 Sunier et al. (n 2) 144–5.

68 Kaplan (n 54).

69 Kaplan (n 54) 45.

colour, sex, religion, political opinion, philosophical belief or sectarian affiliation (Article 10), minority status was granted only to these designated groups of non-Muslim citizens, as an international obligation within the Lausanne framework, and not to ethnic or linguistic groups. As such, the new republic followed on the path of its predecessor by officially recognizing a communal identity based on religion, while at the same time breaking from the past by recognizing members of communities as individual and equal citizens of the Turkish Republic, doing away with the 'ontological inequality' between Muslims and non-Muslims, intrinsic to the millet system, which is usually praised as an early example of tolerance and peaceful coexistence.[70]

However, this combination of group-specific rights with the principle of equality of citizenship proved to be a fragile one. The recognition of minority rights in the Lausanne Treaty was resented for being a foreign imposition, reminding Muslim Turks of the century-long intervention of foreign powers in the domestic affairs of the Ottoman Empire, beginning with the Tanzimat Edict of 1839.[71] At the same time, the spread of nationalism among the former millets from the early nineteenth century, the later failure of the policy of Ottomanism adopted in the early twentieth century as a means to create an Ottoman identity based on equal rights for all, the emergence of an overwhelming majority Muslim/Turkish population in Anatolia after the Balkan Wars and the separation of even the Muslim subjects of the Empire (Albanians and Arabs) and, finally, the Treaty of Sèvres in 1920 dissolving the empire along ethnic/religious lines, left their mark on the psyche of the new republic.[72] Hence, equal citizenship did not translate into membership of the Nation for non-Muslims, who were perceived as 'foreign' elements. Moreover, the dichotomy in this conceptualization of the Muslim majority/non-Muslim minority also meant a monolithic definition of the Muslim majority, regardless of ethnic, linguistic and sectarian diversity within. Thus, group-specific rights or public demands for identity recognition by various ethnic/sectarian/cultural groups were denied and deemed as 'dangerous' to the unity of the Nation. As such, a certain homogenization within the majority led to ignoring religious rights for non-Sunni Muslim groups.[73]

Thus, it is possible to say that the current system of state funding of religion and the differential treatment characteristic of it originate from this dual dynamic of a concern for homogenization for the Muslim majority and a perception of 'foreignness' of the non-Muslim minorities, both leading to the problem of double taxation on non-Muslim communities on the one hand, and assimilation with taxation and taxation without representation for the non-Sunnis on the other. As such, recent sociological changes in the religious configuration in Turkish

---

70 İçduygu et al. (n 20) 456–8.

71 Minority Rights Group International Report, *A Quest for Equality: Minorities in Turkey* (2007) 7.

72 İçduygu et al. (n 20) 451–2.

73 İçduygu et al. (n 20) 455–6.

society are perceived from a similar perspective, one of threat to national unity and security. As Akay[74] argues, the Turkish system of State–Religion relations in general, and state funding for religion in particular, suffer from a lack of flexibility necessary to accommodate new religious communities, and it has an even harder time meeting demands for justice and equality from more established groups, such as the Alevis.

Sociological and Political Challenges

It is possible to identify three sociological and political challenges to the current system of state funding for religion in Turkey. In the first place, as noted above, the current regime is not flexible enough to accommodate new sociological realities, such as the emergence of new religious communities. Consequently, Protestant religious groups do not fit into the Lausanne framework, as they are not defined as minorities. Nor do they qualify for funding from the Diyanet. This situation exacerbates the problem of differential treatment within the Turkish system of state funding and creates further discrimination among different religious communities. At the same time, a security perspective also defines the perception of demands for freedom of religion from Protestants and their activities are mostly viewed as 'missionary work', which has long been categorized as a threat to national unity by political parties of all persuasions[75] and by the Diyanet.[76]

Secondly, another sociological/political challenge is the increasing disjuncture between Nation-State and cultural/ethnic/religious/sectarian identities. Since the 1980s, there has been a growing intensification of identity-based politics in Turkey, which is challenging a homogeneous and unitary conception of national identity. On the one hand, this has led to increasing assertiveness of Islamist identities and politics. On the other hand, Kurdish and Alevi demands for recognition of their distinct identity and claims for equality have shown remarkable visibility in internal as well as external debates on democratization in Turkey. As far as religious communities and state funding for religion are concerned, the criticisms by the Alevis and other minority groups within the broader Muslim community

---

74 Akay (n 20) 46.

75 'Sağcı da solcu da misyonerlik alarmı veriyor', *Radikal*, 20 April 2007.

76 There is information on missionary activities under the 'Religious information' heading on the Diyanet's website <www.diyanet.gov.tr/turkish/dy/DiniBilgilerDetay. asppx?iD=305>. See also the article (Şinasi Gündüz, 'Misyonerlik ve Hristiyan Misyonerler' (2002) 38, 2 *Diyanet İlmi Dergi*) published in a Diyanet publication, which talks about the history of missionary activities in Turkey and what can be done about it. For an official statement on how the European Union accession process encourages missionary activities, see *Radikal* (n 75).

have particularly targeted compulsory courses of religion and the Diyanet.[77] Alevis have begun to politicize the issue, especially since the 1990s and recently filed complaints with the European Court of Human Rights,[78] which ruled in favour of the applicant, an Alevi parent, on the basis that these lessons are not general knowledge courses, as claimed by the government, but rather they basically follow Sunni Islamic doctrine and worship in their curriculum.[79]

While the Diyanet has been a major target of criticism from various sectarian groups in Turkey such as the Alevis, Caferis and Baha'is, it has, in fact, been a very controversial institution ever since the end of the single party regime in Turkey. Interestingly, the dual nature of the Diyanet has manifested itself in the arguments of various groups against the Diyanet. While, for the Islamists, the Diyanet has long been a promoter of Islam *à la* Kemalism, for the Kemalists, this institution has itself been an actor in the Islamization of Turkish society, and hence, not living up to its controlling mission that it was originally designed for. However, neither of these groups is seriously considering the complete abolition of the institution. In fact, both groups are fearful, for different reasons though, of a 'religious anarchy' in the absence of the State's regulatory power.[80] Those who advocate the abrogation of the Diyanet, either secular or religious conservatives, seem not to be in a majority. According to a 2006 poll, popular support for religious services being financed by believers' voluntary contributions amounts to about 49.3 per cent, which is still higher than those who oppose it or who are not sure.[81]

In the debate on the Diyanet, one could also find arguments for assigning more autonomy to the Diyanet. While it is not always clear what autonomy means in this context and what it exactly entails, nevertheless, the common point among arguments for an autonomous Diyanet is the need to remove it from the influence

---

77   While, in principle, non-Muslim students are exempt from attending these courses, there has been confusion in practice due to contradictory directives from the Ministry of Education. While a 1990 directive exempts them from these courses, one from 1992 grants them exemption only from topics that specifically cover Sunni prayer and worship, but holds them responsible for other subjects related to religion and morality in a more general way (Buket Türkmen, 'Kemalist İslam'ın Dönüşümü mü Yoksa Yeni Sünni Yurttaş Ahlâkı mı?: 'Din Kültürü ve Ahlâk Bilgisi' Ders Kitapları Üzerine Bir İnceleme', (2011) 120 *Toplum ve Bilim* 57–8). As Buket Türkmen points out, non-Muslims have not been publicly very vocal about their grievances on this issue, due to their traditional quietism and in order not to offend the authorities. For an example of public criticism by the Protestant community, however, see the petition addressed to the Ministry of Education by the Protestant Churches, available at: <http://www.protestankiliseler.org/index.php?option=com_content&view=article&id=1 and http://firatnews.com/index.php?rupel=nuce&nuceID=27266> 1 June 2010.

78   *Hasan and Eylem Zengin v. Turkey*, No. 1448/04 (ECHR, 9 October 2007).

79   For accounts of Alevis' experiences with the compulsory courses in religion, see Aykan Erdemir et al., *Türkiye'de Alevi Olmak* (2010) 104–19.

80   Bein (n 49) 157–62, and Gözaydın (n 42) 273–87.

81   Ali Çarkoğlu et al., *Değişen Türkiye'de Din, Toplum ve Siyaset* (TESEV Yayınları 2006) 80.

of political power.[82] Another proposal is to make room for representation of – and state funding for – other faiths as well. Nevertheless, the 2006 poll suggests that there has been a decrease in popular support for Diyanet funding to support the *cemevis* of the Alevis, from 69.2 per cent in 1999 to 43.5 per cent in 2006, which, according to Çarkoğlu and Toprak, demonstrates the increasing sectarian polarization in the Turkish context.[83] Thus, while the sociological challenge of increasing demands for recognition of sub-national identities seems to challenge the current regime of state funding for religion in Turkey, at the same time, this demand for enhanced pluralism feeds into fears of religious chaos on the part of those who advocate the present system, notwithstanding their own criticisms for different reasons *vis-à-vis* the Diyanet.

The Diyanet, however, is also challenged in the transnational dimension of funding of religion, a factor that has often been overlooked in the literature. The realization of the permanence and increasing visibility of Muslim communities in Europe initially led to an enhanced role for the Diyanet. As a representative of the secular Turkish State, and moderate in its interpretation of Islam, the Diyanet soon became one of the main interlocutors for various European States. Nevertheless, efforts to create European Islam(s) through various processes of institutionalization of Islam aim at eliminating the role of the host country's influence and network in Muslim communities and creating an Islam endogenous to Europe. In that respect, the Diyanet's claim to represent the Turkish/Muslim community and its continuing financial and organizational influence are being challenged.[84] The Diyanet continues to send and pay salaries to imams, which most likely will not change in the short-term. However, the emergence of European Islam(s) has the prospect of changing transnational funding in the future.

A third challenge is the European Union accession process for Turkey. In fact, it is possible to argue that identity politics, demands for increasing pluralism and the ensuing recent criticisms and challenges to the current regime of state funding in Turkey have been closely connected to the nature of relations between Turkey and the European Union. The European Union has been putting increasing pressure on Turkey for democratization, and protection of minority rights has been one of the most important components on the agenda of Turkey's relations with Europe since the early 1990s. Thus, it is impossible to examine improvements in the rights of non-Muslim minorities independently of the reform packages of the 2000s, as they relate particularly to the Law on Foundations. Again, the ruling of the European Court of Human Rights in relation to the Alevis' exemption from compulsory courses in religion has been an important variable in the debate on the legitimacy of these courses.

However, it is important also to recognize the limitations of the European Union factor in reforming the current state-funding regime in Turkey. One limitation is

---

82   Gözaydın (n 42) 282.
83   Çarkoğlu et al. (n 81) 80.
84   Çitak (n 36).

the salience of entrenched and established structures and practices, whose origins can be found, as examined previously, in the peculiarities of Turkish secularism and the Lausanne framework, as well as in the evolution of the place of religion in Turkish society since the late 1940s. While some structures and practices can be more susceptible to pressure from external actors, others might prove to be more resilient. Secondly, and related to the previous limitation, one should also take into consideration the possible counter-productive effects of pressure from the European Union. As has been discussed above, European interference in Turkish domestic affairs is stigmatized, due to the weight of the historical experience of Ottoman modernization and minority rights in the nineteenth century. In fact, Alevis' demands for recognition of their rights has frequently been labelled as 'provoked from the outside' and a consequence of the European Union's attempt to create 'new minorities' beyond the Lausanne minorities in Turkey. Thirdly, the pace of Turkey–Europe relations is also an important factor, determining the capacity of the European Union to influence reform in Turkey. The cooling of relations between the European Union and Turkey since 2005 – for various reasons that are beyond the scope of this chapter – and the distancing of Turkish foreign policy from Europe, turning rather towards the Middle East, seem to have resulted in a loss of leverage on the part of the European Union to effect political reform in Turkey. Fourthly, the effect of Europe can at times amount to no more than cosmetic changes, such as in the incorporation of a section on Alevism as 'one of the interpretations of Islam' in the textbooks of compulsory courses in religion. Not only did the AKP government show incredible resistance to making compulsory courses in religion optional, the new textbooks have exacerbated the problem by shaping how Alevism will be portrayed in the curriculum, which continues to follow the Sunni doctrine.[85]

Policy Suggestions

As we have discussed throughout this chapter, the differential and often discriminatory treatment of religious communities in Turkey stems from the current regime of state funding of religious institutions and services. The most significant step towards improving the current arrangement is to reform state funding of religion and the institutional structure of the Diyanet. Only through equal treatment and support of all religious communities in Turkey can one begin to transform the religious domain into a fairer and inclusive system. We, therefore, recommend the following policy suggestions be implemented in Turkey:

1. Establishment of a Regulatory Agency of Religious Services (İnanç Hizmetleri Üst Kurulu), representing all existing religious communities in Turkey and authorized to regulate and audit religious institutions;

---

85   For Alevi activists' criticisms of the new textbooks, see Türkmen (n 77) 59.

2. Lifting of the Diyanet's privileged legal and financial status, transforming it into an autonomous and privately funded Sunni institution;
3. Allowing each religious denomination to be fully in charge of running and funding its own religious institutions, services and affairs;
4. Recognition of the equal legal status of places of worship belonging to all religious communities;
5. Abolishing compulsory courses in religion from school curricula and allowing each religious community to offer elective classes in schools;
6. Lifting of the legal and financial privileges provided to the Diyanet Foundation to bring it on a par with other religious foundations;
7. Allowing each religious community equal access to broadcasting on state radio and television.

List of References

(2005) 'Diyanet: Misyonerler AB sürecinden yararlanıyor' *Hürriyet*, 5 January 2005 <http://hurarsiv.hurriyet.com.tr/goster/ShowNew.aspx?id=286458>
(2007) 'Sağcı da solcu da misyonerlik alarmı veriyor' *Radikal*, 20 April 2007, <www.radikal.com.tr/haber.php?haberno=218964>
Akay H, 'Uygulamada Laiklik: Devlet-Din Ekseninde Özgürlükler, Hizmetler ve Finansman' (2011) 120 *Toplum ve Bilim*
Bein A, *Ottoman Ulema Turkish Republic: Agents of Change and Guardians of Tradition* (California: Stanford University Press 2011)
Berkes N, *The Development of Secularism in Turkey*, with a new introduction by Feroz Ahmad (Hurst & Co. 1998)
Çarkoğlu A et al., *Değişen Türkiye'de Din, Toplum ve Siyaset* (TESEV Yayınları 2006)
Çitak Z, 'Laïcité et nationalisme: une comparaison entre la France et la Turquie' in J Baubérot et al. (eds), *De la séparation des Eglises et de l'Etat à l'avenir de la laïcité* (Editions de l'Aube 2005)
—— 'Between 'Turkish Islam' and 'French Islam': The Role of the Diyanet' in Conseil Français du Culte Musulman (2010) 36, 4 *Journal of Ethnic and Migration Studies*
—— 'Religion, Ethnicity and Transnationalism: Turkish Islam in Belgium' (2011) 53, 2 *Journal of Church and State*
Dere A, 'The PRA of Turkey: The Emergence, Evolution and Perception of its Religious Services Outside of Turkey' (2008) 98, 2–3 *The Muslim World*
Diyanet İşleri Başkanlığı Faaliyet, *Raporu* (2010) <www.diyanet.gov.tr> accessed 13 October 2011
Erdemir A et al., *Türkiye'de Alevi Olmak* (2010)
Gökaçtı MA, *Türkiye'de Din Eğitimi ve İmam-Hatipler* (İletişim Yayınları 2005)

Gözaydın İ, 'A Religious Administration to Secure Secularism: The Presidency of Religious Affairs of the Republic of Turkey' (2006) 11, 1 *Marburg Journal of Religion*

—— '*Diyanet* and Politics' (2008) 98, 2–3 *The Muslim World*

—— *Diyanet: Türkiye Cumhuriyeti'nde Dinin Tanzimi* (İletişim Yayınları 2009)

Gündüz Ş, 'Misyonerlik ve Hristiyan Misyonerler' (2002) 38, 2 *Diyanet* İlmi *Dergi* <www.diyanet.gov.tr/turkish/DIYANET/ilmi_dergi/ilmi/main.asp?makro=1>

İçduygu A et al., 'Turkish Minority Rights Regime: Between Difference and Equality' (2006) 42, 3 *Middle Eastern Studies*

Kaplan S, *The Pedagogical State: Education and Politics of National Culture in post-1980 Turkey* (Stanford University Press 2006)

Kara İ, *Cumhuriyet Türkiyesi'nde Bir Mesele Olarak* İslam (Dergâh Yayınları 2008)

Macar E et al., *Heybeliada Ruhban Okulu'nun Geleceği* Üzerine *Tartışmalar ve* Öneriler (TESEV 2005)

Mahçupyan E, *Türkiye'de Gayrimüslim Cemaatlerin Sorunları ve Vatandaş Olamama Durumu* Üzerine, Ekonomik ve Sosyal Etüdler Vakfı (TESEV 2004) no. 1, <http://www.tesev.org.tr/etkinlik/demokratiklesme_cemaatler.php>

Minority Rights Group International Report, *A Quest for Equality: Minorities in Turkey* (2007)

Oran B, *Küreselleşme ve Azınlıklar* (İmaj Yayınevi 2000)

Rustow DA, 'Politics and Islam in Turkey, 1920–1955' in RN Frye (ed.), *Islam and the West* (Mouton & Co. 1957)

Sunier T et al., *Diyanet: The Turkish Directorate for Religious Affairs in a Changing Environment* (VU University Amsterdam and Utrecht University 2011)

Türkmen B, 'Kemalist İslam'ın Dönüşümü mü Yoksa Yeni Sünni Yurttaş Ahlâkı mı?: 'Din Kültürü ve Ahlâk Bilgisi' Ders Kitapları Üzerine Bir İnceleme' (2011) 120 *Toplum ve Bilim*

Yıldırım M, 'TURKEY: The Diyanet – The Elephant in Turkey's Religious Freedom Room?' (2011) *FORUM 18 News Service*, 4 May <http://www.forum18.org>

Chapter 12

Religious Communities, Public Funding and Economics

Niels Kærgård

What is Economics?

The science of economics deals with institutions, allocation of resources and the rational organization of society. The basic assumption behind most economic theory is that the best society is the one whose members are the happiest; economists call happiness 'utility'. In most situations, this is the case when individuals have considerable freedom to maximize their own utility through free choice.

This is most explicit in allocation via the market mechanism. Given some ideal assumptions, the price mechanism will generate an allocation of the resources in the society, which is optimal in the sense that all other allocations will be worse for at least some people. In a market economy, producers decide what they want to produce independently of other producers and consumers, and they only maximize their own individual profit given the prices and wages in society. Similarly, consumers buy what they want independently of the other agents in society given their own income and the prices. The coordination is established via the price mechanism. If there is excess supply of a commodity, the price will fall and fewer firms will produce the commodity, while more consumers will buy the commodity. The price is the coordinating signal between producers and consumers.

However, sometimes these price signals are misleading or non-existent. Markets do not exist for everything; there can be what economists call 'external effects'. This means that some by-products, which are important as far as society is concerned, are non-market goods which do not enter into the private firms' accounts. Such external effects can be positive or negative. The beekeeper receives money for honey, but not for the important social work the bees perform for farmers and biodiversity by pollinating cultivated and uncultivated plants. This means that the beekeeper does not receive income for all the benefit he produces for society. This means that there will be too few beekeepers if there is no public support for beekeeping. Such reasoning has been part of the argument for supporting farmers in Europe; they not only produce food for the market, but also provide food safety, landscape preservation, labour in peripheral rural areas etc. However, external effects can also be negative. Factories not only produce commodities for the market, but also, for example, pollution, smoke, noise etc. To regulate this, society introduces 'green taxes', also known as Pigou-taxes because of Arthur Pigou's pioneering book *The Economics of Welfare* of 1920.

Another problem with market regulation is what economists call 'public goods'. These are goods for which there is no competition between users and for which it is impossible to exclude anybody from their use. The standard television signal is an example of a public good. Viewers do not compete over the signals; I can watch television regardless of whether my neighbour is watching the same programme. And when the signals are sent, everybody can use them. Public defence, the police, most infrastructures, knowledge gained from research, etc. are further examples of public goods. Regulation through the market mechanism is not possible, because there is a serious free-riding problem; everybody can use the goods and, consequently, nobody is willing to pay individually. For this reason, public goods are normally produced by society. This is indicated by the common use of the word 'public' in both 'public goods' and the 'public sector'.

It is important to stress that economics deals with the whole of human life, not only material products which are exchanged via the market. This means that materialism and commercialism have no foundation in economics. Agents in economic models receive utility from everything that influences their well-being. Sunshine, love, spring water and a beautiful landscape are as economically relevant as food and cars.

But it is of course difficult to quantify the importance of non-market goods. However, a lot of work has been conducted to quantify the value of, in particular, environmental goods such as public recreational areas, national parks etc. One can ask people what they would be willing to pay for a walk in a forest, if it was not free, or one can calculate how much people have spent on transportation to travel to the forest. Also, house prices in different areas can be a good indication of the value of access to a beach or forest.

Economic cost–benefit analysis attempts to measure all the costs and benefits of a specific decision including non-market goods. It is complicated. If too few immaterial goods are included, there will be a bias towards materialism. But if all immaterial goods are to be taken into account, it will necessitate a lot of very difficult or perhaps even impossible valuations. For example, what is the value of good health or beautiful flowers? It is, however, important to remember that, even if we do not quantify, decision makers implicitly make such valuations every time they take decisions about health care or city planning.

Another relevant branch of economics deals with economic growth and development. Why are some countries becoming rich while others are becoming poorer and stagnating? Institutions play a very important role. A key figure in the analysis of institutions and economic performance is the Nobel Prize winner, Douglass C. North. In his seminal book, *Institutions, Institutional Change and Economic Performance*, he defined institutions thus:

> Institutions are the rules of the game in a society or, more formally, are the humanly devised constraints that shape human interaction. In consequence they

structure incentives in human exchange, whether political, social, or economic. Institutional change shapes the way societies evolve through time and hence is the key to understanding historical change ... Institutions reduce uncertainty by providing a structure to everyday life ... Institutions include any form of constraint that human beings devise to shape human interaction.[1]

According to Douglass North, institutions can be divided into three different parts: formal constraints, informal constraints and enforcement. The difference between informal and formal constraints is one of degree ranging from taboos, customs and traditions to written constitutions. An important part of institutions is the enforcement of rules. This can be based on a wide range of institutions from an effective judicial system to moral restriction and loss of moral reputation.

According to North, society is characterized not only by 'institutions', but also by 'organizations':

A crucial distinction ... is made between institutions and organizations. Like institutions, organizations provide a structure of human interaction ... Organizations include political bodies (political parties, the Senate, a city council, a regulatory agency), economic bodies (firms, trade unions, family farms, cooperatives), social bodies (churches, clubs, athletic associations), and educational bodies (schools, universities, vocational training centers). They are groups of individuals bound by some common purpose to achieve objectives.[2]

North's conclusion is that institutions are crucial to the economic performance of societies:

Institutions provide the basic structure by which human beings throughout history have created order and attempted to reduce uncertainty in exchange. Together with the technology employed, they determine transaction and transformation costs and hence the profitability and feasibility of engaging in economic activity. They connect the past with the present and the future so that history is a largely incremental story of institutional evolution in which the historical performance of economies can only be understood as a part of a sequential story.[3]

This includes many different forms of institutions:

---

1   Douglass C North, *Institutions, Institutional Change, and Economic Performance* (University Press 1990) 3–4.
2   North (n 1) 4–5.
3   North (n 1) 118.

Informal constraints matter. We need to know much more about culturally derived norms of behaviour and how they interact with formal rules to get better answers to such issues. We are just beginning the serious study of institutions.[4]

Another crucial element in North's understanding of human behaviour is the interpretation of the realities or, in the words of another Nobel Prize winner Herbert Simon, 'the distinction between the real world and the decision maker's perception of it'.[5] In this perception, both ideology and religion play an important role:

The subjective and incomplete processing of information plays a critical role in decision making. It accounts for ideology, based upon subjective perceptions of reality, playing a major part in human beings' choices ... By ideology I mean the subjective perceptions ... all people possess to explain the world around them. Whether at the micro level of individual relationships or at the macro level of organized ideologies providing integrated explanations of the past and present, such as communism or religions, the *theories* individuals construct are *colored* by normative views of how the world should be organized.[6]

Other parts of economic theory are also relevant to the discussion of churches and religious communities, but in the following discussion, the above-mentioned key elements of market theory and institutional economics are the most important.

What is a Religious Community?

A religious community, for example the Danish Public Church, consists of many very different elements, including what North calls 'institutions' and 'organizations'. It also consists of some very tangible elements, such as buildings, land and cemeteries, but a lot of them have considerable sentimental value. They are historical places which are part of the society's cultural inheritance. Almost all Danish buildings from the Middle Ages are churches. Some of these will have a higher sentimental value for a nationalistic atheist than for a spiritual Christian.

Sentimental value is not only connected to the buildings themselves, but also to the ceremonies that take place inside them. For many romantic couples who are doubtful about Christian dogma, it is still of great value to get married and have a traditional ceremony in an old church containing art from the Renaissance period. Many Danes like to sing old Christmas hymns in church as part of the family's Christmas tradition. For concerts where the music of Bach and Handel are

---

4   North (n 1) 140.

5   North (n 1) 22–3, and Herbert Simon, 'Rationality in Psychology and Economics' in Robin M Hogarth et al. (eds), (1986) 59 (supp.) *The Behavioural Foundation of Economic Theory, Journal of Business* 210.

6   North (n 1) 23.

being played, a church with an organ is almost essential, even for a non-religious music enthusiast.

In many countries, churches and their ceremonies are part of the national identity and the coherency of the population; at least until very recently, this has been the case in Denmark. But there are of course also societies in which religious conflicts have a very negative effect on the coherency of the population; Northern Ireland and the former Yugoslavia are clear examples of this. The relationship between coherency and religion is obviously a very important, but also very difficult, question. In modern social science, coherency and what is called 'social capital' are considered to be very important for the success of a society. No doubt, there are dominating elements of what historians call 'path-dependency' in these relations. Whether religious communities have a positive or negative influence on the coherency and economic performance of a nation is highly dependent on the history and the institutions of the society.

Religious communities are not just buildings, historical places and ceremonies; they also consist of beliefs and attitudes, which are also of vital importance to society. These attitudes can have a significant effect on how agents act. They constitute institutions as defined by Douglass North. Religious rules significantly restrict how members act: for example, practising Catholics do not accept divorce; Muslims do not eat pork meat; Protestants are sometimes said to be especially hard-working and many religions demand ascetic behaviour, just to mention a few obvious examples. Even in the secular USA, there are close links between religion and formal institutions in the form of laws, as formulated by John Witte Jr:

> Law and religion also balance each other by counterpoising justice and mercy, rule and equity, discipline and love. This dialectical interaction gives these two disciplines and dimensions of life their vitality and their strength. Without law, religion slowly slides into shallow spiritualism. Without religion, law gradually crumbles into empty formalism.[7]

The position of economists regarding the role of religion in the discussion of the development of societies has changed over time. In the first decades of the twentieth century, there was intense debate about religion, which was considered very important, also for the economic development of society, although this debate disappeared in the 1930s. However, interest in religion has witnessed a revival in the last couple of decades. The next section will present a short discussion of the debate among economists.

---

7 John Jr Witte, 'Introduction to American Law and Religion Discourse' in Lisbet Christoffersen et al. (eds), *Law & Religion in the 21st Century – Nordic Perspectives* (Djof Publishing 2010) 43.

Religion and Economics

At least since Max Weber's contribution at the beginning of the twentieth century, there has been an ongoing debate about the relationship between the influence of religion and economic forces. This debate has not yet reached a consensus and, until very recently, few modern economists were interested in the debate. In a survey, Heine Andersen (1999) asked 788 Danish social scientists about the researchers they found most important in relation to their discipline. The top three were:

1. Max Weber
2. John Maynard Keynes
3. Karl Marx

But it is characteristic that, whereas Max Weber was number one among sociologists and political scientists, he was not in the top ten among economists. Theories concerning less economics-based subjects, such as religion, have until very recently not been classed as high priority by modern mainstream economists.

Nevertheless, Max Weber (1864–1920) has a central place in the debate about religion and economics. He was an unorthodox pupil of the German economic-historical school. He was professor in Freiburg and Heidelberg in the 1890s and, after a long personal crisis, he became active again and was professor in Vienna and Munich from 1918–19. His most well-known contribution is *Die protestantische Ethik und der Geist des Kapitalismus*, which was published in 1904–05. In this contribution, he tried to draw parallels between the spirit of capitalism and Protestant ethics.

According to Weber and his pupils, a special attitude to work can be traced back to Christian reformers in the sixteenth century. Jean Calvin and Martin Luther argued against the Catholic Church's beliefs about internal ecclesiastical activities, monks and monasteries, but instead considered it to be the duty of Christians to become involved in activities in society outside the ecclesiastical sphere. This was a request to Christians to view labour as a duty and a calling. Thus, it was a Christian's duty to work in civil society in the interests of his community and neighbours. Tawney (1926) and Samuelson (1957) are perhaps the most well-known discussions of Weber's theory.

Such rather general discussions of the relation between religion and economic behaviour were common among economists of the historical and institutional schools in the period before 1930. Werner Sombart (1863–1941), with his contributions *Der moderne Kapitalismus* (1902) and *Die Juden und das Wirtschaftsleben* (1911), is another prominent example from the period. Sombart, like many others at the time, saw a close relationship between the capitalist market economy and the Jewish religion.[8]

---

8 This attitude can also be found among Danish theologians during the period. See, for example, Bishop Hans Lassen Martensen, 'Den Christelige Ethik' (Christian Ethic) of 1878.

During the inter-war period, this attitude degenerated into fascism and so did Sombart himself, while at the same time, mainstream economics moved in a mathematical and statistical direction. In 1933, Hitler came to power in Germany and, at the same time, the first volume of the mathematical-economics journal, *Econometrica*, was published in United States and it soon became the most prestigious of the economic journals. Both of these independent events are symbols of a development which almost totally excluded the relationship between religion and economics from serious economic research for many decades.

During the very last couple of decades, religion has once again begun to appear in economics – as both qualitative and quantitative variables in statistical studies. Martin Paldam, for example, used a classification of ten religious groups (four Christian groups – Orthodox, Catholic, Anglican and Protestant – as well as Islamic, Hindu, Buddhist, oriental, tribal and atheist groups) as an explanatory variable in a statistical study of corruption in 135 countries. He found a statistically significant lower level of corruption in Protestant and Anglican countries, while these countries have an income which is more than four times as high as the average level in the sample.[9] In a study of Irish agriculture in the nineteenth century, Kevin H. O'Rourke found a significant difference in the establishment of dairies between Catholic and Protestant counties in Ireland and a significant negative effect of counties with mixed religions.[10] A considerable number of such studies could be mentioned.

At the same time, there was a revival of interest in mainstream economics about 'institutions', as previously mentioned. A more theoretical formulation is found in 'new institutional economics', with names such as Douglass North and Oliver E. Williamson. Not only have formal institutions found their way into mainstream economics and economic history, but so have 'softer' institutions in the form of 'social capital'.[11]

This means that attitudes, confidence and credibility have been reintroduced into economics and old Weberian questions about ethics and spirit have been taken up once again in new forms. They are important informal institutions in

---

9   See Martin Paldam, 'Corruption and Religion: Adding to the Economic Model' (2001) 54 *Kyklos* 383–414.

10   Kevin H O'Rourke 'Culture, Politics and Innovation: Evidence from the Creameries' (2002) *CEPR Discussion Paper* 3235.

11   Pierre Bourdieu, 'The Forms of Capital' in Richardson, John (ed.), *Handbook of Theory and Research for the Sociology of Education* (Greenwood Press 1986); Robert D Putnam, *Making Democracy Work, civic traditions in modern Italy* (Princeton University Press 1993); Robert D Putnam, 'Bowling alone: America's declining social capital' (1995) 6, 1 *Journal of Democracy* 65–78; Martin Paldam, 'Social Capital: One or Many? Definition and Measurement' (2000) 14, 5 *Journal of Economic Surveys* 629–53 (Special Issue on Political Economy); Martin Paldam et al., 'An essay on social capital: Looking for the fire behind the smoke' (2000) 16 *European Journal of Political Economy* 339–66; Martin Paldam et al. (eds), *Trust, Social Capital and Economic Growth: An International Comparison* (Edward Elgar Publishing 2003).

Northian terms; religious condemnation and reputation within religious societies are important ways of enforcing the rules among agents. Since Weber's time, a huge stock of statistical data has, however, been calculated and estimation methods have improved considerably. This has resulted in a number of empirical studies which have investigated economic hypotheses including religion. Religion has for instance been reintroduced as an explanatory factor for economic growth. Blum and Dudley[12] investigate economic growth in European cities from 1500 to 1750 and find a considerable difference between Catholic and Protestant cities. For example, Landes[13] and Acemoglu, Johnson and Robinson[14] find that religion has a statistically significant, but not very important, effect on economic growth.

A number of remarkable statistical studies have been conducted by one of the most prominent mainstream economists of the last four decades, Robert J. Barro from Harvard University.[15] He explains economic growth in a large cross-country sample with a number of variables including church attendance and belief in Heaven and Hell. Furthermore, he uses a number of dummy variables for the different religions, but his main interest is in attendance and belief variables, irrespective of the religion. His theory – which has been significantly confirmed by his statistical investigation – is that 'church attendance' has a negative effect on economic growth. People use time and energy on religious activities instead of productive activities. On the other hand, belief in Hell, but also in Heaven, stimulates a good work ethic and conscientiousness which have a positive effect on economic growth. Belief in Heaven and Hell is a central part of the enforcement of moral commitments. Consequently, the net effect of religion is insignificant in Barro's investigation because of the contradictory effects. Barro found small, but significant differences between the different religions; Orthodox, Hindu and Muslim faiths – in that order – have a negative effect on economic growth, while Catholic, Jewish and Protestant faiths – in that order – have a positive effect.[16]

Barro is just one example of the new interest in religion among economists. Recent decades have witnessed a rapid growth in literature in the border area between economics and religion. For a profound overview of the first wave of this

---

12   Ulrich Blum et al., 'Religion and Economic Growth: Was Weber right?' (2001) 11 *Journal of Evolutionary Economics* 207–30.

13   David S Landes, *The Wealth and Poverty of Nations: Why Some Are So Rich and Some So Poor* (W.W. Norton & Co 1998).

14   Daron Acemoglu et al., 'The Rise of Europe: Atlantic Trade, Institutional Change and Economic Growth' (2005) 95 *American Economic Review* 546–79.

15   Robert J. Barro (born in 1944) has been professor of economics at Harvard University since 1987 and is very well known for a number of important contributions to economic science, mainly in monetary theory, economic policy and growth. He was the second most cited economist in the 1990s. His contributions on religion and economics are all from the last ten years.

16   See Robert J Barro et al., 'Religion and Economic Growth' (2003) *NBER Working Paper* W9682, and Robert J Barro et al., 'Religion and Economic Growth Across Countries' (2003) 68, 5 *American Sociological Review* 760–81.

literature see Laurence Iannaccone.[17] The *Association for the Study of Economics, Religion and Culture* held its first conference in 2002.

A major problem for statistical studies of the effect of religion on economic performance is that a considerable number of variables, of which religion is one, are characteristic of a specific geographical area. Is the development in the Scandinavian countries due to the fact that Scandinavians are Protestants, that they have a specific climate, that they have a lot of natural harbours, or that they have a common history going back to the Vikings? An area with a common religion, such as Scandinavia or the Middle East, normally has many other common characteristics and this makes it difficult statistically to separate which of the area's characteristics is the cause of the development in the area. We are far from the ideal statistical situation with the different causes varying independently of one another.

This is also the problem for the considerable semi-economic literature on the effect of Islam on the economy and society.[18] Muslim countries are geographically concentrated around the Middle East, North Africa and Southwest Asia and share many common characteristics, not just religion.

Barro and McCleary[19] formulate the following statement about the relationship between economics and religion:

> Our central perspective is that religion affects economic outcomes mainly by fostering religious beliefs that influence individual traits such as thrift, work ethic, honesty, and openness to strangers. For example, beliefs in heaven and hell might affect these traits by creating perceived rewards and punishments that relate to 'good' and 'bad' lifetime behaviour. In this perspective, organized religion – and, more specifically, attendance at religious services – would affect economic performance mostly indirectly, that is, through influences on the religious beliefs. Hence, we envision a chain whereby church attendance affects religious beliefs, which affect individual traits, which affect economic outcomes.[20]

The idea can be illustrated as in Figure 12.1.

---

17   Laurence R Iannaccone, 'Introduction to the Economics of Religion' (1998) 36 *Journal of Economic Literature* 1465–96.

18   See Samuel P Huntington, *The Clash of Civilizations and the Remaking of World Order* (Simon & Schuster 1996); Sven Burmester, *Fred og Fare. Islam, Østasien og Vesten set af en dansk kosmopolit* (Gyldendal 2007); Rodney Stark, *The Victory of Reason: How Christianity led to Freedom, Capitalism, and Western Success* (Random House, Inc. 2006); and many others.

19   Barro et al. (n 16), 'Religion and Economic Growth'.

20   ibid 23–4.

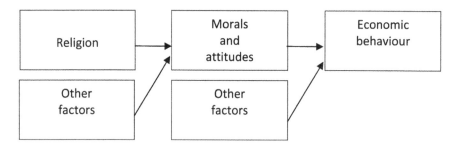

Figure 12.1 The causal chain from religion to economic behaviour

As an example of such effects, one can consider the development of the Danish welfare state. There seem to be good arguments for believing that at least some of the roots of this welfare state can be traced to the Christian pioneers' mercifulness and charitableness towards the weak and poor members of society.[21] In 1873, a law to protect children and youngsters against working in industry was passed (work was forbidden for children younger than ten years, while children aged between ten and fourteen were only allowed to work six hours per day). In 1891, a general pension was introduced for poor elderly people and, at the same time, support for people who had undeservedly lost their income. In 1892, a law was passed to establish health insurance associations (*sygekasser*) and the public paid half of the hospital costs for members of these associations. In 1907, unemployment insurance associations received public support. A major social problem in Danish society at that time was poor farm workers. A land reform, which gave small pieces of land to farm workers was passed by Parliament in 1899 and was further developed in 1904, 1907 and 1919. All these early reforms were implemented before the important influence of the socialist movement and many of the most prominent personalities who participated in the social and political debate from 1870 to 1914 were Christians.[22] The most remarkable contribution to the debate was perhaps from Hans Lassen Martensen and his pamphlet *Socialisme og Christendom* [Socialism and Christianity] of 1874.[23] In the 1870s, Martensen

---

21 Niels Kærgård et al., 'Harald Westergaard: From Young Pioneer to Established Authority' in WJ Samuels (ed.), *European Economists of the early 20th Century*, vol. 1 (Edward Elgar 1998) 349–69.

22 Niels Kærgård, 'Cooperation not opposition – Marginalism and Socialism in Denmark 1871–1924' in Ian Steedman (ed.), *Socialism and Marginalism in Economics 1870–1930* (Routledge 1995), and Niels Kærgård, 'Economic thought and economic development in Denmark 1848–1914' in Michalis Psalidopoulos et al. (eds), *Economic Thought and Policy in Less Developed Europe* (London: Routledge 2002) 21–36.

23 Martensen (1808–84) was at the pinnacle of the official Danish church. He was Professor of Theology at the University of Copenhagen from 1840 to 1854 and in 1854 he became Bishop of Zealand (which includes Copenhagen).

worked on Christian ethics and his pamphlet was incorporated into volume III – *Den Sociale Ethik* [The Social Ethics] – of his Christian Ethics in 1878; it is clear that he did not consider the pamphlet to be of a more polemical nature, but rather a part of his 'official' Christian ethics.

These Christian-Socialist movements seem to have played an important role in the very early welfare state, but their importance began to decrease from around World War I when the Social Democratic Party (*Socialdemokratiet*) achieved a dominant position in the social and political debate. It is difficult to estimate how important the Christian movement was compared to the Socialist, but it is always the winner who writes history and, while the Christian-Social parties have disappeared from Denmark, the power of the Social Democrats has grown. It seems reasonable to assume, therefore, that the importance of the Christian movements is usually underestimated today.

It is well known that the Catholic Church has even more specific social ethics than the Lutheran. Whereas Lutherans have a very distinct separation of the religions and the secular regime, Catholics have more specific social ethics. So if there are correlations between the development of the Danish Welfare State and Christianity, it is not unfair to conclude that a society's religion generally has an important effect on the nature and form of a society's institutions.

It is also worth remembering that the state and its role have changed radically since America's great founder, Thomas Jefferson, formulated the axiom of 'a wall of separation between Church and State'. The modern welfare state regulates education, charity, welfare, childcare, healthcare, family rules, the workplace, taxation and security. 'Both confrontation and cooperation with the modern state are almost inevitable for any religion that peeks of its cave'.[24]

Society and Religious Communities

Given this description of economics, churches and religion, perhaps we cannot – from an economic point of view – say much about the optimal relationship between the State and religious communities. The arrangements are very different from country to country, and these arrangements are highly dependent on the history of the different countries.

What can be said, is that religion and religious institutions have a very important influence on economic institutions and citizens' well-being. The religious sector has significant sentimental value and important effects on social capital. No doubt this includes both production of public goods and external effects. Consequently, very few countries have a clear logical distinction between state and religion, where all buildings and ceremonies related to religion are purely private.[25]

---

24 Witte (n 7) 51.

25 See for a discussion of a different organization of religion and society, Silvio Ferrari, 'Introduction to European Church and State Discourses' in Lisbet Christoffersen

One main conclusion is that it is impossible to separate religion from other parts of society. In many cases, morals and attitudes in a society have their roots in historical religion. This means that many institutions in a society are based on religion, even in secular countries.

There are societies, such as in the USA, which have free competition between different religious communities[26] and there are societies, such as in Denmark, where a special church has a close relationship with the state.[27] But in all cases, there is some division of labour between the religious communities and other parts of society.

In all Western countries, there is a high degree of religious liberty. This sort of freedom may partly have a rational 'economic' reason. The alternative could very well be a number of dissatisfied and aggressive minorities. Dissatisfied and aggressive minorities are problematic for the coherency and the social capital of a society.

There are, however, also clear economic advantages to having a dominant religion. Solidarity between the different groups in society will perhaps be higher if all are included in the same religious community. There are potential advantages to having common religious holidays.

Some European countries have witnessed economically expensive conflicts between different religions; clashes between Christian majorities and Muslim minorities are ongoing in a number of countries and, further back in history – and still today in Northern Ireland – there are clashes between Protestants and Catholics.

A discussion about the economically optimal religious structure for a society is, however, completely irrelevant. Even if social scientists achieved a consensus of results to support the conclusions of Max Weber and Robert Barro, which indicate that a society of Protestants, who are disciplined at working hard through their strong beliefs in Hell and who do not spend much time on religious ceremonies, will become richer than all other societies, there are no instruments to create such a society. The religious structure of society is highly determined by history and is very stable and inflexible even in the very long term. This is illustrated by the revival of the Orthodox Church in modern Russia after the State in the Communist period tried to suppress it for almost 75 years.

It is furthermore worth stressing that almost all findings on the relationship between religion and society are very uncertain. We perhaps know that the effect can be significant, but we do not know the causal mechanisms and we cannot estimate the extent of the effects or sometimes not even the sign of the effects with any certainty. We simply do not know enough. Nevertheless, it is clear that the

---

et al. (eds), *Law & Religion in the 21st Century – Nordic Perspectives* (Djof Publishing 2010) 23–41.

26   For a more detailed discussion of the American situation, see Witte (n 7).

27   See for a more detailed discussion of the Danish case, Lisbet Christoffersen, 'State, Church and Religion in Denmark' in Lisbet Christoffersen. (eds), *Law & Religion in the 21st Century – Nordic Perspectives* (Djøf Publishing 2010) 145–61.

church provides a considerable number of public goods and external effects, some of which have been discussed above.

We cannot say anything substantial about religion and society in general, but perhaps something more relevant can be said in relation to specific countries. In a country such as Denmark, with an old State Church which has an organization in almost every village, many of the formal and informal institutions are based on an ecclesiastical tradition and morals and attitudes have their roots in Lutheran theology. The only public organization in many peripheral rural villages is the church, and so concerts and public debates are arranged there (98 secular municipalities exist in Denmark today compared to approximately 2,000 ecclesiastical parishes). The only university-educated individual in rural villages is often the priest. The traditional economic, commercial and administrative centre of the village, such as the dairy, shops and the school, has, in many cases, moved to a larger city. Historically, but also to the same degree today, the community around the church has included the whole population of the village, regardless of whether their faith is strong or weak.

All this means that we have to be very careful if we want to change the established institutions. Furthermore, the underlying structures are so different from country to country that it can be problematic to use experiences from one country in another. A strong statement or a rash reform can do irreversible damage in the form of conflicts and loss of coherency. This is not an area for fast reforms and intense public debate. It is perhaps better to continue with a partly illogical system, if 'logical' reform would result in incalculable damage and conflict. This is a potentially explosive subject where care and humbleness are needed.

Such a conclusion is stressed by the important Canadian philosopher Arend Lijphart, who has analysed conflicts involving religious and ethnic subcultures in a number of books and articles.[28] Lijphart is interested in differences relating, for instance, to the importance of religion, language and class, and he argues that such conflicts can rarely be handled by normal democratic processes because:

> ... this sort of conflict is too explosive to be managed by ordinary parliamentary opposition, bargaining, campaigning, and winning elections. Instead, the principal ways in which such conflicts are dealt with are (1) violence and

---

28   See Arend Lijphart, 'Consociational Democracy' (1969) 21, 2 *World Politics* 207–25; Arend Lijphart, 'Cultural Diversity and Political Integration' (1971) 4, 1 *Canadian Journal of Political Science* 1–14; Arend Lijphart, *Democracy in Plural Societies: A Comparative Exploration* (Yale University Press 1977); Arend Lijphart, 'Religious vs. Linguistic vs. Class Voting: The 'Crucial Experiment' of Comparing Belgium, Canada, South Africa, and Switzerland' (1979) 73, 2 *American Political Science Review* 442–58; Arend Lijphart, *Pattern of Democracy: Government Forms and Performance in Thirty-Six Countries* (Yale University Press 1999).

repression, (2) secession or separation, (3) mutual veto, (4) autonomy, (5) proportional representation, and (6) assimilation.[29]

According to Lijphart, most researchers who work with integration predict possible outcomes 1, 2 or 6; either 1 or 2, if integration fails, and 6 for successful integration. However, what interests Lijphart are the possibilities in-between. This is what he calls a 'consociational' solution. And this is what he finds in traditional pluralist societies. He finds that stable consociational societies are characterized by a number of checks and balances, which are mainly arranged by agreements among the elites of the different subgroups. Consociational arrangements are not established by interrelations among the masses of the subgroups; typically there is little interrelation between the different groups. This stresses the explosiveness of public political debate about this sort of problem.[30] The success of many populistic anti-Muslim parties in European countries in the last decade is perhaps indicative of the problematic effects of discussions about religious questions in the political system. Historically fruitful cooperation in the parliament about economic and social questions is often ruined by hateful debate about integration, immigration and religion.

List of References

Acemoglu D et al., 'The Rise of Europe: Atlantic Trade, Institutional Change and Economic Growth' (2005) 95 *American Economic Review*

Andersen H, 'Prestige og indflydelse i samfundsvidenskaberne' (1999) 6 *Samfundsøkonomen*

Barro RJ et al., 'Religion and Economic Growth Across Countries' (2003) 68, 5 *American Sociological Review*

—— 'Religion and Economic Growth' (2003) *NBER Working Paper* W9682

Blum U et al., 'Religion and Economic Growth: Was Weber right?' (2001) 11 *Journal of Evolutionary Economics*

Bourdieu P, 'The Forms of Capital' in J Richardson (ed.), *Handbook of Theory and Research for the Sociology of Education* (Greenwood Press 1986)

Burmester S, *Fred og Fare. Islam, Østasien og Vesten set af en dansk kosmopolit* (Gyldendal 2007)

Christoffersen L, 'State, Church and Religion in Denmark' in L Christoffersen et al. (eds), *Law & Religion in the 21st Century – Nordic Perspectives* (Djøf Publishing 2010)

---

29 Lijphart (n 28, 'Cultural Diversity and Political Integration', 11).

30 See Niels Kærgård, 'Social cohesion and the transformation from ethnic to multicultural society: The Case of Denmark' (2010) 10, 4 *Ethnicities* 470–87.

Ferrari S, 'Introduction to European Church and State Discourses' in L Christoffersen et al. (eds), *Law & Religion in the 21st Century – Nordic Perspectives* (Djof Publishing 2010)

Huntington SP, *The Clash of Civilizations and the Remaking of World Order* (Simon & Schuster 1996)

Iannaccone LR, 'Introduction to the Economics of Religion' (1998) 36 *Journal of Economic Literature*

Kærgård N, 'Cooperation not opposition – Marginalism and Socialism in Denmark 1871–1924' in I Steedman (ed.), *Socialism and Marginalism in Economics 1870–1930* (Routledge 1995)

—— 'Denmark and the marginal revolution' in W Samuels et al. (eds), *Research in the History of Economic Thought and Methodology*, vol. 14 (JAI Press Inc 1996)

—— 'Economic thought and economic development in Denmark 1848–1914' in M Psalidopoulos et al. (eds), *Economic Thought and Policy in Less Developed Europe* (Routledge 2002)

——'Social cohesion and the transformation from ethnic to multicultural society: The Case of Denmark' (2010) 10, 4 *Ethnicities*

Kærgård N et al., 'Harald Westergaard: From Young Pioneer to Established Authority' in WJ Samuels (ed.), *European Economists of the early 20th Century*, vol. 1 (Edward Elgar 1998)

Landes DS, *The Wealth and Poverty of Nations: Why Some Are So Rich and Some So Poor* (W.W. Norton & Co 1998)

Lijphart A, 'Consociational Democracy' (1969) 21, 2 *World Politics*

—— 'Cultural Diversity and Political Integration' (1971) 4, 1 *Canadian Journal of Political Science*

—— *Democracy in Plural Societies: A Comparative Exploration* (Yale University Press 1977)

—— 'Religious vs. Linguistic vs. Class Voting: The 'Crucial Experiment' of Comparing Belgium, Canada, South Africa, and Switzerland' (1979) 73, 2 *American Political Science Review*

—— *Pattern of Democracy: Government Forms and Performance in Thirty-Six Countries* (Yale University Press 1999)

Martensen HL, *Socialisme og Christendom* (Den Gyldendalske Boghandel 1874)

—— 'Den Sociale Ethik', *Den Christelige Ethik, Den Specielle Deel*, vol. 2 (Gyldendal 1878)

North DC, *Institutions, Institutional Change, and Economic Performance* (University Press 1990)

O'Roucke KH, 'Culture, Politics and Innovation: Evidence from the Creameries' (2002) *CEPR Discussion Paper* 3235

Paldam M, 'Social Capital: One or Many? Definition and Measurement' (2000) 14, 5 *Journal of Economic surveys* 629–53 (Special Issue on Political Economy)

—— 'Corruption and Religion: Adding to the Economic Model' (2001) 54 *Kyklos*

Paldam M et al., 'An essay on social capital: Looking for the fire behind the smoke' (2000) 16 *European Journal of Political Economy*

—— (eds), *Trust, Social Capital and Economic Growth: An International Comparison* (Edward Elgar Publishing 2003)

Pigou AC, *Economics of Welfare* (Macmillan & Co 1920)

Putnam RD, *Making Democracy Work, civic traditions in modern Italy* (Princeton University Press 1993)

—— 'Bowling alone: America's declining social capital' (1995) 6, 1 *Journal of Democracy*

Samuelsson K, *Religion and Economic Action* (1957, Reprinted University of Toronto Press 1993)

Simon H, 'Rationality in Psychology and Economics' in Robin M Hogarth and MW Reder (eds), (1986) 59 (supp.) *The Behavioural Foundation of Economic Theory, Journal of Business*

Sombart W, *Der Moderne Kapitalismus*, vol. 1–2 (Duncker & Humblot 1902)

—— *Die Juden und das Wirtschafts leben* (Duncker & Humblot 1911)

Stark R, *The Victory of Reason: How Christianity led to Freedom, Capitalism, and Western Success* (Random House, Inc. 2006)

Tawney RH, *Religion and the Rise of Capitalism* (John Murray 1926)

Weber M, *Die protestantische Ethik und der Geist des Kapitalismus*, English translation 1930 (Charles Schribner's Sons 1904–05)

Witte JJ, 'Introduction to American Law and Religion Discourse' in L Christoffersen et al. (eds), *Law & Religion in the 21st Century – Nordic Perspectives* (Djof Publishing 2010)

Chapter 13

A Theory of Church Funding – One Answer, Two Problems

Rik Torfs

One Answer

Unlike the United States of America, most European countries have a system of organizing, in various ways, public funding for religion.[1] Of course, this does not mean that all religious groups obtain subsidies, nor does it imply that nearly all these groups' expenses are covered by the State. However, the principle of Church funding is implicitly accepted in most European countries, very often without much overt discussion. The situation is as it is: that is the way many citizens have tended to look at things.

Yet, whereas until several years ago the principle of religious groups being financially supported by the State had hardly ever been challenged, public opinion today is becoming more reticent about this phenomenon. Separation of Church and State is invoked as an argument against Church funding. The argument makes some sense, as a strict separation – implying the complete absence of contacts between both entities – is incompatible with funding mechanisms. However, pure separation is difficult to achieve. It is like dealing with something that exists, as if it did not exist. The latter is even true in the United States, since this country allows tax exemption for religious groups.[2] Other arguments against Church funding include the idea that everybody should pay for their own hobbies, for the survival of sects or other groups he or she wants to be part of. These are some arguments against Church funding. What does the other side of the picture have to offer? Are there possible arguments for a positive approach, for accepting the principle of granting money to religious groups? I see three arguments. Let me start with the weaker ones, explaining what Church funding is not.

Firstly, Church funding is not the outcome of a collectivist idea that believes that religion should be subsidized, relying upon the idea that all people need it. This is, of course, not true. In this regard, religion enjoys the same position as

---

1   See Gerhard Robbers (ed.), *State and Church in the European Union* (Nomos 2005) 589.

2   On the problem of naming religion in that regard, see Collin R Mangrum, 'Naming Religion (and Eligible Cognates) in Tax Exemption Cases' (1986) *Creighton Law Review* 821–56.

emotions do. They both belong to people's privacy. The latter is valid for both the presumed need for religion, as well as with regard to any practice or content given to it. Some people live happily without religion, whereas others live unhappily with religion. Some people like it, other people need it, whereas others like or need it at certain moments in their lives. So what? Few things in life are used or needed by all the people. Public transport facilities, including railways, will not be important for every single member of society. Some prefer endless traffic jams to the grey misery of ugly stations and trains arriving late. One can argue that many people support the public funding of railways, bearing in mind that they may need them one day, when old age prevents them from driving a car. However, this idea is too vague a justification for comprehensive funding. Yet, there are activities which are subsidized and which it is even less plausible that everyone will participate in. A good example of this is the opera. Without public funding there would no longer be room for any opera. Too many people are involved in both performance and decor. To put it bluntly: society as a whole funds activities only enjoyed by some. Yet, is that necessarily reprehensible? Teaching Sanskrit at university is of direct importance to a tiny minority of the population only. At the same time, many people would feel unhappy living in a world where absolutely nobody is aware of Sanskrit, its linguistic beauty and its cultural relevance. To sum up this first point: the reason why religion should – or can – be funded is not the collectivist idea that all people need it or should need it at some stage in their lives.

Secondly, the utilitarian approach is also not the right one to underpin Church funding. Jeremy Bentham (1748–1832), following Cesare Beccaria (1738–1794), was in favour of 'the greatest happiness of the greatest number',[3] a formula he himself criticized in later years. That was a good move. Few things are less sure than the ideas of the younger Bentham. If he were right, the common good would be nothing more than the sum of the good of all individuals. Following that line of thought, there would be nothing that interests all people together, in community, without already being part of the individual good of one or more individuals. Bentham is right to focus on the individual dimension of happiness, but he is wrong to neglect its collective aspect. Moreover, utilitarian thinking has yet another weakness: it is built around a completely rational approach to happiness, as if the latter were empirically measurable.[4] Admittedly, many people love this method. Why do they do so? Because transcendental thinking finds itself in a crisis. If God is no longer responsible for happiness, there should be a place for happiness without a god. However, this form of happiness can be qualified as reconstructed rational thinking. As a result of this approach, not only does a definition of happiness

---

3   For more details on this magical and often misunderstood formula, see James E Crimmins, 'Contending Interpretations of Bentham's Utilitarianism' (1996) *Canadian Journal of Political Science* 751–77.

4   This is not always true. See Friedel Bolle, 'A Note of Interdependent Happiness' (2009) *Journal of Socio-Economics* 713–21.

seem possible, so does evaluating the quality of it in concrete cases. I am afraid such a method will lead us nowhere. To put it briefly, Church funding cannot find its rationale as a tool achieving the greatest happiness of the greatest number. Religion should not be funded as an element potentially leading to happiness. Such a construction fails for two reasons: because it presupposes the absence of any common good beyond that of the individual and because it uses a rational notion of happiness.

As has become clear, both the 'collectivist' and the 'utilitarian' approaches fail to successfully underpin Church funding. The only strong argument is that of protecting the interests of certain groups in society, namely religious people. That is sufficient. Other arguments are redundant. The State very often helps a limited number of people for the sake of the common good. Two examples may clarify this point: firstly, freedom of expression, as developed by the jurisprudence of the European Court of Human Rights in Strasbourg, includes disturbing, shocking and hurtful ideas.[5] Why? Because accepting these ideas, as painful as it is for some, belongs to the common good. It is good for society as a whole that people can express themselves freely, even if at first glance others suffer as a result of this freedom being exercised. Their pain is more than counterbalanced by the benefits it offers to society, in which freedom of speech never should be an idle notion.[6] Secondly, specific groups, including minority groups, need specific treatment, which contributes to the common good. For instance, handicapped people increasingly enjoy advantages.[7] They have reserved parking spaces at their disposal. Access to buildings is adapted to their needs. A considerable amount of public money is spent to improve their physical and material condition. But then, not everybody is handicapped. However, the support given to the minority of handicapped people confirms and strengthens the common good shared by all. To formulate it in a more precise way: privileges attributed to specific groups can lead to more justice in society as a whole. Perhaps it is not a sign of good taste to compare religious to handicapped people, although both groups represent minorities. That said, what I am aiming at by making the comparison is the basic concept that the common good requires specific, detailed attention, at times including financial support, and focused on certain groups in society.

---

5 See *Handyside v the United Kingdom*, no. 5493/72 (ECHR, 7 December 1976).

6 Today, the human rights oriented approach, as expressed by Handyside, is increasingly being challenged. Some see the protection of moral culture as limiting rights. See on this issue Amitai Etzioni, *The Common Good* (Malden MA, Polity Press 2004) 47.

7 Michael S Cummings, *Beyond Political Correctness. Social Transformation in the United States* (Lynne Rienner Publishers 2001) 64, offers a discussion on structural positive discrimination *vis-à-vis* handicapped people.

Two Problems

Funding and Equality

At the RELIGARE conference in Copenhagen (11–13 May 2011), Pierre-Henri Prélot drew attention to the problem of equality between religious groups and other groups in society. This concern is a legitimate one.

In Europe, where majority religions have long enjoyed considerable privileges, solely founded in history and without any further in-depth discussion, the idea of equality is gaining ground in legal thinking, as well as in public debate. Obviously, religion too is concerned. With regard to equality and religious freedom, two different strategies are possible. They depend on the answer to the basic question as to whether equality among religions is an issue of religious freedom or of law and religion. Why is this initial choice important? If equality is an issue of religious freedom, it is an intrinsic part of human rights. Equality is an element of the very notion of religious freedom. This approach joins with the American tradition: no religious freedom without equality between religious groups before the law. Such is how the crucial point of Thomas Madison's legacy can be seen.[8] Yet, a second approach is also conceivable. In that hypothesis, equality is part of public policy on law and religion. The second option leads to a different central question: is it acceptable, once religious freedom for all is guaranteed, that some religions are treated more generously than others?

The question is far from being innocuous, not only in its conceptual shape, but also with regard to its practical consequences. If equality is intrinsic to religious freedom, any form of public funding of religion is hazardous. Indeed, support means discrimination, as public authorities are unable to finance all religious groups without distinction. Indeed, which groups deserve the epithet 'religious'? Is claiming to be a religious group sufficient as a condition giving rise to support?[9] The answers remain as ambiguous as the questions. Especially in a secularized society, an increasing number of people do not want to be involved in this type of pseudo-philosophical debate. An attractive solution, respecting equality, consists in suppressing any form of financial support for religion. Such is the extent of debate, when equality is classed as part of religious freedom.

However, if equality is disconnected from religious freedom and transferred to the discussion on granting advantages to certain groups, once complete freedom for all is safeguarded, a larger space emerges that allows for differing treatment

---

8   See Steven D Smith, *Getting over Equality. A Critical Diagnosis of Religious Freedom in America* (New York University Press 2001). However, the author argues that the definition by Thomas Madison (1746–1798) was compatible with some religions, but not with others.

9   On the idea of self-definition, see Kerry A Mitchell, 'The Politics of Spirituality: Liberalizing the Definition of Religion' in Markus Dressler et al., *Secularism & Religion-Making* (New York: Oxford University Press 2011) 125 and following.

of religious groups. Yet, increasingly rigid criteria applied to funding groups or not, as well as to the amount of money granted, will be at the heart of the debate. To put it in another way: even if preferential treatment of some religious groups is acceptable, the criteria leading to such a distinction will become more objective and will be scrutinized with greater rigour than before. Public authorities are obliged to treat equal groups equally and unequal groups unequally. Determining when and why groups are equal or unequal is a difficult task leading very often to fierce public criticism.

The Supremacy of Emotions over Institutions

Another difficulty affecting possible funding of religious groups concerns the dominant mentality in society. Certainly in Europe, people remain lifetime members of religious institutions and other groups less than in the past. There is an overall sceptical attitude towards institutions.[10] People come and go. They are inclined to follow their emotions. These emotions are not the traditional emotions people cherish deep in their hearts without expressing them easily.

Today, emotions are supposed to be very direct, overt and expressive. One can argue that, increasingly, a 'compulsory' code of public emotions is in the making. People are invited to show their immediate feelings. Not crying at sad or dramatic moments is perceived as ethically despicable. This contribution is not the right place to analyse this current phenomenon in depth. And yet, an important cause of the triumph of overt, violent emotions may precisely be the weakening of religions that structure people's spiritual lives. Consequently, an interesting paradox emerges: emotions resulting from abandoning institutions affect the attitude of people towards the financial situation of the same institutions. There follow three examples illustrating the supremacy of emotions over institutions.

Firstly, in today's European society, individual faith is more important than institutional adherence. In the past, people belonging to religious institutions were exempted from personal faith: the experts legitimized by the institution were taking care of that. Again, this point may sound paradoxical. A person joins a religious group because of his or her faith, and once he or she is a member, personal faith no longer matters. This is an easy solution to an existential question, yet, at the same time, a scant one. Some people just do not want to be exempted from thinking about God. But then again, the practice described above is becoming exceptional in the European landscape. Institutions are suspect. People cannot rely upon them all their lives. Consequently, they are obliged to formulate their own faith, independent from their personal desire to be exempted or not from profound religious reflection. Yet, here is a consequence of this evolution: personal thinking

---

10   This scepticism is not new. *Cf.* Maria Letizia Cravetto, *A partir de Michel de Certeau: de nouvelles frontières* (Presses Universitaires de France 1999), more specifically p. 92. Michel de Certeau (1925–1986) was very critical towards institutions, without ever abandoning the Catholic Church he belonged to.

happens with or without the support of the institution. Very often, the institutional contribution is limited or absent. In this hypothesis, personal religious faith is defined as the counterpart of institutional and official teaching.

Secondly, all systems and institutions are distrusted. Churches are not the champions of contemporary Western society. However, the same is true for more secular concepts with a rich past including the magical notion of *laïcité*.[11] People are not in search of an alternative to churches as institutions. They are in search of an alternative to institutions. This may affect the way to fund religion. The latter may become less structural and more project-oriented. Should this hypothesis be confirmed, one should not be blind to possible dangers counterbalancing obvious advantages. Advantages include temporary funding and quality control of the projects submitted. Disadvantages include structural uncertainty (also with regard to staff and job positions) and bureaucracy. Indeed, who is going to evaluate the quality of certain projects? How does one measure the quality of religious projects? What about the risk that practical proposals will be welcomed more easily than spiritual ones? Moreover, who will evaluate? Where do authorities find brilliant people to do the job? In any case, evaluators should never be weaker than those being evaluated.

Thirdly, ethical issues of paramount importance are looked at from a non-structural, emotional angle. For instance, with regard to accepting euthanasia or not, a key notion in current debate is the preservation of human dignity at the end of life. Why is this notion emotional? It is emotional because 'human dignity' in its contemporary form does not focus on the mystery of death. It deals with the elegance of dying. Dignity does not mean that all people who die are less radically dead than they used to be before. There is no more dignity in being dead today than there was in previous times. Something else is at stake. Dignity as such is no longer a solidly rooted philosophical notion. It deals with the fact of being surrounded by loving people, the opportunity to say *adieu* with style, the pleasure of drinking a last glass of champagne before darkness comes. To put it both bluntly and briefly: death stands for institutions and dying for personal emotions. It goes without saying that the triumph of emotions over institutions is not neutral with respect to funding religious institutions in the future.

List of References

Baubérot J, *La laïcité, quel héritage? De 1789 à nos jours* (Labor et Fides 1990)
Bolle F et al., 'A Note of Interdependent Happiness' (2009) *Journal of Socio-Economics*
Cravetto ML, *A partir de Michel de Certeau: de nouvelles frontières* (Presses Universitaires de France 1999)

---

11   This crisis is not brand-new. See Jean Baubérot, *La laïcité, quel héritage? De 1789 à nos jours* (Labor et Fides 1990) 87 and following.

Crimmins JE, 'Contending Interpretations of Bentham's Utilitarianism' (1996) *Canadian Journal of Political Science*

Cummings MS, *Beyond Political Correctness. Social Transformation in the United States* (Lynne Rienner Publishers 2001)

Etzioni A, *The Common Good* (Malden MA, Polity Press 2004)

Mangrum CR, 'Naming Religion (and Eligible Cognates) in Tax Exemption Cases' (1986) *Creighton Law Review*

Mitchell KA, 'The Politics of Spirituality: Liberalizing the Definition of Religion' in M Dressler et al., *Secularism & Religion-Making* (Oxford University Press 2011)

Robbers G (ed.), *State and Church in the European Union* (Nomos 2005)

Smith SD, *Getting over Equality. A Critical Diagnosis of Religious Freedom in America* (New York University Press 2001)

Chapter 14

Religious Activities and Public Funding – Concluding Observations

Jean-Marie Woehrling

As shown in the preceding contributions, the issue of public funding of religious activities is becoming increasingly important in the political and scientific discussion. This is due as much to the economic crisis in some way putting restrictions on public resources, as to the multiplicity of contradictory arguments concerning the justification or the critic of the existing situation. Numerous studies and reports are dealing with this subject without providing more clarity or increased consensus in this debate.

Nevertheless, having a close look at the results of the various contributions developed in the course of this volume, there is a set of conclusions which can be summarized in seven points:

1. Public Funding for Religions: A General Phenomenon

All countries have mechanisms for providing public financial support for religious activities, even if this funding is more significant in certain countries and more limited in others. This support is sometimes direct, but at the very least indirect in the form of tax advantages of various types.

This public financial support exists even in countries which declare themselves to be secular or claim the existence of a strict separation between state and church or which have an anticlerical tradition, despite there being general principles theoretically prohibiting such aid. France and the United States are good examples of this.

2. Increasing Discrepancy Between Legal Rules and Concrete Reality or Increasing Gap Between Enounced Objectives and Actual Practice

No national system can be considered to be consistent in this area, that is to say, adequately applying stated political or legal principles, such as those of separation, neutrality or the principle of equality. The reality of public funding and the official objectives don't fit each other. This clash is emphasized by a tendency towards giving a more rigid interpretation to the referred principles.

3. Dominance of Historical Factors

Despite all the efforts made to base the issue of public funding (or not) for religious activities on objective and rational principles, in practice it is, in all countries, the historical factors, traditions and characteristics of society which remain overriding and play the most important part.

4. Existing Solutions Under Criticism

In every country, the system put in place for dealing with the question of public funding for religions finds itself 'under pressure' – subject to discussion, criticism and proposals for reform.

A need to adapt to the new social and religious context can be felt everywhere. This is partly due to the frequent inconsistency, identified previously, between principles and concrete application, to the difficulty in achieving the declared objectives and also to the profound change in the religious landscape, which means that traditional solutions are less and less well-adapted.

But in every country, changes, passing laws or reforms are very difficult and largely improbable.

5. Significant Change in the Criteria for Discussion

One can, however, notice in every country an important change in the methods of discussion or the evaluation criteria relating to legitimacy/illegitimacy of public funding for faiths.

The nature of the arguments relating to this issue has witnessed a real paradigmatic shift: everywhere, one notices the shift from arguments of a political kind towards those of a legal kind.

The traditional form of discussion on the legitimacy of public funding for religions revolved primarily around political or ideological considerations or even arguments of political and social philosophy.

The decisive criterion was political and the decision ultimately taken by political institutions and thus by the movement which possessed the political power.

The political arguments employed for or against public funding for religions were, for example:

- the historical and cultural bond between a religion and national society;
- the willingness to compensate for former despoliation inflicted on the religious authorities;
- the contribution of religious convictions in moralizing or pacifying society;
- the issue of conflicts or co-operation between State and Churches;
- the advantages and risks of the public funding of faiths from the point of view of governance.

The idea that public money should only be used for secular activities is also a 'political' kind of reasoning, the interest for public authorities being that they can have the means to influence all areas of social life and so on.

During recent times on the other hand, primarily legal arguments have been put forward in the discussion and the bodies called upon to take the ultimate decisions have been judicial bodies using reasoning of the 'legal' kind.

These legal arguments rely primarily on the following concepts:

- the principle of freedom of religion;
- the principle of the religious neutrality of the State;
- the principle of equality between citizens irrespective of their religious views, sometimes also the principle of equal treatment of the various faiths;
- the prevalence of the principles of public order and public interest.

The ultimate decisions no longer belong to political bodies (government, legislature), but to jurisdictional bodies (constitutional courts, European Court of Human Rights).

The above-mentioned legal principles are supposed to be objective and rational, but they are open, however, to a broad degree of interpretation, which results in the choices of the supreme courts appearing as arbitrary as those made by political authorities. Nevertheless, it remains important to note that this passage from political argument to legal reasoning results in a change to the essential concept of reference: previously, this was ideological – 'secularization' – and henceforth it is legal – 'neutrality'.

6. Towards a 'Trivialization' of Religious Activities

From now on, the resulting tendency is to treat religious activity like any other social activity. 'Neutrality' and 'non-discrimination' are understood to imply that religious activities must be treated (and thus funded) in the same way as other social activities, neither better, nor worse.

Religious activities are therefore regarded as belonging to the general rules and obeying the general principles similar to those characterizing social activities: non-discrimination, transparency, respect of individual rights, democratic principles, loyalty and morality, non-violence, a mission of integration and so on.

These are the criteria which henceforth will be put forward to evaluate the appropriateness of public funding.

7. A New Dimension of Secularization

What are the consequences of these changes in the nature of the justifications judged to be appropriate when evaluating the grounds for funding (or not funding) religious activities? Is the public funding of religious institutions favoured or brought into question by this evaluation?

On the one hand, the legal approach to the issue of the legitimization of public funding for religions serves to counter demands for an outright ban on such funding.

A complete and systematic exclusion of public funding for religious activities is difficult to justify from the moment when one passes from ideological reasoning to legal reasoning, because such an exclusion creates discrimination between religious activities and other philosophical, cultural or social activities of the same type, which are not subject to the same ban.

On the other hand, religions can be considered impaired by the fact that they are treated like any other activity. This reduction to 'common law' deprives them of a specific status illustrating their particular importance.

This evolution is in fact a new dimension of secularization: the latter does not take place any more by dividing profane activities from religious ones, but by the assimilation of religious activities to any other profane activities. It is another way of making religion disappear from public space, by denying its specificity: it will be subsidized if necessary by the authorities, but according to the same criteria as any other private activity.

The way in which Community legislation treats religious activities illustrates the trivialization of religion: ordinary law also applies to religious activities.

From now on, to benefit from public financial support, a religious activity is subjected more and more to 'common law' criteria: this activity has to correspond to a public interest, be assigned in a non-discriminatory way, be exercised according to criteria of transparency, respect the rights of the individual and democratic rules, be compatible with general market and competition rules, meet criteria of effective management and saving resources and offer guarantees from the point of view of integration and so on.

At the end of this investigation, the remaining question is how will this evolution continue? How far will this trend of negating the specificity of religion go? Can religion perhaps become a privatized object, subject to the law of the marketplace like any other? Is such a trivialization appropriate to the profound nature of religious activity?

On one hand, it should be considered that religious activities correspond to a very structuring element of society which calls for the recognition of a certain specificity, including in its legal status and the rules of funding. On the other hand, the understanding of religion is changing. Secular forms of belief like the role assigned fundamental rights are not so different from traditional 'religious' beliefs. In this sense, the issue of the funding of religious activities is questioning the very nature of religion.

Chapter 15
Funding of Protestant Churches

Jean Volff

Protestantism is extremely diverse, to state a cliché, as much on dogmatic and ecclesiological levels, as on that of its Church–State relations. Built on a denominational base and a – national, regional or local – geographical context, Protestant Churches have only one common reference – the Bible – from which they have developed doctrines and special traditions, as well as organization of varying complexity. No universal Protestant Ecclesial Law therefore exists that is comparable to the Canon Law of the Roman Catholic Church. The internal laws of Protestant Churches have evolved to varying degrees, are specific to each church and rarely address the issue of resources.

It is mainly by examining church practices in this area that it is possible to identify their main approaches.

A quick historical overview and an analysis of the current context clearly show the existence of two trends, sometimes exclusive of each other, but which join together in the twenty-first century.

A Practice Evolving over Centuries

Over more than two centuries, post-Reformation Churches adopted a quasi-unanimous stance on the question of their resources. From the second half of the eighteenth century, a second approach, which had already been outlined at the start, was to acquire ever greater importance, without, however, supplanting the first.

The First Two Centuries

In the sixteenth and seventeenth centuries, which mark the beginning and the settling of the Reformation in Europe, the Evangelical doctrine of universal priesthood favoured extending political authorities' powers over the Church, erasing the traditional distinction between laity and clergy. Reformers also considered the Christian magistrate to be the representative of the community, thereby justifying his intervening in ecclesiastical affairs. Protestants, whether Lutheran, Reformed or Anglican, naturally considered that their churches be financially supported by public authorities, kings, princes or free imperial cities. At that time, there was no real problem and neither Luther nor Calvin took up this issue, unless incidentally. It was to become the dominant model in the Protestant world up until the twentieth century.

In the Empire, the principle *cujus regio, ejus religio*, established by the Peace of Augsburg in 1555 and corrected by the *jus emigrandi*, confirms the existence of a mosaic of states of homogeneous faith. In Protestant States, the Church was placed under the authority of the prince or magistrate, with its pastors, schools and academies being funded by the State. Such was the case in Alsace, which was then still part of the Empire.

Also, Martin Luther wrote: 'Thus, the Apostle (Paul) teaches us clearly that, in Christianity, each town should choose from within its community a pious and educated citizen, to be entrusted with priestly duties, fed at the community's expense and given complete freedom to marry or not to marry'.[1]

In the free imperial city of Strasbourg, the Synod of 1533 approved the text of the so-called XVI Articles, Article XIV of which states: 'The Magistrate, who has the sword and the supreme exterior power, is a servant of God and must therefore, as God commanded in His law and as the Spirit of Christ teaches and promotes in all those He leads, do his utmost so that among his subjects God's name is sanctified, that His Kingdom increases and that people live according to His will, as much is possible through his duties'.[2]

However, as early as 1525, the Anabaptists (led by Grebel, Mantz and Menno Simons) and Spiritualists (guided by Sébastien Franck and Caspar Schwenckfeld), emerging from the radical Reformation and hostile to any ecclesiastical institution, formed small communities separate from the other churches, living away from society and with the help of internal resources alone. They clearly advocated the separation of the Christian community and the State and treated pastors paid by the political authorities as 'mercenaries of the princes'. They ended up being persecuted by all the established churches – Catholic and Protestant – and were marginalized for a long period.[3]

In France, after an era of persecutions, followed by religious wars, the Edict of Nantes of 30 April 1598 recognized the existence of the Reformed churches, granting them freedom of conscience and limited freedom of worship, and providing three methods of funding for these churches.

Special Article 42 allowed donations and legacies for the maintenance of the 'So-called Reformed Religion' and special Article 43 gave synods, under the control of a Royal Commissioner, the right to levy contributions from their followers, to meet the expenses of these assemblies and maintenance costs of ministers and it made these decisions binding (it was a kind of church tax before

---

1   Martin Luther, *à la noblesse chrétienne de la nation allemande*, coll. *La Pléiade, tome I* (Gallimard 1999) 636.

2   François Wendel, *L'Église de Strasbourg, sa constitution et son organisation, 1532–1535* (PUF 1942) 167.

3   Marc Lienhard, *'L'apport des dissidents du XVIe siècle à l'émergence de la laïcité'* in *Genèse et enjeux de la laïcité* (Labor et Fides 1990) 15–27.

its time). The first letters patent, annexed to the Edict, finally provided for an annual payment by the Royal Treasury to the Reformed churches of a sum of 45,000 écus, earmarked for the remuneration of pastors and the functioning of colleges and academies where they were trained.[4]

It is worth mentioning here that the Edict and its annexes were the result of two years' bitter negotiations between the King and the Reformed Assembly of Loudun, which was later moved to Saumur and Châtellerault. The French Reformed Churches therefore allowed resorting to donations from the faithful, as well as financial support from the political authorities.

This was in line with the thinking of Jean Calvin, who considered these two methods of funding to be legitimate.

He wrote: 'Scripture, in leading us to this reason, shows us again that everything that we have received by grace of the Lord has been committed to us on condition that we entrust it to the common good of the Church'.[5] But, on political authority, he also maintains: 'But the aim of this temporal system is to feed and maintain God's external service, pure doctrine and religion, to keep whole the State of the Church, to agree with one another and preserve a common peace and tranquillity'.[6]

After the revocation of the Edict of Nantes by the Edict of Fontainebleau on 18 October 1685, the French Reformed Churches went into hiding and, deprived of temples, schools, academies and pastors, lived solely on donations from the faithful and particularly on assistance from exiled Protestants. Yet, in Alsace – that had now become French – the situation of the Protestant Churches, guaranteed by the treaties of Westphalia, remained unchanged and consisted with the Peace of Augsburg.

In England and Scandinavian countries, national Protestant Churches formed, fully dependent on the sovereign and funded in whole or part by the State and from income from property inherited from the Catholic Church.

Very early on (as early as the reign of Elizabeth I) English Protestants demanded that the established Church be further purified and, in the seventeenth century, these Puritans separated from it. Others were to follow the movement, forming dissenting churches, which lived solely on donations from their faithful. Some, inspired by the tithe mentioned in the Old Testament, even required their flock to contribute one-tenth of their income. These dissidents then spread and thrived in the English colonies of America (Congregationalists, Baptists, Presbyterians and Quakers).

So, from the beginning of the Reformation, two stances emerge among Protestants that are more pragmatic than doctrinal, as regards funding their churches. For Lutheran, Anglican and Reformed Protestants, the overwhelming majority, it seemed natural that the State should help the churches fund the training of pastors and their remuneration, as well as the construction and maintenance of

---

4   Janine Garrisson, *L'Édit de Nantes* (Atlantica 1997).
5   Jean Calvin, *Institution de la religion chrétienne, livre III, chapter VII* (Vrin 1960) 5.
6   *Calvin (n 5) livre IV, chapter XX*, 2.

academic and religious buildings. For the Anabaptists, Spiritualists, Puritans and dissidents – in the minority and tolerated more or less – churches had to be free from the powers that be and depend solely on the offerings of their believers.

The Turning Point

The end of the eighteenth century and the nineteenth century were to see these positions shift. Born at the start of the eighteenth century, John Wesley came from a family environment that drifted between Anglicanism and Puritanism. Ordained in the Church of England in 1728, he founded the following year, at Oxford University, a religious society called the 'Holy Club', rapidly labelled with the nickname 'Methodist'. It was the start of a wide-ranging, Evangelical revival. Its members took part in prison visits, assisting the poor and the sick, observing fasts, taking communion each week and preaching in the open air. These kinds of secular congregations, on the fringes of the established Church, developed in England and North America. Little by little, faced with the increasing hostility of the Anglican clergy, these societies joined together and eventually broke away from the Church of England to open a new dissident front. The Methodist Church, independent of public authorities, organized itself as a society and lived from its members' donations.[7]

In France, Reformed Protestants and Lutherans welcomed with satisfaction the Organic Articles of 1802 promulgated by First Consul Napoléon Bonaparte, who made their Churches recognized faiths funded by the State, equivalent to the Roman Catholic Church. They are still in force in Alsace and Moselle and Protestants in these three French *départements* remain largely favourable to this system of funding, with pastors directly paid by the State.

In North America, under the increasingly predominant influence of the Puritans and other dissenters, the Protestant Churches organized themselves independently of public authorities and without direct funding from them. An amicable and pragmatic system of separation of Church and State was established alongside the independence of the United States. Article IV of the 1787 Constitution prohibited 'any professing of religious faith as a condition of fitness for public office or duties' and the First Amendment states: 'Congress will not pass a law regarding the establishment of a religion or prohibiting its free exercise'.

In Europe, internal conflicts between Orthodox and Liberals and *Réveil* movements resulted here and there in the creation of so-called Free Churches, which, having broken away from the official Churches, were organized along the lines of societies. Independent of the State, they lived from members' donations and in 1843, Thomas Chalmers left the long-standing Presbyterian Church of Scotland, along with hundreds of pastors, to found the 'Free Kirk' – the Free Church.

It was a Swiss theologian, Alexandre Vinet, who, in the middle of the century, was to give a doctrine to this movement, which would thrive in the French-speaking

---

7   Bernard Cottret, *Histoire de la Réforme protestante* (Perrin 2010) 285–399.

Reformed Churches. In 1826, he published a first book, *Mémoire en faveur de la liberté des cultes*, and then a second in 1842: *Essai sur la manifestation des convictions religieuses et sur la séparation de l'Église et de l'État envisagée comme conséquence nécessaire et comme garantie du principe.*

He wrote in the first of these books: 'State and Church can have no act nor institution in common. In other words, neither of the two societies can call upon support for acts and institutions which are respectively their own'. He goes on to explain his thinking: 'Religious freedom entails the absolute separation of the civil State and the religious State, the absolute independence of political society and spiritual society'.[8]

In the second work, he states: 'It is not that religion has no needs or material needs; but it cannot accept it from anyone. It is *via* the faith, that is, through itself, that it wants to be helped'. He further adds: 'Its capital is in the faith and charity of its members; its resources are in principle all spiritual, and woe to any institution which ensures its existence'.[9]

Thus, Alexandre Vinet defends the necessary and full separation of Church and State, including on the financial level, this being in his view the only guarantee of genuine religious freedom.

In reaction to attempts by the Government of the Canton of Vaud to bring Reformed Church pastors into line, in 1846 he reacted by creating the Free Church of the canton and became its leader. For him and those who were to follow him, a living Church is made up of converts; it obeys solely the Law of Christ and must not depend on civil authorities for anything.

He contrasts the People's Church with the Professing Church and civil servant pastors with missionary pastors.

Vinet's work and thinking would later foster the creation of Free Churches in France, largely funded by the aristocracy and the *grande bourgeoisie*. They also prepared the way within the Reformed Church for the idea of a separation of Churches and State. In 1849, Free Church supporters founded the Union of Protestant Churches, which voluntarily left the concordat mould and was to show great vitality.

The Current Situation

At the beginning of the twentieth century, the context became favourable. The Law of 9 December 1905, establishing the separation of Churches and State in France, was in part written by a Protestant jurist, Louis Méjean, *attaché* in Aristide Briand's Cabinet. It was welcomed by the majority of Reformed Protestants and,

---

8   Alexandre Vinet, *Mémoire en faveur de la liberté des cultes* 2nd edn (Les éditeurs 1852) 211–31.

9   Alexandre Vinet, *Essai sur la manifestation des convictions religieuses et sur la séparation de l'Église et de l'État* (Paulin 1842) 332–54.

furthermore, Protestant Churches were the only ones, alongside Israelites, to comply fully with it.

The Law of Separation

The Law of 1905 allowed religious associations to have as their sole resources: membership dues, the fruits of collections for the expenses of worship, various payments for acts of worship, hiring benches or interior, funerary or other decorations. In Articles 2 and 19, it forbade public subsidies for faiths.

The first reads: 'The Republic does not recognize, does not pay for, nor subsidize any faith. Accordingly, with effect from 1 January following the publication of this law, all expenditure relating to the practising of religion shall be abolished from the budgets of the State, the *départements* and communes. There could, however, be incorporated into the budgets expenditure relating to running chaplaincies intended to ensure the free exercise of religion in public establishments, such as high schools, primary schools, hospices, asylums and prisons'.

The second, in sub-paragraph 9, states: 'They [religious associations] will not be able, in whatever form, to receive subsidies from the state, the *départements* or the *communes*. Not considered as subsidies are amounts provided for repairs to historic buildings'.

Contrary to appearances, these two articles are not redundant. The first, of general scope, aims to abolish and in future prohibit the system of recognized faiths (Catholic, Lutheran, Reformed and Jewish faiths, legally recognized by the State, whose ministers were employed by the State and whose activity was supported financially by the State), with one notable exception in the case of chaplaincies. The second, particular to the new associative system of faiths, bans public subsidies (from the State or local authorities) for religious associations. It also provides an exception – to ensure the maintenance of monuments placed at the disposal of these associations. Article 2 draws a line under the past, Article 19 organizes the future.

From the outset, exceptions are envisaged to the principle of 'no public funding' laid down in these two articles – for maintaining historical monuments and running chaplaincies. Also, Articles 12 and 13 of this law make an additional exception benefiting older, recognized faiths, insofar as buildings of worship built prior to the law are left available to them without charge. It is an indirect and everlasting subsidy. Therefore, financial support directly or indirectly provided by public authorities to faiths was never entirely excluded from the moment the separation was introduced.

The 1905 Law was considered by the majority of French Protestants as an act of freedom that placed them on equal legal footing with the Catholic Church. Furthermore, 'free' or 'independent' Protestant Churches welcomed this law for reasons of principle and practicality: henceforth, they were no longer victims of discrimination within Protestantism.

Since 1905, this law, which is not in force over the whole of French territory, has been changed nine times and various other regulations have extended the scope of aid granted to faiths by public authorities.

A 1908 Law authorized the state, *départements* and *communes* to participate fully or partly in the expenses of repairing and maintaining buildings of worship that they owned and left for faiths to use free of charge.

Another law in 1942 authorized local authorities to pay subsidies to religious associations for repairs to buildings of worship they owned. The same law also authorized these religious associations to receive donations and bequests, which are totally exempt from transfer duties. Finally, the 1987 Law on patronage allowed religious associations and congregations (some Protestant, such as the Salvation Army) to receive individual donations of unlimited value and with total exemption from tax. This law also provided that these individual donations be deductible at 66 per cent of the taxable income of the donors, up to a limit of 20 per cent of their total revenues.[10]

Not only have Protestant Churches seen no obstacles to this of a doctrinal nature, they have by and large taken up such aid.

The Context Today

At the dawn of the third millennium, when tax and social deductions are tending to attain 50 per cent of gross domestic income, we can see that a large association, in need of buildings and employees for its activity, can no longer live solely from the contributions of its members. Various charitable associations, trade unions and political parties today derive the key part of their resources from government aid.

Faiths, which must fund the training, salaries, and then the pensions of many ministers and provide for maintenance and the recurrent upgrading of their buildings open to the public, can no longer do without the help of the state and public authorities. It is a question of their survival. At the same time, it is also a problem of freedom of religion.

Nowadays, the Protestant Federation of France, which has been a strong defender of secularity, highlights the limitations of the Law of 1905 and is advocating tidying it up to better ensure religious freedom and equality of all religions, not only in legal terms (already achieved), but also as regards its tangible benefits, including funding. According to the organization, in fact guaranteeing religious freedom goes beyond simple legal protection and should include the possibility of ensuring the practice of worship in material conditions of security and decency.

So, in December 2005, they gave the Prime Minister a document entitled *Faiths, fairness, secularity*, in which they underlined that, beyond the separation of Church and State, the latter must develop and give today a concrete guarantee of genuine religious freedom, including for people recently settled in France. In

---

10   Jean Volff, *Le droit des cultes* (Dalloz 2005) 78–94.

particular, it called for financial support for the construction of places of worship by the new Evangelical Churches which are witnessing strong growth, as they had not been able to receive the free allocation of buildings of worship in 1905. This support could, in their opinion, take the form of special conditions for loans and leases. Finally, it is also seeking state intervention to assist in the training of ministers of religion, in the areas of language, culture, secularity and religious laws, with the churches solely providing theological training.[11]

In late 2005, the then Minister of the Interior, Nicolas Sarkozy, created a commission of jurists, responsible for legal reflection on relations between faiths and public authorities. Chaired by Professor Jean-Pierre Machelon, it issued its findings in September 2006. After recalling that the Republic could not become disinterested in religious reality, as it is social reality, the report found that the constitutional principle of secularity has three aspects: neutrality of the State with respect to religions, religious freedom and respect for pluralism. It thereby concludes that Article 2 of the Law of 1905, which prohibits all public subsidies for faiths, does not have constitutional value and can be changed by a new law.

The report specifically recommends amending various Articles of the Law of 1905 to allow *communes* to subsidize the construction of religious buildings (temples, halls of worship, mosques etc.), as well as works to secure and make older places of worship compliant with norms, in order to enable new faiths (including Evangelical Churches) to meet and celebrate their rites in a decent location, visible and secure, and to enable older faiths to undertake the essential and expensive works necessary to bring their buildings up to standard. Welcomed in Protestant circles, this report was widely criticized by the lay community and has not yet been followed up.[12]

Nowadays, everywhere in Europe, even in some former Communist countries, public authorities are, directly or indirectly, providing financial support to Protestant denominations, in a variety of different ways (church tax, grants for religious buildings and faculties of theology, subsidized social work undertaken by churches, paying pastors' salaries and pensions, various tax rebates etc.).

Conclusion

For Protestant Churches, the issue of funding is not an element necessary to obtain salvation, but arises from *adiaphora* – indifferent things – according to the well-known distinction by Philippe Melanchthon. It is resolved differently according to places and eras and it can even have different forms within the same country or

---

11   Fédération protestante de France, 'Protestantisme et société, documents, cultes, équité, laïcité'(2002) <www.protestants.org>

12   Jean-Marie Woehrling, *'Le rapport Machelon: une utile contribution à la démystification du droit français des cultes'(2006) 48 La Semaine Juridique, Administrations et collectivités territoriales 1292.*

the same confession, as is the case in France. The solutions adopted are therefore pragmatic and depend greatly on social and historical circumstances and the political attitude of the State towards religions.

Two major trends emerged as early as the sixteenth century in the Churches of the Reformation, levelling out in the nineteenth century. For some, the State has a duty to financially assist faiths which contribute to the moral education of citizens, to creating and maintaining social bonds and public peace. For others, for the Church to remain faithful to Christ, it must be totally independent of the State and therefore survive and evolve relying only on contributions from the faithful, following the example of the Hebrews (tithe) and the Paul the Apostle (collections).

In the twenty-first century, combining these two approaches seems to attract consensus among the churches which, unlike the Church of England, do not have a historical heritage. These Protestant Churches intend to live mainly thanks to members' donations, but they consider that public authorities should help them directly or indirectly, as happens for other types of associations (charitable associations, trade unions, political parties), at least as regards training their personnel, constructing new buildings and bringing up to standard the existing ones. By doing so, without saying it openly, they are challenging the religious discrimination inherent in the application of Article 19, paragraph 9 of the Law of 1905, which is in violation of Articles 9 and 14 of the European Convention of Human Rights and Fundamental Freedoms.

For this reason, proposal number 46 put forward by the then candidate for the Presidency of the Republic, François Hollande, (in which the first two Articles of the Law of 1905 would be incorporated into the Constitution), greatly concerned officers of the Protestant Churches, just as much in Alsace-Lorraine as in the rest of the country and overseas, because its implementation would call into question any form of public subsidy to faiths.

So, apart from any doctrine or ecclesial regulations, the issue of funding Protestant faiths remains open, with its solution depending mainly on the society in which they are involved and on the rules of the State to which they are subject.

List of References

Calvin J, *Institution de la religion chrétienne, livres III & IV* (Vrin 1960)
Cottret B, *Histoire de la Réforme protestante* (Perrin 2010)
Fédération protestante de France, 'Protestantisme et société, documents, cultes, équité, laïcité' (2002) <www.protestants.org>
Garrisson J, *L'Édit de Nantes* (Atlantica 1997)
Lienhard M, *'L'apport des dissidents du XVIe siècle à l'émergence de la laïcité' in Genèse et enjeux de la laïcité* (Labor et Fides 1990)
Luther M, *à la noblesse chrétienne de la nation allemande, coll. La Pleïade, tome I* (Gallimard 1999)

Vinet A, *Essai sur la manifestation des convictions religieuses et sur la séparation de l'Église et de l'État* (Paulin 1842)

—— *Mémoire en faveur de la liberté des cultes*, 2nd edition (Les éditeurs 1852)

Volff J, *Le droit des cultes* (Dalloz 2005)

Wendel F, *L'Église de Strasbourg, sa constitution et son organisation, 1532–1535* (PUF 1942)

Woehrling J-M, *'Le rapport Machelon: une utile contribution à la démystification du droit français des cultes'* (2006) 48 La Semaine Juridique, Administrations et collectivités territoriales

Chapter 16

Management of Goods in the Catholic Church and its Relationship with the Laws of the State: Principles and Implementation

Patrick Valdrini

The Church's Jurisdiction over Its Goods

Managing the goods of the Catholic Church is the subject of an entire book of the 1983 Code of Canon Law.[1] On some key points, the rules it lists have been modified from those promulgated in the first Code of Canon Law published in 1917.[2] The latter had introduced the principle of codification for all matters relating to the organization of church activity. Consequently, the conciseness of the method

---

1   This study focuses on the Latin Code of Canon Law promulgated in 1983 for the Latin part of the Catholic Church (CIC of 1983). The second – *Codex canonum Ecclesiarum orientalium*, promulgated in 1990 by Pope Jean-Paul II (CCEO), targets the Eastern part of this same Church, that is to say 21 churches organized to a large extent according to a law which is their own. One title of this Eastern Code deals with temporal goods of the Church (Title XXIII), canons 1007–1054 of which are strongly inspired by the Latin Code. These two codes are similar on many points. See the comment by Jobe Abbass, 'The Temporal Goods of the Church: a comparative Study of the Eastern and Latin Codes of Canon Law' (1994) 83 *Periodica* 669–714. Their differences mainly arise from their references to diverse traditions. The Eastern code is rooted in the experiences of the Eastern churches (which are mainly located in the Near, Middle and Far East), having remained outside European streams of thinking.

2   Before the CIC of 1983, an initial code had been promulgated in 1917 by Pope Benedict XV (CIC of 1917) which contained 56 canons (can. 1499–1551) assembled under one title: *De bonis Ecclesiae temporalibus.* Previously, 79 canons (can. 1409–1488) were devoted to ecclesiastical benefices, that is to say stable responsibilities entitling those concerned to receive revenue provided via an allowance attached to it. For commentary on all these canons, see Raoul Naz (ed.), *Traité de droit canonique* Tome III (Letouzey et Ané 1948) 222–266. On the superseding of the benefice system in the CIC of 1983, following the CIC of 1917 which still recognized it, see Velasio De Paolis, *I beni temporali della Chiesa*, nuova edizione aggiornata e integrata a cura di Alberto Perlasca (EDB 2011) 162–170. And to read a study on the history of the revision of the 1917 CIC standards by the Revision Commission, see Jean-Claude Périsset, *Les biens temporels de l'Eglise. Commentaires des canons 1254–1310*, coll. Le nouveau droit ecclésial. Commentaire du Code de droit canonique. Livre V (Tardy 1996) 17–27.

of presenting legislation in short articles – as had been done in Emperor Napoléon Bonaparte's French Civil Code at the beginning of the nineteenth century – allowed the principles and rules (which were to be respected by all believers, especially those holding power in government) to appear more clearly.[3] The Catholic Church has a hierarchical structure organized by positions, some of which are reserved for ministers who have been ordained. The latter are distinguished among the faithful by virtue of a specific sacrament in addition to those of baptism and confirmation, and have authorization or ability to assume stable ecclesiastical responsibilities; these include hierarchical duties of leadership in all three main orders described by the Second Vatican Council: education, sanctification and government.[4]

The governmental duties allow the promulgation of laws and for these to be enforced by individual acts or to be applied when sentencing. This means that managing goods and the presentation of the rules and principles that inspire and govern it, will have to contain the power of ecclesiastical jurisdiction as an essential element to it being understood; its basis and legitimacy are of canonical nature, namely internal to the Catholic Church. This is no doubt what best explains the struggles of the Catholic Church against its opponents: there are those who challenge it from the inside, such as movements in favour of radical purification and a return to the declared origins of the organization;[5] then, those who have turned away from the Church, rejecting the jurisdictional principle of sacramental foundation and replacing it by organizational elements that can no longer claim any real difference or autonomy compared to secular jurisdictions;[6] finally, those who – using direct opposition and for political and philosophical reasons – have despoiled its religious heritage.[7]

These three most effective kinds of challenge underlie many official documents, which present a Catholic ecclesiology that included the idea of synodal participation – a constant in the Church, even if it had been less important during some epochs, but which contains the principle of hierarchical organization, the essential character of which stands in contrast to the organization of democratic societies.[8]

---

3   Albert Ortscheid, *Essai concernant la nature de la codification et son influence sur la science juridique d'après le concept du Code de droit canonique* (Recueil Sirey 1922).

4   Patrick Valdrini et al., *Droit canonique* (Dalloz 1999) 41–5; Ludwig Schick, *Das dreifache Amt Christi und der Kirche. Zur Entstehung und Entwicklung der Trilogien* (Peter Lang 1982).

5   'Vaudois' in Jean-Yves Lacoste (ed.) *Dictionnaire critique de théologie* (PUF 1999) 1205–7. See also article 'Catharisme' in Jean-Yves Lacoste (ed.) *Dictionnaire critique de théologie* (PUF 1999). 209–11.

6   Gianni Long, *Ordinamenti giuridici delle chiese protestanti* (Il Mulino 2008) spec. 11–16.

7   Francis Messner et al. (eds), *Traité de droit français des religions* (Litec 2003) 88.

8   See Patrick Valdrini, 'Fedele, uguaglianza e organizzazione della Chiesa nel CIC del 1983' *Ambula per nomine et pervenies ad Deum. Studi in onore di S.E. Mons. Ignazio Sanna* (Studium 2012) 513–53.

An Innate, Own and Exclusive Right

The first canon of Book V of the CIC of 1983 declares that the Catholic Church has, by virtue of an innate right, the ability, independently of the secular power, to acquire, own, administer and dispose of temporal goods to pursue its own purposes. It describes these main purposes as: organizing public worship, enabling an honest livelihood for the clergy and other ministers and performing works of the holy apostolate and of charity, especially towards the poor. The first paragraph of the canon is declaratory.[9] It lays down the principle that the Church enjoys independence in relation to civil authority in exercising its jurisdiction over its heritage.[10]

All the Catholic authors and canonists of the nineteenth century who were dealing with the relationship between Church and State within the context of the so-called science of *public, ecclesiastical law*, drawing inspiration from the theories of schools of natural law,[11] already asserted this independence of the Church as *societas iuridice perfecta*. The canon does not use this expression, but it remains, due to its content and purpose, a working reference marking out the respective boundaries of ecclesiastical and secular authorities in their capacity and desire to govern the Catholic Church's own affairs.

Based on this reasoning, the Catholic Church possessed, in the spiritual order, the traits of sovereign, independent societies that the state, sovereign in the temporal order, could not deny. Of an apologetic nature, the expression set the terms of the relationship between sovereignties within the field of law, using its strength to prohibit action and intervention in areas where the state was declared not competent.[12] In the 1983 Canon Law Code, this innate, own and exclusive right is made explicit, being declared and claimed in legal terms; the same applies when activities organized under canon law relate to exercising the magisterium[13] or are identical to those governed by state law – judicial activity internal to the

---

9   Can. 1254 § 1: 'To pursue its proper purposes, the Catholic Church by innate right is able to acquire, retain, administer, and alienate temporal goods independently from civil power'.

10   Jean-Pierre Schouppe, *Droit canonique des biens* (Wilson et Lafleur 2008) 15–27. Périsset (n 2) 29–31.

11   See Alberto La Hera et al., 'Le droit public à travers ses définitions' (1964) 14 *Revue de droit canonique* 32–63.

12   Roland Minnerath, *Le droit à la liberté de l'Église. Du Syllabus à Vatican II* (Beauchesne 1982) 81–110.

13   Can. 747 § 1: 'The Church, to which Christ the Lord has entrusted the deposit of faith so that with the assistance of the Holy Spirit it might protect the revealed truth reverently, examine it more closely, and proclaim and expound it faithfully, has the duty and innate right, independent of any human power whatsoever, to preach the gospel to all peoples, also using the means of social communication proper to it'.

Church (trials),[14] the imposition of sanctions on the faithful (canonical penal law)[15] and administering goods itself[16] – three areas in which the Catholic Church demands to exercise its jurisdiction, but cannot avoid coming up against state law and getting to grips with it. This legal and political reference is solemnly stated, at a time when the Second Vatican Council was helping the Church's design to evolve for the benefit of a richer ecclesiology, as one of the key passages of the Dogmatic Constitution, *Lumen gentium*, explains; here, the Church, which is no longer called *Societas iuridice perfecta*, but sacrament of salvation, is described as a reality made up of a divine and human element, compared by way of analogy with the Incarnate Word.[17]

Goods for Church-Specific Purposes

In the Conciliar Constitution, the societal nature of the Church is not denied, but included within a more theological and biblical understanding of the Church; this lends it the character of a place where the divine plan can be carried out in history, an apocalyptic plan including what has already been done and what there is still to do, since the element of mystery depends on this tension between the divine and the human, between what has been accomplished and what remains to be done throughout history.[18] This richer understanding means determining the

14   Can. 1401: 'By proper and exclusive right the Church adjudicates: 1) cases which regard spiritual matters or those connected to spiritual matters; 2) the violation of ecclesiastical laws and all those matters in which there is a question of sin, in what pertains to the determination of culpability and the imposition of ecclesiastical penalties'.

15   Can. 1311: 'The Church has the innate and proper right to coerce offending members of the Christian faithful with penal sanctions'.

16   Can. 1254 § 1.

17   Dogmatic Constitution *Lumen gentium*, Number 8: 'Christ, the one Mediator, established and continually sustains here on earth His holy Church, the community of faith, hope and charity, through which He communicated truth and grace to all. But, the society structured with hierarchical organs and the Mystical Body of Christ, are not to be considered as two realities, nor are the visible assembly and the spiritual community, nor the earthly Church and the Church enriched with heavenly things; rather they form one complex reality which coalesces from a divine and a human element. For this reason, by no weak analogy, it is compared to the mystery of the incarnate Word. As the assumed nature inseparably united to Him, serves the divine Word as a living organ of salvation, so, in a similar way, does the visible social structure of the Church serve the Spirit of Christ, who vivifies it, in the building up of the body'.

18   Gérard Philips, *L'Eglise et son mystère au IIe Concile du Vatican. Histoire, texte, commentaire de la Constitution Lumen gentium* Tome I (Desclée 1967) 98–105; Yves Congar, *L'Eglise. De Saint-Augustin à l'époque moderne*, coll. Histoire des dogmes, Tome III, Christologie-Sotériologie-Mariologie, Fascicule 3 (Cerf 1970) 462: 'The concept of society was not enough to express the richness of the mystery. You could even doubt the ability to define the Church'.

ecclesiological nature of purposes in all orders of activity, including the subject of our study – managing goods.[19] The Second Vatican Council contains a mixture of elements that can be used to ascertain, on the one hand, a general understanding of the possession and management of goods by the Church and, on the other hand, the limits to heritage-related activities over which the Church is claiming autonomy in this order, in the face of external authorities.

On the first point, the texts serve to indicate envisaged sources of current legislation, either as a reminder that goods have an instrumental nature,[20] or as affirmation of the principle according to which their management should highlight evangelical virtues and be consistent with the true nature of the Catholic Church, particularly with a view to ensuring the funding of works and persons exercising a responsibility there. The Pastoral Constitution *Gaudium et Spes* states that the Church uses temporal instruments, insofar as its own mission requires it,[21] that it must create activities to serve everyone, including the poor, charitable organizations and the like[22] and highlights the ideal of poverty which must prevail in the evolving activities of the Church.[23] This last statement is given particular

---

19   Peter Erdö, 'Chiesa e beni temporali: principi fondamentali del magistero del Concilio Vaticano II (can. 1254–1256)' in Velasio De Paolis (ed.) *I beni temporali della Chiesa* (Libreria editrice Vaticana 1999) 26–8.

20   Lumen Gentium, § 8, al. 3: 'Thus, the Church, although it needs human resources to carry out its mission, is not set up to seek earthly glory, but to proclaim, even by its own example, humility and self-sacrifice'. The CIC of 1983 does not describe scriptural or magisterial foundations of the possession and management of Church goods. We must seek them in studies of a doctrinal nature, such as De Paolis (n 19) 11–33 or Erdö (n 19) 26–34.

21   Gaudium et Spes, § 76: 'The Church herself makes use of temporal things insofar as her own mission requires it … '. This way of presenting the instrumental nature of assets was taken up in the plan of the *Lex fundamentalis* 1970 in canon 82, § 2 and is better highlighted in the CCEO at c. 1007.

22   Gaudium et Spes, § 42: ' … Christ, to be sure, gave His Church no proper mission in the political, economic or social order. But out of this religious mission itself come a function, a light and an energy which can serve to structure and consolidate the human community according to the divine law. As a matter of fact, when circumstances of time and place produce the need, she can and indeed should initiate activities on behalf of all men, especially those designed for the needy, such as the works of mercy and similar undertakings'.

23   Presbyterorum Ordinis, § 17: 'Those goods which priests and bishops receive for the exercise of their ecclesiastical office should be used for adequate support and the fulfilment of their office and status, excepting those governed by particular laws. That which is in excess they should be willing to set aside for the good of the Church or for works of charity … They are even invited to embrace voluntary poverty which will make more obvious similarity with Christ and will be more available to the Holy Ministry … Priests, moreover, are invited to embrace voluntary poverty by which they are more manifestly conformed to Christ and become eager in the sacred ministry. A certain common use of goods, similar to the common possession of goods in the history of the primitive Church, furnishes an excellent means of pastoral charity. By living this form of life, priests can

emphasis when the Council mentions the religious institutes that express and institutionalize religious vows requiring people to live in material detachment.[24]

These statements are accompanied by a fundamental claim that the very mission that Christ entrusted to his Church is neither of political, economic nor social order, but religious.[25] Such statements by the Council serve as the basis and the viewpoint for the 1983 Code of Canon Law and supplement the traditional desire, described above, to preserve the principle of sovereignty of ecclesiastical jurisdiction. This explains why canon law focuses on goods when they serve specific purposes and, in doing so, promulgates norms for acquiring these goods, for administering and disposing of them, for establishing heritage contracts, for the creation and management of so-called 'pious' foundations necessary for the Church's activity.

The Development and Diversification of Specific Legislation

The 57 canons of Book V describe the universal legislation for managing goods that applies to the entire Church, because the Code is promulgated by the Roman Pontiff for all institutions and the individuals of which they are composed. It contains specific legal categories which determine the degree of autonomy of the various owners of goods.

It does, however, leave room for specific legislation; how this is created, formed and applied depends on each established community that benefits from legal autonomy. Such is the case of specific churches or dioceses at the head of which diocesan bishops or similar individuals have law-making authority, allowing them to introduce laws relating to diverse local cultures.[26] It is part of the nature of these churches to be close to them, to find a means of expression of their own elements, to promote reception of laws and universal rules, while taking into account, as we will see, civil law in each state.

This founding principle of the Church, which prevents it being considered as solely a centralized institution, finds first expression within the specific field

---

laudably reduce to practice that spirit of poverty commended by Christ'. See Yves Congar, 'Les biens temporels de l'Eglise d'après sa tradition théologique et canonique' in Georges Cottier et al. (eds), *Eglise et pauvreté* (Les Editions du Cerf 1965) 234–58.

24   Perfectae Caritatis, § 13: 'Due regard being had for local conditions, religious communities should readily offer a quasi-collective witness to poverty … ' Valesio De Paolis, 'Temporal Goods of the Church in the New Code with particular reference to Institutes of consecrated life' (1983) 43 *The Jurist* 343–55; Schouppe (n 10) 219–223.

25   Gaudium et Spes, § 42: Among the means to acquire goods, the Code grants an important part to offerings from the faithful. See Luis Navarro 'L'acquisto dei beni temporali. Il finanziamento della Chiesa' in Velasio De Paolis (ed.) *I beni temporali della Chiesa* (Libreria editrice Vaticana 1999) 45–57; Schouppe (n 10) 98–151.

26   Patrick Valdrini, 'Unité et pluralité des ensembles législatifs. Droit universel et droit particulier d'après le Code de droit canonique latin' (1997) 9 *Ius Ecclesiae* 3–17.

of canon law. In fact, the diocesan bishop – but this also applies to the various religious institutes that have to manage goods in the countries where they exercise their activity – has the ability to establish norms, either personally or within the traditional participation structure of the Diocesan Synod. In the same way, norms could be established at a broader level than that of a diocese, for reasons of consistency, by a conference of bishops or possibly by special councils that legislate for a territory that generally corresponds to a state or nation.[27]

The creation of specific legislation can take place in complete autonomy when it comes from a diocesan bishop, but, in the case of the conferences of bishops and councils, it requires an intervention by the supreme authority of the Church in the form of recognition or approval with a view to preserving the legislative unity of the Church.[28] This fundamental, customary element of canon law explains why a set of rules exists for managing goods, norms or other documents of legislative scope other than those of the Code of Canon Law, which would need to be assembled as collections of laws in the manner of the old *collectiones*, which grouped together legal texts at a time when codes did not yet exist.

This work is often undertaken by the doctrine for different geographical areas that correspond to territories where civil laws apply. It is not undertaken by the authority, which admits that in this domain great diversity may exist, provided that the norms expressed in the 57 canons of the Code be respected, because they contain what the Church wants to keep as universal, founding elements, elements of unity therefore, as regards management. To assist this practice, the Code declares that the Roman Pontiff, by virtue of his rule, is the supreme administrator and provider of all ecclesiastical goods[29] and that diocesan bishops must exercise vigilance when managing them.[30] No doubt this statement explains the extreme diversity of specific legislation, but the right of ownership of assets under the authority of the Pope belongs to the legal person who has legitimately acquired them. Church law makes the many legal owners responsible for finding the best normative framework to manage their goods, a responsibility which falls as much to local government institutions, as it does in many cases to the legal persons themselves.[31]

---

27   Valdrini et al. (n 4) 95–189.

28   De Paolis (n 19) 187–204.

29   *Francesco* Saverio Salerno, 'I beni temporali della Chiesa ed il potere primaziale del Romano Pontefice' in De Paolis (n 19) 103–139.

30   Adolfo Longhitano,'L'amministrazione dei beni: la funzione di vigilanza del vescovo diocesano (can.1276–1277)' in De Paolis (n 19) 83–101.

31   Can. 116: '§ 1. Public juridic persons are aggregates of persons or of things which are constituted by competent ecclesiastical authority so that, within the purposes set out for them, they fulfil in the name of the Church, according to the norm of the prescripts of the law, the proper function entrusted to them in view of the public good; other juridic persons are private. § 2. Public juridic persons are given this personality either by the law itself or by a special decree of competent authority expressly granting it. Private juridic persons are given this personality only through a special decree of competent authority expressly

Another way of looking at the principle of determining rules close to local cultures – directly related to the creation of a special law or community local law or even specific to legal persons rather than universal persons – is to consider the relation to state laws and legal culture.[32] This area is the subject of statements scattered throughout the Code that can be distinguished as three ways to legislate or three ways to envisage the relation with civil law: firstly, a request or recommendation to respect civil law; secondly, a recommendation to refer to this law to utilize its effects; thirdly, its canonization. These three ways are close to one another. In practice, due to the complexity of the situations, they come together or even merge, but, on the theoretical and legal level, they have diverse legal consequences from case to case.

The Principle of Referring to Civil Law

First, as if a general principle, the Code requests or recommends, for certain determined activities of management, respect for state law. For this reason, when

---

granting it'. The distinction is important, as only goods of public legal persons are called ecclesiastical goods and belong to the Church as such. The property of private persons is the property of the persons themselves, as indicated in canon 1257: '§ 1. All temporal goods which belong to the universal Church, the Apostolic See, or other public juridic persons in the Church are ecclesiastical goods and are governed by the following canons and their own statutes. § 2. The temporal goods of a private juridic person are governed by its own statutes, but not by these canons unless other provision is expressly made'.

32   Studies on the application of canon law exist for various countries, for example for Italy, see *I beni temporali della Chiesa in Italia: nuova normativa canonica e concordataria*, coll. Studi giuridici XI (Libreria editrice Vaticana 1985). For Belgium, see Jean-Pierre Schouppe et al., 'Sur les traces du droit canonique des biens temporels en Belgique' in Jean-Pierre Schouppe (ed.), *Vingt-cinq ans après le Code. Le droit canon en Belgique*, prefaced by Cardinal Godfried Daneels, coll. *Droit et religion* (Bruylant 2008) 147–55. For France, see Francis Messner, *Le financement des Eglises. Le système des cultes reconnus (1801–1923)* (Cerdic-publications 1984); Jean-Paul Durand, 'Biens ecclésiastiques. Droit canonique et droit français. Propos conclusifs' (2005) 47 *L'année canonique* 83–5; Philippe Greiner, 'Les biens des paroisses dans le contexte des diocèses français' (2005) 47 *L'année canonique* 37–50; Olivier Echappé, 'Les « biens » des associations d'Eglise' (2006) 47 *L'année canonique* 51–62; Patrick Valdrini, 'La gestion des biens dans les diocèses français' (16 Oct 1997) *Documents Episcopat* 1–6; Messner et al. (n 7) 761–76 and 878–94. For Germany, Hans Heimerl et al., *Handbuch des Vermögensrechts der katholischen Kirche unter besonderer Berücksichtigung der Rechtsverhältnisse in Bayern und Österreich* (F. Pustet 1983) 131–250. For Africa, Sylvia Recchi (ed.), *Autonomie financière et gestion des biens dans les jeunes Eglises d'Afrique*, coll. Eglises d'Afrique (L'Harmattan 2003); Jean-Marie Signé, 'L'administration des biens temporels et l'avènement des Eglises pleinement constituées' (2008) 50 *L'année canonique* 63–75. For North America, Francis G Morrisey, 'The alienation of temporal goods in contemporary practice' (1995) 29 *Studia canonica* 293–316.

it requires the establishment of a council for economic affairs in each diocese, this will consist of experts 'in economic affairs as well as civil law'.[33] Then, when the Code describes the way in which administrators should perform their management duties, using the well-known formula *bonus pater familias*, it requests that the provisions not only of canon law, but also of civil law, be observed, with failing to do so damaging the goods being administered.[34]

One canon envisages the case of a disposal of assets that is invalid in canon law, but valid in civil law. The competent authority shall decide 'whether and what type of action, namely, personal or real, is to be instituted by whom and against whom in order to lay claim to the rights of the Church'.[35] In this case, the priority of canon law over civil law is asserted and will serve as a criterion of judgement about what action to take. But alongside the simple principle of recommended or required respect for state law, the Code of Canon Law uses the principle of forced referral. So, the area of administrators' contracts is subject to particular attention and a canon is dedicated to this, demanding – and not only recommending – that, when employing staff, 'civil employment and social legislation' should be followed to the letter, according to the principles of the social doctrine of the Church.[36] This is a sensitive point when the Church lacks a specific legal status in state law. Such is the case in France, as shown by the issue of laypersons appointed temporarily or permanently to a particular department of the Catholic Church. It is said that they are entitled to obtain payment related to their ability to provide for their own needs and those of their families. Canon 231, § 2 adds: 'also by respecting civil law'.

This declarative recommendation has been at the root of theoretical studies and practical proposals in France, because the ecclesiastical authority has found itself faced with a communication problem between ways of thinking in both types of laws – canon and civil. While, for the former, a layman is appointed to a department

---

33　Can. 492: '§ 1. In every diocese a finance council is to be established, over which the diocesan bishop himself or his delegate presides and which consists of at least three members of the Christian faithful truly expert in Financial affairs and civil law, outstanding in integrity, and appointed by the bishop'.

34　Can. 1284: '§ 1. All administrators are bound to fulfill their function with the diligence of a good householder. § 2. Consequently they must: ... 3) observe the prescripts of both canon and civil law or those imposed by a founder, a donor, or legitimate authority, and especially be on guard so that no damage comes to the Church from the non-observance of civil laws'.

35　Can. 1296: 'Whenever ecclesiastical goods have been alienated without the required canonical formalities but the alienation is valid civilly, it is for the competent authority, after having considered everything thoroughly, to decide whether and what type of action, namely, personal or real, is to be instituted by whom and against whom in order to vindicate the rights of the Church'. For commentary on the canon, see Périsset (n 2) 217–20.

36　Can. 1286: 'Administrators of goods: 1) in the employment of workers are to observe meticulously also the civil laws concerning labor and social policy, according to the principles handed on by the Church'.

by an act of unilateral appointment conveyed by letter (which is in canon law a particular decree given by a person holding governmental authority), for the latter (state law), hiring a service is a contractual act contained within a contract of employment. Marrying the approaches, in the spirit of canon law, must be able to preserve the autonomy and sovereignty of the internal, legal *ordinamento*, that is to say the exercising of the Church's jurisdiction.[37]

In some precise cases, the Code states that civil law will serve as a framework to establish the formalities of an act. Contrary to the previous principle – that made civil law a passive entity and recommended its application – the state law referred to by the Code is an instrument of organization which, without being imposed as such, is used to give acts a legitimacy guaranteed by the legal system in which the activity is carried out. From being passive, the relation with state law becomes active. With civil law remaining state law – and not being canonized, as in other cases to be discussed below – civil law applies its effects in its own order and not in the canonical order. In this case, canon law uses state law for its technicality and the binding force that it could not impose itself. Administrators are then asked to take care to guarantee ownership of ecclesiastical goods by means valid in civil law.[38]

Furthermore, it is envisaged to create a special institute which will gather together goods and offerings with a view to paying for the upkeep of the clergy in dioceses, as well as their social security, a duty mainly performed by conferences of bishops. If possible, these bodies are, it is stated, to be 'set up in such a way that they also apply in civil law'.[39] The sovereignty of the canonical judicial system is assured in this way, as it is an organization created and run by dioceses or a collection of dioceses. At the same time, this guarantees the search for effects that could provide greater efficiency to the body within the order of the state. This is then a civil addition to the canonical legal field, a form of cooperation by civil law in pursuing goals established within the Catholic Church and the opportunity for which is evaluated according to canonical criteria.

Canon 1299 is another example of this utilitarian relationship and its motivation. It solemnly declares that the faithful are free, under natural law and canon law, to dispose of their goods so as to leave them to pious causes (*causes pies*), by *inter vivos* acts or upon death. In the latter case, it is specified that 'the legal formalities

---

37   René Rémond et al., 'Les animateurs pastoraux. Statut civil et canonique des "permanents" en pastorale' (1992) 35 *L'année canonique* 19–100. See also Messner et al. (n 7) 1030–33.

38   See canon 1284: 'Administrators must take care that the ownership of ecclesiastical goods is protected by civilly valid methods'.

39   Can. 1274: '§ 1. Each diocese is to have a special institute which is to collect goods or offerings for the purpose of providing, according to the norm of can. 281, for the support of clerics who offer service for the benefit of the diocese, unless provision is made for them in another way ... If possible, these institutes are to be established in such a way that they also have recognition in civil law'.

of civil law are to be observed as much as possible. If they have been omitted, the heirs must be admonished regarding the obligation, to which they are bound, of fulfilling the will of the testator'. On the one hand, the principle of referral gives state law an instrumental character. It is a means of ensuring the desired aim, since the law applied gives legitimacy to the act that any people not wishing to follow the will of the testator could not challenge. On the other hand, the canon introduces the principle of the priority of canon law, because, if formalities had been omitted (and it is assumed that they would not invalidate an act *ipso jure*), the heirs would be called upon to themselves limit their ability to claim invalidation, out of respect for the will of the testator.[40]

The Canonization of Civil Law

The third type of relationship between canon law and state law in relation to civil law for managing temporal goods is that of canonization – in the precise sense of the term used by the Code. In this case, civil law is integrated into canon law as a law that applies to such an extent that external parliamentary, governmental or jurisprudential modifications may have a knock-on effect on the internal legal domain of the Church.

The canonization of civil law is an ancient principle in the tradition of the Church. The history of canon law sources shows the application of this principle where there are legal systems from which the Church has drawn elements of legislation, in particular Roman law. The current law has made it a principle: the civil laws referred to in Church law must be observed in canon law with the same effects, insofar as they are not contrary to divine law and unless canon law provides otherwise.[41]

The canon speaks of referral, but this is not the mere referral upon which we commented earlier, nor the search for legitimate and efficient legal effects, but rather civil law that has become canon law. As expressed in canon 1290 (on negotiations relating to heritage), the provisions of civil law in force within a territory, in terms of contracts (whether general or particular) and methods of

---

40 This possibility will also depend on the qualification of elements of civil law that applies to the validity of the act of donating. For commentary on this canon, see Périsset (n 2) 229–32. The concept of self-limitation when exercising rights on behalf of believers is a thread present in can. 223 § 1. On this, see Maria d'Arienzo, *Il concetto giuridico di responsabilità. Rilevanza e funzione nel diritto canonico* (Pellegrini editore 2012) 147–51.

41 Can. 22: 'Civil laws to which the law of the Church yields are to be observed in canon law with the same effects, insofar as they are not contrary to divine law and unless canon law provides otherwise'. For a commentary on this canon, see Francisco Javier Urrutia, *Les normes générales. Commentaire des canons 1–203* (Tardy 1992) 90–91; Jesús Miñambres *La remisión de la ley canónica al derecho civil* (Pontificia Università della Santa Croce 1922).

discharging obligations, are to be observed with the same effects in canon law for matters subject to the governance of the Church. Two limitations oppose this canonization: on the one hand, divine law, which is the original law, the basis of which is that the will of God be expressed positively in the texts or discovered by work of reason; and, on the other hand, canon law, which expresses once again its nature as instrument and means of sovereignty, as it will always obtain priority over civil law.[42]

De Paolis gives the example of legal prescription, for which canon law has always demanded good faith. Canon 197 refers to secular laws to organize it, but 'outside of the exceptions laid down by the code'. The author shows that canon law on this point was opposed to Roman law, which accepted that dishonesty did not affect the validity of the prescription. In this light, and referring to Pio Fedele, he reads that this clause, unknown of in secular legislation, shows that 'civil laws are an abstraction of natural law and conscience, whereas canon law considers natural law as the essential basis of all human laws and posits that the latter only have meaning if they do not oppose it. It is' – he adds – 'about acknowledging the proclamation of an absolute, superior, legal principle to which the entire human legal order must yield'.[43]

Compared with the other two ways to legislate on the relation with civil law, canonization is the clearest legal instrument. However, the difficulty remains as to how to bring together the diverse ways of thinking contained in both canonical and civil laws, which, as we have shown, relies on the existence of a sovereign ecclesiastical jurisdiction in its order. Such an operation is facilitated when agreement can be established at sovereignty level by means of a concordat-style text, in this case giving a guarantee to the Catholic Church that its jurisdiction may be exercised in the respect of the principles which it maintains.[44]

List of References

Abbass J, 'The Temporal Goods of the Church: a comparative Study of the Eastern and Latin Codes of Canon Law' (1994) 83 *Periodica*

Congar Y, 'Les biens temporels de l'Eglise d'après sa tradition théologique et canonique' in Cottier, G. et al. (eds), *Eglise et pauvreté* (Les Editions du Cerf 1965)

—— *L'Eglise. De Saint-Augustin* à *l'époque moderne*, coll. Histoire des dogmes, Tome III, Christologie-Sotériologie-Mariologie, Fascicule 3 (Cerf 1970)

---

42   Périsset (n 2) 194–8.

43   Velasio De Paolis, 'Les biens temporels au regard du Code de droit canonique' (2005) 47 *L'année canonique* 27.

44   Roland Minnerath, *L'Eglise catholique face aux Etats. Deux siècles de pratique concordataire.1801–2010*, coll. Droit canonique (Les Editions du Cerf 2012).

D'Arienzo M, *Il concetto giuridico di responsabilità. Rilevanza e funzione nel diritto canonico* (Pellegrini editore 2012)

De Paolis V, 'Temporal Goods of the Church in the New Code with particular reference to Institutes of consecrated life' (1983) 43 *The Jurist*

—— 'Les biens temporels au regard du Code de droit canonique' (2005) 47 *L'année canonique*

—— *I beni temporali della Chiesa*, nuova edizione aggiornata e integrata a cura di Alberto Perlasca (EDB 2011)

Durand J-P, 'Biens ecclésiastiques. Droit canonique et droit français. Propos conclusifs' (2005) 47 *L'année canonique*

Echappé O, 'Les « biens » des associations d'Eglise' (2006) 47 *L'année canonique*

Erdö P, 'Chiesa e beni temporali: principi fondamentali del magistero del Concilio Vaticano II (can. 1254–1256)' in V De Paolis (ed.) *I beni temporali della Chiesa* (Libreria editrice Vaticana 1999)

Greiner P, 'Les biens des paroisses dans le contexte des diocèses français' (2005) 47 *L'année canonique*

Heimerl H et al., *Handbuch des Vermögensrechts der katholischen Kirche unter besonderer Berücksichtigung der Rechtsverhältnisse in Bayern und* Österreich (F. Pustet 1983)

I beni temporali della Chiesa in Italia: nuova normativa canonica e concordataria, coll. Studi giuridici XI (Libreria editrice Vaticana 1985)

La Hera A et al., 'Le droit public à travers ses définitions' (1964) 14 *Revue de droit canonique*

Lacoste J-Y (ed.), *Dictionnaire critique de théologie* (PUF 1999)

Long G, *Ordinamenti giuridici delle chiese protestanti* (Il Mulino 2008)

Longhitano A, 'L'amministrazione dei beni: la funzione di vigilanza del vescovo diocesano (can.1276–1277)' in V De Paolis (ed.) *I beni temporali della Chiesa* (Libreria editrice Vaticana 1999)

Messner F, *Le financement des Eglises. Le système des cultes reconnus (1801–1923)* (Cerdic-publications 1984)

Messner F et al. (eds), *Traité de droit français des religions* (Litec 2003)

Miñambres J, *La remisión de la ley canónica al derecho civil* (Pontificia Università della Santa Croce 1922)

Minnerath R, *Le droit à la liberté de l'Église. Du Syllabus à Vatican II* (Beauchesne 1982)

—— *L'Eglise catholique face aux Etats. Deux siècles de pratique concordataire.1801–2010*, coll. Droit canonique (Les Editions du Cerf 2012)

Morrisey FG 'The alienation of temporal goods in contemporary practice' (1995) 29 *Studia canonica*

Navarro L, 'L'acquisto dei beni temporali. Il finanziamento della Chiesa' in V De Paolis (ed.) *I beni temporali della Chiesa* (Libreria editrice Vaticana 1999)

Naz R (ed.), *Traité de droit canonique* Tome III (Letouzey et Ané 1948)

Ortscheid A, *Essai concernant la nature de la codification et son influence sur la science juridique d'après le concept du Code de droit canonique* (Recueil Sirey 1922)

Périsset J-C, *Les biens temporels de l'Eglise. Commentaires des canons 1254–1310*, coll. Le nouveau droit ecclésial. Commentaire du Code de droit canonique. Livre V (Tardy 1966)

Philips G, *L'Eglise et son mystère au IIe Concile du Vatican. Histoire, texte, commentaire de la Constitution Lumen gentium* Tome I (Desclée 1967)

Recchi S (ed.), *Autonomie financière et gestion des biens dans les jeunes Eglises d'Afrique*, coll. Eglises d'Afrique (L'Harmattan 2003)

Rémond R et al., 'Les animateurs pastoraux. Statut civil et canonique des "permanents" en pastorale' (1992) 35 *L'année canonique*

Salerno FS, 'I beni temporali della Chiesa ed il potere primaziale del Romano Pontefice' in V De Paolis (ed.) *I beni temporali della Chiesa* (Libreria editrice Vaticana 1999)

Schick L, *Das dreifache Amt Christi und der Kirche. Zur Entstehung und Entwicklung der Trilogien* (Peter Lang 1982)

Schouppe J-P, *Droit canonique des biens* (Wilson et Lafleur 2008)

Schouppe J-P et al., 'Sur les traces du droit canonique des biens temporels en Belgique' in J-P Schouppe (ed.), *Vingt-cinq ans après le Code. Le droit canon en Belgique*, prefaced by Cardinal Godfried Daneels, coll. *Droit et religion* (Bruylant 2008)

Signé J-M, 'L'administration des biens temporels et l'avènement des Eglises pleinement constituées' (2008) 50 *L'année canonique*

Urrutia FJ, *Les normes générales. Commentaire des canons 1–203* (Tardy 1992)

Valdrini P, 'Unité et pluralité des ensembles législatifs. Droit universel et droit particulier d'après le Code de droit canonique latin' (1997) 9 *Ius Ecclesiae*

—— 'La gestion des biens dans les diocèses français' (16 Oct 1997) *Documents Episcopat*

—— 'Fedele, uguaglianza e organizzazione della Chiesa nel CIC del 1983' *Ambula per nomine et pervenies ad Deum. Studi in onore di S.E. Mons. Ignazio Sanna* (Studium 2012)

Valdrini P et al., *Droit canonique* (Dalloz 1999)

Chapter 17

Issue of the Funding of Worship in Islam – Worship, Imams and Mosques, as Viewed through Texts and Practice

Franck Frégosi

Raising the issue of public funding for faiths with regard to the internal laws of the major religious traditions (Judaism, Christianity, Islam...) can be, to say the least, anachronistic, if we neglect to specify that these normative systems, and especially that of Islam, have often evolved in historical, religious and cultural contexts that were very different from those with which we are familiar in Europe today. This Europe can be characterized in its western part by both a deep process of secularization[1] and the diversification of its religious landscape, not to mention the existence of a number of legal systems governing the relationship between 'Religion' and 'State', which guarantee, limit or challenge (at least formally!) public funding for faiths.

There are so many new developments which cannot fail to have an impact on the self-understanding that a religious group generates within itself, such as for Muslims – a minority in Western Europe, but in the majority elsewhere.

In the whole of the Muslim world, with very rare exceptions (Lebanon, Indonesia, Senegal, Turkey etc.), Islam is often recognized as the religion of the State and of the Head of the State, with Islamic law (*sharî'a*), especially in Arab States, being presented there as one of the sources of state law in terms of personal status. The Muslim religion also benefits from direct public support (notably financial), from public authorities, whether in terms of ministers becoming state officials or of increasingly centralized training for religious personnel or of aid for the construction of places of worship. Similarly, where in majority Muslim areas regimes of authoritarian secularity long prevailed,[2] public authorities continue to keep the practice of Muslim worship under their financial and political wing. Should one then consider this to be the norm and that the future of the faith itself is inevitably linked to the state budget?

---

1 Peter Berger et al., *Religious America, secular Europe? A theme and variations* (Ashgate 2010).

2 Pierre-Jean Luizard, *Laïcités autoritaires en terres d'islam* (Fayard 2008).

At this first stumbling block, we should add that very often the available Muslim normative corpora contain vast numbers of clichés and stereotypes,[3] which reinforce a fixed vision of a historical reality that turns out to be more complex. This applies firstly to what might be the theoretical outlines of a hypothetical Islamic doctrine, dominant in terms of financial links between a state ideally perceived as Muslim[4] and the faith itself (its buildings, staff and so on). Beyond the rarely explicit texts, there also exist institutional practices and social customs that have contributed over time to shaping attitudes and forging habits, without these necessarily being supported higher up, nor challenged by specific texts of a canonical nature.

Nowadays, these remarks also relate to the contours of what we might understand by a secular State, according to state traditions and distinct socio-cultural contexts,[5] and equally to what public funding for faith includes!

In these circumstances, what might be the specificity of ancient (or contemporary) Muslim societies, in terms of funding relationships between religious institutions and public institutions, when compared to modern secular societies in which a system of public funding for religions persists?

Throughout history, does systematic public funding for faiths constitute the alpha (*alif*) and omega (*nun*) of relations between public authorities and religions in Muslim societies?

And how should we view the situation of minority Islam in European societies from a funding perspective?

These are just some of the questions that will arise during the course of this discussion.

Firstly, our subject-matter will be limited to clarifying the idea of faith from the Muslim perspective, what it includes in theory as in practice, what objectively are the places concerned and who the officials of the Muslim faith are.

The second part will attempt, from a resolutely diachronic viewpoint, to clarify the nature and types of financial links that have existed between the traditional Muslim State and religious institutions. This analysis will base itself on the available legal sources, the so-called literature of 'sound advice', not to mention references to the historical practices of ancient Muslim societies.

Thirdly and finally, our attention will turn to some contemporary Muslim societies, in order to see how relevant the issue of public funding of faiths is for them today. By way of contrast, we will examine the corresponding situation in France.

---

3   Jocelyne Dakhlia, *Le divan des rois. Le politique et le religieux dans l'islam*, coll. Historique (Aubier 1998).

4   There remains the question of the institutional contours of this type of state: Caliphate, Sultanate, Monarchy, Republic and so on.

5   Jean Bauberot et al., *Laïcités sans frontières*, coll. La couleur des idées (Seuil 2011).

Places of Worship and 'Men of God' in Islam

In Islam, the concept of worship (*al'ibadat*), seen from a doctrinal point of view, covers all legal prescriptions, rules, required attitudes and behaviour, as well as statements of dogma relating to the observance of the five pillars of Islam[6] at the heart of the faith. To take the example of prayer, canonical regulations outlined in the *Risala* of *Al Qayrawâni*[7] detail the prerequisites necessary for it to take place (wet or dry ablutions, clothing required to pray, the call to prayer); they then describe how it will be brought about (the ritual and gestures), as well as the different types of prayers prescribed (five daily prayers, community prayer, Eid prayers etc.) and finally the officers who can preside over it (*imâmat* of the five daily prayers and the Friday prayers etc.). Prayer is the summit of Islamic religious practice. Canonist Ibn Taymiyya liked to write that 'the essence of the religion indeed lies in prayer and legal war (*jihad*)'.[8]

The same applies to fasting and pilgrimage, with legal rules detailing the procedures; as for the *zakat*, the method of its calculation and its foundations are explained.

The Places

With regard to places of worship in which Muslims can perform their devotions, some clarification is needed. Ideally, a Muslim is not canonically required to visit a particular shrine in order to perform the rites of his religion. In the words of a famous *hadith*: 'When time for prayer has come, you must perform it and this is a *masjid*'. Also, the Qur'an says little, if anything, about the form that the place dedicated to prayer should ideally have, leaving men to take care of giving it the appearance they choose. However, the need for a space destined primarily for community religious service was to lead to the creation of specific buildings. As early as the seventh century, a distinction was established between the simple private oratory or *masjid* and the building used for Friday's community prayer, the *jama masjid*, which became the most important public building in the Muslim city. In Islamic history, the mosque (*masjid*) therefore emerged as the dominant form of the *Bayt Allah* – the House of God – irrespective of the fact that the word *masjid* is not itself specifically Islamic. Before the advent of Islam, it in fact designated any place in which people celebrate God by kneeling down and touching the ground. A Bukhari *hadith* uses the term to refer to an Abyssinian Church. It was only after the forced exile of the Prophet Muhammad to Medina in 622 that the

---

6   These consist of: professing faith, prayer, fasting during the month of Ramadan, the so-called legal tax (*zakat*) and lastly pilgrimage to Mecca.

7   Abû Zayd Al Qayrawani, *La Risâla. Epître sur les éléments du dogme et de la loi de l'islam selon le rite malikite* (trans. Léon Bercher) (Editions Iqra 1996).

8   Ahmad Ibn Taymiyya, *Le traité du droit public* (trans. Henri Laoust) (ENAG 1994) 63.

word came to specifically designate the space where Muslims gathered for prayer. The first mosque was therefore the courtyard of the residence of Mohamed.[9] The actual religious building referred to in Islam was actually the *kaaba* in Mecca. It is a cubic building located in the centre of the Court of the Grand Mosque in the Holy City, around which Muslims, during the annual pilgrimage, perform ritual circumambulations. It is the building to which symbolically every Muslim turns to perform the five daily ritual prayers. Its existence is said to go back to the dawn of humanity.[10] Although custom was to designate the mosque as the House of God, it is not strictly speaking a *domus dei*, a place where the deity primarily resides, where a divine presence reveals itself, as was the case in ancient Egypt and in Catholic and Eastern Churches endowed with a Eucharistic reserve. The mosque is more a *domus ecclesiae*, a place for the community. As such, it is more like the Protestant temple or synagogue (*beth knesset*), both house for the community and place of study (*schule*).

The first grand architectural mosques were often incorporated by the Muslim conquerors into the buildings of worship of those had been defeated or else built in new garrison towns on virgin soil (for example, Kairouan in Tunisia). In their simplicity and their austere functionality, these mosques were close to the house of the Prophet. The golden age for the construction of mosques lasted from the seventh century to the sixteenth century. The first mosques to be built were those of Medina, Mecca, *Al Aqsa* (690) and Damascus (mosque of the Umayyads, 714), using public funds.

In addition to mosques, a Muslim also has *mussalah* at his disposal, which are simply marked-out, open-air spaces, in which the Eid prayers are usually performed. Other places, past or present, continue to host other religious ceremonies and to fulfil a major role in the dissemination of the religion. So, popular devotion is channelled towards mausoleums and tombs, generally called *qubbas* in the Maghreb, or *mazar* elsewhere; here, persons deemed to be 'holy' were actually or symbolically (catafalques!) laid to rest,[11] for example *Sidi Boumediene* (Tlemcen),

---

9   Once settled in Medina, he set about organising a personal dwelling that could simultaneously be used as a community centre. A brick wall with three entrances bordered a square courtyard. The wall of the courtyard was first pointed towards Jerusalem and then, following a falling out with Jewish tribes, Mecca. It was covered to provide a place of protected prayer (*haram*). The buildings were a kind of huts, composed of clay roofs and palm leaves supported by trunks of palm trees. This initial layout around the courtyard was to become the template for all mosques. A part of the building was used as a classroom during the day and as a dormitory for the homeless at night. It was common for whole caravans to 'park' in the courtyard of the Prophet's residence, which took on a 'caravanesque' air; one of the wives of the Prophet had apparently even attended Abyssinian war games there.

10   According to Muslim hagiography, this building is supposed to have been built by Adam, then destroyed by the flood; the *kaaba* was probably rebuilt by Abraham (*Ibrahim*), who had started the annual pilgrimage to this sanctuary described as the 'House of God' and considered to be first temple on Earth.

11   Emile Dermenghem, *Le culte des saints dans l'islam maghrébin* (Gallimard 1954).

Sidi Mahrez (Tunis), *Sidi Aaron* (Algiers), *Sidi El Houari* (Oran) *Moulay Idriss* (Meknes), *Al Ghilani* (Baghdad), *Rumî* (Konya) and so on. There can also be simple places of spiritual retreat (*khalwa*), which evidence their passing by. Here, the faithful have free rein as to forms of devotion, mixing Islamic prayers of supplication (*du'a*) and popular religious practices (lighting candles, hanging votive fabrics, songs and trances, animal sacrifice, collecting water reputed to be beneficial). Adjacent to these mausoleums sometimes stand *zawiyas*, where believers, members or simple sympathizers of a religious fraternity would meet and perform ceremonies that typically involve repeated, rhythmic recollection (*dhikr*) of the divine name, which can result in sessions of ecstasy and particularly significant mystical manifestations.

Obviously, spaces for prayer are also located in other buildings, such as *medersas* or *ribats* (fortress convents), today transformed into museums.

Religious Officials

The Muslim religion is often said to be ignorant of the idea of a clergy – in the sense of a hierocratic bureaucracy exercising a monopoly on managing the goods of salvation. This is one of the clichés about Islam that Muslims willingly re-appropriate for themselves in order to put forward the egalitarian character of their religion that apparently rejects any difference in status between believers. However, the reality is less black and white. The effective absence of any concept of priesthood does not eliminate the existence in Islam, as elsewhere, of a particular form of holy orders. It is therefore necessary to distinguish religious personnel, including the *imâm* as their major figure, since it is he who presides over and leads religious celebrations, and personnel made up of theologians and jurists who are themselves the true Muslim clergy – that of scholars and experts in Islamic sciences linked to religion (*usul ad din*) and law (*usul al-fiqh*).

In accordance with Sunni Muslim law and the history of Muslim societies, besides the temporal *imâmat* (the Caliphate), it is usual to distinguish three types of religious *imâmat*: the role of *imâm* for the five daily prayers, in supporting and leading the five daily prayers in a mosque; that of *imâm khâtib*, responsible for preaching and the Friday prayer; and the *imâm* of recommended prayers (the community prayers of the Eid festivals,[12] the prayer to invoke rain and so on).

The *imâm* in the religious sense has only 'a role presiding over and anticipating ritual gestures'.[13] Supposedly there is hardly any difference between a believer and his *imâm*. Both are subject to the same obligations, carry out the same rites of ablution and sanctification, they recite the same prayers and pray in the same direction. What really sets the *imâm* apart from the simple believer is his knowledge of the Qur'an, which he is supposed to have learnt partially or entirely

---

12   Eid-El-Fitr, Eid-El-Adha.

13   Michel Reeber, 'La fonction d'*imâm* dans la *Risâla* d'Ibn Abî Zayd al Qayrawânî' (1997) 47, 2 *Revue de droit canonique* 336.

by heart. Basically, the religious *imâmat* is a functional responsibility, with no ordination necessary to assume this role.

Moreover, neither the Qur'an nor Sunnah specify the identity of the person capable of leading prayer. At the very most, it is acceptable that he should be a good Muslim whose skill and moral reputation are recognized by all. These details are clearly set out in all the *fiqh* treatises, in those relating to administrative science,[14] as well as in treatises dedicated to ritual issues,[15] and in more general treatises.[16] To be *imâm*, eight qualities are generally required. Being a Muslim is the first; the Grand Imam *Shafi'ï* considers, however, that the existence of any doubt about the Muslim status of the one presiding over prayer does not as such invalidate him.[17] In the same spirit, it is customary to consider that praying behind an uncircumcised person is perfectly valid. Next, full knowledge of the Qur'an is required. Most of the schools agree in recognizing that the future *imâm* should, at least, know by heart the first sura of the Qur'an and the prayer rules. In the absence of a statutory *imâm*, when it is time for prayer, the faithful there present choose either the oldest[18] or the most educated from among them to perform this role, in accordance with the famous *hadith* which says: 'May he who is the expert in reciting the Qur'an lead you!' However, the Maliki jurist, Al Qayrawani, adds that the *imâm* must also be versed in *fiqh* (Islamic jurisprudence).[19] Ibn Qudâma, the Hanbalite jurist, quotes another *hadith* which states that: 'We will accept as imâm the one who best reads the Qur'an. If all read the Qur'an equally well, we will take the one who knows the Sunnah best; If all know the Sunnah equally well, we will choose the one that was the first to emigrate'.[20] The condition of masculinity is required by almost all schools of jurisprudence and applies to exercising the *imâmat* of the five daily prayers in the community as well as to weekly prayers. Although the majority view, it is, however, based on no established consensus.[21] Following an initiative by an American Liberal Muslim group to admit a woman skilled in the religion to preside over the Friday collective prayer and deliver the sermon, just as the academic *Amina Abdel Waddoud* did in New York on 18 March

---

14   Ali Habib Al Mawardi, *Les statuts gouvernementaux* (trans. Charles E. Fagnan) (OPU 1984).

15   Al Qayrawani (n 7).

16   Muwafffaq al-Dīn Ibn Qudâma, *Le précis de droit* (trans. Henri Laoust) (Adrien Maisonneuve 1950).

17   Ralph Stehly, 'L'*imâmat* des cinq prières selon Châfi'î et Ibn Qudâma' in Franck Frégosi (ed.), *La formation des cadres religieux en France. Approches socio-juridiques* (L'Harmattan 1998) 25–33.

18   *Cf. hadith* 'When it is time for prayer, let one of you two start calling and the elder serve as imam', as told by Malik B. Al Huwairi.

19   Al Qayrawani (n 7).

20   Ibn Qudâma (n 16) 34.

21   Zyed Krichen, 'Femme *imâm*: ijtihad ou hérésie? Que dit le Coran? Que disent les Ulémas?' (31 March 2005) *Réalités* <http://www.realites.com>

2005, controversy and a wave of disapproval shook the Islamic world.[22] At the time, differing opinions were expressed in public.[23]

Being an adult is also a pure convenience and not an absolute imperative! Several sources argue that praying behind a pre-pubescent is not unacceptable, similarly a slave or an unholy person. Excluded from the *imâmat*, however, are: women (except in certain circumstances and according to some opinions), hermaphrodites, the dumb or anyone with defects in pronunciation. Another requirement is to have correct pronunciation, to be devoid of problems and defects of speech and pronunciation (stuttering, mutism etc). Any defect or disability affecting speech is considered to be unacceptable. It is requested that the future *imâm* have exemplary moral behaviour. The one who presides over and edifies the faithful by his word is assumed to himself be exemplary in his everyday life. The fact of practising or being a good Muslim is also implied and represents a truism in the Muslim context. Finally, it has become customary to place emphasis on the fact that the one at the front – in the sense that he is leading prayer – was directly and explicitly chosen by those standing behind him, or at least selected with their implicit endorsement. A famous *hadith* narrated by *Shâfi'î* adds that 'no *imâm* should lead prayers if he chose himself against the wishes of the faithful or against their will, without consulting them'. The *imâmat* therefore implies the existence of a *ma'mûn* – of someone who follows the *imâm* and models himself upon him in his way of acting. In mystical Islam, the *imâm* is supposed to represent the unity and the specificity of the community of believers. For Charles André Gilis, the *imâm* 'achieves in synthetic manner the unity of those he directs and for whom he is the model'.[24]

According to historian Ibn Khaldun, 'leading public prayer is the highest of all responsibilities: it is even above royal power, which is similarly subject to the Caliphate ... Public prayer is superior to political leadership'.[25] The responsibility of *khâtib* usually fell to the Prophet himself, then it was passed on to the first

---

22   Sabah Sabet, 'Lorsque la femme monte au minbar' (April 2005) *Al Ahram Hebdo* <http://hebdo.ahram.org.e.g./arab/ahram/2005/4/13/femm2.htm>. See also Fawzia Zouari, 'Une femme *imâm*, et alors?' (19 April 2005) *Jeune Afrique*. Some sources argue that the *imâmat* of a woman would be contrary to the letter of the religion. In fact, the majority of schools agree in recognizing that the *imâmat* of women is put down to the fact that women are not capable of pronouncing the call to prayer, to raising their voices.

23   *Abu Thaour* and the illustrious *Tabari* (838–923) fully accept the *imâmat* of women, even before a group of mixed believers. As for the mystic *Ibn Arabi* (1165–1241), he also viewed this *imâmat* as legitimate, insofar as the perfection of the soul is accessible to all, men and women. The current Grand Mufti of Egypt, *Ali Guma'a*, has for his part considered that a woman leading prayer in front of a mixed assembly is permitted as long as said assembly is happy with her.

24   Muhammad Ibn Arabi, *La prière du jour du Vendredi* (trans. Charles André Gilis) (Al Bustane 1994) 17.

25   Abd-ar-Rahmân Ibn Khaldun, *Discours sur l'histoire universelle. Al Muqaddima* (trans. Vincent Monteil) (Actes Sud 1997) 340.

Caliphs of Islam, who, equipped with a stick, sword or lance, would solemnly address the faithful. Tired by this task,[26] the latter progressively entrusted it to the *qâdis* (Islamic judges), to the provincial governors, then to the chief of police under the Abbasids. Thereafter the responsibility was entrusted to a permanent official paid for by the Public Treasury.[27]

After the *imâm*, the *mu'adhin* is the second key person in the faith. It is he who is responsible for carrying out the *adhan* five times a day, the call to prayer from the top of the minaret or from inside the mosque, inviting the faithful to fulfil their religious obligations. In Muslim societies, this function had partly become hereditary.

Among the other religious officials, we may mention the corporation of the *qora*, readers of the Qur'an. They were entitled to recite two *hizbs* per day, the entire Qur'an in a lunar month. This paid responsibility did not, however, enable them to earn a living from this, so they also exercised another profession alongside.[28] They also visited individuals on certain occasions and were rewarded for recitations performed on-site.

We may also mention the figure of the *Muftî*, the legal adviser capable of issuing fatwas (legal opinions) who, apart from presiding over Friday and exceptional prayers (during drought), from time to time took care of the administration of the mosque and the supervision of its many serving officials. Lastly, there is the figure of the *qâdi*, the judge appointed by the Caliph, whose responsibility it was to ensure the application of the principles derived from *sharî'a*.

The Muslim State, the Believers and Funding the Faith

What about the existence in the foundations of the Muslim religion of a set of rules establishing obligatory public financial support for expenditure related to the daily practice of religion?

If we keep to the commonly accepted meaning that the generic term 'public funding of religion' means the existence of legal mechanisms and procedures to publicly fund the Muslim faith by granting religious officers as part of a religious bureaucracy a regular salary, accompanied by the state's active participation in the construction of buildings of worship, there is no trace of any explicit doctrine on the subject in the major canonical sources of Islam (Qur'an and Sunnah) or in treatises of specific law devoted to the faith (*fiqh al 'ibadat*).

Is this to say that this type of funding was ignored, indeed contested, or that it was simply implicit?

---

26   Lucien Golvin, *La mosquée: ses origines, sa morphologie, ses diverses fonctions, son rôle dans la vie musulmane plus spécialement en Afrique du Nord* (Institut d'études supérieures Islamiques d'Alger 1960).

27   Golvin (n 26).

28   ibid.

The Faith – Above All A Collective Matter

It has to be said that the situation is simple and more complex at the same time.

First of all, finding very few canonical texts on this topic can be put down to the fact that this issue of public funding for faiths does not by itself seem to be a major issue requiring an explanation of the same length as those dedicated for example to the Caliphate or the judiciary. For jurists writing treatises of public law and from the viewpoint of societies, for which Islam is the common reference for the vast majority of the population (other religious groups descended from one of the 'book' religions see themselves being granted autonomy to manage their religious affairs), the question of faith falls within the competence of all Muslim believers; it is a social obligation incumbent on all and not the exclusive domain of just public authorities. To quote a famous *hadith*: 'For he who builds a mosque (on Earth), God will build a mansion in paradise'. Add to this the fact that, with the exception of the Friday *imâm*s who officiate in the large mosques and who are often chosen from among the knowledgeable families of renowned scholars, other officials of the faith – the *imâm*s of the five prayers and their assessors (*mu'adhin*, readers of the Qur'an) – perform alongside these ad hoc roles other unpaid tasks for believers who appeal to them to do so.

We may note that, in the tenth century, under the reign of the Abbasids, *Al Mawardî*, the famous Shafi'i author who wrote a treatise explaining the Sunni doctrine of the Caliphate, only addresses this issue of funding faiths in a very elliptical way, whether from the perspective of constructing buildings of worship or else that of the appointment and payment of religious personnel. He restricts himself to differentiating official mosques from so-called 'private' mosques. In the former, where Friday prayer takes place, it is the Caliph who appoints and normally pays religious officials. As for the *imâm* in charge of preaching, he is the one who has the power to appoint his other collaborators, the *mu'adhin*. 'The *imâm* in question and muezzins appointed by him may receive fees from the State Treasury from the sum reserved for works of public interest; but this is not allowed by Abu Hanifa'.[29] We note in passing that the remuneration of serving officials from public treasury funds is, however, contested by the founder of the Hanafi school of jurisprudence, *Abu Hanifa*.

There then remains the case of the other mosques, the private ones. As they are connected to a district or to a tribal group, central government has no authority over them, whether in respect of the choice of *imâm* or their remuneration. These sites are managed autonomously using their own funds. 'In private mosques which were built by the inhabitants of the neighbourhood or tribal members in their streets or respective tribes, the prince has not to interfere with interested parties as regards the imams in these temples, who are those agreed upon to exercise their *imâmat* there. The people cannot remove the *imâmat* from the person they have

---

29   Al Mawardi (n 14) 214.

approved, unless, however, his way of being should come to change'.[30] We should add that inspecting the detail of the assignments that are usually conferred on the Caliph in religious matters shows that his powers are quite limited. According to the same Sunni theorist, 'the institution of the *imâmat* has as its purpose to replace prophetism (of which the Prophet was the last representative), so as to safeguard the religion and the administration of earthly interests'.[31] This text is loud and clear: the Caliph, as regards religion, only has a duty of preservation, of safeguarding it. The first of his duties is to 'maintain the religion according to the principles fixed and established by agreement of the oldest Muslims'.[32]

The theory of the Caliphate then acknowledges a two-way splitting of powers between the political body responsible for earthly affairs and the religious body that oversees the content and interpretation of divine law. The *'ulamâ* and *mujtahidun* are *de jure* the real holders of religious power and as such will ensure respect for the true religion alongside the Caliph and offer him advice, so that he acts in accordance with the general principles of the law.

Diversified Funding Sources and Methods

What if public funding for faiths belonged to the register of things unsaid, as with the distinction between political power and real religious power in Islam, without being claimed or theorized as such?

We see in fact this is not the case, if we refer to other doctrinaires of Islam or historians eager to describe their experiences of reality.

So it was with the thirteenth century Hanbali Jurist, *Ibn Taymiya*, who wrote in his famous treatise on religious policy (literally translated: *Sharî'a policy for reforming the shepherd and his flock*) an entire chapter devoted to public expenditure (*masârif*), in which he explicitly mentions the fact that all state assets, except those from the *zakat* (allocated to the poor, prisoners etc.) and from spoils of war (reserved for the Caliph and fighters), must be used to cover expenditure in the common interest, including the payment of state officials. Besides the governors and *qadis*, the beneficiaries include the *'ulamâs*, *imâm* and *mu'adhdhins*. They are therefore paid in respect of services rendered to the community of believers. All public service agents must bear in mind that their mission is to 'improve the religious condition of men, because men who lack religion suffer an obvious loss and do not take advantage on this Earth of the benefits which God has showered upon them'.[33] Nothing is said, however, about the mosques. The writings of *Ibn Khaldun* (1332–1406) provide the most precise indications. 'The maintenance of mosques-cathedrals falls to the Caliph or his representatives, viziers or qadis. An imâm is appointed in every mosque, to preside over the five daily prayers ...

---

30   ibid.
31   ibid 5.
32   ibid 30.
33   Ibn Taymiyya (n 8) 63.

this custom of appointing an imâm to lead the prayer is not required, but simply preferable'.[34] The implicit rule actually intended that the various rulers, their representatives in the provinces, the governors and prominent citizens of the court build mosques in which Friday prayers were uttered in the name of the sovereign, sometimes by the local emir. The Caliphs always took care to associate their names with the construction of majestic mosques for which they had raised funds. Therefore, in 691 *Abd El Malik* built the famous dome of the rock – *Qubbat As-Sakhrah* – in the city of Jerusalem in place of the first mosque built by Caliph Umar. The former was supposed to cover the rock on which Ibrahim allegedly sacrificed his son Ismail and on which is embossed the footprint of Prophet Mohamed, who stopped off there on his night journey from Mecca. In 705, *Al Wâlid* also erected the *Al Aqsa* mosque in Jerusalem and the grand mosque of the Umayyads in Damascus on the site of the Theodosian Basilica of Saint John the Baptist. *Imâm* and *mu'adhdhins* officiated in these mosques, alongside professional readers of the Qur'an directly paid for by the State Treasury (*bayt al mal al muslimin*).[35] One small, but important, detail is that some mosques from the Umayyad era, including that of Damascus, housed within them State Treasury funds. The sovereign power was therefore directly responsible for the maintenance of the grand mosques, which was in fact funded using income from assets put aside for this purpose, which were known as *ahbâs* (literally, put in reserve).

Apart from the grand mosques, there were also other more modest places of worship. Let us listen once again to the words of *Ibn Khaldun*: 'The mosques reserved for a community or a city district are administered by those who live in their neighbourhood. They do need to be monitored by the Caliph or Sultan'.[36]

Alongside public funding, officials of the faith in mosques of lesser importance could be paid from income from so-called pious foundations (*ahbâs* or *awqafs* goods), a part of which was allotted to the faith and its serving officials. This could involve private as well as public foundations. In fact, the *awqafs* were an old institution the origin of which is ancient and hybrid (probably the Byzantine *piae causae*, Jewish *qôdesh*). It allowed goods to be extracted from the commercial network (usually properties) and placed under the protection of the community personified by the *qâdi*.[37] Revenues from the use of these assets were allotted

---

34 Ibn Khaldun (n 25) 340.

35 This concept could include different areas of Muslim history, according to the era and the doctrines professed. Under the Umayyad dynasties of *Al Andalus*, this term designated exclusively all revenues from pious foundations, distinct from the Public Treasury, strictly speaking. This term is generally used to consider all of the funds or property belonging to the Muslim community as a whole, use of which is at the discretion of the Caliph and his representative; it corresponds to one fifth (*al khums*) and must be spent in the interests of the whole community.

36 Ibn Khaldun (n 25) 340.

37 Sylvie Denoix, 'Introduction: formes juridiques, enjeux sociaux et stratégies foncières' (1996) 79–80 *Revue du monde musulman et de la Méditerranée* 9–22.

to various recipients or works. Initially instituted for private use (*waqf ahlî*) to provide income to the donor family, little by little we also see its usage evolve for purposes of general interest (*waqf khayri*), revenues from which benefited a public monument and its officials.

If the first mosques were built by leaders and those responsible for various groups, little by little and alongside initiatives by public figures, wealthy individuals also came to provide for the construction and maintenance of mosques out of their own funds. During the eighteenth century, rich spice traders had contributed significantly to Cairo's numerous mosques. These achievements were as much pious works as demonstrations of prestige extending the traders' power and influence.[38] It was then often the income from properties transformed into pious foundations that provided for the upkeep of mosques and religious personnel. The foundations' constitution stated precisely the amount of funds allocated to the salaries of various staff officiating in these buildings.

At the head of these mosques was a *nâzir* (administrator) who was in charge of administrative affairs (sometimes a descendant of the family of the donor). The responsibility often reverted directly to a *qâdi*. From the Shi'a dynasty of the Fatimides the foundations of a centralized administration of mosques and religious foundations came into existence (transfer of *ahbâs* funds to the Public Treasury), and the process of centralization was strengthened under the Sunni dynasties that succeeded it. Therefore, their management was gradually entrusted to a central administration (*dîwân al ahbâs*) presided over by a *qâdi* who was to ensure their effective management and respect for the clauses relating to the allocation of the revenue generated by their operations. It is through this system that, since the eleventh century, many madrasas and Sufi sheikh (*khânka*) residences had been financed, likewise many urban infrastructures, for example mosques, hospitals/ hospices or fountains.[39] The Mamluks finally set up a specific administration split into three: the Shafi'i *qâdi* had control over *awqafs hukmiyya* assets, the revenues from which had a philanthropic or charitable goal, then family goods (grand foundations of sultans or individuals funded by income from farmland or urban areas used for maintaining a religious institution, while providing an income to the donor's offspring), and finally the *rizka*, which corresponded to the disposal of land by the Treasury for the benefit of individuals and in exchange for specific services. This technique was systematically used to provide services to rural areas, including *zawiya* and mosque staff, craftsmen or construction workers.[40]

This type of funding was designed to ensure the sustainability of the faith and its funding, as well as a relative operational autonomy of religious institutions

---

38   André Raymond, *Artisans et commerçants au Caire au XVIIIe siècle* Tome II (Institut français de Damas 1974).

39   Jean-Claude Garcin, *Etats, sociétés et cultures du monde musulman médiéval X-XV siècles* Tome II (PUF 2000).

40   Doris Behrens-Abouseif, 'Wakf dans les pays arabes', *Encyclopédie de l'islam* Tome XI (Brill 2005) 71.

in relation to the central state. It was the same with the caste of *'ulamâs*, part of whose members cumulated various sources of remuneration: revenues from religious foundations, payment from the Treasury, raw materials provided free of charge, income from farmland, not to mention revenue from property and other speculative products.[41]

As for direct public funding for religion, all modern States in the Muslim world ended up making it a rule or the absolute norm, even those who had already experienced proactive secularization, like Turkey.

The Current State of Public Funding for the Muslim Faith in the Muslim World and Beyond

This issue takes on a certain topicality in contemporary Muslim societies where, via the public funding of the Muslim faith, regimes tend to base their hegemony on public religious practice.

In Western Europe, where Muslims make up large minorities within non-Muslim societies dominated by secularized States, this issue is equally subject to debate.

The Case of Modern Turkey

Take the case of Turkey, which is constitutionally a secular State with a predominantly Sunni Muslim population, with large non-Sunni minorities (Alevis, Ja'fari Shi'ites, Nusayris etc.) and non-Muslim minorities (Orthodox, Gregorian and Catholic Armenians, Syriacs, Assyro-Chaldeans, Jews etc.). The complete absence of state religion and the total secularization of public services do not enable us to declare a complete absence of interactions between religious and political realms – far from it! Turkish secularity should not be confused with secularity of abstention which, having rid itself of the presence of religion in the state apparatus, has sought to limit the social influence of religious institutions on society, by relegating them to being managed privately.[42] 'The Turkish secular State', as Paul Dumont puts it, 'has, unlike France, not broken bridges with religious institutions; on the contrary, it has made every effort to maintain control over them'.[43] Apart from the complete absence of any reference to Islam as the State religion and to *sharî'a* as source of inspiration for state law, the Turkish configuration is similar to that prevailing in most of the States in the Arab and Muslim world, with the state

---

41   Raymond (n 38).

42   Ahmet T Kuru, *Secularism and state policies toward religion. The United States, France, and Turkey* (Cambridge University Press 2009).

43   Paul Dumont, 'La direction des affaires religieuses en Turquie' in Samim Akgönül (ed.), *Laïcité en débat. Principes et représentations en France et en Turquie*, coll. Société, Droit et Religion en Europe (PUS 2008) 156.

aiming to hold onto (with varying degrees of success) the monopoly on production of legitimate religious expression by having themselves be assisted by religious personnel (public servants) trained in faculties or specialized institutes and duly supervised by the public authorities. The intervention of the modern Turkish State apparatus in the national domain of Islam is part of an indisputable historical continuity that appears to prolong rather than break with the policy established by the Ottoman authorities towards Sunni Islam. During the Ottoman period, Sunni Islam was already structured in a hierarchical manner[44] with, at its head – in addition to the symbolic authority of the Sultan Caliph – a *cheikh ül islam*, with directly under him the muftis, who themselves officiated over the entire Empire and acted as guardians over those officiating in mosques and *medrese*. Even the area of the *tekke* and places which were the terrain of popular religiosity (*türbe* – tombs of saints) attracted sustained attention from central government in the form of various donations. Government intervention was not merely limited to the granting of financial rewards, it could lead to a restriction on their activities.[45] The entire strategy employed by most of the Ottoman Sultans during the nineteenth and early twentieth centuries (*Selim II* and *Mahmud II*) consisted in distancing temporal affairs from religious institutions, while ensuring at the same time increasingly tighter control over Islam through the centralization and bureaucratization of religious personnel.[46]

If the spirit of most reforms driven by Mustafa Kemal was to prolong the Ottoman secularization process initiated by the last reformist Sultans, the Kemalist project was nevertheless distinguished by its ideological element of control and, in particular, reform of Islam. 'Mustafa Kemal and his partisans', writes Thierry Zarcone, 'do not aim to eradicate Islam, but to separate it from political affairs and reform it'.[47]

There were in fact several facets to the 'secular' politics of the new Turkish Republic: firstly, a plan to reform Islam, to promote a new Islam which was to be taught by the new faculty of theology created in 1924 (Turkification of rituals, modernizing buildings of worship, training religious leaders and so on); next, a distancing of Islam from political and public life; and lastly restricting it to personal practice. To carry out these plans, it seemed essential that the State

---

44   Gilles Veinstein, 'Les Ottomans: fonctionnarisation des clercs, cléricalisation de l'Etat?' in Dominique Iogna-Prat et al. (eds), *Histoire des hommes de Dieu dans l'islam et le christianisme* (Flammarion 2003) 179–202.

45   Such was how the *Bektachiyye* brotherhood, which was historically linked to the Janissary corps, was to suffer the wrath of central government and was condemned to surviving underground, after this elite army corps had been disbanded in 1826.

46   Only duly recognized non-Muslim religious minorities (Jews, Greek Orthodox and Gregorian Armenians) enjoyed relative autonomy in religious affairs and with regard to personal status. These domains were reserved for their respective religious authorities. By contrast, there was nothing similar for other Muslim minorities (or assimilated ones like the Alevi) or Christians (Assyro-Chaldean, Syriacs, Catholics or Protestants).

47   Thierry Zarcone, *La Turquie moderne et l'islam* (Flammarion 2004) 136.

exercise direct control over religious institutions responsible for administering the faith and nothing else. In the wake of the abolition of the Caliphate on 4 March 1924, the Presidency of Religious Affairs and Pious Foundations established in 1920 was to be abolished in favour of two separate administrations: Religious Affairs and the Directorate of Pious Foundations, both reporting directly to the Prime Minister. After the abolition of the *medrese*, the training of the *imâm* was entrusted to specialized schools that ensured teaching of Kemalist thought, positivism, science and nationalism. These schools were to have a fairly hieratic way of operating. It was only from the 1940s, with the first measures relaxing anti-religion laws, that they were to experience a real boom, until becoming real denominational establishments at the very heart of state education.

Efforts to modernize the religion also extended to reforming the language of prayer and redeveloping places of worship; this was brought about through the abolition of all mystical orders in 1925, the closure of the *tekke*, the confiscation of their foundations, not to mention the closure of saints' mausoleums and the ban on pilgrimages thereto.

Breaking with pan-Islamic thinking largely linked to the Caliphate, the new Directorate of Religious Affairs (*Diyanet*) was initially limited to intervening on Turkish territory. Its sphere of action amounted primarily to managing the faith and property of Sunni Islam, in accordance with the ideals of the Kemalist Republic and the appointment and remuneration of *imâm* in Turkey. Management of pious foundations was the responsibility of the Directorate of Pious Foundations. Training future religious leaders reverted to the Ankara Faculty of Theology, created in 1924, which was then to close in 1930 and 1933, to permanently reopen in 1951. Today, there are more than twenty faculties.

While the Kemalists had ended up banning any teaching of religion in the official schools, the lessons returned in 1942 for military personnel, then from 1948 as an option in primary schools, in junior high schools from 1956, extending to senior high schools in 1967. This process of standardization of religious policy would continue during the 1970s, with permission granted to graduates from *imâm* schools to enrol at universities. In 1980, religion lessons became mandatory in state schools. In parallel, lessons on the Qur'an were also delivered in mosques under the control of the *Diyanet*.

As Turkish society evolved, the Directorate of Religious Affairs, once more a 'Ministry' for modern Islam, came to experience a gradual redefinition of its scope. From 1960, its role was also to 'inform society about religion', which amounted to defining the contours of Islam consistent with the ideological orientation of the regime, organizing the pilgrimage to Mecca, overseeing the translation of the Qur'an and monitoring religious publications imported from abroad and, last but not least, responding to the cultural needs of the Turkish diaspora.

This plan is consistently subject to criticism from Liberals and the most radical of laypersons, who wish its budget to be removed, considering it unjustified; then, there are other sectors of Turkish society who, in contrast, would want public support to be no longer reserved solely for Sunni Islam. Such are the demands made by the Ja'fari Shi'ite minority (predominantly Azeri) and part of the Alevi religious movement group together under the name *Çem vakfı*. These two minority groups would wish for the Directorate of Religious Affairs and Pious Foundations to be more 'ecumenical' and bear the expenses incurred by their respective faiths, relating to both personnel and buildings of worship.

Other European States with a majority Muslim population are strictly secular States too, in which the State does not bear the costs of religious instruction or the faiths themselves. This is the case in Albania,[48] Kosovo[49] and the Turkish Republic of Northern Cyprus. In Bosnia and Herzegovina, where the majority of the population is of Muslim origin, the State – even though secular in the sense of non-denominational – does, however, provide public funding to various recognized religious communities (Catholic Church, Serbian Orthodox Church and the Islamic Community of Bosnia and Herzegovina), while religious studies remains optional in state schools.[50]

Public Funding of the Muslim Faith: an Affair of State during the Colonization!

In 1830, on the eve of the landing of French troops and the beginning of the colonization of Algeria, then under the authority of the *Beys* (local rulers of Turkish origin), Muslim religious officials derived the bulk of their income from *ahbâs/habous* goods. The new colonial power, in the words of Marshal Bourmont, undertook the solemn declaration on 5 July 1830 to 'respect the exercise of the Mohammedan religion and ... to not violate the freedom of people of all classes, their religion, their properties, their businesses and their industries'.[51] Very soon afterwards, the French administration went back on its word and embarked on a comprehensive policy of land appropriation that had implications on a religious level. Therefore, by order of General Clauzel, dated 8 September 1830, the former properties of the *Dey*, of the *Beys* and Turks, as well as pious foundations whose revenues were allotted to the Holy Places of Mecca and Medina, were re-assigned to state ownership. In the light of protests by Muslim religious leaders, a complementary clause specified that these goods would nevertheless continue to be managed by Muslim administrators placed directly under the control of the French Government. Via various other legal measures, the government gradually granted itself total control over all Algerian *ahbâs/habous*.[52] By awarding itself the management of Muslim property, the colonial power thus deprived the Muslim

---

48   Olsi Jazexhi, 'Albania' in Jørgen Nielsen (ed.), *Yearbook of Muslims in Europe* vol. 1 (Brill 2009) 15–23.

49   Xhabir Hamiti, 'Kosovo' in Nielsen (ed.) (n 48) 193–8.

50   Mirnes Kovac, 'Bosnia and Herzegovina' in Nielsen (ed.) (48) 49–59.

51   Jacques Carret, 'Le problème de l'indépendance du culte musulman en Algérie' (1957) 37 *L'Afrique et l'Asie. Revue politique, sociale et économique.*

52   A decree of 23 March 1848 re-attached the budget of the religious establishments to the budget of the colony. A second decree of 3 October 1848 re-attached the *habous* to

faith of a major source of income and caused it to fall directly under its financial dependence. The task of paying staff and maintaining Muslim buildings of worship now reverted to the French State. For further details, see the testimony of Alexis de Tocqueville, who undertook two trips to Algeria, in 1841 and 1846. In particular, he wrote a report on the situation of the Muslim faith, charitable foundations and schools and he directly addressed the Chamber of Deputies during the discussion on the general budget of Algeria, in order to denounce the despoliation of goods belonging to pious foundations.

> The Chamber knows that public charity, the religion, the schools are strangers to the Public Treasury in Muslim countries; they are pious foundations, like in Europe during the Middle Ages, created to meet both religious and social needs. A few years ago, the French Government removed the administration of Muslim foundations from Muslim authorities throughout the whole of Algeria; in my view, it was wrong to do so. I would have understood perfectly, if we were bringing increased light into the darkness of its administration, if we were supervising it, if we were ensuring the use made of money entrusted to it. But entrusting Christian administrators with the management of pious foundations established by Muslims, leads me to believe that we wanted less to regularize the use of funds than to divert them from their objective and devote them to another use. ... As to the faith, I will say with certainty and without fear of being proved wrong, that the Muslim faith has fallen, as a result of this unjust and inexpedient suppression, into a state of poverty that shames not only us, but the whole of civilization. ... Apart from people of a privileged rank, at the head of the Muslim faith, huge numbers of Muslim priests find themselves in shameful poverty. Most of them are paid less than most of the porters in Algiers.[53]

At the same time as the annexation of mortmain property, the colonial administration was to consolidate its grip on the functioning of religions. An order by the Commander in Chief, dated 11 May 1848, created a special department of the Indigenous Civil Administration responsible for monitoring the Muslim faith.[54] The various roles of this department included, *inter alia*: monitoring Muslim religious establishments, such as mosques and Sufi convents; paying religious personnel; maintaining religious buildings; putting forward candidates for senior and junior positions in the faith. In so doing, the non-Muslim French Government obtained complete power of guardianship over the Muslim faith, which had

---

the public domain. A law of 16 June 1851 sanctioned the confiscation of mortmain property, integrating it into the domain of the state.

53   Jean-Louis Benoît, *Alexis de Tocqueville. Notes sur le Coran et autres textes sur les religions* (Bayard 2007) 60–62.

54   That was how, at the beginning, Muslim affairs came under the mandate of the Ministry of War; a royal decree of 24 July 1846 re-attached the Office of Justice and Faiths to the Directorate of Algerian Affairs.

until then been officially recognized as falling within the exclusive competence of the Sultan of Istanbul in his role as Caliph of Islam, and in whose name the Friday prayer was pronounced. A new circular dated 17 May 1851 provided for a complete reorganization of the Muslim faith in Algeria and, in particular, the classification of religious buildings according to their size and location. It also created a hierarchy of religious personnel, determining salary levels and money destined for maintaining buildings.

In fact as in law, the Muslim faith in Algeria became, under the terms of the decrees of 26 August and 6 September 1881, the fourth religion officially recognized by the State, after Catholic, Protestant and Jewish faiths. Historian Charles Robert Ageron notes, however, that efforts made towards the Muslim faith remained minimal, as much towards officials of the faith, as to the construction of places of worship and their maintenance. Part of the religious heritage was used to cover the costs.[55]

At the time, the official numbers of Muslim personnel integrated into the civil service was estimated at 16 *Mufti*, 83 *imâm* and 390 junior officers for a population estimated in 1890 at three and a half million believers.[56] The section on faiths in the Law of 29 December 1883 mentions the sum of 160,400 francs allotted to the remuneration of Muslim religious officers and 40,850 francs intended for equipment. In the years preceding the adoption of the Law of 1905, the expenditure allocated to the Muslim faith was to rise to 337,000 francs or 0.075 francs per person, compared to 337,000 francs for the Catholic faith or 1,320 francs per person.[57]

Far from wanting to ensure the sustainability of the practice of the Muslim faith in Algeria, government interventionist practice in fact relayed the implicit objective of the body of colonial elected representatives: the progressive decline of the practice of the Muslim religion in favour of a forced secularization of mindsets.

The modification to the political climate at the beginning of the century (1880–1900) in France was to result in the passing of the Law of 9 December 1905, which was to bode well for the end of state guardianship over the Muslim faith, but had no impact on the administration's general attitude in relation to Islam in Algeria. The Law of separation remained unimplemented in Algeria.

In the country, it was the Muslim religious leaders, the reformist Ulama alongside other local, secular Muslim forces, who demanded in vain for the principle of separation of religion from the State to be applied in the interests of the Muslim faith.

Diverting attention to the example of Algeria demonstrates that the legal regime of these foundations that met objectives of general interest, guaranteed the

---

55   Charles-Robert Ageron, *Les Algériens musulmans et la France (1871–1919)* Tome I (Presses universitaires de France 1968).

56   Ageron (n 55) 394.

57   Jean Boussinesq, *Laïcité et islam en France. Rapport d'étape d'une commission de travail de la Ligue de l'enseignement* (Ligue de l'enseignement 1998) 49.

faith a degree of autonomy and a continuity of funding that colonization brought partly into question.

This system was to continue in most Muslim countries until their accession to independence. If some states retained this system and modernized it, most transferred all their pious foundations into the public domain (Algeria, Tunisia, Syria, Libya etc.).

Towards Subsidized Public Mosques?

Apart from the special situation of Alsace-Moselle, where public subsidies for faiths (Catholicism, Protestantism, Judaism) is the rule, raising the issue of public funding for faiths across the rest of France remains problematic and highly controversial. Nevertheless, the gradual inclusion of Islam in the public agenda over the last decade has contributed to conferring a certain topicality on the issue of public funding of the so-called minority faiths, such as Islam; its many facets, the underlying arguments and approaches will now be examined.

The objective situation of the Muslim faith (absence of Muslim religious heritage (real estate)), heterogeneous funding of places of worship, inconsistent local public management of building permits) was in fact supposed to render a semblance of social legitimacy to this question of the liberalization of public funding for the benefit of minority religions.

Equally, left and right-wing politicians did not hesitate to declare themselves favourable to public funding, whether *ad hoc* or systematic, for the construction of mosques by local authorities.

It was Jean-Pierre Chevènement, who, in 1995, was the first to clearly mention this idea. Describing the various ways of implementing a 'grand integration policy', the political leader with his stated republican and lay convictions and at the origin of a proactive policy towards the Muslim faith[58] was to raise the issue of public funding for mosques, alongside the creation in Strasbourg of a Faculty of Islamic Theology.

> ... I add [he wrote], at the risk of causing a shock, public funding of mosques, where a large Muslim population live ... It is neither normal nor worthy that the second religion in our country only has as places of worship cellars, abandoned hangars, or former social housing, barely refurbished. They'll tell me that such funding would be contrary to the principle of secularity. Of course, it should remain exceptional, in its duration and scope.[59]

Apart from Jean-Pierre Chevènement, we can also cite the very real case of the client-oriented management of Islam put in place by George Frêche, when he

---

58   Franck Frégosi, *L'islam dans la laïcité* (Hachette Pluriel 2011).

59   Jean-Pierre Chevènement, *Le vert et le noir. Intégrisme, pétrole, dollar* (Grasset 1995) 207.

was Socialist Mayor of Montpellier from 1983 to 1997. This elected representative had his City Council vote on funding the construction of several multi-purpose rooms, designed to become spaces reserved exclusively for Muslims to worship in.[60] Manuel Valls (the current Minister of the Interior), when also Mayor of Evry, declared himself in favour of financial participation of the State in planned construction of places of worship or in training *imâm*.[61]

> ... secularity is experienced [he said] as a pretext to weaken the confessions of those who arrived last, a subtle system to help religions selectively. A feeling of religious discrimination was thus born ... the Law of 1905 must therefore evolve. It can be amended without being distorted ... I am favourable for my part, to responsible, public evolution to allow the Republic to send a strong sign; ... the modification would consist in authorising public finances for the purpose of construction, using foundations ... That would make it possible to avoid, on the one hand, too strong a structuring of the community, an undesired, but quite real effect of our incapacity to understand the limits of our model and, on the other hand, to avoid funding from abroad with its various influences.[62]

Unlike the Foundation for Islam in France, set up by Dominique de Villepin and which was intended to receive, under state supervision, funds from abroad intended for Muslim communities in France and to ensure transparency, Manuel Valls suggested a foundation in which the state and local authorities would be present and participate directly in the funding of construction of places of worship. 'To refuse foreign funding and want to establish a certain balance between faiths requires the State to call for it'.[63]

On the Right, a few voices emerged, demanding the opening of a debate on public funding of mosques by local authorities.

In 2004, Nicolas Sarkozy, then Minister of the Interior, in a book of interviews, implied – without committing himself explicitly to such an option – that an evolution of the Law of 1905 to support public funding for faiths, and particularly Islam, could be considered in the long term.[64] This was not to prevent him responding negatively to two UMP representatives (Arlette Grosskost and François Grosdidier) who wanted the Muslim faith to enjoy the same benefits in law as the recognized faiths across three Eastern French *départements* (Lower Rhine, Upper Rhine and Moselle) and public funding for any public institutions of worship and to pay the *imâm*.

---

60   Lydie Fournier, *Le fait musulman à Montpellier entre réalités sociologiques et enjeux politiques* (Dalloz 2008).

61   Manuel Valls, *La laïcité en face* (Desclée de Brouwer); Manuel Valls, *Les habits neufs de la gauche* (Robert Laffont 2006).

62   Valls (n 61) *Les habits neufs de la gauche* 84–5.

63   Valls (n 61) *La laïcité en face* 116.

64   Nicolas Sarkozy, *La République, les religions, l'espérance* (Cerf 204).

Such was the proposal made by the Moselle MP from Woippy, François Grosdidier. He was clearly in favour of not only the Muslim faith becoming the fourth religion in Alsace-Moselle, but that, in the rest of France, *communes* be also allowed to fund the construction of places of worship. 'According to the case law of the Council of State, they (the communes) can even build and/or manage a café, if no applications from the private sector are received. A bistro, yes, but a prayer room, no. It is time to lift the ban on the communes building places of worship to respond to a real social demand'.[65]

An official commission was finally appointed by Nicolas Sarkozy in 2005 to examine what progress was necessary to modernize legislation governing the relations between religion and the State. Chaired by the publicist Jean Pierre Machelon, the commission reminded us that the principle of 'no public subsidies', which did not figure in the constitution, should be separated from the principle of secularity and then, under certain conditions, the *communes* should be able to subsidize an investment made by a religion.[66] These proposals went unheeded.

The progressive installation of a climate of moral panic around Islam in France helped to curb any initiatives seeking to reopen the case of public funding for the Muslim faith. The controversy that ensued following the announcement made by the UMP party (in power!) to hold a seminar on proposed incompatibilities between Islam and secularity was to contribute to making any alternative approach inaudible, such as that of Club 89 led by Benoist Apparu, then Secretary of State for housing. His intention was to raise anew the issue of public funding for religious needs in clear terms:

> ... we must facilitate the construction of mosques in our country, even if it means that the state participates. Even if it is contrary to the Law of 1905, which needs adapting. ... We cannot on the one hand denounce the Islam of the cellars and streets and not assume the consequences. Being happy to denounce, that's what the National Front does. We, we must provide answers.[67]

Here again, his suggestions fell on deaf ears.

Now let us unravel the various approaches towards public action that have led to the issue of public funding for the Muslim faith figuring on the public agenda or at least being omnipresent in public debate.

Both in France and in the rest of Europe, the principle of public funding for religion appears to respond to a three-way approach that can result in asymmetrical situations as regards minority faiths.

---

65   François Grosdidier, *Les you you et la république des tabous* (Mettis Editions 2008) 46.

66   Jean-Pierre Machelon, *La laïcité demain. Exclure ou rassembler?* (CNRS Editions 2012).

67   'Benoist Apparu veut faire financer les mosquées par l'Etat' 17 February 2011 *Planète UMP Blog*.

Firstly, there is a tendency to make the principle of public support for faiths subordinate to the recognition of a religion's stable base and social legitimacy, duly guaranteed by criteria laid down in law. Such is the general philosophy prevailing in most European States, in which mechanisms of public support exist for statutorily recognized faiths (Federal Republic of Germany, Belgium, Austria, Italy, for example). For the time being, it is only in Belgium, Spain and Austria that the Muslim faith enjoys public support offered to other recognized faiths.

A detour via the study of local, communal and regional policies in force, particularly in Alsace, shows that in fact there is also an opening-up, even a progressive exit from a selective system of faiths that are officially and explicitly supported (Catholic, Protestant, Jewish) in favour of a more pragmatic management of other implicitly recognized faiths from which Islam has benefited (allocation of grants for the construction of buildings of worship by the *communes*, general councils and the Council of the Alsace Region). The policy followed by the City of Strasbourg towards minority faiths fits totally with this alternative approach. At local level, it means establishing public voluntarism aimed at reducing disparities between statutory faiths (Catholic, Protestant, Jewish) and others (Islam, Orthodox). The granting of public funding in the form of a financial contribution by the *commune* to the expenses of buildings of worship, in addition to indirect aid (emphyteutic lease), is supposed to compensate for the inequality – in fact as in law – between faiths with historical roots, supported in law, and more recent religions. As for Islam, it is a well established fact that the principle of self-funding remains socially unpredictable, due to the high proportion of members from economically disadvantaged social classes in these communities, hence their resorting to funds from abroad. Add to this the fact that public support remains purely optional and of variable scale. Strasbourg's municipal majority, supported by the local law on religions, intends to manage the needs of all faiths on a level playing field.

In terms of public funding, a different way of thinking also prevails, which aims to conceive of public funding as a way for governments to ensure a means of control over the 'subsidized' faith. In France, the proposal to promote public funding for Islam via local authorities tends to follow this approach to the subordination or public guardianship of the Muslim faith. Public funding is often presented as the obvious way to help communities without their own funds to acquire places of worship, but above all to limit calling abroad for funds, so as to guard against any possible ideological guardianship of Muslim places of worship funded too unilaterally. Rather than having to resort to reputedly unsafe funding from abroad, some political leaders prefer therefore to opt for the approach of direct funding by public authorities. Such a solution, besides implying an amendment to Article 2 of the Law of 1905, could, in the long term, lead to the establishment of what are called 'municipalized Islams'[68] and granting public funding could give rise to, or be born from, client-oriented approaches involving politicians and Muslim leaders.

With regard to the demand for a possible modification to the Law of 1905 separating religion and State, Islam's institutional players in France themselves seem rather prudent, if not reserved.

Like representatives of other faiths, they rely more on flexibility – in the construction of places of worship and granting of building permits – rather than on a total redesign of the system, which clearly favours public funding for minority religions.

If some Islamic federations, such as the UOIF, remain resolutely opposed to any public funding, other groups linked to national networks would like to be able to count on state aid, such as the Muslim Institute of the Grand Mosque in Paris. As for the *Rassemblement des Musulmans de France*, it is standing back from this debate, knowing it can count on foreign (including Moroccan) funds for its mosque projects. Behind these two strategies that reveal the difference in stance between Muslim communities and public authorities we can also detect two diametrically irreconcilable, ideological approaches. Although the UOIF was involved in the process of institutionalization of the Muslim faith set in motion by the French Government 20 years ago, this federation has always counted on the emergence of Muslim communities that are autonomous from governments in Muslim countries as well as from the French State. As such, it intends to formally favour a more intra-community, national regulation of faiths in France and formally refuses to tolerate political and financial interference from foreign States. The UOIF has also opened a dedicated website (http://www.alwakf-alislami.fr) aimed at collecting funds intended to promote autonomous funding of the activities of the Muslim faith along the lines of the classical pious foundations. By way of contrast, if the Federation of the Grand Mosque in Paris benefited from state aid from the Algerian regime in the recent past, now it had to reckon with less of it. Although still sensitive not to offend authorities in Algiers, it competes in loyalty terms with the French public authorities, expecting to reap some symbolic benefits or, even at local level, some additional resources from politicians supporting its cause.

It must be also recognized that on the fringes of large Muslim federations, many local Muslim associations count not only on the generosity of the faithful, but also have to opt for bank loans and therefore build up debt to equip themselves with places of worship, rather than resorting to external funding or to soliciting funds by forming associations in accordance with the Law of 1901. The financial independence of the faith has its price too.

We must also take into account the fact that certain positions can change over time, depending on economic conditions and new opportunities.

---

68 Françoise Duthu, *Le maire et la mosquée. Islam et laïcité en Ile-de-France*, coll. Logiques sociales (L'Harmattan 2008); Franck Frégosi, 'Regards contrastés sur la régulation municipale de l'islam' (2006) 62 *Les Cahiers de la Sécurité* 71–92.

This is particularly the case in Alsace with the stance taken by the *Milli Görüs* organization with respect to the public funding of mosques. The position adopted by this conservative Turkish Muslim organization was traditionally to not apply to local authorities, usually the *communes*, for any funding whatsoever for their places of worship, but simply for the issuance of building permits. The organization indeed emphasized self-sufficiency and being able to own places of worship. Recently, it changed its doctrine in Strasbourg. With plans to rebuild the Eyyup Sultan Grand Mosque in the Meinau district (with its 1100m² prayer room), it now envisages, in turn, requesting the help of the municipality of Strasbourg. This change can largely be explained by the funding opportunity that local law offers, by the probably high cost of the work planned, not to mention the chance of a lifetime that the city's bold policy towards public funding represents, in accepting requests from various religious groups – Muslim or non-Muslim – present in the Strasbourg urban area.

Finally, one cannot totally rule out as an explanation for this reversal the desire to provide a counterbalance to the new grand mosque in Strasbourg, funded for the most part by funds from the Kingdom of Morocco, Gulf States and public funds from Alsatian local authorities (the *commune*, General Council of the Lower Rhine and the Alsace Region). It seemed difficult for the Turkish community to allow the Moroccan community to become the single official showcase of Strasbourg's Islam!

Several Findings by way of Conclusion

If, throughout the course of history, no official Islamic doctrine exists on public funding for the Muslim faith, we have seen that, in fact, the faith was an eminently collective affair in which public authorities, private individuals (rich traders, prominent people, corporations), leaders and their citizens – all as believers – played an active part in funding the construction of buildings of worship and in remunerating officials. Many buildings of worship and their staff were financially supported through pious foundations. The situation then changed with the emergence of modern Nation States, most of which favoured exclusive supervision by state powers of the practice of worship, whether in terms of appointments and training *imâm* or supervising construction projects, and which were content to provide public funding for places of worship.

Approaching the end of this contribution, it becomes clear to us that this issue of public funding of the Muslim faith is still topical in a majority Muslim context. Where Islam gives rise to bidding wars between regimes in place and more radical sectors of society (state Islam versus political or Salafist Islam), the strengthening of state control over Islam means, *inter alia*, maintaining public funding for the Muslim faith and supervising the sermons.

Where Islam remains in a minority, as in the societies of Western Europe, things are different. Very often access to public funding is presented rather as a means to equality, as a means of enabling the Muslim faithful to have places of worship in sufficient numbers without needing to seek funds from abroad.

So far, the example of France compels us to state that reluctance towards such a plan is real, felt as much by defenders of a secularity which rejects any direct financial link between state and faiths, as by the Muslim communities themselves. The latter reflect first a sense of resolute defiance towards any model of an Islam that is administered from the top down in line with a neo-colonial or paternalistic approach, while also expressing willingness to take as read the ideal of secularity, in that it promotes autonomy of operations and organization of the faiths in relation to the State.

All in all, Muslims in France appear to be more favourable to the secularization of the funding of faiths than some Western Churches which, over more than a hundred years, have taken full advantage of state generosity in the name of legally preserving religious heritage. These same Churches were also offended at the idea that we can reform the 1905 Law to liberalize the public funding of faiths for the benefit of the minority ones.

List of References

Ageron C-R, *Les Algériens musulmans et la France (1871–1919)* Tome I (Presses universitaires de France 1968)

Al Mawardi AH, *Les statuts gouvernementaux* (trans. Charles E Fagnan) (OPU 1984)

Al Qayrawani AZ, *La Risâla. Epître sur les* éléments *du dogme et de la loi de l'islam selon le rite malikite* (trans. Léon Bercher) (Editions Iqra 1996)

Bauberot J et al., *Laïcités sans frontières*, coll. La couleur des idées (Seuil 2011)

Behrens-Abouseif D, 'Wakf dans les pays arabes' *Encyclopédie de l'islam* Tome XI (Brill 2005)

'Benoist Apparu veut faire financer les mosquées par l'Etat' *Planète UMP Blog*, 17 February 2011 <www.planete-ump.fr/t18095-Benoist-Apparu-veut-faire-financer-les mosquées-par l-Etat.htm>

Benoît J-L, *Alexis de Tocqueville. Notes sur le Coran et autres textes sur les religions* (Bayard 2007)

Berger P et al., *Religious America, secular Europe? A theme and variations* (Ashgate 2010)

Boussinesq J, *Laïcité et islam en France. Rapport d'étape d'une commission de travail de la Ligue de l'enseignement* (Ligue de l'enseignement 1998)

Carret J, 'Le problème de l'indépendance du culte musulman en Algérie' (1957) 37 *L'Afrique et l'Asie. Revue politique, sociale et économique*

Chevènement J-P, *Le vert et le noir. Intégrisme, pétrole, dollar* (Grasset 1995)

Dakhlia J, *Le divan des rois. Le politique et le religieux dans l'islam*, coll. Historique (Aubier 1998)

Denoix S, 'Introduction: formes juridiques, enjeux sociaux et stratégies foncières' (1996) 79–80 *Revue du monde musulman et de la Méditerranée*

Dermenghem E, *Le culte des saints dans l'islam maghrébin* (Gallimard 1954)

Dumont P, 'La direction des affaires religieuses en Turquie' in S Akgönül (ed.), *Laïcité en débat. Principes et représentations en France et en Turquie*, coll. Société, Droit et Religion en Europe (PUS 2008)

Duthu F, *Le maire et la mosquée. Islam et laïcité en Ile-de-France*, coll. Logiques sociales (L'Harmattan 2008)

Fournier L, *Le fait musulman* à *Montpellier entre réalités sociologiques et enjeux politiques* (Dalloz 2008)

Frégosi F, 'Regards contrastés sur la régulation municipale de l'islam' (2006) 62 *Les Cahiers de la Sécurité*

—— *L'islam dans la laïcité* (Hachette Pluriel 2011)

Garcin J-C, *Etats, sociétés et cultures du monde musulman médiéval X-XV siècles* Tome II (PUF 2000)

Golvin L, *La mosquée: ses origines, sa morphologie, ses diverses fonctions, son rôle dans la vie musulmane plus spécialement en Afrique du Nord* (Institut d'études supérieures Islamiques d'Alger 1960)

Grosdidier F, *Les you you et la république des tabous* (Mettis Editions 2008)

Hamiti X, 'Kosovo' in J Nielsen (ed.), *Yearbook of Muslims in Europe* vol. 1 (Brill 2008)

Ibn Arabi M, *La prière du jour du Vendredi* (trans. Charles André Gilis) (Al Bustane 1994)

Ibn Khaldun A, *Discours sur l'histoire universelle. Al Muqaddima* (trans. Vincent Monteil) (Actes Sud 1997)

Ibn Qudâma M, *Le précis de droit* (trans. Henri Laoust) (Adrien Maisonneuve 1950)

Ibn Taymiyya A, *Le traité du droit public* (trans. Henri Laoust) (ENAG 1994)

Jazexhi O, 'Albania' in J Nielsen (ed.), *Yearbook of Muslims in Europe* vol. 1 (Brill 2009)

Kovac M, 'Bosnia and Herzegovina' in J Nielsen (ed.) vol. 1 (Brill 2008)

Krichen Z, 'Femme *imâm*: ijtihad ou hérésie? Que dit le Coran? Que disent les Ulémas?' (31 March 2005) *Réalités* <http://www.realites.com>

Kuru AT, *Secularism and state policies toward religion. The United States, France, and Turkey* (Cambridge University Press 2009)

Luizard P-J, *Laïcités autoritaires en terres d'islam* (Fayard 2008)

Machelon J-P, *La laïcité demain. Exclure ou rassembler?* (CNRS Editions 2012)

Raymond A, *Artisans et commerçants au Caire au XVIIIe siècle* Tome II (Institut français de Damas 1974)

Reeber M, 'La fonction d'*imâm* dans la *Risâla* d'Ibn Abî Zayd al Qayrawânî' (1997) 47, 2 *Revue de droit canonique*

Sabet S, 'Lorsque la femme monte au minbar' (April 2005) *Al Ahram Hebdo* <http://hebdo.ahram.org.e.g./arab/ahram/2005/4/13/femm2.htm>

Sarkozy N, *La République, les religions, l'espérance* (Cerf 2004)

Stehly R, 'L'*imâmat* des cinq prières selon Châfi'î et Ibn Qudâma' in Frégosi, Franck (ed.), *La formation des cadres religieux en France. Approches socio-juridiques* (L'Harmattan 1998)

Valls M, *La laïcité en face* (Desclée de Brouwer 2005)

—— *Les habits neufs de la gauche* (Robert Laffont 2006)

Veinstein G, 'Les Ottomans: fonctionnarisation des clercs, cléricalisation de l'Etat?' in D Iogna-Prat et al. (eds), *Histoire des hommes de Dieu dans l'islam et le christianisme* (Flammarion 2003)

Zarcone T, *La Turquie moderne et l'islam* (Flammarion 2004)

Zouari F, 'Une femme *imâm*, et alors?' (19 April 2005) *Jeune Afrique*

Chapter 18

Financing of Worship and its Original Symbolic Referents in the Jewish Tradition

Raphaël Draï

The very formulation of our title highlights the current mismatch with its original Hebrew reference. 'Financing' is a recent term that reduces the verb 'finance' to its exclusively monetary and material element. As for the word 'worship', it also refers to a dated, institutional and even administrative definition of religious practice. From this point of view, financing the 'Jewish faith' in France, Europe and the State of Israel, is provided for under laws and regulations of the countries concerned and according to their degree of 'secularism', friendly or not. Here we find comparable items: public funding when authorized, funding according to current laws on associations, funding via foundations, donations and bequests, all controlled, once again, by the legislation in question. It is not sure that this approach, as indispensable as it is in positive law, completely accounts for the causes and ways in which the Hebrew people – *Bnai Yisràel* – allocated a significant proportion of its members' resources to the functioning of the Temple of Jerusalem and its attached institutions, as well as to supporting and providing for the tribe of Levi, from whom descended the *cohanim*, the priests, and from among them, the high priests, the *cohanim guedolim*, from among whom the high priest – the *cohen gadol* – himself came. However, transposing this formulation into the context of the so-called biblical institutions – to use this expression in its broadest sense that will require defining subsequently – not only has documentary interest, illuminating an aspect of the history of religions that is no doubt instructive, but also archaic and exotic. This reformulation, necessitating careful research so as to understand the original concepts and unique practices of the Hebrew world in this area, will no doubt also help better inform not only the meaning of the two words used in this initial formulation: 'financing' and 'worship', but, more broadly, to better understand how a human community invigorates its own transcendence by the manner in which it attends to its relationship with its God: relations of hospitality and welcoming, validated by the way it behaves towards the priesthood in charge of this welcome, without interruption and without irregularity. This raises two questions that will form the essence of this investigation.

First of all, this sacerdotal group – to give it the most utilitarian and neutral term available – does it actually constitute a 'caste', burdened on the entire people for whom it would be, without euphemism, the prebendary and parasite?[1] Then, if this is not the case, how does the group of Levites and *cohanim* restore to the people what they inherited from them? For such is the most noticeable difference between the *levi'im* tribe and a caste, in the derogatory sense attached to this term in common usage: it is *an exchange* that occurs between these two sections of the people of *Bnai Yisra'el*, in the manner and for reasons that we will need to consider. Through the relationship between *levi'im*, *cohanim* and *israelim*, we will see that, in reality, it is a way to understand society in its relations with transcendence and everything economic that offers itself up to the analyst.

The Institution of 'Worship' in Hebrew Biblical Institutions

The concept of worship is so marked by that of caste or ecclesiastical apparatus that first and foremost we need to recognize what distinguishes the tribe of Levi, the sacerdotal tribe *par excellence*, instituted by God's Word (Numbers 18). What is the genealogy of this institution? It should be noted first of all that it was not created, but a by-product, and a by-product from a very serious accident involving the people of Israel: the adoration of the Golden Calf, which occurred just after the liberation of the slave State of Egypt. Only a by-product, because originally it was the entire people as such, that God – to designate Him by His name in the biblical narrative – established as a sacerdotal entity, facing Mount Sinai, and in preparation for the gift of the Torah, the Decalogue: 'Now therefore, if ye will obey my voice indeed, and keep my covenant, then ye shall be a peculiar treasure unto me above all people: for all the earth *is* mine. And ye shall be unto me a kingdom of priests, and an holy nation' (Exodus 19: 5– 6). It is the people as a whole which is the subject of divine choice and this sacerdotal love, according to the conditions laid down, the main one of which – that regroups all the others – is the keeping of the Covenant, explained in the Ten Commandments of the Decalogue with the positive rules, the *michpatim*, for putting them into practice. This means, in terms of the narrative, that *Bnai Yisràel* become, so to speak, the *pontifex* of humanity, dedicated to spreading knowledge of the One God, the unifying God, He who created what is human in His reflection (Genesis 1:26). This institutionalization does not imply any of the parasitic connotations of the word 'caste', as at the same time we are reminded that the Earth belongs to God and God alone. And it is through exercising such a sacerdocy that this belonging will be recognized and consecrated or, rather, sanctified.[2] In what circumstances and for what reasons

---

1 Louis Dumont, *Homo Hierarchicus. Essai sur le système des castes* (Gallimard 1979).

2 Without radically opposing the meanings of these two terms, one can distinguish them as follows: the sacred distances, the holy calls to approach, but gradually, *cf.* Rudolf Otto, *Le sacré* (Payot 1969).

will the Levites be distinguished among the people? And does this distinction constitute a caste? We must return to the biblical tale of the Golden Calf.

This spiritual accident, which is to be understood as a very serious regression into idolatry, takes place while Moses is on Mount Sinai where God had summoned him to receive the Torah. Indeed, the Ten Commandments had already been the subject of a prior collective revelation. However, Moses was called directly by God to be taught how to apply these Ten Commandments, to move from ideal to reality, to make them *effective*. However, barely a few hours before Moses' planned return, the people finds itself in a frenzy of impatience that it cannot control. Threatening, the frenzy reaches Aharon, brother of Moses, like him descended from the Levites: they have him make an effigy which is to serve as guiding and tutelary God for the rioters! And it is faced with this threat that, after having used all possible delaying tactics while awaiting the safe return of Moses to him, that Aharon fabricates this effigy, in the form of a compact figurine, that of the Golden Calf. And the people devote themselves to the regressive 'hilarion',[3] as if just a few weeks ago, faced with the divine proposal for the Torah, they had not answered with one voice: 'We will do and we will listen'. Moses is warned of this and the rest is history: the descent – as if Mount Sinai were coming to land – the breaking of the tables, the pulverising of the idol and the judgement of the people. But, before this judgement, Moses had encouraged everyone to make a clear and unambiguous statement: 'Then Moses stood in the gate of the camp, and said, "Who is on the Lord's side? let him come unto me". And all the sons of Levi gathered themselves together unto him'. (Exodus 32:26). In such circumstances, the Levites were not singled out *a priori*, in a discriminatory manner. All in all, it was the rest of the people, convened as a collective, that chose them by default. It remains to understand the reasons for this choice, what motivated their attitude. To assist, we will compare the two blessings that this tribe received in the biblical narrative.

The first is to be found in the general and individual blessings that Jacob, on death's doorstep, gave his sons who had finally gathered together, as well as to each of them personally (Genesis 49). Turning to Levi, inseparable from his brother Simeon, he directly uttered these words: 'Simeon and Levi *are* brethren; instruments of cruelty *are in* their habitations. O my soul, come not thou into their secret'. For a 'blessing' one would have expected rather different remarks. Those of Jacob are nevertheless justified in the light of the massacring of the inhabitants of Shechem, visited by two brothers after their sister Dinah had been raped and treated as a prostitute by the son of the King of Shechem. Their father in no way shouldered the responsibility for this violence, and did not absolutely condemn the intentions which had led this shady pair to behave likewise with regard to their sister's dignity. And this is why Jacob adds this phrase that we will meet again, but in another context – and it is important to translate it precisely here: 'I will divide (*ah'alkem*) them in Jacob, and scatter them in Israel' (Genesis 49: 5–7).

---

3   Philippe De Félice, *Foules en délires, extases collectives. Essai sur quelques formes inférieures de la mystique* (Albin Michel 1947).

The vocation of the two brothers, a vocation that will be borne eventually by Levi alone, is this 'scattering' – which is not random, but means sowing seed within other tribes, as if they should become their salt or leaven.

The transformation of what Levi embodied was to emerge centuries later, after the liberation of Egypt and the crossing of the desert, when entering the land of Canaan, in Moses' blessing this time in the form of spiritual *viaticum*: 'They shall teach Jacob thy judgments, and Israel thy law: they shall put incense before thee, and whole burnt sacrifice upon thine altar' (Deuteronomy 33:10), which exposed them to the condemnation of their enemies, in other words of those that deny this sacerdocy. From one blessing to the next, one is led to understand that the tribe of Levi is not singled out ontologically or genetically from the people as a whole, but on the contrary they represent and elevate to the level *that had become their own*. How was this level reached? Not by unpredictable mutation or by magical substitution, but after considerable work on one's self; from a deep, intense, broad and communicative awareness that led the *levi'im* to the psychic and moral preparation of this impulsive act of violence, irrespective of what may have been legitimate motives; it was intimate work that henceforth protected them against destructive outbursts or nostalgia. The tribe of Levi will be that of loyalty and constancy, one that knows how to take on a commitment and honour a promise. It will be the *balancing* tribe of *Bnai Yisra'el*. It will not yield to ruthless ambition, because it does not feel perfect, but will take care to improve itself. It is not even immune to regressing to states that one would believe to have surpassed, as evidenced by the attempted coup against Moses and Aharon by other *levi'im*, those descended from Korah and from his associates, who judged that they had had 'enough' of Moses and Aharon, as the people in general had already reached the level of full sainthood, individually and collectively. As a result, they were to be severely judged and punished (Numbers 16:32).

In this sense, the *levi'im*, from which we have said the *cohanim* descended, assumed a formal sacerdotal mission within *Bnai Yisra'el*. Acts, liturgies and duties conferred to them as a result (which we will consider) only find their true meaning in the light and constant reminder of this mission which did not yield to any mystagogy. The true sacerdotal character of this tribe is identifiable by its *exemplary nature*. So was it to be distributed and disseminated among the people and not by forming an enclave or mysterious citadel. The *levi'im* give *Bnai Yisra'el* the hope of elevation that drives themselves. They were the bosom of the *cohanim and* became their officiating priests at the heart of a people from whom they do not separate, because they are committed to its care and dependent on its solidarity. Rabbis would be today's equivalent.

Of what specifically does the *cohenat* consist? According to the cognitive processes appealed to by Hebrew exegesis, the term is revealed by the letters forming the name it designates: *CHN*. The middle letter, *hei*, is symbolic of the Divine Presence, which is also called the Shekinah. It is surrounded by letters *kaph* and *nun*, which, when joined, mean the assertion 'yes' – confirmation and validation. In Genesis, the term validates the successive phases of Creation. In other words, and in this algorithmic form, the mission of the *cohanim*, within the tribe of Levi, is to welcome the Divine Presence within the breast, in the *tokh*, of *Bnai Yisra'el*, among whom the Levites, as has been said, had been divided and scattered. This welcome takes on a particular gravity on Yom Kippur, for this reason called '*The* day' (*yoma*). On that day, it is for the *cohen gadol*, the high priest and him alone, to enter the Holy of Holies; it is his under his sole authority and sole responsibility, but equally at his own risk, to pronounce the Unutterable Name of God: Shem Hameforash, in order to obtain forgiveness for errors and bad conduct by the entire people, of which he is an intrinsic part, from which he does not exempt himself. And it is also from this viewpoint that we can better understand the role of the Temple and the service accomplished there by the Levites, at least for those of its members who were specifically assigned there, the rest being scattered throughout the territory of Israel.

The Synagogue and the Temple

Nowadays, the funding in question concerns what are called synagogues, a term sounding Hellenic or Greek in spirit, which means: teaching and common way of life. Any synagogue envisaged in this sense is inseparably a place of prayer (*beth knesset*) and a place of study (*beth hamidrach*). These institutions are not autonomous entities. They are said to be *homothetic* to the Temple in Jerusalem, called *Beth Hamikdash*, 'the House of the Sanctuary', or else *Beth Habeh'ira*, 'the House of Choice', and are linked to it. In times when Judea was independent and sovereign, a tribunal was attached to each local synagogue as it was to the Temple in Jerusalem; in this court, everyone was obliged to have their differences with others – Jewish or not – judged.[4] Suffice to say that, since then, all construction and planning of synagogues must be accomplished in accordance with the construction of the Sanctuary in the desert first, with the two Temples of Jerusalem next, while awaiting the third Temple of Ezekiel's prophetic vision.

The architecture of the original Sanctuary and the two Temples has given rise to numerous comments. We need to understand the general spirit and intentionalities. Of course, the latter control the construction and management of synagogues today, at least in France and according to French law – which fully plays its part in European Community law, as evidenced by debates on circumcision or ritual slaughter. Why and how was the Desert Sanctuary built? Lack of common sense attributes it to the desire to build a house for the Divine Presence, inside which the latter would reside, could be consulted and – why not – met, at least in a spiritual sense, if not in an ecstatic manner. This is not the general intent of the Sanctuary, nor that of the two Temples in Jerusalem, following the principle that God is free

4   Shemuel Safrai et al. (eds), *The Jewish People in the First Century. Historical Geography, Political History, Social, Cultural and Religious Life and Institutions* (Van Gorcum Fortress Press 1974).

to manifest Himself and reveal Himself at His chosen place. Depending on the features of a biblical geography of holiness, and without being able to go further into detail, if He preferred Jerusalem, it is because this place is known to the *mother mediator* of the universe, for which it constitutes the generic point of equilibrium.

In the book of Exodus, instructions for construction, assembly, then edification of the Sanctuary, obey the following request: 'And let them make me a sanctuary; that I may dwell among them (*betokham*)' (Exodus 25:8). Commentators of the Jewish Tradition interpret this as follows: 'Let them make me a sanctuary, so that I reside not in this *sanctuary*, but in their own *private, individual and collective sphere*'. But it is nevertheless necessary to construct this 'them', this inner site of welcome, of human hospitality for the Divine Presence. As it happens, the implementation of the Sanctuary is at least as important as its outcome, precisely because it embodies a work accomplished by a human collective, by a people, an *âm*, worthy of this name. It is a true working through of a propensity to idolatry. Does this repeat the previous question? Why, following the liberation of *Bnai Yisra'el* from the Pharaonic house of slavery, did this project become indispensable? We have started to provide an answer in the regression of the Golden Calf, one of the multiple causes of which lay in the slave mentality which *Bnai Yisra'el* had not yet completely shaken off. The shaping of this massive, opaque effigy was the result of a crowd in revolt against Moses and his brother.[5] The irrefutable order had been given to Aharon: '*Make us* a God who walks at our head'. There followed the false, yet immediate, reconstitution of the story, and then the orgiastic worshipping of a metal imitation, while the 'hilarion', as we have seen, consumed the loss of consciousness and the moral decline of those giving themselves up to it until the moment of sanctioning. It left people feeling lost, 'headless', until Moses, confirming the divine pardon that he promptly requested, received the second tablets of the law. The construction of any place of Jewish worship must take inspiration from the project to build the Sanctuary, which is precisely about where the tablets must be deposited, in just as symbolic a gesture.

How will the materials be gathered? Not by taxation and compulsory levies, but by voluntary donations and offerings, made with the intention of an open mind and the volition of the heart. In reality, it is about operating in the opposite direction to the acts and intentions which led to the Golden Calf. Gold alone will not suffice. All other minerals and materials will have to contribute, so that all the elements of Creation are represented there.

However, if the work required to achieve this should naturally be entrusted to a contractor with the necessary knowledge, Bezaleel – to name no names – we will note in the light of our previous explanations precisely did not belong to the tribe of Levi, but that of Judah, meaning that this Sanctuary is not the preserve of a tribe apart that could be inclined to form a caste. On the other hand, if Bezaleel (Exodus 31:2) is the prime contractor and site manager, the work on the Sanctuary

---

5   Michel Gad Wolokowicz et al. (eds), *La psychologie de masse aujourd'hui*, Shibboleth/Actualité de Freud (Les Editions des Rosiers 2012).

should be carried out by *anyone* from among the people, men and women, with this essential quality: wisdom of the heart. The very terminology of such work indicates its spirit since, *inter alia*, assembling panels and draperies will take place according to the vocabulary of the brotherhood (Exodus 36:29). This symbolism and terminology are those prevailing up to today, when it comes to building a new synagogue or redeveloping a pre-existing one, so as to inspire the behaviour of the officiating priests and their followers.

As for symbolic elements that will be arranged inside the Temple, one should not create either confusion or contradiction. By approaching more and more what is called the Holy of Holies (*Kodech hakodachim*), you first recognize the Altar of Sacrifice, that it would be better to call for reasons that we will see, the altar of the 'liturgies of reconciliation' – of the *korbanot*. And then in a less exposed, more intimate location, three main elements should be positioned in line with three of the four cardinal points, which are also the directions of the spirit: the Candlestick with seven branches representing the seven major faculties of human consciousness able to perceive and welcome the Divine Presence; tables welcoming 'the bread of the face' (*leh'em panim*) that can be considered as revealing symbols of the social link, and the Holy Ark where the second Tablets of Stone were placed alongside the fragments of the first, these two types of tablets fitting together and forming a structure. As to the Candelabra, we must emphasize that it should be lit daily, its lighting being a task for the people and not the *cohanim* or *levi'im*, who were exclusively responsible for preparing the assembled light, individual and collective, the purpose of which we can better understand. As to the fourth cardinal point – the East, the direction of the origin, of the front, where one entered the Temple – following the required procedures, it was supposed to remain completely free and open, which requires no comment. With respect to the Holy of Holies, where only *cohen gadol* was allowed to enter on the day of Yom Kippur, for reasons we know, it should not remain empty in a negative sense, but free, available, corresponding to the welcome area for the Divine Presence similar to the one that the Creator had arranged, so that Creation itself could take place.[6]

Still today, such are the rules governing the building and development of synagogues and the material resources required have to be inspired by them. One may then wonder where the Holy of Holies was relocated. Is it in the *hekhal*, in the place where the *Sifrei Torah* are now stored – the scrolls of the Law and counterparts to the Tablets of the Decalogue? Or else on the *bama*, on the dais where these scrolls are unrolled and read? No doubt in both these places, without forgetting the journey which leads from one to the other.

So what were the specific duties assigned to Moses and Aharon? Moses' mission – this word is preferable to that of 'responsibility' – was to ensure the work in progress was adequate and corresponded to the divine plan that had inspired it, then to proceed with assembling its elements and next erecting the construction

---

6   Not to mention the bones of Joseph, memorial from Egypt in its contrasting faces, and that of the absolute necessity to obtain liberation, rightly by means of the law.

before the final edification, with each phase having its specific risks. The book of Exodus describes these steps and how Moses dealt with them until the time of abundant divine consecration came (Exodus 40:34).

As to Aharon, his mission, that the *levi'im* in the Sanctuary will be assisting with, is referred to as *âvodat hakodech* – 'holy service'. To put it in more cursory terms, it consists in accomplishing the aforementioned *korbanot* and blessing the people in quite specific ways. The *korbanot* are not sacrifices in the usual sense. The word *korban* contains the root *KRB* which means reconciliation, reduction of a fracture, the shortening of physical, mental, emotional and spiritual distance. The precise nomenclature and typology of these *korbanot* – one of which was called *tamid*, or perpetual, to mark the continuity of the history of this people and the spirit thereafter describing its states of consciousness – is to be found in the corresponding treatises of the Talmud and in the 'Mishneh Torah' by Maimonides. Their *internal logic* is not unfathomable and can be understood as follows: for each event – happy or unhappy – of individual or collective existence and for the latter especially when a split or rupture could result, the protagonists had two obligations: firstly, if a conflict had already been declared, to bring it before a court. The Sanhedrin, both Supreme Court and Parliament, sat in Jerusalem, physically and symbolically adjacent to the Temple. Secondly, they were encouraged to go to the Temple itself in order to meet a Cohen or a Levite and speak with him about the reasons for coming, to determine if necessary the extra-judicial reasons for the dispute or ongoing conflict and to decide from among all the *korbanot* which one would allow spirits to be recovered and if possible find paths of reconciliation accompanied by new peace of mind. Moreover, it should be noted that, in its own order, this was the objective of the formal judicial trial.

Since the destruction of the Temple in Jerusalem and the impossibility of carrying out these *korbanot* according to their specific instructions, the corresponding duties have not been dropped and have not fallen into disuse, instead being *transferred* to the synagogal liturgy and its associated prayers. Every day, these *korbanot* are methodically recollected so that their spirit, if it can thus be described, can be found not only within the modern functions of the synagogues, but also in the behaviour of the faithful, which explains that synagogues were also places of study – and of a 'non-academic' one. By studying there the meaning of the liturgies and gestures devoted to the accomplishment of the *korbanot*, one is also committed to understanding the causes of conflicts within society or between individuals, possibly of breakdowns and splits in progress, so as to prevent them continuing or repeating. The development, operation and management of synagogues is to be seen within the context of a never abandoned hope for construction of the third Temple and the re-establishment of these liturgies of reconciliation, including those performed at the Festival of Sukkot destined for *all* the other nations on Earth and mankind. One can better measure the consequences of Napoleon convening the 'Sanhedrin' in 1807, with the intention of forcing the Jews of the Empire to abandon this hope which was certainly not ethnocentric. Remember that access to the Temple of Jerusalem was open to foreigners, at least to those who respected the Noachide Laws, and that they could adequately perform *korbanot* there. This now brings us to examining the material conditions for the functioning of the Temple in Jerusalem that inspire, or must inspire, the smallest of synagogues in Israel and the diaspora.

Elements of Sacerdotal Management

The *cohanim* and *levi'im*, as has been said, were responsible for maintaining and operating the Temple in Jerusalem. As in this context they could not perform other duties, how was their day-to-day existence provided for? It was dedicated to the solidarity of the other members of the community. However, it was not a form of parasitism, but an exchange of goods – to keep this term about 'goods of the soul' – ensuring the continual movement from the material to the spiritual, from the raw or roughly fashioned material to its 'sublimation'. It was indeed for the *cohanim* to perform the liturgy of the *ketoret* – incense – which can also be understood as the sublimation stage of the phases that preceded it.

Without going into detail about the conditions of this maintenance, the *cohanim* were entitled, above all, to the offerings called *terumot*, of the same nature as those used in the construction of the first Sanctuary in the desert, and following the same intentionalities. The *terumot* are not simple donations, but offerings dedicated to the sanctification of their author, to their spiritual elevation to the level where the *cohen* is supposed to be found. How can we characterize that level? We will retain just a single criterion: the *cohenat* involves an unbinding of whatever could be linked to death, morbidity or to splitting and breakage. It embodies the decisive choice for life in an existential field where the reverse and opposing choice remains conceivable. He pays emotionally – a *cohen* is not allowed to enter a cemetery, including to bury close relatives. The *cohen* shall remain the embodiment of life. One exception is nevertheless possible: when no-one is in a position to ensure a decent burial, to accompany a deceased person having no family or other form of assistance to his final resting place; physical, social and emotional accompaniment appears to be one of the most characteristic behaviours of Levites. For the same reasons, it is forbidden for a *cohen* to marry a woman who has already divorced, who has experienced rupture and rift; his responsibility is to rebuild the social link and proceed with reconciliation within and between individuals, knowing that his wife will be spiritually and legally authorized to receive the *terumot*. Being exemplary does not go without the requirement of consistency. Otherwise, it proves fictitious and is subject to derision. Incidentally, and at least for this last prohibition, these rules are valid today for all Jews with the name 'Cohen'; what designated in the beginning a duty became a family name, a name whose genealogy has been validated from century to century, ever since the first exile to Babylon and the first scattering, in the sociological and historical sense, of the people of Israel. Still today, when going up to read the Torah, anyone who is named 'Cohen' will precede anyone who is named Levi, before believers with other names are called upon. This ordering does not correspond to an outdated 'privilege'. It recreates the sequence of duties prevailing at the Temple in Jerusalem. In this way it reminds any synagogue – and even any oratory of minor importance – of its imprescriptible homothety in time and space with the matrix-like House of Holiness in Jerusalem.

Let us be clear that significantly the word *TeRuMah* is built on the root *RM*, which means 'raise' – also found in the name of AbRahaM, the embodiment of human devotion through the example of divine devotion. The *terumot* come from the part that must be deducted from goods produced by the people and assigned by them for another purpose than immediate consumption, like the portion named *h'alla*, removed by the woman who kneads bread and reminds us that humans do not feed exclusively on this bread, which we cannot physically do without anyway. Other donations or voluntary assignment of goods grouped together under the term *h'ekdech*, are also included in the *terumot* for the proper functioning of the Temple; these were 'consecrated' or rather 'sanctified' goods, once they had satisfied, by their nature and their initial method of acquisition, the conditions required for that use and purpose.

Furthermore, the *cohanim* were to receive fixed portions of any pure beast dedicated to the *korbanot*, the right or left parts, with these two directions corresponding to two of the most essential attributes of the Divine Presence: the justice attribute on the left and the attribute of compassion on the right; these two attributes must remain closely interrelated in case of need and according to the prayer of the *cohanim*, the symbolism of right prevails over the symbolism of left. In turn, the *cohen* also had to involve himself personally in this liturgy via private prayer, especially when it involved a request for forgiveness. The intercession so heard and practised would require a perfect ductility of thought and non-opacity of the heart; the concern of others whose actions and operations of liturgy strictly speaking were only the external and public manifestation. It is this sacerdotal sequence that the man referred to as 'Korah' will attempt to denigrate in his 'putsch' attempt against Moses and Aharon (Numbers 16), accusing them of parasitism and exploiting the gullibility of a human community already assumed to be completely holy in his eyes; it was a violent, demagogic affirmation that his own behaviour showed to be wrong in every respect.

The *levi'im* assigned to the Temple of Jerusalem received subsidies and voluntary donations in the form of shares intended directly for their use. Similarly, they were entitled to the product of the first two tithes; the third, called 'the poor tithe' was specially assigned to supporting humans in need, whoever they were, among the people of Israel. A similar observation to that concerning the *cohanim* can be made. The *levi'im*, as we have already underlined, did not constitute a separate group, enclosed within a population and dependant on them for their livelihood. We may recall the threefold mission of the descendants of Levi. During the crossing of the desert, their mission was, when the people were moving, to transport the elements of the sanctuary that they alone could disassemble, carry and reassemble in order to ensure its integrity and to respect the profound symbolism in the same spirit which they were able to demonstrate during the crisis of the

Golden Calf and its aftermath. The Sanctuary is in the image of the people: it is not a room. It was configured as a consistent and connected whole. Disassembling it in order to move it did not mean breaking it up. Those who did not participate in the breaking up of the people during the aforementioned crisis will have the mission of embodying this unity, but according to two conditions.

If the *levi'im* assigned to the Temple in Jerusalem were then to assist the *cohanim* in the performance of their duties, they also had the distinctive mission this time of ensuring the service of singing and in particular singing the Psalms of David, one for each day of the week, and a special one for the Sabbath. This mission should not be confused with that of simple musical accompaniment. In the Temple of Jerusalem, singing the Psalms meant first recalling their contents, which related to the teachings of King David or of those who claimed to be his followers; they addressed the relationship to God and the personal, human experiences of the Anointed King, *Melekh Hamachiah'*, the Messiah-King, as well as the trials that sometimes tested this relationship.

A large number of other *levi'im* – those who were scattered among the rest of the people and did not constitute a mendicant population – were sent to cities of refuge (*ârei miklat*), where the perpetrators of accidental, unpremeditated murder had to go in order to be far from victims' relatives seeking revenge, when this was to be feared. These cities were not reduced to simply refugee cites. A murderer, if he had committed his deed by simple oversight – anyway an irreversible and as such irreparable act – must wonder about the reasons why he did so, attempting to elucidate the psychological, but also moral, causes, so that any recurrence could not be envisaged. The other *levi'im*, if not part of a mendicant order, did not figure either in a contemplative one. Possessing no personal property amidst the people, they dedicated themselves to acts of social welfare, to *guemilout h'assadim*, demonstrating availability and selflessness by their own example. They trained, so to speak, the mobile and available section of the people, not relieving it of its own duty of solidarity, but *preaching by example* to those even less well endowed than they might be, to visit the sick, to comfort prisoners pending release, to perform the 'last duty' *vis-à-vis* deceased without families. This is why the allocation of the proceeds from the tithe was given to them by law. Contrary to conventional wisdom, the eminent significance of the tithe was not fiscal, but societal and person-to-person. In practice, the biblical tithe was not about taking a tenth of a herd or a monetary amount, but to *constitute sets of ten elements*, in Hebrew *minianim*, preparing for the establishment of human groups of this size, conducive to the reception of the Divine Presence.

In summary, such are the original, spiritual and symbolic, not to say metaphysical, references determining the operation and maintenance of the Temple of Jerusalem and now serving as guide to the current funding of places of Jewish worship. As was said by way of introduction, nowadays and in the societies concerned, provided that they met the requirements of what is known as the Rule of Law, the rules of this funding obey general laws and specific regulations on the subject, as more often it is about the laws and regulations pertaining to associations of religious or cultural nature. Such rules take their meaning from the laws and regulations (*takannot*) prevailing at the Temple in Jerusalem, resulting in, despite the loss of political independence particularly from the first century of the Christian era, a translation almost term-by-term being provided in each place of prayer and study, but also in every Jewish residence; any family table is considered as a 'mini-sanctuary' (*mikdach méât*), a table- altar where any meal shall in principle be accompanied by words of the Torah, so that the Divine Presence can be welcomed there.

No financing, no method of management can be appreciated *in abstracto*.[7] Recalling the genealogy also helps to ensure the best match to their current purpose.

List of References

De Félice P, *Foules en délires, extases collectives. Essai sur quelques formes inférieures de la mystique* (Albin Michel 1947)

Dumont L *Homo Hierarchicus. Essai sur le système des castes* (Gallimard 1979)

Otto R, *Le sacré* (Payot 1969)

Safrai S et al. (eds), *The Jewish People in the First Century. Historical Geography, Political History, Social, Cultural and Religious Life and Institutions* (Van Gorcum Fortress Press 1974)

Savatier R, *Le droit comptable au service de l'homme* (Dalloz 1969)

Wolokowicz MG et al. (eds), *La psychologie de masse aujourd'hui*, Shibboleth/ Actualité de Freud (Les Editions des Rosiers 2012)

---

7   René Savatier, *Le droit comptable au service de l'homme* (Dalloz 1969).

Index